TWO DAYS ONE

in 1958,

the greater part of Burton Bradstock and east of the river at West Bay, which formed part of the extensive estates, of the Pitt-Rivers family, came under the hammer.
Nothing was ever the same again.

1. Burton Bradstock from the air in the 1950s.

ELIZABETH BUCKLER GALE

Published by Time & Tide in 2007

© Mrs Elizabeth Buckler Gale
Salway Ash
DT6 5JF
Email: eg.gale@virgin.net

ISBN: 978-0-9508717-1-4

Printed by

Creeds the Printers, Broadoak, Bridport, Dorset DT6 5NL

CONTENTS

CONTENTS *Ctd.*

Acknowledgements

Two Days One Summer has been written with the assistance of a large number of people.

I am extremely grateful to **Anthony Pitt-Rivers, Esq., OBE, DL**, for his interest in my work and for giving permission for me to copy from the 1958 Sale Catalogue. Mr Pitt-Rivers read the draft Preface and advised on family biographies and assisted me in compiling the Freke/Pitt/Pitt-Rivers Family Tree. Mr Pitt-Rivers's valuable contribution has enabled me to produce the interesting inheritance details regarding the Burton Bradstock 'block' of the Estate.

Permission to quote from the works of Eden Phillpotts kindly granted from the Royal Literary Fund.

The staff of the following - Dorset County Reference Library, Dorset History Centre Dorchester, West Dorset Research Centre, Bridport and Dorchester County Reference Libraries, Yeovil County Library, Bridport Museum and History Centre, The Bridport News, The Dorset Evening Echo, The Western Gazette, Freshwater Caravan Park, West Dorset District Council, *(Jill)*.

Also: Miss Rebecca Bevis, *Secretary to The Rushmore Estate, Tollard Royal,* Mr Stephen Case of Sturminster Newton Museum, Miss Helen Mann and Mr Roland Moss of the West Dorset Branch of The National Trust, *Curator*, The [Military] Keep, Dorchester, Miss Susan Anders, *West Dorset Parish Council Coordinator*, Captain Michael Southgate, RN, Rtd., *Chairman* and Mr Fel Moore, *Clerk*, Burton Bradstock Parish Council, Mr Mark Strata, *Headmaster*, Burton Bradstock School, Mr MJS Harris, *Headmaster,* Sandroyd School, Rushmore, Messrs Symonds and Sampson, (formerly Senior and Godwin) Sturminster Newton, Mrs Ann Smith, BA, *Archivist Sherborne Estate*, Mr Christopher White of Milne and Lyall Bridport, Mrs Patricia Cook *President* and *Members* of West Bay Women's Institute.

My appreciation is extended to the numerous people who gave interviews and information:

Mesdames Rita Atwooll, Thelma Aylott, Valerie Aylott, Mary Bailey, Jacquie Basden, Beverley Benham, Jeanne Berry, the late Barbara Bishop, Agnes Bowditch, Christine Bugler, Suzanne Bugler, Kathleen Burton, Nancy Camm, Mary Catton, Winifred Dales, Helen Dommett, Sylvia Elsworth, Betty Fitzpatrick, Joan Gillett, Rebecca Hansford, Greta Heal, Lindsey Hartman, Beryl Hyde, Joyce Hyde, Pamela Ingram, the late Gillian Johnston, Doris Klopper, Jennifer MacAllister, Mary Payne, Sally Parker, Betty Starkey, Cynthia Stevens, Gillian Styman, Gillian Summers, Heather Thomson, Paula Todd, Madeleine Wakely, Mary Ward and the Misses Sandra Brown, Alice Legge, Gillian Legge and Sue Wheeler.

Messrs Geoffrey Ackerman, Philip Baker, John Barnes, David Barnikel, Andrew Bullock, William Bullock, John Burton, Winston Churchill, Andrew Collins, John Copp, Roger Day, Basil Dent, Colin Derryman, Geoffrey Derryman, Brian Galpin, John Gurd, Julian Harvey, Christopher Hutchings, William Ives, Alex Johnston, Harry Lenthall, Paul Loud, Justin Mallinson, Kenneth Mullins, Alan Musgrove, Roy Nethercott, David Perrin, the late Richard [Dick] Ramsden, John Riggs, Allan Rodway, James Rowe, Sidney Shipp DSM, Colin Sibley, Trevor Sturgess, Tony Warren, Arthur Watson, David Weston, Gilbert White, Jonathan Wyatt, Richard Wylde and Drs Philip Shemilt and CA Smith.

Mr and Mrs John Bull, Mr and Mrs Dennis Bullock, Mr and Mrs Ben Bryant, Mr and Mrs John Case, Mr and Mrs Peter Chick, Mr and Mrs RD[Bob] Conway, Mr and Mrs Geoffrey Guppy, Mr and Mrs John Layflurrie, Mr and Mrs Philip Hutchings, Mr and Mrs Peter Parsons, Mr and Mrs John Parsons, Mr and Mrs Peter Pattinson, Mr and Mrs Philip Milner, Mr and Mrs AE [Tony] Legg, Mr and Mrs David MacDermott, Mr and Mrs Roger Saint, Mr and Mrs Norman Saunders-White, Mr and Mrs Kenneth Short, Mr and Mrs Richard Stevens.

I have used comments made by **some others who are not listed.**

Mr and Mrs Tony Legg have kindly given me hospitality on numerous occasions and enthused me with their interesting and useful memories.

Mrs Carolyn Drewitt read the draft copy of the book and lent great encouragement. Mrs Barbara Brook read the draft and offered constructive ideas as well as undertaking some proof reading. Mrs Sue Kane and Mrs Marion Wrighton have also lent encouragement and gave their opinions regarding selection of photographs. Mr David Barnikel has kindly made copies of some photographs.

I appreciate the advice and attention given by the Directors and Staff of Creeds the Printers, Broadoak.

My daughter, Mrs Amy Knight, assisted me in researching the Census Returns and Parish Registers and was enthusiastic about the book, as was my husband Guy Gale, who has advised me with details regarding building technicalities and country matters, besides giving overwhelming support to the whole project.

The Gale families mentioned in the book are not immediately related to the author or in all cases, to each other.

PHOTOGRAPHS

The photographs have been reproduced by courtesy of:

Plates:

1, 2, 5 and 113, Anthony Pitt-Rivers, Esq.

1, also courtesy former Director, Airpic, *(not now trading)*.

4, Mr MJS Harris, Sandroyd School, Rushmore.

7a, 16, 30a, 60, 60a, 62, 62a, 63, 79, 99a, Mr Roger Saint and Mrs Jaquie Basden.

8, 8a, b, and 52 and 52a, Mrs Beverley Benham and other members of the Lenthall family.

10, 69 *(photographer)*, 94, Mr David Barnikel.

12, 23a, 39 and 39a, 44, 44a and 50b, Mr and Mrs Philip Hutchings.

24, Mrs Valerie Aylott.

51, 69a, Mr Tony Legg.

25a, 29, 85, The Imperial War Museum, London.

26, *(named with assistance from Mr Dennis Bullock)*, 31a, 33a, 34, 36 and, 78, Mrs Sylvia Elsworth.

35, Mr Kenneth Mullins and Mrs Madeleine Wakely.

(34, 35 and 36 were named with assistance from Mrs Sylvia Elsworth, Mrs Mary Ward, Miss Alice Legge and Miss Gillian Legge).

37, Mr Sidney Ship, DSM.

43, Mr Roy Nethercott.

48, and 48a, Mr Andrew Collins.

50, The Spiller and Hutchings families.

55, and 55a, Mr Dennis Bullock.

57, Mr M Cheron, *photographer* and Mrs Kathleen Burton and Mr John Burton.

58, 59 and 59a, Mrs Madeleine Wakely.

78a, b, 84, 106, 107, Mrs Greta Heal.

61a, 100, *(named by Mr Basil Dent and Mr Robert Rodway)*, 101, 109, 109a, 110, Mrs Joan Gillett.

63a Mr Jonathan Wyatt.

64 (with Mrs Valerie Aylott), 79a, Mr Allan Rodway.

65, Mrs Betty Starkey.

72, 72a, Mrs Thelma Aylott and Mr Peter Aylott.

74, 82, Mrs Mary Bailey.

76, 76a, 111, the late Mrs Barbara Bishop.

77, Mrs Janet Guppy.

83a, Mrs Gwenda Brown.

87, Mr Geoffrey Derryman.

90, Mrs Vivien Batten.

91, Mrs Doris Klopper.

92, Mrs Cynthia Stevens.

95, Mr and Mrs Peter Broomhead.

99, Mrs Jill Chick.

104, Mr Frank Clarke, *photographer.*

105, Mr and Mrs Peter Pattinson.

105a, 116, Mr and Mrs Peter Parsons.

108, Mrs Heather Thomson.

115, 115a, 117, 119, Mrs Sue Kane , *photographer.*

15, 15a, 20, 21, 31, 40, 49a, 56, photographs by Maurice Ouseley, MA .The collection, (now in the Bridport Museum), was entrusted to the author, by his widow, with permission to take copies.

All other photographs and paintings are from the author's collection, with credit to:

Front cover: [discovered by Tony and Ann (née Spikes) Packham of Northants who have sentimental connections to the village.] Burton Hive Beach, Circa 1920s.

Back cover: 1958 catalogue, Anthony Pitt-Rivers, Esq, recent portrait by Colin Davis.

18a, WG Morris, 46, 45, John Clist, 114, Aerial Pictures, *photographers.*

19a, 83, J. Valentine & Co. Dundee

67, Beatrice Mercer, 103, Henry Redwood, *artists.*

Mr Philip Baker, Mr David Barnikel and Mr and Mrs Bernard Paull have assisted in obtaining copies of photographs from owners.

Map of Burton Bradstock showing the Lots sold by the Pitt-Rivers Estate in 1958, drawn and painted by Karen Justice, Bridport.

Every effort has been made to obtain permission to print photographs where copyright might still exist.

No responsibility can be accepted for any reports that are subsequently considered inaccurate.

PREFACE

INHERITANCE AND THE PITT-RIVERS ESTATE

and significant women in Burton Bradstock's history.

The Sale of the Pitt-Rivers Estate in Burton Bradstock and West Bay, in 1958 by the eleventh holder of the title "Lord of the Manor" was a significant happening. The inheritance which had been held since the sixteenth century, had come to General Pitt-Rivers, in 1880. As there was no heir in the direct line, the succession had fallen to him, through his paternal grandmother, Marcia Lane-Fox, née Pitt.

Much earlier, it was another woman, Elizabeth Taylor, the daughter and only child of John Taylor, an Alderman of London and merchant, with important trade connections to Bridport, who brought the Burton Bradstock Manor with her, on her marriage to Sir Thomas Freke, *1563-1633*, of Shroton [Iwerne Courtney], Member of Parliament, who had acquired various manors in Dorset.

John Taylor, descended from the Taylors of Carlisle, had held the tenancy of Burton Manor since 1590. Elizabeth is commemorated in the church at Iwerne Courtney on a memorial tablet of black marble, erected by her two surviving sons, Raufe and William, in 1654.

Sir Thomas Freke's grandson, also named Thomas Freke, disinherited his surviving second son, William Freke, of Hinton St Mary, in favour of his daughter-in-law, another Elizabeth, née Pile. (William had written subversive books, under a pseudonym, although it was fairly apparent who was the author). Elizabeth had married the elder brother, Thomas. On Elizabeth Freke's death the reversion passed to her nephew, George Pitt, son of her sister Lucy. He died in 1745 and it was his son, GeorgePitt, *1720-1803*, who was created the first Lord Rivers of Stratfield Saye, (a pleasant village on the Berkshire border), when the family was raised to the peerage, in 1776. He inherited the vast estates, including Burton Bradstock and an area at Bridport Harbour.

Baron Rivers's status and interests required a substantial residence from which to ride out to hunt in Cranborne Chase, on the Dorset/Wiltshire county borders and he rebuilt the house at Rushmore, using it as a hunting box. It became apparent that his son, George, *1751-1828*, although having fathered several illegitimate children, would have no rightful heirs and he obtained a second barony of Sudley Castle, in 1802, of which the remainder favoured his daughter's male offspring. In 1817, Stratfield Saye, was sold by the second Lord Rivers to the Crown. This estate was presented to the Duke of Wellington, in recognition of his services to the nation.

When the second Lord Rivers died in 1828, his nephew, William Horace Beckford, son of Louisa Pitt, (the second daughter of the first Lord Rivers), found himself the third

Baron Rivers of Sudley Castle and holder of the extensive estates. Under his grandfather's will, Beckford adopted the name Pitt-Rivers by Royal Licence. His son, born in 1810, the sixth to bear the name George, became the fourth Baron Rivers and fathered thirteen children, the four eldest being boys. As this immediate line of inheritance fell like ninepins, presumably the deaths of these children being accountable to tuberculosis, it was the fourth son, Henry, who survived to become the fifth Lord Rivers in 1866 but died shortly after, aged eighteen and unmarried, in 1867. Then, with yet another deviation, the title passed (back) to his uncle, Horace, who became the sixth and last Lord Rivers, who died childless in 1877. The failure of this line of inheritance, eventually had a marked effect on Burton Bradstock.

★★★★★★★★★★

Lieutenant General Augustus Henry Lane-Fox, DCL, FRS, FSA, had distinguished himself in his military career and married into the Stanley family who were prominent, aristocratic and intellectual. The Honorable Alice Stanley's father, the second Lord Stanley, of Alderley, had refused permission for them to marry, at first, as with the rank of Captain, Lane-Fox could not boast the sort of income her father would have wished. A few years later he still found himself without sufficient money to please Alice Stanley's father, although her aunt, as the women in families often do, was supportive and pointed out in a letter to her brother, Lord Stanley, that at least Augustus was a gentleman. There had been no better offer for Alice's hand and there were four more daughters yet to marry!

Alice Stanley and Augustus Lane-Fox married in 1853 but his prospects of ever having money of any consequence were still very remote. Matters were to change, when in 1880, Lieutenant General Lane-Fox, (having been promoted), on the death of the sixth and childless, Baron Rivers, inherited the Pitt Estates, through his grandmother, Marcia Pitt. The younger son of a younger son, (his infirm elder brother, William Edward, having predeceased him in 1852, aged forty-six), by the hand of Fate, or a Gypsy, the inheritance had fallen to Augustus.

The seat of the Lane-Fox family was Bramham Park, in the West Riding of Yorkshire. It was here at Hope Hall, in 1827 that Augustus was born, son of William Augustus Lane-Fox and Caroline, née Douglas, a Scottish aristocrat [later Lady], daughter of John Douglas, descending from the Earls of Morton. Research by MW Thompson, revealed that William Fox inherited a large estate from his mother, Frances Lane and by Act of Parliament in 1751, took the surname and arms of "Lane". He was succeeded, in 1773, by his nephew, James Lane-Fox. It was then that the family connected with the "Pitts", as James Lane-Fox married the third daughter of Lord Rivers, [The Honorable] Marcia Lucy Pitt, in 1789, *another significant woman in the history of Burton Bradstock* and who was the grandmother of Augustus Lane-Fox. (The Family Tree is shown on page 312.)

Desmond Hawkins, in *Concerning Agnes,* the life story of one of the General's daughters, who met Thomas Hardy, the writer, recounts that there was a curse on the family. The numerous deaths were said to be as a result of a prediction by a betrayed Gypsy woman, that the Rivers's line would become extinct. By1880, the curse, (supposing it were true), had gone some way to fulfil the Gypsy's intentions.

GENERAL AUGUSTUS LANE-FOX PITT-RIVERS, DCL, FRS, FSA.

There was a condition imposed that the General was to take the name of Pitt-Rivers. At the same time, his eldest son, Alexander Edward, took the name "Lane-Fox Pitt-Rivers", by Royal Warrant dated January 24th 1881, both officially posted in the London Gazette. The remaining seven children took Pitt as their surname (the first child was stillborn in 1853). The family moved into Rushmore House, on the Dorset and Wiltshire county boundaries, which lay surrounded by the villages of Tollard Royal, Ashmore, Sixpenny Handley, Tarrant Gunville and Berwick St John. Included in the inheritance was Cranborne Chase, (where King John had hunted and met his huntsmen and hounds at a boundary tree) and the Manor of Burton Bradstock.

At Rushmore, the beautiful formal gardens and extensive parklands of two thousand acres, allowed the family absolute privacy and a delightful place in which the children could grow up. The General could pursue his passion of excavating for ancient remains and set up a private museum. Besides Rushmore Lodge, at Berwick St John, there was a beautiful manor house at Hinton St Mary and another at Tollard Royal, in Dorset, as well as a London house, in a smart area, not far from Buckingham Palace, easily accessible for the younger members of the family to ride out in Rotten Row.

The Tithe Report of 1841 recorded 4,068 acres in the Burton Bradstock parish, of which 3,297 were subject to tithes, of this, 992 acres were cultivated, 2,038 pastureland and 30 acres consisted of woodland and plantations. By 1880, General Pitt-Rivers, held the largest amount of land in Burton Bradstock, his major tenant being Job Legg, at Manor Farm, with 499 acres. A Return of the Owners of Land, at the time of the last Lord Rivers's death, stated that he held 24,942 acres in Dorset, with additional land in Wiltshire.

When Rural District Councils replaced the Courts Leet, the General foresaw the growth of beaurocracy and crippling taxes. The title of Lord Rivers ceased with the death of the sixth baron and General Pitt-Rivers never received similar recognition, even after a distinguished military career and a lifetime of dedicated, scientific work, particularly in archaeology, although he wrote to Gladstone suggesting that the title might be recreated and if it was, offered to support the Liberals in the House of Lords. Anthony Pitt-Rivers,

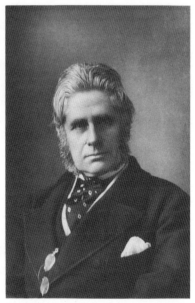

2. *General Lane-Fox Pitt-Rivers, DCL, FRS, FSA. 1827-1900.*

great-grandson of the General, referring to the subject, comments that General Pitt-Rivers received a polite but non-committal reply.

There is no record of any visits that the General made to Burton Bradstock but shortly after inheriting the Burton 'block', the villas on the cliff were built as summer residences. By then his domestic life had soured somewhat and his bouts of ill health, bronchial ailments and diabetes, probably contributed to his ill temper, even rage. Mrs Pitt-Rivers was always a careful account keeper, although the General was by then comparatively wealthy and like many of their class, they dallied over paying the bills or only settled them annually, making life for the would-be recipients difficult. The General, absorbed in his archaeological activities, expended a great deal of his income on these projects. He appeared to get on well with the workers he employed on the Estate, even if he put them on the excavating work and paid them less than they could earn on other labouring jobs.

Mark Bowden, in a biography, writes that the General and Mrs Pitt-Rivers travelled in separate carriages. With such a large family, the villas would have been well used and the sea and the patchwork West Dorset countryside would have been viewed from the modest heights of Burton, a complete contrast to the wide, open, inland, bleak expanse of Cranbourne Chase, which lay some eight hundred feet above sea level. The retinue of carriages, servants and luggage would have been a fascinating sight for the villagers as it passed through Burton, snuggling in its valley. It is known that General Pitt-Rivers did visit on several occasions, for the twice yearly Rent Days.

★★★★★★★★★★

Augustus Lane-Fox was educated at Sandhurst and commissioned in the Grenadier Guards in 1845. He saw service in the Crimean war, with distinction and great hardship. He was at the Battle of Alma and the Siege of Sevastopol. Here, in the battle on the south bank of the Alma, Lane-Fox would have come in contact with Codrington, a superior officer, whose descendant, in due course, would come to live in Burton Bradstock. As a young officer, he served at the Hythe School of Musketry and was involved in the introduction of the Minie rifle, writing a drill book on the subject.

His thinking led him to consider the development of mankind from primitive beginnings. His writings were far ahead of his time wrote Harold St George Gray, a clerk to the excavations. The collections brought him immense recognition and he was elected as a Fellow of the Royal Society of Archaeologists, excavating for three decades. When he inherited the Rushmore Estate, he had every opportunity to work on his own land, as well as in other parts of the country and abroad.

Augustus Lane-Fox, an imposing figure, first established a museum at Bethnall Green, in 1874, illustrating the evolution of the design of implements of primitive tribal people. This then formed the Pitt-Rivers Museum of Oxford University. Besides these interests, the General kept a zoo in his park and was a Fellow of the Zoological Society, opening the collections to the public and sharing his findings with them. The Larmer Tree pleasure grounds were planned in 1880 at the spot where King John had met for the Royal hunt. Set in some ten acres, on the lawns of Rushmore, the grounds were created by the General and immortalised by Thomas Hardy. Annually, in September, a public event was held there which consisted of 'elegant' attractions, pony racing and other sports and the provision of light refreshments, in the form of tea, coffee, minerals, (rarely

3. *The mouth of the River Bride at Freshwater, circa 1900. The lynchets, [ridges], were cultivated in the Middle Ages and in Victorian times, flax was spread on them to [dew] rot and bleach.*

alcohol, except on special occasions) and simple meals.

The General's private brass band played, as they did, every Sunday, to the disapproval of some 'who held the Sabbath Day in strict regard'; the bandstand, a Singing Theatre, the General's Pavilion, the Temple, a croquet lawn and golf links, were constructed over a period of around fifteen years, forming part of these unique gardens. The annual gathering was attended by hundreds of the general public and amongst the many attractions, the open-air theatre provided further entertainment for the visitors. There were no charges made as Pitt-Rivers was committed to letting the working man view and thereby educate himself.

Captain George Pitt-Rivers, grandson of the General, noted that, at its peak of popularity, 44,417 visitors went to the Larmer Tree grounds in 1899 and a further 12,611 to the Pitt-Rivers Museum, at Farnham. These people had travelled up to thirty miles, by horse-drawn vehicles, as well as by the new fashion of travelling on a bicycle, from Bournemouth and other destinations.

General Augustus Lane-Fox Pitt-Rivers, the father of British archaeology, Inspector of National Monuments and a great supporter of the Dorset County Museum, was in failing health as the new century dawned, after a full life and one greatly benefiting the community. He died in May 1900 and his ashes were interred in a carved marble niche, contained in a black marble sarcophagus, set in the wall of the church at Tollard Royal. Cremation was uncommon in England and he broke family tradition by this unconventional disposal of his body.

At his funeral were representatives from the Burton Bradstock Estate. The brass band, of which he was so proud, in their livery of the Lords of the Chase, were in attendance. He was survived by five sons and three daughters, all of whom were exceptional people, marrying into the prominent and distinguished families of the day. The eldest son,

Alexander, inherited the Estate and the second son, St George, was the inventor of the first incandescent light bulb which was commercialised in association with Edison of the Edison Bell Company.

★★★★★★★★★★

On the death of his father, Alexander Lane-Fox Pitt-Rivers, JP, FSA, 1855-1927, moved to the family seat at Rushmore and listed his summer residence as "Cliff Villa", Burton Bradstock. He had married Ruth, daughter of The Right Honorable The Lord Henry Thynne, younger brother of the second Marquess of Bath. Alexander Pitt-Rivers, of Rushmore and Hinton St Mary, continued the interests of his father, serving for a time in the Royal Wiltshire Regiment and the Dorset Yeomanry. He was a Justice of the Peace and at one time High Sheriff of Dorset.

In his younger days, Alexander spent seven years as an articled clerk to George Edmund Street, RA and was an accomplished water-colour artist and throughout his life, was devoted to the management of his estates. During the Edwardian period, Mr and Mrs Pitt-Rivers entertained, in elegant style, at Rushmore. On his death, in 1927, he was succeeded by his eldest son, George.

4. Rushmore House.

THE LAST LANDLORD *or almost*

George Pitt-Rivers, 1890–1966, JP, BSc. (Oxon.), FRAI, FRGS, and Mrs Pitt-Rivers moved to the Manor House at Hinton St Mary in 1929, where he had made alterations and necessary restoration. He first married The Honorable Rachel, daughter of the First Lord Forster in 1915. During the period when the Manor of Hinton St Mary belonged to the Benedictine Abbey of Shaston, [Shaftesbury], the barn would have held the tithes brought in from the land cultivated by lay brothers. Its conversion to a delightful theatre was a clever architectural and social plan and today it is selectively used, courtesy of Mr and Mrs Anthony Pitt-Rivers.

Educated at Eton, George Pitt-Rivers gave his recreations as hunting and polo. He joined The Royal Dragoons in 1910 and continued through the First World War rising to the rank of Captain. Although severely wounded in the army, he did not allow this to curtail his ambitions and his career took him into the field of social psychology and as an ethnographic field-worker. After the First World War, he accompanied his father-in-law, Lord Forster, as ADC, on his appointment as Governor General to Australia, in 1920. This enabled George Pitt-Rivers to tour in the Pacific and visit remote tribes. Continuing his grandfather's interests, he brought back artefacts to the family museum. He resigned his post after some three years and undertook research on Awa island off New Guinea, writing a book entitled *"The Clash of Culture"*. Through this he was admitted to Worchester College, Oxford, as a fellow commoner and was awarded a Bachelor of Science degree on this published work.

In 1923 he accepted the Presidency of the Anthropology Section of the Australasian Association for the Advancement of Science, at a meeting in Wellington, New Zealand and during a tour of the islands, was able to study the Maori peoples and delivered lectures on the *"Passing of the Maori Race"*, to the Royal Institution, in 1929, writing books and papers.

A World Congress was held in 1927, revolving around the problems of population. Pitt-Rivers became the organiser of the International Central Bureau of the International Union for Scientific Study. The third Congress was held in 1937, in Paris but already war was rearing its ugly head again. The concern of the delegates to this Congress was that of maintaining a balanced population. It boiled down to encroachment by the ever growing industrial workforce and factories, becoming 'urban sprawl' onto land required for food production. Pitt-Rivers wrote and lectured on these subjects and campaigned that *'swords should be turned into ploughshares'*.

5. *Captain Lane-Fox Pitt-Rivers, JP, BSc. (Oxon), FRAI, FRGS. 1890-1966.*

At Hinton St Mary, George Pitt-Rivers continued to host, many eminent anthropologists, archaeologists and genetisists. His interest and concern for mankind and agriculture during the depression years of the 1920s and 1930s, resulted in a huge rally of agriculturalists being held at the Larmer Tree pleasure grounds, on September 11th 1935. Pony racing, sheep dog trials and the usual brass bands, competing with each other, regaled some 10,000 people. This gathering was heralded as a farmers' protest concerning tithes which led to the proposal to march on London. Captain Pitt-Rivers was to the fore as the leader.

Six thousand farmers from twenty-five agricultural counties were represented; albeit it was the middle of the haymaking season. These farmers arrived in London by train, coach and road and paid their own expenses. It was a comely sight, led by two brass bands, with decorated farm wagons, live animals, loads of hay and accompanied by pikemen from the home counties. At Hyde Park the procession, was greeted by its leaders and important speakers of the day. Members of Parliament who had risked the barrage, were heralded with blasts from hunting horns, provided by liveried, Cranborne Chase gamekeepers. A deputation of farmers, to Number 10 Downing Street, found that Prime Minister Stanley Baldwin was not at home. Slightly Fascist and anti-tithes, in 1936, at an election, George Pitt-Rivers stood for his own party, Wessex Agricultural Defence Association, his slogan being, *"Peace and the Plough"*.

A petition signed by 15,000 farmers and delivered to the King, to withhold the Royal Assent to the Tithe Bill, became lost in the seemingly more important politics of the day. The Manor House at Hinton St Mary was requisisioned, yet again, for use by the army when the population of the village doubled, with soldiers and evacuees billetted in the surrounding cottages, throughout the Second World War. George Pitt-Rivers's eldest son, Michael, held a commission in the Welsh Guards and Julian followed his father into the Royal Dragoons as did their half-brother, [George] Anthony, later. These brothers were the fifth generation of the family to serve their country.

Shortly after the outbreak of the Second World War, Captain George Pitt-Rivers was interned as a British political suspect. He was incarcerated in Brixton Prison and the elephant house of Bertram Mills's Circus winter quarters, at Ascot, which he said was hurriedly turned into a concentration camp for six hundred political suspects. The loyal tenants at Burton Bradstock spoke, in whispers, about his political persuasion. A man of spirit, he always took a stance on matters for which he held strong views. At the start of the war, the family house, at Rushmore, became a preparatory school [Sandroyd]. Although it was set in a splendid park, the family were not too enamoured with the house and it was finally sold some years later.

As soon as hostilities ceased, Captain George Pitt-Rivers, (he had his opinion about the Peace Treaty), threw himself back into the good works, for which he was both well known and well qualified. Soon after, Captain Pitt-Rivers's son, [Professor] Julian, was entrusted as English tutor and equerry to twelve year old King Faisal II of Iraq. The King and another equerry stayed at the Manor House and were able to visit the museum where there were some ancient Assyrian exhibits.

As a distinguished gentleman, Captain Pitt-Rivers, pursued his interests and served the county. This eleventh holder of the title " Lord of the Manor", which included within the vast estates, the village of Burton Bradstock and east of the river at West Bay, for personal reasons, decided to offer this area in West Dorset, on the open market, in 1958.

6. General View over Burton Bradstock before the Pitt-Rivers Estate Sale, circa 1940s.

TWO DAYS ONE SUMMER

in 1958,

the greater part of Burton Bradstock and east of the river at West Bay, which formed part of the extensive estates, of the Pitt-Rivers family, came under the hammer. Nothing was ever the same again.

This book is dedicated to those with whom I share our heritage, the summers gone and those who went with them.

AUTHOR'S INTRODUCTION

*T*wo Days One Summer is an account of life in Burton Bradstock before the Sale in 1958 and the happenings that followed which changed the village for ever.

Few people, who are new to the area, or many of the younger generation, are aware of the upheaval that occurred when Captain George Pitt-Rivers decided to sell the West Dorset section of his Estate. Research has shown that the Sale had more effect on the community and the village, in general, than ever could be imagined. Some stories have been left untold, respecting privacy. Others will come to light.

It is with thanks to my contemporaries for the interest that they have taken and the time they have spent recalling their memories, as well as finding the faded photographs, that the story of the Sale, has unfolded and appears in print. Even during the period of writing this book, some of them are no longer with us. Recollections by others, now long gone, have also been included. There are only a few of us left who were directly caught up in the event. In addition to my memories about the Sale, particulars in the catalogue and comments recorded by my mother, the rest of the details, come from newspaper reports and research undertaken.

Everyone, in Burton Bradstock, the working folk, the tradesmen, fishermen and the farmers, had lived and worked side by side, harmoniously, for generations. Together they had dealt with all manner of incidents, helping each other, sympathetically, whatever their standing in the community. There were very few disagreements. Life had gone on uninterrupted for hundreds of years. New life and mortality, fire, famine, floods, disease, tragedies at sea, work on the farms and in the mills, fishing from the beach; a hard existence with little financial reward. All that and wars, had not broken their spirits. This book is about that spirit too, as they found time to enjoy themselves and make the best of their situation.

Although, after 1958, it was a peaceful and happy time, there was an undertow of problems and disturbance generated by the Sale. It was mainly to do with new residents bringing their ways and wants, planning applications and the resulting building projects. Other villages, since, have experienced similar happenings but at a much steadier pace.

★★★★★★★★★★

For keen scholars I wish to point out the style that I have used in the book. "Sale" and "Lot" are of sufficient importance to warrant capital letters. As a little girl, at the village school, in the 1940s, our teacher, Mrs Rodford, a local woman, insisted that we did not put a comma after the joining words 'and' and 'but'. Still with a degree of fear, throughout the book, I have adhered to her teaching! On occasions, I have only used the first element (consisting of two compounds – *the farm*/ *Bride*), of the name of the village. Those of us born and bred there, call it "Burton" which is how it appears in the earliest records. There are a variety of references to individuals; a mixture of formal address, Christian names and surnames, or the names by which they were commonly known, just as they came to mind as I wrote.

Figures and measurements (Imperial) rather than words, for easier understanding have, at times, been used. The price of property today has increased so very much that the apparently small sums, paid in 1958, cannot be compared with today's asking prices. Conversion to today's value is not just a matter of reckoning that one old shilling is equivalent to today's five pence. It isn't!

★★★★★★★★★★

In bringing the situation up-to-date, I talked to some new residents and have tried to give a balanced view. From the time of the Sale to the present day much water has gone under the bridge. The waters were often rough and muddied but finally seem to have settled and cleared as Burton presents its new face.

Two Days One Summer is written with the sincere hope that the account of the Sale will be passed on down through the generations. It is a tribute to the tenacity of the people who made Burton Bradstock the place where so many wish to settle or visit.

To quote some words of General Augustus Lane-Fox Pitt-Rivers is apt: "I cannot myself see how human conduct is likely to be affected disadvantageously by recognizing the humble origin of mankind. "

Elizabeth Buckler Gale
2007

7. *Burton Hive Beach circa 1885 shows the route to the village up over the cliff and the newly built villas. Fishermen's Green and boathouse to the fore, with eleven leret type boats laid up. 7a Fishermen spreading their nets on the beach, circa 1900.*

THE MANOR OF BRIDETON

A traveller along the River Bride to the coast, through any century, would have happened upon a sleepy little village, set in the fertile silted valley, nestling in the hills beside the sea. This would have been Burton Bradstock.

There, in the past one thousand years, the visitor would have found an industrious people going about their daily tasks, unfettered by concerns about their home, as long as it was dry and warm. The crumbling cob and stone walls, the thatched roofs and low chimneys, animals everywhere and rough lanes, the lush meadows with the beach beyond, littered with nets and boats, would have been their haven. These people, dependent on each other, whatever their calling, might have been born in the village, descended from Iron Age man, the Romans, Saxons, Danes who had invaded, or from Spaniards, shipwrecked along the treacherous coast, who had arrived to inhabit the place, or they may have been 'newcomers' who ventured to Burton Bradstock to rent some land, or to find work as farm labourers, be orphans sent from Westminster to the flax factory or bound as a fisherman's apprentice. When they arrived they would have been soon accepted into the community as part of the workforce to become part of the long and fascinating story of Burton Bradstock.

This history of the village goes back to time immemorial. Called Brideton in the Domesday Book, meaning the farm [tŭn] on the River Bride, pronounced *Briddy*, it consisted of two manors which were held, one by the King and the other by the Church. The word *bride* comes from an old, British tribal word, *brydoi*, which means boiling or throbbing water. The river rises at around 350 feet above sea level and falls some 100 feet in three miles, starting its course as a spring, coming out of the chalk hills at Little Bredy and bubbles and meanders, (or' boils' in bad weather), its way, some nine miles, until it meets the sea at Freshwater, Burton Bradstock.

The village centre lies three miles east of the town of Bridport and about half a mile from the mouth of the River Bride. Its outstanding feature is that it developed along the Chesil Beach, which was formed by wind and tide, making is so unique as to warrant being part of a World Heritage Site, (recording 185 million years of the Earth's history), consisting of a stretch of cliffs and pebbles, (which graduate in size and are constantly shifting back and forth), from West Bay, eastwards, for some eighteen miles. Chesil means *pebble*.

Prior to the Norman Conquest, the larger section of Brideton was held by King Edward the Confessor. In due course, King Henry I gave it to the Abbey of St Stephen of Caen, in France, to redeem regalia handed to the abbey by his father, attaching it to the Benedictine Priory of Frampton. Hutchins, in his *History of Dorset*, clarifies the complicated ownership details, by stating that the village came to the church of St Stephen's, in Westminster, following the suppression of foreign monasteries.

The church and some land, which formed a smaller manor, were exchanged in 1286, according to the researches of C J Bailey, for land held in Normandy, France, by the Priory of Bradenstoke, in Wiltshire and hence the second part of the name of the village. Sometime around then, the two parts were amalgamated and extended the Manor of Brideton(e). This dates the joining of the manors to somewhere in the mid-fifteenth century. It was not until this period that the two parts of the name were used. It was originally 'Burton' or variations of that name, just as those born and bred there still refer to the village by the first element of the title. After the dissolution of the monasteries, to which the nearest, Abbotsbury, fell victim, the Burton Manor belonged briefly to the Crown until 1570.

8. *[Burton] Manor Farmhouse in 1958, where a house had stood for hundreds of years. Inset 8a and b (L) Henry Lenthall, 1841-1924, (R) John Lenthall, 1881-1949.*

The Burton Manor had been surveyed with several other Royal Manors and it was in 1452 that the tenancy of Burton Bradstock Manor was sold by the Dean and Canon of St Stephen's Church for three lives. Shortly after 1590 the tenancy was granted to John Taylor, who was a merchant and Alderman of London and had important connections with Bridport, in the flax and hemp trade. Sir Thomas Freke, a distinguished Dorset gentleman, married, Taylor's only daughter and heir, Elizabeth. Through Elizabeth, the Burton Bradstock Estate, eventually, came to the Pitt-Rivers family. *(See Preface).*

9. *Southover, the street of fishermen and mariners, prior to 1898, before the cottages (L) and far (R) had burnt down.*

HOW THE VILLAGE EVOLVED

Surviving records indicate that early man had settled in the vicinity of the present village of Burton Bradstock. He would have hunted and gathered, eventually remained in one place, farmed the land and fished from the sea, growing the crops and rearing the types of animals that thrived in the heavy clay valleys and the alluvial soil deposited along the river banks, in the damp, mild, climate. Predominant was the growing of flax and hemp and the rearing of cattle, pigs and sheep. The latter were reared on the slopes, for meat and milk, as well as wool.

The Romans, arrived in the village in the first century AD and established a settlement, or look-out post on the top of the cliff, where items of that period have been found. They brought the art of farming as well as rope making and the Vikings, who came later, were skilled spinners. The growing of flax and hemp, spinning, weaving, rope and net making, became second nature to the inhabitants of the village. From 1213, when King John commanded that Bridport should make ropes by day and by night, mainly for the navy, in the defence of the Kingdom, Burton Bradstock competed with Bridport and other villages, in the production of flax and hemp for processing into twine, nets, rope and the manufacture of many allied products.

This veering away from the centre of the industry in Bridport, eventually led to a decree, issued by Henry VIII, that hemp, grown within five miles of Bridport must be sold in the town. Merchants had moved out to the countryside, including the area around Burton Bradstock and set up farms, and were doing too well.

What had started as a cottage industry later became one of the three main occupations of the inhabitants. Behind many of the dwellings in Burton Bradstock could be found plots, much later turned into gardens, where the cottager had grown flax and/or hemp for his own use. Workers would club together to dress the raw materials, in a shed at the end of the plot and with the assistance of the women and children, spin and turn the stricks into twine, ropes and nets. Even when a factory was started later, by Roberts, there were still people braiding and rope making at home.

In Victorian times, at Harvest Festival, a bundle of flax was used in the decorations in St Mary's Church. There was a marked fall in the acreage, in Dorset under flax in 1894 and to shore up the industry, flax and hemp were imported to Bridport Harbour, from the valleys of Italy and the Baltic States, whilst fishing and farming provided the other two main livelihoods for the inhabitants.

Some of the men worked at several occupations and were farmers, fishermen and flax and hemp workers. The last of these, in Burton Bradstock, was Joseph Buckler, 1859 –1933, who was employed as a master flax dresser and as a waterman, controlling the river for the mill. He rented a smallholding from the Pitt-Rivers Estate, owned a boat and was a skipper of a fishing crew, all concurrently.

10. The oldest surviving photograph of Burton Bradstock, taken from North Hill, circa 1890. Note the large number of cottages that there were in Southover.

THE MANORIAL COURT LEET

The Manorial Court Leet and Court Baron of the Burton Manor, (Manorial Rolls [records] survive from 1744), was originally held twice a year. The Steward was sent to oversee the proceedings where a number of senior men of the village assembled, to impose fines on those who had infringed the rules of the Manor. The jury was familiar with the situation and the person before them. They witnessed the transfer of tenancies and set standards for the maintenance of the cottages, roadways and river banks. Most of the cottages were held for three lives with a rule of the Manor appertaining to this system.

The Court made certain that the clearance of the river and highway was carried out and that hedges, bridges and the stocks, (in place beside The Pound), were maintained. No one was allowed to carry naked lights through the village or to let their chimney fall into disrepair, on pain of a fine, as the low thatched roofs caught on fire all too easily. Stray animals were impounded and anyone found throwing 'dung' out onto the street was brought before the Court. Fishing with a seine net on Sunday was illegal.

An early record of the rental paid by Burton Bradstock tenants to George Pitt, Esquire, exists for the period, 1744-1752. Abraham Lawrence paid 15/2d for the mill below the church. Elizabeth Perrot rented a part of the orchards in the village and William Hallett had been charged 6d for a small house adjacent to The Pound, that *was now rented by Robert Row*.

A similar system of local government, landlord and tenant, continued for another two hundred years; the Feudal ways giving way to the Estate system. Men of the village had been employed as carpenters, painters, glaziers, thatchers, watermen and as other artisans, by the Pitt/Pitt-Rivers Estate, for many years and this was operating up to the time of the Sale. There was an Estate workshop and yard and a foreman who was responsible to the Agent.

By 1900, the Landlord's Agent was visiting the village on the Quarter Days, in March and September to collect the rents and discuss local matters. There was great excitement in the village when, on occasions, General Pitt-Rivers, treated like royalty, had come to the village in person and addressed the tenants, standing on The Pound, outside the Inn.

The end of the nineteenth century saw an agricultural depression and the large estates suffered throughout the country. The agricultural worker demanded higher wages and the farmers found it difficult to meet these increases and keep up with the rent. A rent book for Burton Bradstock shows a decrease in the amounts charged to the tenant farmers around this period.

Joseph Hawkins had written to the Agent in 1891 to apologise for the delay in forwarding the rent of The Three Horseshoes. He enclosed postal orders for £4. *'It is the best I can do at present',* he wrote. Henry Prout, the same year, was sorry not to have sent the money, *'but the butcher can't take my piggs not till a week after Christmas, then I will send it on'*.

The Pound is one of the oldest parts of Burton Bradstock. Here, was the chapel to St Laurence and a burial yard, the original village pound, used to pen stray animals, (the later pound being situated at the bottom of Shipton Lane where it converged with Annings Lane) and the stocks; all mentioned in the Manorial Rolls. The church would appear to have been called St Laurence's. Reputed to be buried under the old chapel, near to The Anchor Inn, was a stone cross.

The chapel was converted to a cottage and features in the accounts of the Overseers of the Poor, as it was used later as the village Poor House, until about 1834, when a Union Workhouse was established to cater for the poor and needy, built in Barrack Street, Bridport, formerly Bradpole parish.

This pretty cottage, which became number 9, Burton Bradstock, that had been so much part of the history of Burton Bradstock, was one of the places that had been sold, entirely for reasons of economy, as early as 1951.

11. *Mrs Julia Legg braiding at her cottage door, circa 1905. She is wearing a Burton bonnet and wooden shoes.*

WHO WERE THEY?

THE SPINNERS AND CORVISARS

By the late 1700s, Richard Roberts, from Welsh origins, whose family came to settle in the eighteenth century at Chilcombe, a hamlet overlooking the Bride Valley, was living in Burton Bradstock. Roberts had the foresight to bring together the flourishing cottage industry to his mills, using the water from the fast flowing river as power. He had married well, circa 1789, to Martha Best, née Hoskins, of Symondsbury, the widow of Samuel Best, the tenant of Burton Manor Farm, who rented from the Pitt Estate. Roberts took a leading part in village activities serving as a Churchwarden, Overseer of the Poor, choirmaster and Foreman of the Manorial Court Jury.

12. Mill Street circa 1897, probably for Queen Victoria's Diamond Jubilee (L) The factory chimney stands proud and (R) Lot 39 Shadrach Dairy Farmhouse, is thatched. Inset 12a Mill Street looking towards Manor Farmhouse, early 1950s.
Note the "flower knots" outside the cottages.

During Roberts's era, the two mills, with in excess of two hundred looms, were recorded as having manufactured, twine, ropes, nets of all kinds, particularly for fishing, hammocks for the navy, sheeting, (naval and domestic), towelling, napery, thread for boots, harness and Dorset button making, mail and bread bags, tarpaulins and sailcloth. Roberts traded throughout the West Country, London and the Channel Islands, besides having contracts with the Royal Navy. He demolished a cottage, using men from the village to dig the channel, in Church Lane, to create a leat from The Grove to the spinning mill.

After Richard Roberts's death in 1820, the business was put up for auction on the

5th of February 1821. Advertised were, a substantial dwelling, outhouses, garden, two acres of excellent orchard and both mills, (The Grove and Mill Street), with fixtures and machinery, comprising two hundred and twelve spindles ready for carrying on the lint and tow spinning, complete with a booking house, weaving shops and fixtures complete for an extensive linen and sail cloth manufactory, also a leasehold meadow. (Did Lord Rivers buy the whole?)

Robert's sons and grandsons found a more lucrative income from the sea. For the grandsons, the era of the cross-Atlantic liners lured them away. A directory of 1830 for the county, lists Darby and Roberts running a flax spinning mill. By the middle of the century The Grove mill was grinding corn, held by three generations of the Rendall family. In 1874, the factory off Mill Street was operated by tenants John Clarke Andrews and his brother, Albion.

In Roberts's time, the men and women from the village, were skilled retters, hacklers, flax dressers, spinners, weavers and corvisars [rope-makers]. Children were brought in from orphanages and worked long, gruelling hours in the mills, doing the dirty, menial and dangerous jobs. Roberts supplied them with food and lodging and arranged for them to receive two hours' schooling on Sundays, to learn to read, say the Catechism and write their names. They were obliged to come with two suits of clothes, supplied by the orphanages. In a letter to the parish overseers of Westminster, Roberts wrote, *'I beg to ask the ages and numbers of each sex also if it will be agreeable that they should be bound to the linen trade. '*

By the time these orphans had reached their twenty-first birthday, they were off Roberts's hands and had to provide their own accommodation. Some of this workforce stayed on in the village, marrying into the local families.

★★★★★★★★★★

'A BAD JOB FOR BURTON'

So read the headline in *The Bridport News* of May 8th 1874. The previous Tuesday, the factory had been gutted by fire, very early in the morning. This was to have been a joyous day for the village as it was the wedding day of Miss Florence Templar, the Rector's daughter.

Albert Burwood, the waterman, had attended to his crack-of-dawn tasks which involved seeing that there was a sufficient head of water to power the water wheel for the day's spinning and rope making. Generally, he would oversee the flow of the river water and raise and lower the hatches that intersected the River Bride right up through the valley, as required. During floods this presented added duties.

On the morning in question he was about at the factory, below the church, at five o'clock and rang the 'warning bell', as was his custom, to summon the workers, when soon after, the men, women and children, about sixty of them in all, came streaming in to the factory. One of these was young George Symes, a lad from Loders, who had only started work there for the first time, the previous day.

The factory was owned by Lord Rivers and was under the proprietorship of the Andrews brothers who were sons of a Cattistock yeoman farmer, James Andrews. John, the eldest of the family of six children started his working life in the flax mills and was a clerk in a flax factory by the time he was aged thirty-four, living at Gore House, Bradpole. In 1871, he was managing a sailcloth factory in Crewkerne and was the father of seven children. He lived in a row of cottages at number one, Tail Mill. His status advanced when, in his mid-forties, he took over the tenancy of the flax spinning mill in Burton Bradstock.

13. St Mary's Church and the spinning mill factory chimney, at its full height, circa 1897. The yew tree, from which the bows were cut, spreads its branches. Inset 13a, the lowered chimney viewed from a camp at Magnolia Farm, circa 1910.

This towering building was 100 feet in length by 30 feet across and four storeys high, with three rows of windows of eight in each. It was a well built structure of local stone and had a slated roof. Inside were some of the latest machines for cording and spinning. The rooms were spacious and all kinds of manufactured goods were turned out in this busy place.

Young Symes went up to the third storey, on his arrival and began feeding a cording machine with tow. The water-wheel was not yet at full speed but as it was hot and dusty, Symes opened a window whereupon the tow burst into flames and he ran for his life and raised the alarm. 'Consternation followed'.

The men started to implement 'counteracting measures' said the report in *The Bridport News*. A messenger was sent, to Bridport, presumably on horseback, to fetch the West of England fire engine. A typical May day, stiff north-east breeze was blowing, taking the billowing smoke out to sea. This was a blessing as there were thatched buildings in its path - the Mill House and stables, Magnolia Farmhouse cottages and Shadrach Dairy House, the home of Mrs Ann Cousins. Assisted by volunteers, the household goods were removed from all these premises.

Plenty of water was available and everyone attempted to save the building and materials by forming a human chain, with buckets, to keep the flames in check. This proved impossible. The wooden floors, soaked with tar and the [linseed] oil from the flax, together with the highly inflammable dry flax itself, tow and accumulation of twine, ropes and other assembled products, fuelled the flames. It was an hour before the fire engine arrived, drawn by two pairs of horses obtained by Fire Chief, George Squibb, from the Bull Hotel.

By 7.10 a. m. the roof had fallen in and heavy 'advance' machinery was 'thundering into the yawning furnace below'. The nearby warehouse and the northern end of the factory so far, were escaping as Boreas kept his course, regaled the report in *The Bridport News*. People had gathered in droves aghast at what was happening. By eight o'clock the greater part of the premises was 'beyond all human aid'. The walls were strongly built and were still standing and the fire engine was being worked 'most zealously'.

At this juncture it was thought that two cording machines worth about £500 each, on the ground floor, might be salvaged, if that part of the ceiling stayed intact. Some of the men found ladders and scaled the burning factory walls to get in at what remained of the second storey to the north of the building. They threw out burning tow but there is no account that the cording machines were saved. Everything that was left there was severely damaged by water and the whole of the factory was soon completely gutted and volumes of thick black smoke belched forth, still heading towards the sea.

By nine that morning, the whole lot had burnt itself out and the smouldering wreck caused great distress to the management, workers and onlookers. Cog-wheels, massive shafts and machines lay in a great heap. Large iron bars had snapped and twisted with the intense heat and lighter parts lay in 'innumerable shapes'. 'This noble building' was no more. Within a short time, people were pouring into Burton from Bridport and the surrounding villages, to view the scene.

What had caused the disastrous fire? Had it been spontaneous combustion or arson? Only days before a 'fuse' had been found hidden in the tow. Was there a match in the tow that was ignited by the machinery or had boy Symes got matches in his pocket? This he vehemently denied. The tow could have been smouldering all night and had burst into flames when the boy opened the window. The cause remained a complete mystery.

The report stated that the building was insured for £1,500, with the London and Liverpool Company, for whom Mr C Wilson of Bridport was the agent and the machinery was covered up to £3,000. Everyone felt for Mr Andrews. He was a 'painstaking' employer and had recently increased the amount of business that went out of the factory. The whole village was going to feel the blow.

In conclusion, *The Bridport News* stated *'We can only express hope, an earnest wish that despite the serious extent and grave nature of the contretemps the trade of the village may speedily attain that prosperous and flourishing condition which it has hitherto and especially recently enjoyed. '*

On the 17th May, John Andrews penned a letter, on small sheets of crisp sea-blue note paper to Mr Creech, Agent to Lord Rivers, stating that the damage was to be assessed by the insurers. The insurers agreed on 30th May that the mill was a total loss.

A further letter to the Agent, from Andrews, said that Harry Gerrard, a builder of Barrack Street, Bridport, had been invited to produce plans to reinstate the mill and that he [Andrews] would call on his way to London, for the Agent's perusal and Lord Rivers's sanction, as he was anxious that no time should be lost as the machinery 'will be here in September'. Andrews was overseeing the rebuilding, the costs of which would be met by Lord Rivers. Alexander and Daniel of Bristol estimated that the claim to rebuild would be £700. Gerrard submitted an estimate of £1,190 and a further £140 to reinstate the shafting, gearing and other machinery. Repairing damage done to the dwelling house would cost £9.5/- and £4.10/- to repair the adjoining stables. A revised estimate of May 22nd quoted £710. Gerrard's handwritten Specification stated that he would carefully take down the walls of the old mill and use the stone in rebuilding as well as other stone from the ruins of Barn Cottage. Trenches for good firm foundations were to be dug six feet deep and three feet wide. The mortar would be composed of fresh Beaminster lime and clean sand from the beach, obtained free of cost. An internal wall was be built to divide the card[ing] room from the mill with nine inch brickwork, using the bricks from the ruins. Iron doors and a frame, with a stone arch over the entrance door, the walls to be neatly pointed and 'twice whitened' steps, Portmadoc slates for the roofs, fixed with two stout zinc nails and good hard, burnt Bridgewater crease tiles, pointed in cement, for the ridge, would be carried out. Gerrard had quoted to ram the ground down well to receive the floor and lay it with self-jointed Bothenhampton stone.

Ten iron columns measuring six inches in diameter with one inch thick iron would be put in place and imported timber would be used for the 'common' rafters, measuring 3½ inches by 2½ inches, 'free of shakes, sap, large and dead knots or any other imperfections, 16 inches apart'. A Red Deal wrought, rebated and beaded door frame 6 inches by 4 inches, filled in with tongued boarding and hung folding, fastened with a good lock to the value of 10/-, twenty-four glazed openings of sheet glass, and guttering between the roofs concluded the precise and detailed specifications.

This Specification was accepted by the Andrews brothers and a contract was signed by them, assuring Lord Rivers that the rent would be met. A new factory materialised, two feet longer than the old mill but of only two single storey bays (the common practice for factories at that time) and with the roof well glazed. Was the property underinsured?

Lord Rivers had received £103.15/- for the destroyed mill gear and £813.15/- for the loss of the mill from the insurers. Andrews thought that Gerrard should pay half of the cost of the rebuilding contract and be paid when the work was completed. It is presumed that Andrews replaced the actual machines. What happened to the workers in the meantime? Did they manage to pay the rents of their cottages?

14. *Church Lane circa 1900. (R) Lot 53, Rookery Cottage, (C) Lot 51 The Magnolias. Inset 14a. (L) Lot 52, The Rookery. (R) Polly Gale's cottage and two others burnt down in 1902.*

★★★★★★★★★★

At the appointed hour, that day, shortly after fire had demolished the spinning and cordage factory in Burton, Miss Florence Templar walked to church from the nearby Rectory, on the arm of her young brother, Master John Templar, (along a carpet of coconut matting strewn with flowers), to St Mary's Church for her marriage to Mr John William Alexander, of Middlesborough. Many villagers had gathered, in spite of the terrible events of a few hours previous, to see the procession and in particular, the bride attired in a rich white silk dress trimmed with satin and adorned in a veil of Honiton lace. She wore a sprig of orange blossom in her hair and was attended by six bridesmaids.

How the winds and waves governed the lives of the inhabitants! Had the wind been blowing in another direction, then the whole of the centre of the village could have gone up in flames and the church, the Rectory and the waiting participants in the forthcoming nuptials, been engulfed in thick, black smoke. Fortunately, no one had been physically injured although several men had gallantly given no thought to their safety in trying to save the premises and their livelihood.

OUT OF THE ASHES

By the following August *The Bridport News* confirmed that the new factory, considerably reduced in size, was well underway and would be ready in two months. The Census Return of 1891 records some fifty workers, from the village, were employed in the mill and other employees would have come in from the surrounding district so that the workforce was about the same as sixteen years previous. Had the proprietors already switched to steam-driven turbines by the time of the fire? The magnificent factory chimney, which stood as high as the church tower, was not mentioned in connection with the event. It remained at that height until after another fire, when it was lowered.

★★★★★★★★★★

The fire in 1902 did not affect the mill but set alight cottages below the school. A spark from this gigantic chimney was the cause. Joe Buckler, then aged forty-three, scaled the roof between the burning cottages and his home, Magnolia Farmhouse and with a special tool, for that very purpose, pulled a wide strip of thatch out from between the properties, thereby preventing the fire from spreading further.

By 1911 when viewed by the writer, Eden Phillpotts, the spinning mill was more of long, high roofed sheds with sundry smaller buildings around it. For the villagers, the mills had provided a living for one hundred and fifty years. The final tenant was the company of Rendall and Coombs, who styled themselves as 'hemp, flax and tow spinners' with another factory at 13 West Allington. From the office there, a clerk would cycle out, each week, to Burton, with a bag on his back, containing the wages for the Burton employees. (Rendall and Coombs, continued to operate in Bridport until taken over by Bridport Industries in the 1950s. The wages for a number of factories under that umbrella received the payments, in cash each week. A van took the clerk around to the various factory offices, the driver having armed himself with a gun).

In the 1930s, the men, women and youngsters were employed, in Burton, in the same capacities as their great-grandparents had been before them. The significant difference was that no children under fourteen years of age, worked in the mill. Its closure soon after was a blow to the village. Several of the redundant workers then walked, or cycled, to Bridport to work in the rope and net factories. Others took up different employment. No one could afford to be without work. The rent had to be found.

The Burton factory bell, in the tone of "D", which Roberts had installed, still rang out at the hour for reporting to work and the end of the working day, until the last. AE [Bert] Williams, whose mother had died and left five small children, remembered as a youngster, around 1910, waiting for the bell to toll, at six o' clock in the evening, as it signalled that his two sisters would soon be returning from the factory, to prepare a meal. The spinners and corvisars, had competed with those in Bridport for well over six hundred years.

"Smakem" Joe Swaffield, from Shipton Gorge, had pulled down the high factory chimney, after the second fire, and left the base, which was later demolished altogether. By 1958, the retting ponds were overgrown and the path and bridge across the river, from Magnolia Farm, where several of the manufacturers had lived after Roberts's time, had fallen into disuse. At the former flax spinning mill the empty bell-turret still dominated the roof.

The spinning mill, ended its days as a vehicle repair shop and winter store for caravans, as part of Cheney's Garage business. It was stripped of its machines and net-hanging frames but left with the ghostly wheels and engine belts.

THE SEAFARERS

It was inevitable that being born in a coastal village and having contact with the sea from an early age, that the men of Burton Bradstock would be called to earn a living on the water. Throughout the centuries, men had sailed the seas. If they survived, they retired back to the village, never losing the pull of the sea and many took up seine and trawl net fishing. The wealthier sons, of land owners, also joined the Royal Navy, taking command in the many wars. When there was a lull in activities, they returned home, to their estates and resumed farming.

Burton Bradstock tenant, John Anning's will of the early 1700s, states that he had left his watch and *'two table bordes',* to his son, *'if he do come back safe from the Enges'*. Burton could boast numerous naval connections.

One Burton son, Sidney Shipp received a medal for gallantry, for the part he had played during his service in the Royal Navy detecting enemy U-boats in the Atlantic in 1943. Born at Norburton, he was called up at the age of twenty, just before Christmas 1939 at the same time as, Bill Bullock, another young man from Burton. Modest about what was involved in being awarded a Distinguished Service Medal, it is obvious that Sidney Shipp had experienced some dangerous, unpleasant and haunting times in the war. The particular U Boat that his ship sunk, was the pride of the German Navy, with the latest technology and was carrying ammunition to restock other U boats. "There is no glory in war", Shipp revealed later. "It was them or us but those men on board were young like us and were somebody's sons, husbands, brothers and sweethearts. " Although he was invited to receive the award from the King at an Investiture, it meant disruption to his meagre, precious leave and as he said, "We didn't know if we would be here tomorrow. " Unique to this, was that his father, Albert Shipp had been awarded the Army equivalent, the DCM, in the First World War, for his bravery in saving an officer, under fire, in France.

Early in the 1900s, Albert Shipp was a newcomer to Burton. Moving for advancement, at the request of Edward Sturdy, of Norburton, on the recommendation of a Sturdy

15. *Tommy Swaffield and Mabel Hussey mending nets at Burton Hive Beach 1935. Inset 15a Tommy Swaffield DSM.*

relative, where he was a gardener, (probably Teddington). He settled into village life and took a full part in its activities.

When the village was sold, in 1958, there was still a long list of men in Burton who had seen service in the armed forces. All these men were courageous, good, practical

16. *Mackerel fishing with a seine net, Burton Beach 1930s.*

and unassuming. The village was proud of them. When Tommy Swaffield, DSM, died in 1955, RB Howarth was rowed, by Ted Hitt and Louis Brown, a mile out to sea, to Tommy's favourite fishing ground and a casket containing his ashes was confined to the deep.

★★★★★★★★★★

Some of the Merchant Navy men had sailed out of Bridport Harbour. Many had served an apprenticeship, learning a trade before signing-on. Those with naval connections could be distinguished by their attire of navy blue jumpers, dark, serge trousers and a navy peaked cap. The fishermen without a naval background were often seen in bowler hats, (the original hard hat, for working purposes). None of them ever killed a seagull. These birds that nested in the cliffs, frequented the shore and followed the shoals of fish, or the plough far inland, were believed to carry the souls of dead sailors and fishermen.

Since man had first made a net and caught himself fish from the sea, off the Chesil Beach, the villagers had either earned, or supplemented, their incomes in this manner. As early as 1749, records refer to a lad from Powerstock being apprenticed to a Burton fisherman who agreed to provide him with meat, drink, wearing apparel and lodgings. Seine netting was the predominant type of fishing and the fishermen sometimes flouted the 'No fishing on Sunday' Court Leet law, by bringing their catches, in by the back-way to the village, through the fields near Cogden and Bredy Lane.

The seine net, which was made locally by the fishermen or the women braiders, could be up to one hundred yards long and thirty feet deep. The smaller ones were seventy to eighty feet long with about the same depth. The net resembled a long purse, with a narrow funnel at one end, [the bunt end], with a draw string. Long, strong ropes were attached to the end on board the boat and to the other side, which was held on the beach, [land end], by some of the crew. The top of the purse was strung with corks and the opposite side, with heavy, holed stones, (found on the beach), to weigh it down.

Once mackerel had been seen 'straying' [swimming in a shoal close to the shore], this long net was cast out in a semi-circle, from the boat, which was rowed by one oarsman, or a pair. If the net had trapped the shoal, the ropes would be hauled in gradually on to the beach and the catch would be 'in the bag'. A good catch would require a crew of eight or more men, to bring it ashore.

Crews often tried a 'venture shot' which was when no indication of fish, [usually mackerel] were known to be about. The net was cast out in the hope of getting a haul and the net was weighted so that it sank lower into the water.

With the heavier mesh nets, which dragged the bottom of the sea, plaice and flounders would come in with the catch. Before 1939, these "scoff fish" would go in "the driblet bag" and be put out for sale along the wall opposite the village shop. A pensioner fisherman would stand by to mind the takings which would be shared out amongst the crews, once a year.

Off Burton Ledge [a crop of rocks], a "trot line", was another means of fishing. A row

17. Circa 1932 Reg Buckler, Burton Bradstock farmer and fish merchant, 'the longest serving tenant of the Pitt-Rivers Estate when the Sale took place', with his wife, Gladys and assistants (L) Walty Tucker and (R) Ken Mullins, awaiting a catch of mackerel at West Bay. Note the solid tyres of the Ford lorry.

of hooks was attached to a rope, carrying a buoy at each end and on cold winter nights, just as it was getting dusk, between "two lights", fishermen would drift for herring. This worked best with a crew of three. The boat, manned by a crew member, was allowed to drift with the tide. A rope from the drift-net was held on shore by two others, who moved along the beach with the tide, predominantly from west to east. The fishers could start at Burton Hive and end up at Cogden.

Eels came up the River Bride, in season and were trapped, as were river trout. Young boys went 'tickling' trout and one lad, in 1901, cut his foot badly in the river by the school. He was laid on the kitchen table and the wound, requiring eighteen stitches, was treated without anaesthetic.

All the Census Returns from 1841 to 1901, taken every decade, list men who were serving in the Royal Navy or Merchant Navy, retired mariners and others employed as fishermen, or fish dealers. Fishing boats were built by the Forseys of Eype or by others, further up the Chesil Beach, such as the Toms family. By the 1880s, a man could earn twelve shillings a week, working part-time as a fisherman, which was as much as he earned in a week on the farm. This extra money would keep his children in boots.

The Lord of the Manor had allowed the fishermen to store their nets and boats on the Fishermen's Green, at The Hive Beach. In 1926, William Hutchings and Tommy Swaffield were renting boathouses. Few of the older fishermen could swim but there is no record of a Burton Bradstock fisherman drowning, such was their dexterity with their boats and local knowledge, that kept them safe. There had been loss of life, further up the Chesil Beach, where the beach shelved and the water was deeper. A very heavy catch of fish could weigh the boat down and swamp it. Desmond Gape's grandfather had drowned after he was caught in the nets, as he leaned overboard. Fishermen's heavy waders soon filled with water and clothing became saturated, dragging them down.

Often, shipwrecks had tested the seafarers to the limit. They never hesitated to attempt to save life and vessels. Many acts of bravery are recorded. Lifeboat men once rowed from Lyme Regis past Burton, in a horrendous storm, taking twenty-two and a half hours. That was the sort of tenacity all those local men possessed.

★★★★★★★★★★

The fishermen's wives would hawk the fish, selling from door to door and women were doing this up until 1914. They carried huge baskets on their arms, venturing to the villages inland, often walking as far as Maiden Newton, about fifteen miles, as the crow flies. The grandmothers would mind the children whilst the women were away. If they were unable to get back home within a day, the fisherwomen would sleep rough in barns and under hayricks. Times were always very hard and a few shillings extra, assisted the families to lead a slightly easier life. During the 1914 – 1918 war, it was the women and the older men who kept the fishing business going.

Before the First World War there had been a dozen boats working off the beach at Burton Hive alone but by the early 1930s, this had dwindled to eight working from Freshwater to Bexington. There was always great rivalry between the crews. The motto, for all, was *A dry seine never catch fish.'*

Eventually, motorisation enabled fish touts to make regular calls around the village. In 1939, Charles Moore, was dealing in fish. Reg Buckler, a cattle and pig dealer and Walter Thorner, a coal merchant, were also involved in buying catches off the beach and marketing them to fish shops inland, or selling on to other merchants in Poole. In addition, they travelled, in their solid-wheeled lorries, in the 1920s and 1930s, to Brixham, in the opposite direction, to top-up the consignments.

One of the last of the fish touts[travelling retailers], in Burton, was AE [Bert] Williams, who was born in the village and vastly knowledgeable about the art of fishing off the Chesil. Fred Copp, who came from Dorchester, joined him later as a partner. This was a partnership made on a very open-ended type of verbal agreement which was often fraught with problems. When they were unable to carry on, John Eastwood, a former cider company salesman turned writer, who had moved to the village, writing books and articles about the fisherman's and labourer's lot, took over their modest business, which consisted of an ancient van, a pair of dubious scales and plenty of old newspapers, unfettered by public health regulations.

Fish was the staple diet of the Burton people. Through the seasons, the fisherman's home took the less marketable of the catches. Fish roes were considered very nutritious, especially for children. For the housewives, fish were plentiful. They busied themselves salting sprats and herrings in earthenware jars or wooden barrels which were stored for consumption during the worst of the winter months. Occasionally there was a salmon on the table! A licence was supposed to be held to catch these prize fish but there were times when they were accidentally caught-up in the nets.

The large households, hotels and guest houses were the fishermen's main customers, coveting lobsters, which fetched a good price, found in certain fishing grounds off the Chesil Beach. In the early 1900s, Miss Rachel Lenthall, had witnessed a catch of around 30,000 fish, presumably mackerel. In December 1921, nearly 10,000 herrings were landed between Burton Hive and Swyre. It was a very good season and brought a welcome bonus for the crews.

Following the arrival of the railway, if the catches were good, the surplus bushels were left loose in the bottom of the boat and rowed from Burton or Freshwater to West Bay. At the harbour, the fish were boxed and put on the train for the London markets but the Second World War curtailed the entire business when the beach and immediate hinterland were barricaded with barbed wire and iron defence structures, with the land,

18. Fishermen gather around a 'venture shot' of mackerel on Burton Beach, 1930. Fred White (standing centre holding net), Steve Northover (hands in pockets, third on left of fisherman sorting fish), Walty Tucker (gathering-up seine net front R), Joe Buckler, (skipper extreme R back to camera). Inset 18a Pushing the boat out in the 1950s. AE [Bert] Williams in trilby hat.

close to the foreshore, being mined.

Licences were demanded by the Ministry of Agriculture and Fisheries, in 1939, to retail the catches. Because of petrol rationing the fish merchants were restricted from travelling too far a-field to the inland towns of Yeovil, Chard, Ilminster and Crewkerne, where they had always found ready markets, selling direct to the fish shops and consequently, the numbers declined.

After the Second World War, until the time of the Pitt-Rivers Estate's Sale, a few fishermen still supplemented their normal living with fishing from the Chesil Beach. From Abbotsbury, the Huddy family was the last to give up fishing for a living, some years later. In their heyday, they hired out boats and nets and there were Burton men who had taken advantage of that system.

By 1958, only part-time fishing was practised at Burton and catching mackerel with feathered lines was becoming popular and lucrative. There was still the camaraderie, as well as the excitement, when the fish were seen to *'be straying'*. A good catch meant some extra cash for the crew and a delicious meal. The whole stretch of the Chesil Beach had lost nothing over the centuries but the disposal of the beach, in the forthcoming auction, could bring marked changes to that way of life.

SMUGGLERS

Smuggling had always been part of the fisherman's way of life. Those who participated considered it 'a rightful trade'. From the sixteenth century, goods were brought ashore in the dead of night and distributed along the routes inland, from Burton Bradstock, north to Shipton Gorge, Askerswell and thence to the main Crewkerne to Bath and Bristol roads. In the 1700s, the Customs and Excise officers, known as "the riding men", patrolled the coast on horseback. Some of the smugglers were caught and imprisioned. The majority were never apprehended.

Later, coastguard stations were set-up around the country and along the Chesil, cottages, up to six in number in each block, were built at Bridport Harbour, Cogden, Abbotsbury, Langton Herring and Wyke Regis. The coastguards kept a look-out for invaders as well as vessels carrying contraband. There had always been a trade in smuggled goods across the Channel where the ships from Bridport Harbour sailed, on a regular basis.

Another type of smuggling had been carried out along the Chesil Beach for several hundreds of years. When a ship broke up and the cargo was washed ashore, the locals would be there to retrieve it. They felt it their right to take any wrack [wreck] that washed up on the beach and some of it was declared. The Chesil coast was notorious for disasters and many of the cottages were built with ships' timbers or fires kept going and poor families fed and clothed with stuff that came ashore.

The law was that it had to be handed over to the Receiver of Wrecks. An exception was that in the Burton area, the Lord of the Manor was entitled to take the wreck, as long as ' neither cat, dog or man were thrown up alive, ' depending on what part of the beach, between the tide marks, that the items were washed-up.

In the stormy winter of 1933, Ephraim Hussey assisted by Walter Thorner brought ashore at Burton, a huge butt of wine, totalling some one hundred and four gallons. The undamaged barrel was duly handed over to the Receiver of Wrecks.

During the Second World War, The Three Horseshoes Inn seemed to be the centre for many of the transactions. As in days of old when everyone in the whole village, from the parson to the fishermen, was involved, so, during the war years there were very few who could honestly say that they had not been on the receiving end of some illicit goods. The exception was certainly Frank Bishop, who felt that men were risking their lives to bring in fuel and needed commodities. Generally, the black economy caused little harm.

19. Warehouses at West Bay, circa 1890s. (R) The railway station. Inset 19a West Bay circa 1960s.

Most of the fishermen were involved in a bit of black market trading. The wife of one dealer, received an unexpected visit from the Customs and Excise officials who arrived, clutching a warrant to search their home and premises. The husband was away on other business and she had to convince the lawmen that there was no contraband to be found.

Leading the Excise men into the spare bedroom of the cottage, she portrayed a melancholy air and related how it had been her dear old parents' room. "They were such good folk and have now passed away," she informed the officials. It would have been far too insensitive to search the bedroom and they moved on, finding nothing anywhere to implicate the couple in any illegal trading. Little did the officers realise that secreted under the bed and hidden by the pretty valance, were the illegal goods, for which they were searching.

There were numerous dealers, throughout the war years, in the village, who bought and sold goods that were on ration, or in short supply, which they had obtained by irregular means. There were many, from all sections of the community, who were only too willing to buy from them in order to bolster their rations of sugar, dried fruit, tea, butter, cheese, coal, and other commodities, or to 'make a few bob'. One young man was sent to prison for six months, although unbeknown to the magistrates, he was shielding others.

Another local dealer, had obtained two large packs of tins of condensed milk which he had hidden in the hay of the cow stall manger. Before he ever sold on the goods or attempted to use any of the forty-eight cans, he became uncomfortable about the situation and buried the packs in one of his fields, completely forgetting about the incident. Twenty years later, he was working in a field and sat down on the grass to have a rest. Suddenly he discovered that he was covered in ants. On close inspection, he found that he was sitting on the very spot where he had buried the tins which had rusted through and the ants had made their nest where sweet and tasty food was on-tap.

THE FARMERS

The major mode of life, that was apparent in West Dorset, was farming. Records survive that tell of extensive sheep husbandry on the slopes of the hills. The Domesday Survey stated that there were eight hundred sheep in the Manor of Burton Bradstock and as early as 1598 there was a court case over sheep rustling. A visitor to Dorset, wrote of early factory farming with lambs being fattened in dark sheds, in the eighteenth century.

The Manorial Rolls record the keeping of cattle and pigs in Burton Bradstock and there was a communal bull, penned in Bull Lane [Grove Road], in the eighteenth century. At this same time, societies sprang up to improve agricultural methods and to instruct farmers and their labourers. The West Dorset Agricultural Society was in existence in 1840 and the Melplash Agricultural Society, replacing the former, was inaugurated in 1847. For Burton Bradstock, records survive of the payment of tithes, when one tenth of the crop or dairy produce, had to be given to the incumbent. The income from a few acres of land off Gages Lane, known as Parson's Hill, was paid to the church.

Agricultural depressions had hit the farmers who rented from the Pitt-Rivers Estate, like others involved in agriculture, throughout the British Isles. In the latter half of the nineteenth century and again in the 1920s and 1930s there were bad times. During these periods, men left the land and sought work elsewhere, particularly on the railways and to naval ports where rope making was still needed. Others went to Somerset and Wales to the mining towns. During the two recent wars, agriculture had progressed and the farmers prospered.

★★★★★★★★★★

Farmers' wives turned to earning extra money, during the lean-time, by taking paying guests. Staying on a farm, helping to feed the animals, collect eggs straight from the nest, eat fresh bacon, cheese, butter, fruit and vegetables was a new adventure for city dwellers. Those who took advantage of these farm holidays were the wealthier class and at Manor Farm, Mrs Jack Lenthall, with her daughter Jeanne and only limited help in the house, fed and entertained visitors. Jeanne organised

20. Harvesting on Manor Farm, 1930s. Dave Legg on top of the wagon, Fred White pitching up the sheaves of corn.

tennis parties, as Manor Farm lawn lent itself as a full-sized grass court. In these carefree days after a dreadful war, tennis was fashionable for both the men and women who had the free time and money to take holidays.

Then came subsidies and the government's encouragement to plough up land, to produce more food, from 1939 to 1945. This production drive saved the farmers. Land that had lain permanently fallow, or had been covered in gorse for hundreds of years, came under the plough for the first time. The hills and slopes of Burton were some of the first to be rid of acres of gorse, brambles and bracken. Farmers were purchasing machinery and modern equipment, encouraging the workers to become skilled in using it, whilst the farm labourer was beginning to be seen in a better light and had a Workers' Union to protect him.

During the First World War some 90,000 women were recruited into the Women's Land Army and by 1945 there were 230,000 in employment. Land girls came to Dorset and were invaluable in the assistance they gave on the farms whilst the men were absent. Many had never been to the countryside before. Every morning a lorry collected those who lived out and drove them to the farms and the market gardens, where they worked. Several were employed on the Burton farms; some were billetted with Mrs Hutchings at Somercotes.

In Burton, in 1958, around two hundred dairy cows, occasionally accompanied by the herd bulls, ambled their way through the village streets, to and fro, from the meadows along the River Bride, twice daily, to be milked. Beside the River Bride lay the lush fields where they grazed. When the weather warmed up, the farmers moved young stock to pastures new. The fields that went with the farms, were scattered around the village and in spring the animals would be taken through the streets. This was quite a 'circus act'

as the calves were frisky, having been housed all the winter. Several helpers were required to run on ahead, or stand in the gateways, whilst the animals scampered past. In the autumn, the procedure was reversed. Moving stock was usually done very early on a Sunday morning when few, except the fishermen, who could be coerced into standing on guard, were about in the village.

21. Grove Road, formerly Bull Lane. William Gale, butcher and farmer who had riding hacks for hire, on his horse, around 1935. (R) Butcher's shop. (Standing far L) farm workers, Mrs Ward, in bonnet and possibly older relative. (C), "Willy", Rob Gale and brother Reg. Other unknown.

The high output from "intensive farming" was far away. The pigs lived and grubbed around the farmyard, whilst the porkers remained confined in sties, where they had ample space. The Dorset Horn sheep could be seen on the hillsides, brought in for the annual round-up of washing, shearing and culling. On Manor Farm, the shepherd held sway over all the other farm workers. Shep's word was law and definitely no woman was allowed in the vicinity of the flock.

★★★★★★★★★★

Most of the surplus stock on the farms was sold at Bridport Market. As late as 1913, the animals had been penned and auctioned in West Street. The horses that had brought the country people into town, were stabled at the inns and hotels, such as The [Knight's] Bull and Greyhound Hotels, where there were ostlers to attend to them. The traps and wagons were laid-up in the street, row upon row, until the farmers and their families, were ready to harness up and go home.

When the street site was required for a post office, Morey, the auctioneer, moved the market to St Michael's Lane. The market was held on Wednesdays and Saturdays, a grant dating back to the time of Queen Elizabeth I, finally closing post Second World War. Reports refer to *'pigs cheek by jowl in the street'* and once the farmers became mechanised, traffic jams in St Michael's Lane.

★★★★★★★★★★

As for poultry, they were the prerogative of the farmer's wife who saw to the management, collecting, washing and marketing the eggs, claiming the cash, known as "pin money", as their own. Each farm stocked a mixture of poultry breeds. There were regulations about marketing eggs throughout the Second World War. A farmer's wife taking a huge basket of eggs to family and friends, in Bridport, accepted a lift with a ministry inspector, fearing all the time that her young child might divulge the contents of the basket.

Some farmers' wives extended their income by rearing for the table. Table poultry were produced mainly for the Christmas market, although, hotels and the larger houses included poultry on their menus, at other times of the year. Poultry was only served at Christmas by the majority of the working people, in 1958. Those who kept them, ate duck, with the first fresh garden peas and newly dug potatoes, at Whitsun. The farmers who reared poultry, enjoyed the meat more often and regularly ate goose.

There was an outlet for green geese, which had been fed on grass and stubble-land to be eaten at Michaelmas, by the more affluent or superstitious people. The latter thought that if goose was eaten on Michaelmas Day, the 29th September, then they would not lack for money during the coming year. In earlier times, goose was eaten when the Lord of the Manor, or his Agent, came to the village, on the September Rent Day, joining the senior tenants and village dignitaries at The Anchor Inn.

Although some other parts of the country may have always eaten turkey, in West Dorset, it was not popular until the American soldiers, who were stationed in the locality, prior to D-Day 1944, introduced their custom when feasting on turkey, on their Thanksgiving Day and at Christmas. There was one mishap connected with the American soldiers' Thanksgiving Day dinner, when an inexperienced cook did not remove the entrails of some fifty turkeys and cooked them whole. The carcases had to be discarded and were fed to nearby pigs.

★★★★★★★★★★

After the Second World War, the men began to filter back to Burton. A number of farmers' sons had been exempt from service, causing indignation from those whose men had gone off to war. Some, whose backgrounds were far removed from agriculture, became students on farms, under an ex-servicemen's scheme and Bunny Lenthall took-on several of these men. The farm labourers picked up the threads of life but were more restless and aware of better wages and working under improved conditions. Machines were taking over from horses but the farm workers still had to put in long hours, in all weathers and the majority lived in a tied cottage. ('Tied' meant that it came with the farm worker's job).

Up for sale, in the crowded marquee, on that late July day, in 1958, was the largest and most progressive farm, referred to in the old Manorial records as Burton Manor Farm, tenanted by Martin Lenthall, (known as Bunny to everyone). His grandfather, Henry, had taken over Manor Farm in 1911, followed by son, Jack, a pillar of the community, who farmed there until his death in 1949. With the farm were six farm workers' tied cottages. Four other large farms and several smallholdings, belonging to the Pitt-Rivers Estate, were destined to come under the hammer, as well.

22. Looking up the High Street with (R) Buckler and Mullins's general village shop and newsagents, circa 1920. (Centre) Lot 45, The Post Office, Lot 13, Reading Room, with deep windows, and beyond Lot 47, Rock House.

AND THE OTHERS

When war broke out in 1939, the Directory listed twenty-two private residents, three public houses, eleven farmers, several guest houses and holiday apartments, four shops, a blacksmith, a miller, a builder, a motor engineer/garage, two dairymen, a carpenter, three fish dealers, a coal merchant, a carrier/bus service, a post office, a music teacher, a beekeeper, the rating officer and Mrs Alexander Pitt-Rivers, who termed herself as a poultry farmer.

Likewise in 1958, those engaged in the main occupations, needed the support of various services in the form of general shops, a shoe-mender, a dressmaker, a baker, a milkman, a blacksmith/farrier, (who could do an ironmonger's and wheelwright's job), several general shops, a miller, a coal merchant, a carpenter, (doubling as an undertaker), a chimney sweep, a roadman, a motor and marine engineer, who would also repair a bicycle and someone to recharge wireless accumulators. There were itinerant men called "strappers" who could turn their hand to most of the jobs on the land and a few gardeners who plied between the larger houses.

Once a man, had the responsibility to looked after the Barr Lane sewer. He retrieved a lady's false teeth, on one occasion! There was even a man who went around the village, in the evenings, or early on Sunday mornings, to cut the men's hair. At one time, this was Tommy Roper. Burton was progressive in having a garage with petrol pumps, which

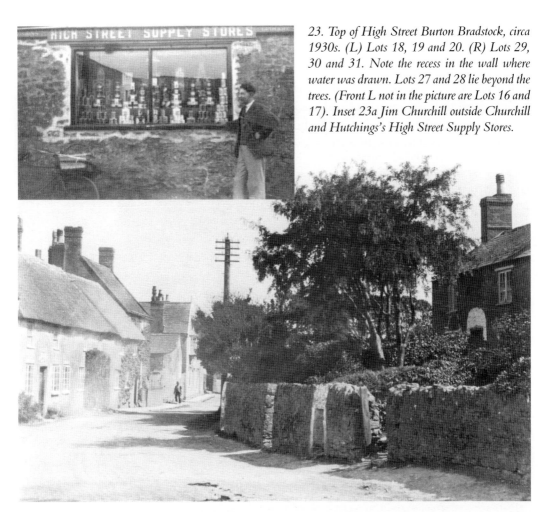

23. Top of High Street Burton Bradstock, circa 1930s. (L) Lots 18, 19 and 20. (R) Lots 29, 30 and 31. Note the recess in the wall where water was drawn. Lots 27 and 28 lie beyond the trees. (Front L not in the picture are Lots 16 and 17). Inset 23a Jim Churchill outside Churchill and Hutchings's High Street Supply Stores.

was being used more and more, by the farmers and businessmen and as people acquired vehicles.

Few owned a television at the time of the Queen's Coronation in 1953 but by 1958, some residents were buying a black and white set, with a fourteen-inch screen. Local man, Henry Aves, a wireless engineer, employed by Best Brothers, Bridport, furniture and electrical dealers, had amazed everyone with his knowledge and he was advising about the buying of sets and installing huge aerials, like flagpoles. Nearly everyone owned a wireless, known later as a radio, as they became connected to the electricity supply. The old cumbersome sets, generated by accumulators, which required recharging, were being replaced by smaller, portable but expensive electrical models.

Most importantly, for the women, was the practice of braiding, from home, to earn extra money. In centuries past, men, as well, had spun, made ropes and braided at home during the winter months, when there was no work on the land, or fishing available. At the time of the Sale, this was done by the housewives, few of whom went out to work.

These women were very industrious, making hay, pig and rabbit nets, billiard pockets and some took on the huge task of making trawl, seine and tennis nets, at home. The work was brought out to the cottages from the factories and had to be completed within a designated time - usually a week, resulting in the women often staying up until the early hours, to get the consignment finished, in order to receive payment.

All these different people, with their various skills, who lived in and around the village, contributed to its self-sufficiency. All of them depended on each other.

24. Crowning the May Queen, on the Rectory lawn, circa 1939.

THE VISITORS

Bridport had been known for its bracing air since 1820 and from the latter part of that century, visitors began to arrive, staying at the few guest houses, that enterprising women had set up, or in rented cottages. Landed gentry had second homes in Burton Bradstock. Prominent, were the villas on the cliff, built in the 1880s, which belonged to the Pitt-Rivers family. They named them "Alpha" and "Omega". Day trippers came to Burton and Freshwater beaches, first by pony and trap and then, in due course, by charabanc and later by a bus service that

25. Visitors on Burton Beach pre-1939. The changing-tents could be hired. Inset 25a 1944, US soldiers practise at Burton Bradstock for the D-Day landing. Note the grapnel in the foreground.

came from Bridport to Burton, via West Bay. Local women provided teas and made some extra money, whilst picnics on the beach were popular, as there were few food and drink outlets.

Freddie Mullins, a shopkeeper in Burton, was enterprising enough to set up a refreshment stall on the beach in the 1930s. His son, Ken, recalled tramping the beach, 'cinema style' selling ice creams from a tray. 'Stop-me-and-buy-one' ice cream sellers, on bicycles, were to be found in the vicinity. For a picnic, wrack was gathered on the beach, pebbles piled up in a heap, a fire was lit and the kettle boiled, although, finding a clean water supply was the main difficulty, in the early days. Some brought the water with them.

Other visitors came to the village, by means of the Great Western Railway, to West

Bay and were brought out to Burton by pony and trap. These were wealthy people, accompanied by their servants, who stayed several weeks. In the 1920s and 1930s, others from working class backgrounds, who now had some free time, besides the Bank Holidays, were camping, in tents, (ex-army tents from the First World War), on the cliffs at Burton Bradstock and a few motor-drawn caravans began to appear whilst horse-drawn, round-topped, (covered wagon style), wooden caravans, could still be seen on Burton cliff, as late as 1939.

Between the wars, the villagers became more adventuresome. Organisations were formed and excursions were taken to other seaside resorts such as Weymouth and Lyme Regis, in open-topped charabancs and later coaches. Going on outings was one of the latest recreations.

George Bonfield, proprietor of a garage and motor works, in Bridport, had motor-cars for hire. His credentials listed that he was *'Official repairer to the Royal Automobile Club, and the Automobile Association and Motor Union.'* Circular tours of the neighbourhood, lasting anything up to four hours, at thirty shillings, or whole day trips, were two, of over a dozen charabanc tours, his firm undertook. A tour to Beaminster, Sherborne Abbey, Shaftesbury, Milton Abbas and Dorchester, taking in all the towns and villages, along the way, was an all-day trip and cost £4.

In the 1930s, Captain Pitt-Rivers, aware of the increase in visitors coming to visit the seaside at Burton, had a private road constructed to the beach, off the Weymouth Road and was charging a toll. A house was built at the bottom of Beach Road and a toll keeper employed. His job was to raise and lower a wooden barrier across the roadway and take the fees, charging sixpence, or a shilling, according to the size of the vehicle. Beside the barrier was a narrow gateway where pedestrians could pass unchallenged.

The Second World War brought a halt to camping and to anyone going on, or near, the beach, unless on military or ministry business. As the dark days of the Second World War became imminent, the village was again giving up its sons and daughters to join the armed forces. The older men who had served in the 1914-18 war, were assigned to the Home Guard, the Civil Defence and the Special Constabulary. Some of the genteel ladies served in the Women's Royal Voluntary Service, administering to the soldiers stationed in and around the village, who came to the servicemen's canteen in Donkey Lane. The women who braided, turned their skills to making camouflaged nets or gun pull-throughs, whilst the visitors to the district were now evacuees and soldiers.

Burton accommodated a great many troops during the war, in camps which were situated at The Hive, Freshwater, Annings Lane and Common Knapp. Army lorries and tanks continuously threaded their way through the village, back and forth to the beach, Bridport, Weymouth, Beaminster and villages up the Bride Valley. In 1943 the American soldiers moved in, preparing for the greatest battle in history. Burton cliffs were used for rehearsals and to prepare them for a dreadful challenge when they landed on the French beaches and scaled the Point du Hoc and similar cliffs, sadly, resulting in huge casualties.

26. *Burton Bradstock Home Guard. 1939-1945. Back row (L to R): ?,Fred Norris, ?, ?, Bill Helps.*
Middle row (L to R): Fred Mullins, Arthur Bartlett, Fred Kerley, Geoff Derryman, Dennis Hawkins, ?,
Archie Mitchell, ?, Ivor Guyatt, Bill Hutchings, Henry Pitman and Bob Hawkins.
Seated front row (L to R): 'Jock' Johnson, ?, Fred Jupp, John Panten, Albert Shipp, DCM, Henry Palmer, Alf
Churchouse, Bill Nethercott, ?, Bunny Lenthall, Dick Ramsden and - Foot.
Seated on ground (L to R): Dennis Bullock, Leslie Chilcott, Cecil Stirke and – Gale.
Frank Bishop is absent.

27. Burton Bradstock Second World War Civil Defence unit.
Back row (L to R): Dicker Thorner, George Downton, Albert Stevens, Dick Galpin, Harold Greenham, Bob Cammell Snr.
Seated (L to R); Dorothy Jones, Elizabeth Shipp, Nancy Wratislaw, RB Howarth, Ruby Gale and Lilian Swaffield.

They had sailed from Weymouth and Portland Harbours, fighting alongside the British, Canadian and other allied forces.

★★★★★★★★★★

Throughout England, immediately after the war, there was a wish to get away and in 1951, the secretary at Manor farm, confirmed the booking for the first car and tent at Freshwater, at 1/6d a night. A caravan and tenting camp sprang-up there and the Hawkins and Kerley families re-established camps in the cliff fields. There had always been camping, in moderation, on these particular sites but the growth in tentage and caravans soared.

During the following seasons, far more visitors arrived in Burton. Camps for organisations such as the Boys Brigade, Boy Scouts and Girl Guides were to be seen on the fields beside the Cliff Road, at Freshwater, Marsh Barn and along Bredy Road. This was the beginning of the real tourist industry. Few working class people ventured abroad. If they did, they travelled by sea. Air travel was still in its infancy, as a means of transport for holiday and business destinations.

When, a seventeen year old, girl from Burton Bradstock was selected to travel to Canada, on a United Kingdom youth exchange scheme, in 1951, she crossed the Atlantic by liner, taking five days, each way. In the 1950s young men were conscripted, for two years, into the armed forces. Many, who were recruited, found themselves being sent abroad, by sea, in troop carriers.

Bridport railway station was still functioning at the time of the Sale and trips by train from Bridport were being offered to Paddington, at 30/- return, whilst an outing to Bath Spa could be made for 14/9d. Shorter journeys to the county town, Dorchester, cost 2/9d return fare.

During the summer of 1957, the Estate recorded that nine thousand vehicles had descended on the fields, used for parking cars, adjacent to the beach. Was the time ripe for a move away from the old system? Captain Pitt-Rivers must have calculated what the Burton part of his estate was worth.

THE SCHOOL

A report of 1846/47, stated that there were 174 children in Burton Bradstock, attending either a day, evening and/or Sunday school in the village. Several of these would have been Dames' Schools, which were often more of a minding service. Any proper schooling was usually directed at the boys. A Church of England school had been established in 1845 and pupils left at twelve years of age. Some stayed on longer but those from the poorer families, quitted school as soon as they were old enough. Other children attended part-time, working on the farms and in the mills, three or four days a week.

The present School was first opened in 1864, on land given by Lord Rivers. Prior to that, a cottage, on the same site, was being used as the schoolroom and the tenant, Zacharia Chick, who was born in Crewkerne, became the Schoolmaster. Chick had married into a Burton family, the Clark Hoskins. He also acted as an insurance agent. By 1851 he was joined by his son, as a pupil teacher. A charge was made for attending school at the time, with a reduction for each additional child. Two cottages, in Church Lane, were demolished to make way for the new school building and the school was built from public subscription, with Lord Rivers contributing £40. The official opening, when all the buildings were completed, was not until 1866.

There were building regulations and the high windows, in the new school, formed part of the plan. Although there had to be six square feet of floor space per child, there were not enough desks. The children stood for many of the lessons and Mrs Daphne Bartlett, née Legg, remembered, around 1900, sitting in tiered seats and writing on slates. She started school at the age of two-and-a-half and often fell asleep, only to be awakened with a blow to the head, from the teacher. There was no requirement for a sports' field!

Reading, writing and arithmetic, religious knowledge and "the object lesson" were deemed the important subjects. Singing, recitation and dancing formed a large part of the curriculum. Every morning started with prayers and a lesson in Religious Knowledge. The children learnt the Ten Commandments and The Lord's Prayer by heart and were tested by the Rector on a weekly basis. In the early 1900s, the school children were taught about Nelson and the Battle of Trafalgar and the Burton Bradstock connection with young midshipman, Richard Roberts, from The Grove, who served on the Flagship, "The Victory". The Rector's wife and other ladies visited the school to be shown the girls' needlework attempts, particularly as these benefactors had contributed a bolt of material, from which aprons, or blouses, could be fashioned.

This was a time when children walked to school from, Cogden, Bredy and Marsh Barn, in all winds and weathers, remaining in their wet clothes all day. Some children came from poor families and were barefoot. The Headmaster, Thomas Milburne, used to beat the boys, who arrived at school with no boots. Pupils journeyed from outlying hamlets (and in due course from Shipton Gorge, when the school there closed in the1950s), for the next fifty years, until school transport was provided.

In 1907, all the harsh regime of the Victorian era, changed with the arrival of the certificated, new Headmaster, Robert Bertrand Howarth, from Lancashire, supported by his wife, Alice, who was also a qualified teacher. Howarth had been brought up in an isolated hamlet in the village of Harwood. He walked to school two miles each way, over a bleak moor. Originally, he had wanted to be a veterinary surgeon but influenced by his father, went into teaching. Prior to coming to Burton, he taught at a school near Rugby. His background fitted him well for his work in a rural community, with spinning mills.

28. Robert Bertrand Howarth, M.B.E., 1881-1972. Born in Lancashire.
Headmaster Burton Bradstock C. of E. School, 1907-1944, Chairman of Burton Bradstock Parish Council, 1914-1972, Church Warden of St Mary's Church, 1919-1972, served on Bridport R.D.C. 1949-1972, Chairman West Dorset Water Board 1958-1972 and Founder and Secretary of the Bride Valley Branch of the Royal British Legion.

RB Howarth's origins were humble. When he was born, in the harsh winter of January 1881, the second of four sons, the family was living at "The Old Green", Harwood, not many miles from Bolton. His young father was a calico bleacher and his wife's three younger siblings were living with them. One of them, Lilian Tootill, aged thirteen, was a cotton weaver. RB Howarth's maternal grandfather was also employed in the cotton trade. Other branches of the family were crofters.

Ten years later, the family could be found at the mill cottages in Bradshaw. RB Howarth, aged ten, was attending school full-time, whilst his fourteen year old, elder brother, James, was a factory "finisher, in the cotton trade". Schooling was compulsory up to age thirteen, although in the Lancashire cotton area, children still often worked part-time in the mills. Howarth, being a clever scholar, probably attended school full-time, where a fee of pence still had to be paid each week.

By 1891, there were two more young brothers and the three Toohills, were still living with the family, bringing in some extra money. There were over four hundred cotton factories in Lancashire in 1900 and a bleaching works was situated where the Howarths lived.

Seemingly having moved back into a more populated area by 1901, the whole family was engaged in cotton manufacturing or as shop assistants, except RB Howarth who was, by now, an assistant schoolmaster. He set off to undertake his studies at Exeter and went back up to Rugby, where he continued to teach until his consequential move to Burton, in 1907. He married in 1906, a young woman, Alice Hannaford, from a middle-class, West Country, journalistic family, who he had met at college.

RB Howarth introduced a wider curriculum in Burton school and set up a football team. A hardy individual, with a marked accent and of medium height, throughout his long service as schoolmaster, the sound of his approach was detected by the clatter of his wooden clogs, a left-over from his days in the North Country!

The girls, under Mrs Howarth, learnt cookery, knitting and sewing (which included darning), at first in her home and later in the Women's Institute Hall. All the children took part in country dancing, with either Mrs Howarth, or Mrs Rodford, née Marsh, at the piano or the ancient harmonium. The older boys were encouraged to do woodwork and gardening, equipping them for later life, in a practical way. Evening classes, that had been started in conjunction with the school, were expanded and encouraged by the new headmaster, enabling many a clever pupil, forced to leave school at fourteen, to benefit from extra tuition.

Medals were awarded for regular attendance and whilst there were some sickly children who missed school on account of their health and others who were taken out to help at home or on the farms, there was a surprising number of pupils who never missed a day. Some gained medals for six and seven years' regular attendance. Inspectors' visits were regular, too and the school always received high commendation, both under the headship of Milburne and Howarth.

The same pattern of schooling continued through the two wars. Howarth served in the Royal Navy during the First World War but came back to educate yet another generation of village children. He was a strict disciplinarian but was fairer in his approach than his predecessor, although the boys still feared a caning with a whippy, ash stick, which he had cut from the hedge.

At the School, the timetable was disrupted in 1939, when evacuees from London, were billeted locally. With their own teachers, the evacuees attended school in the afternoons and the village children had lessons in the mornings. Gradually this scheme was dispensed with, as many of the London children returned home, leaving behind a few who stayed throughout the war.

In the Second World War, the Headmaster encouraged the children to save in the National Savings scheme, to raise money for war weapons, [ships and aeroplanes], and to collect waste paper. The older children in the school, some only nine years old, were paired off and collected the paper and cardboard from the households, on a weekly basis. They were termed "cogs in the wheel" and wore a badge of a little red cog-wheel, on their lapels.

As it was a Church of England school, Ascension Day was marked by the older children climbing the steps to the church tower from where they marvelled at the view of their village and sang hymns such as "Hail the Day that sees Him Rise". Empire Day was no less important and a map of the Empire was displayed and patriotic songs were sung in school before the announcement that it would be a half-day holiday.

The senior boys spent a great deal of time at the school gardens. Tony Legg remembered the march to the Jubilee allotments, set back from Beach Road and the other school gardens, in Annings Lane; Howarth being a great advocate of the National effort to "Dig for Victory". As an air raid warden, he did 'dummy-runs' for air raids at the school and the children had to put on their gasmasks and get under the desks, to become familiar with the procedures, in case of an attack. All the windows were stuck, in a criss-cross fashion, with gummed paper, to minimise the fall-out of glass in the event of an air raid. The children got used to hearing 'planes, friend and foe, passing overhead. Sometimes there were "dog fights", in the air, to witness. When an aeroplane crashed at Freshwater there was great curiosity.

29. Headmaster RB Howarth's final class at Burton Bradstock school 1944. Howarth is standing by the window whilst an US army officer speaks to the children.
Back row (L to R): Elizabeth Buckler, John Riggs, Bernard Thorner, Tony Legg
Middle row (L to R): James Churchill, Andrew Collins, Enid Price, Robert Cammell, June Downton, Gordon Legg.
Front row (L to R): Frederick Kerley, David Kerley, Benjamin Bryant, Pamela Darby, Alice Legge and Amy Collins.

R B Howarth retired in 1944, staying on to see-in his successor. He was to continue to serve the community in his 'retirement' for another twenty-five years and for most of those years was a widower.

Things changed dramatically when Miss Gwendoline Boddy, a woman who towered over everyone at six feet tall, took over the running of Burton School. Her 'town' methods and teaching were frowned on and many of the children were bewildered. She did not spare the cane and some children were frightened. She changed the method of handwriting with a system called "pot hooks" and the children wrote in "jotters", where should a blot fall, the result was a hard rap across the hand with a solid, round ruler. She used an official cane on the boys. It is for her hard-line and the amusing writing method for which she is remembered, by those she taught. The older girls of nine and ten were taught needlework, in The Magnolias [schoolhouse] by Miss Boddy's colleague, Miss Cowgill. These little girls, queuing at the back door, to go in to the kitchen, where they worked at the wooden table covered with a chenille cloth, eyed up the gleaming red apples growing in the garden.

Miss Boddy's redeeming act was to hire a taxi, at the eleventh hour, to get Audrey Huxter, an evacuee, to the Bridport Grammar School, where she was due to sit the entry examination; her guardians were not aware of her brilliance and that she would be sure to obtain a scholarship.

About this time, school dinners, which were delivered in heat-proof metal canisters, were introduced at 4d each per day. Previously, children who lived in the village went home from noon to one-thirty and children who came in from the outlying hamlets brought some food in a tin or tied up in a cloth. The first school dinner to arrive at Burton School was macaroni cheese. This was a ridiculous meal for country children who were being brought-up on plain foodstuffs. Most of it was sent back to the canteen in Bridport where it had been cooked.

Throughout RB Howarth's headship, an examination took place at around eleven years of age. Those who passed the scholarship were sent to Bridport Grammar School, in St Andrew's Road, [formerly the Secondary School, until Latin, as a subject, was introduced]. Those who were not to go to the Grammar School, remained at the village school until they were fourteen years old. There was a certain amount of expense associated with the Grammar School and some children were denied the opportunity, as their parents could not afford the extra costs. The wealthier families sent their children to private schools in Bridport and then on to the Grammar School or boarding schools. Until 1945, a place at the Grammar School was possible by paying fees. With the 1944 Education Act, at around eleven years old, the segregation was either to the Grammar School, Bridport General School or the Secondary School, in Allington. Bobby Cammell had been accepted for the Technical College in Weymouth. Quite an adventure, travelling there daily!

When the children left school, they either went on to further education, mostly with teaching in mind, or joined the services, the greater number preferring the Royal or Merchant Navies, whilst the rest found apprenticeships locally, in various trades. The majority of the girls worked as domestics, or in the factories, shops and offices, until they married. Marriage, was generally the goal set for young women but a few went on to further education. For some farmers' daughters, places were found in banks, as women clerks became more acceptable. All wages were low, amounting to a few pounds a week, in the 1950s. As the housing needs of Burton began to be met, following the war, there was talk of a new, modern school building, with a recreational field in Annings Lane.

In 1958, the playground games were still similar to those that the grandparents had played, Tag, "Farmer's in His Den", Hop-scotch, "I Sent a Letter to My Love", and war games for the bigger boys.

The school, now under the headship of Leonard Starkey, the eleven year olds were being transferred to the Alfred Colfox Comprehensive School in Bridport, collected by bus. For some, this was the first introduction to their counterparts in the town. At the time of the Pitt-Rivers's Sale, three generations of Burton Bradstock pupils had passed through the village school. The education had given them a good start in life, considering the limitations of the day and the disruption caused by the wars.

THE THIN EDGE OF THE WEDGE, *'not selling away'*

Shortly after the Second World War, Captain Pitt-Rivers decided to test the market with a sale of some cottages in Burton. In the past, the Estate had bought and sold off, in a limited manner but this had never affected the momentum of the village.

On June 13th 1951, seventeen freehold cottages were auctioned at The Greyhound Hotel, Bridport. The sale particulars emphasised the sporting amenities in the district, in particular, the private fishing, golf and rough shooting. The distance from Bridport and Yeovil railway stations and the proximity of the county town of Dorchester, the picturesque appearance of Burton Bradstock, its sheltered position and the shops, the advantage of a post office, three inns and the church, were all considered most important. The particulars were aimed at wealthier people with money to spent on second homes.

The Bridport News, of the previous week, had heralded a sense of sadness. It would be a fateful day for Burton families. Frank Cowley, the Pitt-Rivers Estate's Agent said, "The sale is due totally to present economic conditions. That was the sole reason. " RB Howarth, Chairman of the Parish Council, feared that weekenders would buy the properties and would be prepared to spend hundreds of pounds to secure a cottage in the country.

There was a housing problem. Twenty-one applicants were on the waiting list, confirmed RB Howarth. He was afraid that outsiders might make the situation even worse. The tenants were fairly secure and "They can buy through the Rural District Council on a Small Dwellings Acquisition Act, which many do not realise, " he added. No one wanted to leave Burton, particularly a place where their fathers and forefathers before them, had known as home, was the general feeling, in the village.

In the saleroom the atmosphere was tense. All was conducted in a very formal manner. *The Bridport News* stated that it was the largest gathering to attend an auction and there was a great deal of speculation. Village life was about to be disrupted. The auctioneer announced that bids would be accepted in £25 amounts.

★★★★★★★★★★

Surprised and dazed by the decision to sell, the occupiers had very little to say to the Press reporters. The lots offered for sale were, a pair of vacant cottages in Southover, which had once been a single dwelling, two more in Darby Lane and another pair in Donkey Lane. There were two tenanted cottages, numbers 101 and 102 in Southover, making a speculative block of four places. The Stevens family lived at 101. This had been the home of Cynthia Stevens's (née Coombs) grandparents. Her father and his siblings had been raised there, as she and hers had, too. The vacant cottages, numbers, 45a and 46 were on the market, with Arthur and Daphne Bartlett's adjoining cottage, number 45 Darby Lane. In Church Street, the pretty cottage, opposite the church, occupied by Annie Northover and [Mrs] A Jones, at number 47, were sold as a tenanted pair. All were in good condition.

Near The Anchor Inn, engulfed in its historical connection to the lives of many, once the village Poor House, was number 9, occupied by Raymond Walbrin and his wife and family. (Mrs Walbrin, née Nellie Burwood, had an ancestor who had come, from

30. Darby Lane, 2007. (L) cottage included with Lot 39. (R) cottages sold 'to test the market' in 1951. Inset 30a Minnie Bartlett, [Mrs Nethercott] circa 1916.

Norfolk, to the locality, to take up employment as a coastguard in the early 1800s). Living at numbers 53 and 55, adjoining the Pound, were Frank Ward and Louis Thorner, whose homes were to be auctioned, too. Bunny Lenthall's sister, Jeanne Berry, often stayed at number 61 Donkey Lane with Joe Ward living next door. Number 57 Donkey Lane, was another vacant property and William Legg was a sitting tenant at number 59.

A large detached cottage, at the junction opposite the The Anchor Hotel, given as Ivy Cottage in old Estate records, was the home of the Brine family. Their connections with Burton Bradstock went back a long way. Like the rest of the tenants whose homes were to be sold that day, Alice Brine, née Hitchcock, was faced with having to buy her home, 63 High Street. With her sister, Hetty Williams, she travelled into Bridport to the Greyhound Hotel, where the auction was to take place. Mrs Brine was almost overwhelmed with the situation. She started the bidding at £150. As the bidding for her home escalated, she was goaded on by her sister. Her last bid was £400. This was the most money that she could afford and with her head in her hands, she gave a huge sigh of relief as the auctioneer swiftly let the hammer fall to her. "We are not trying to sell away when we have a reasonable offer from the tenant, " concluded Arthur Richards, the auctioneer.

The vacant cottages invited speculators. There had been very few, country cottages, with vacant possession. Most properties belonged to estates. RB Howarth paid £1,000 for the two empty places in Southover and Reg Buckler, a local farmer, bought the two adjacent cottages, with sitting tenants, for £350. Annie Northover had a good family around her, particularly her daughter Edith, [Mrs Scourey], a private nurse. Annie Northover had lived in her cottage, in easy sound of the church bells, for over forty years, celebrating her Golden Wedding the previous year, a rare anniversary in those days. She said, "There has been an ever flowing stream of cars and enquiries. " The Northovers were able to secure their home and number 47 for just over £675.

The three cottages in Darby Lane made £875, bought by a speculator. A loud cheer greeted the purchase of number 9, The Pound, for £350, by Ray Walbrin, the tenant, a "hail-fellow-well-met". The crowd was unaware that Walbrin had obtained a backer. *The Bridport News* reported that, 'Mr Buckler said, "Ray has lost a lot of sleepless nights over this. "' The cottage was later sold on to Mary Beavis, the daughter of RB Howarth, with the Walbrins remaining there as her tenants.

Two cottages, numbers 53 and 55, which lay on the old church path, made £200, bought by another outsider, from Charmouth. Mrs Louis Thorner had lived in her cottage for thirty-three years and had been born, in a cottage, across the road. "It seems hard, " she lamented. Donkey Lane was a quaint street and free from any traffic. The properties, numbers 57 and 59, went to a Mrs Jones of Shaftesbury for a total of £400. Mrs Joe Ward had been adamant, that if she had to get out, she would go and live in the camping field. £500 was paid for the two cottages, believed to have been bought by Jeanne Berry, who continued to visit with her family, for holidays.

This sale firmly established the holiday-cottage business, in Burton. Life was unaltered but the real shock and ultimate changes were still some way off.

The Village in 1958

In quiet Burton Bradstock there was still a lot of post-war austerity. Rationing had been in force only a few years previously but traditions were kept and the age-old pattern of life flowed on.

CHURCH AND CHAPEL

St Mary's Church, was one of only a few churches mentioned in Dorset, in the Domesday Book, although there were numerous others in the county. Maurice Ouseley, in his village survey, in the 1930s, decided that the church was Norman, built on Saxon remains - its tower similar to that of Bridport and Symondsbury. The registers dated back to

1614 and the records of the Church-wardens and Overseers of the Poor survive, housed at the Dorset History Centre, in Dorchester. In order that she could support herself, the Overseers of the Poor paid 2/8d in 1773, *'for a special whele for Hannah*

31. St Mary's churchyard in the 1930s. Inset 31a taking the bells to be recast 1928.

Wheadon.' Many similar entries could be found.

Built of local rubble, thirteenth and fourteenth century remains are visible today and there are interesting additions of around 1570. Prominent are the Tudor roses and shields carved on the north side of the nave and the north transept. The font stem is as early as the 12th century and the remainder dated around 1300. The communion rails from the 17th century, were placed there by the Churchwardens of 1686. The south aisle was added in the 1800s.

★★★★★★★★★★

In the belfry, six bells, of which the earliest dated from 1615, had rung out for all occasions. There was war, victory, peace, homecomings, marriages, deaths and during the 1940s, when the bells were silenced, there was one time when it was thought that the Germans were about to invade the Chesil shore. The bells were rung and the volunteers reported to their stations, only to discover that it had been a false alarm. Ken Mullins remembered, as a young Home Guardsman, turning out in the middle of the night, armed with his loaded gun and a belt of additional ammunition, standing on duty by Cheney's garage, for hours on end, plied with cups of tea, by his cousin, Ruby Churchouse. Had there been an invasion it was rumoured that the women and children would be conveyed to Beaminster Tunnel for safety! Acquiring the transport might have been a problem.

Much earlier, in 1805, the bells had been rung *'until the ropes broke'*, to celebrate Nelson's victory at the Battle of Trafalgar and probably as much for the survival of a young man from Burton, Midshipman Richard Roberts. The news had taken almost three weeks to reach Burton and was brought out to the village by Mr Fish, possibly a local carrier. "Old Jemmy", (a family servant or a horse?) was considered *'would not be quick enough'*, wrote Roberts's young brother, William.

In 1945 the news of Victory in Europe was quicker to arrive, by the technology of the day. The bells rang out again, whilst villagers danced "The Four Handed Reel", in the road, outside the school, accompanied by an accordion. Peals of thanksgiving heralded the end of the war, in August of that year, although men, some from Burton, were still in the Far East and Japanese prisoner of war camps.

★★★★★★★★★★.

The church clock had a fascinating 'story'. It was made by Thwaites of London in 1780 and had previously been purchased by Christ's Hospital, Newgate Street where it had bidden the boys to school and meals. At the turn of the twentieth century when ideas were being put forward for memorials to the late Queen Victoria, the Rector's son, a pupil at the school, heard that the clock was being sold by Blount and Sandford who were London housebreakers. After much wrangling the Burton Memorial Fund committee bought the clock. Mr Sturdy wanted to buy the bell as well to which he was prepared to contribute £5. A total of £70 was needed to buy the clock and install it. Jumble sales and donations funded the purchase and the bell was sold off for £14. Thwaite and Reed packed and despatched the clock to West Bay railway station and Bartletts the local builders fixed it on the north side of the tower, charging 2/6d for transport. Later Thwaites posted a can of oil, costing 2/6d and an extra 4d for postage.

★★★★★★★★★★

During the post-war years, leading up to the Sale, St Mary's Church and the Methodist Chapel remained bastions of the community and attendance, although reduced from pre-war years, was still good. The Rector's wife, captured those with the better singing voices, to join the church choir. Originally the organ, usually played by Sidney Rendall, or Mrs Dittmer, was pumped with bellows but was later modernised and electrified. All classes of village society congregated on Sundays for the services and took part in the activities associated with their calling.

The church had a Sunday School and there had once been one for the Methodist children. Fêtes were held annually, as much for a social gathering, as to raise money. Various venues had been used over the decades but recently, the Rectory lawn, Manor Farm and The Rookery gardens had lent themselves well to such gatherings.

★★★★★★★★★★

St Laurence's Chapel, to the east of The Anchor Inn, had been the main chapel of ease to the village church. Traditionally, a Wake Day was held on the Sunday after August 10[th.] Dancing took place in the street and there were stalls, on the patch of green, outside Manor Farmhouse. In 1934, the old remaining wall of the chapel which was, by then, a private house, had been covered over. It was a law of the Court that there should be a clear path to the church, at all times. This path ran to the main church, crossing a burial ground, which lay between the former chapel and the Women's Institute Hall, which had yielded human bones over the centuries. Bill Nethercott and workmen for the Estate, had once unearthed remains, when digging there. The sites of other chapels that were once situated in the hamlets, around the perimeter of Burton, could be located. St Catherine's [Caddy's Cross], halfway between Burton and Shipton Gorge, where the coffins were rested on their way for burial at Burton, St Luke's, on the outskirts of Shipton and another at Bredy.

The Victorian habit of restoration did not escape Burton church and iron pillars were replaced by stone ones in 1897. The architect for the alterations was Edward Prior, who designed Pier Terrace, at West Bay. It was said that the graves under the church floor gave off an *'unpleasant odour'*. The box pews were removed and the old seating arrangements were gone forever. Once, the congregations had been so large, that, those who could afford it, purchased a seat in the gallery, for one shilling a year, to be sure of somewhere to sit.

In 1928, it was decided that the belfry needed attention, which was then carried out. The altar cross, was dedicated and placed in memory of a Captain Francis Roberts, who died in 1915, reminding of the Roberts's connection with the church, Royal Navy and the village, that had spanned two hundred years. The heating was installed by a clever pipe system and electric lighting replaced the oil lamps, in 1935.

32. *The green is known as "Parish Pump". (R) Lot 2, the Wesleyan Chapel and Lot 3, The White House. (L) Lot 4, Beulah Cottage, with large, purpose built, side window and beyond Lot 5, Ingram House.*

★★★★★★★★★★

There had always been a strong Wesleyan following. Doctor Giles Roberts, born at "The Sloop Inn", [later the Bridport Arms Hotel],

Bridport Harbour, was descended from a Burton family. He was instrumental in setting up a Wesleyan chapel in the village and his father-in-law, Farmer Brown, as well as Doctor and Mrs Robinson, were great supporters. The cottage, used as a meeting place, was tenanted, from Lord Rivers by Brown, which in the early 1800s, was gutted and a chapel was especially furbished, adjacent to the Parish Pump, when the Wesleyan movement had a large following in Burton.

★★★★★★★★★★

At the time of the Sale, Methodist services, with a dwindling congregation of around twenty, were held regularly, with visiting preachers and as usual, on the Sunday, before the great Sale by the Pitt-Rivers Estate, the bells of St Mary's Church, rang out, as they had done for generations. The yew tree, by the west gate, still spread out its presence, a reminder of the days when bows were fashioned from it, used by those called to defend the village, who practised their skills after church, on Sunday mornings.

THE HOMESTEADS

'The roof is down, a standing wall
Waits one more winter storm to fall;
But yesterday this was home…. '
Eden Phillpotts

Some parts of the village dated from the sixteenth and seventeenth centuries, the cottages were newly built or on old sites where even more humble homes had stood. In the late 1700s, when the village began to flourish, with the flax and hemp spinning mills, cottages were renovated, by Roberts, and new ones built. His Letter Books, mention the importing of timber for repairing the workers' cottages.

All around the district, were stone quarries, which had been operational until the mid-1930s. The rubble type had been used in the construction of the inferior buildings and for the walls of the fields and to enclose some of the properties. Better quality stone, for dressing, was used, some from as far a-field as Ham Hill, near Yeovil, Portland and Bath and used in the grand houses and churches in the Bride Valley. All the homes had flagstone floors; huge, flat, slabs of stone, blue-grey in colour. These flagstones were embedded with fossils. There was a problem with this method of flooring, when in thundery, or foggy weather these stones could become wet, referred to locally as *sweating or heaving*. Mould and damp set in, as was apparent in many of the Burton buildings, at the time of the Sale.

The older properties had no proper foundations. The walls rested on broad, flat stones and there were no damp courses, consequently the airing of the cottages was most important and all the doors would be left wide open, as often as practical. The low ceilings and the living room/kitchen had an open fire, later replaced with the kitchen range, the only means of heating and cooking. Backhouses still had earth floors well into the twentieth century and in general, there had been few structural alterations to any of the cottages, over the centuries .

The interiors were whitewashed and the woodwork painted, often a dark brown or green. The grander houses were painted in lighter colours or had fashionable wallpaper

33.(L) fated cottages, (C) Lot 26, Girt House, (R) Lot 70, Townsend Farmhouse. Inset 33a the cottages that burnt down in 1926. Lot 24 Somercotes and Lot 25, New Cottage, were built on the site.

but the woodwork was often still dark in colour. As the cottager could afford it, the front-room might become more decorative and wallpaper used. Dampness was always a problem!

Most cottages had one door at the front and another at the rear, which dated back to the time when the living quarter was of one storey, with the fire in the centre - the smoke going out of the roof, by means of a hole, (not a chimney). The majority of the homes and farm buildings were thatched or had been slated following a fire. Sparrows found the thatch a haven and in the 'old days' were killed for that reason.

There were numerous gaps where homes had burnt down and when one thatched cottage caught on fire, usually, the whole row was destroyed. In 1850 there were twenty houses lost in that way. In 1851 there were twenty-three dwellings recorded in Southover but by 1898, twelve of those had disappeared. (Wrack gathered from the beach splattered everywhere as it burnt in the grates and was another fire hazard). Forty years later, one hot, humid day in August, a bolt of lightning had struck cottages, to the south of The Anchor Hotel which could not be saved.

The cottages and the farm houses, were built in the lower reaches of the River Bride and fanned out from the church, others that were built above the flood-line fared well in bad weather. The long thin gardens that could be located behind many of the smaller cottages bore a Medieval pattern. Swallows and many other species of birds frequented the buildings and gardens.

In time, rooms were put in on the second floor, of the properties. Ladders or winding, wooden staircases went up to a landing/second bedroom and a slightly larger area which formed the main bedroom. Joined on at the back of the ground floor, was a lean-to [back-house] where the dirtier domestic duties were carried out. Those without a separate washhouse had a copper built in and this was used for boiling the weekly wash and heating water for baths, usually a weekly ritual, (in a tin bath). This lean-to also formed a store for outdoor clothing, the family boots, working tools and fishing gear. Few people locked their doors and the businessmen and farmers left their premises and possessions open to all.

The old farm houses appeared to have been altered in the 1700s and 1800s, or smartened up in the wake of the new Victorian era and were superior, in all respects. By this period, kitchens which had been built away from the main house, to prevent fire spreading, had been joined on. This was how the housing had been for decades and in 1958, the Estate properties, many thatched, were painted with dark green doors and were very humble in appearance. Horseshoes were nailed over many of the back doors to bring good luck, (the shoe had to be positioned up the right way or the luck would fall out!). Doorsteps were scrubbed and often 'whited' with a block of chalk. Flower-knots, [clumps], ran alongside the frontages, giving a cheerful look to the streets. This was a hazard, as the cattle, on their way to the milking sheds, would savour the blooms, as they passed.

The Estate saw to house repairs and the maintenance of the walls, re-thatching, painting, glazing and rendering of properties, some ditching and drainage and during the five years leading up to the Sale had laid out over £3,000 on the maintenance of the cottages and larger houses.

Sixteen council houses, of Bothenhampton bricks, had been erected around 1926, along Barr Lane, on land acquired from the Pitt-Rivers Estate. These were well constructed and designed, with good sized gardens and modern facilities. In comparison with the humble cottages, these were luxury dwellings and the status of the occupiers was elevated and envied.

The post-war years heralded a phase of new homes. In the 1950s, council properties had been built at Lower Townsend and others followed in Annings Lane. Privately owned bungalows were springing up, at the same time. In Beach Road, where sites had been sold off by the Estate, one enterprising, up-and-coming builder, Joe Linee, had built one place, sold it on and started on the second. He was fortunate to have a wife who was not afraid of hard work, or heights, as she could often be seen carrying the tiles up the ladder.

In 1952, the Pitt-Rivers Estate relinquished another of the properties in Burton, with vacant possession. This was Darby House, *'an exceptionally nice residential property of moderate size'*. The auction was held on May 14th, in Bridport, by Senior and Godwin, Chartered Surveyors of Sturminster Newton. A pair of cottages, numbers 40 and 41 The Grove, was sold separately.

Many prominent families had lived at Darby House. The cottages had, in the past, been occupied in conjunction with Darby House but were at the time of selling, let to Bertram Bull, at £7 per annum, with one vacant. The two cottages, in excess of a thousand pounds, the pair, were bought by the Bull family, with cash.

DRAWING WATER

From around 1750, drinking water had been drawn from a communal well at the village green, adjacent to the church. A subscription had been raised to provide a well, with a hand-pump, on Doll's Knapp, later referred to as "Parish Pump". River and rain water were used for every other purpose. The large farm houses and gentlemen's residences drew their supply from their own wells.

★★★★★★★★★★

There were many springs in the district, enabling the sinking of wells in the heavy clay areas but presenting more difficulty when rock, similar to the yellow cliffs, was struck. All the digging was done by hand, going down thirty of forty feet, at times. There was great danger from the well caving-in, or the diggers being overcome by gas, after getting to certain depths. At St Catherine's House, in Shipton Lane, the well had to be sunk to sixty feet, when RB Howarth set-out to build a grand house from two cottages. It was said that the cost involved, caused him to run out of money and sell on to the Scudamore family. (One of the cottages had been the home of a labourer who stole a sheep and buried it in the garden, which now is part of Buckler's Bid. He hid in Cathole Wood and the police tracked his wife as she took him food. It was said that he was hung).

★★★★★★★★★★

The Bridport Water Company built a reservoir, under North Hill, to supply the whole of Bridport, to hold water piped from Little Bredy but it became disused when a young woman drowned herself there, in the early 1900s. Another reservoir was built beside it.

The 1958 Sale catalogue, listed a variety of means of obtaining drinking water that was in use; springs, reservoirs, boreholes, wells and standpipes. The mains water supply had been improved and extended in the 1950s to coincide with the start of some council and private development in the village.

'DOWN GARDEN'

Although mains water had been brought to a number of the properties, at the time of the Sale, the majority of the cottages still did not have mains drainage. In some instances, the sewer, which had been put in during the post-war building, was situated in close proximity but it was not in the Landlord's interest to go to the excessive expense of building bathrooms or flush lavatories. Several of the bigger houses had septic tanks or cesspits, whilst only a few, had flush lavatories installed. A mains sewer had been put through the village in 1956, with the plant for it, in a valley at Freshwater. and the businesses and larger properties were gradually getting connected. Earth closets [outside lavatories], of various description had been the normal fixture for the majority of the properties.

Outside lavatories were usually single seated and situated at the end of the garden path, although two households could have their privies side by side or back to back. The "throne" was built inside sentry-box shaped, wooden, stone or brick sheds, thatched, galvanised, slated or tiled. There was a rough wooden box, (either fixed or in a small number of the premises, a free-standing box with a hole cut in the middle) over a pit, known as a vault, which was dug out from the back. Earth, ashes and lime, (lime kilns were located all around the area), were used to cover in the contents of the vault. In some cases, ventilation holes were cut into the lavatory door or let into the walls. Such a 'convenience' was dependent on the lie of the land and built a reasonable distance away from the living quarters. Some lavatories commanded a good view of neighbouring gardens, although the more modest builders had positioned them facing a wall.

Better lavatories were still worked on the vault principle with a wooden or metal hopper fixed above the seat and a handle could be pulled in and out which shot the covering material into the pit below. The Reverend Moule of Dorchester, in the mid-nineteenth century, astounded at the lack of sanitation in Fordington, had patented a free-standing box, with a hopper, in which earth was used to cover the contents that could then be dried and used as fertiliser. Burton Bradstock had adaptations of this; one being at Magnolia Farmhouse, although it was over a vault and had never been dug out, in living memory.

Other tenants had acquired a two handled bucket-type lavatory and the contents were emptied into a trench, usually in the garden. One lady who came to a summer bungalow, on the beach, referred to this type of lavatory, as a 'bucket and chuck it'. Some people went to an additional expense, of using disinfectant in these buckets. Sometimes they were rinsed out after emptying, the rinse going down the drain or into the river.

When the vaults were dug out it was usual to bury the contents in a trench or to spread it on the garden or on nearby rough land. The vegetables that were grown, in the gardens, always seemed to be extremely good! Privet and climbing plants, such as roses and honeysuckle, were encouraged to grow over and around the lavatory and the former contributed to endorsing the name of "the privy". This was no new term as Medieval records referred to it the same, meaning "private".

By August 1958, a number of the tenants, had done away with earth vaults and buckets and had installed Elsan lavatories. There had been a ten pound grant, (a government scheme), towards updating the facilities, when the Elsans were installed. A metal bucket was fitted inside a second free-standing metal casing, with a vent pipe leading from the back of the container out through the building. A dark, strong smelling disinfectant fluid, manufactured by Elsan, was put into the bucket and a loose fitting wooden or Bakelite seat, with a matching lid, topped the whole appliance.

These lavatories, like the bucket types, required emptying on a regular basis. If the Elsan was not fixed on a level base, it was liable to tip over, when in use. Many men were inclined to urinate elsewhere in the garden to avoid having to undertake the emptying too often. Janet Sanderson Crouch, whose family stayed in Burton each summer, for some twenty years, from 1916, recalled that in the later years, the butcher's wife, at Hydrangea House, in Grove Road, who took paying-guests, had erected a canvas screen in the kitchen garden where she said, "The men could 'go front'. "

The buckets and Elsans were not always as practical as the old earth closet and vault system. Visits in the dark by the aid of a candle or lantern, or perhaps by 1958 with a the dull light of a torch, could be hazardous and every home retained chamber pots. One tenant who lived near The Anchor Inn had no garden there and he was obliged to empty the contents of the bucket on a piece of land, he rented on the outskirts of the village, some way from his house, where he grew the household vegetables. This procedure involved getting up before the village was astir, lighting his pipe and trekking along the village street with the bucket, to the dumping ground.

All the privies harboured numerous insects and mice, rats and snakes were not unknown, whilst birds found the surrounding bushes ideal nesting territory. The school and the pub facilities fared little better until around the mid 1930s.

A cleansing company had, by 1958, organised a collection scheme, for which the householder paid direct. This was a very messy, unhygienic operation. The men from the company carried the buckets straight from the lavatories to their vehicle waiting out in the roadway. Depending on how full the bucket happened to be, some of it could be slopped along the way. Those living outside the collecting area continued to dispose of the contents in the same old manner. In order to save costs, the contents were often emptied into the river, at dead of night. The chemical fluid and other disinfectant was costly and was skimped, or watered down, in many cases. The fluid was poisonous but no one ever seemed the worst for the procedure, at the time, although the dangers, in the longer term, were never considered.

WOMEN'S WORK

All the adults, in 1958, remembered the time when there was no electricity in the village or surrounding farmsteads. Oil lamps and candles had been used in the homes. Lanterns were the means of lighting on farms and at the beach. The foundation stone of the Bridport Power Station was laid in 1928, by Mayor Alderman Andrew Spiller and opened the following year, although it was towards the mid-1930s, before Burton Bradstock first received electricity. Basic installations enabled the householders to have a single, central light in the downstairs rooms and in due course the lighting was extended to other rooms.

Most people had a meter, which took sixpenny and later shilling pieces. This was emptied quarterly by the Bridport Electricity Company's collector. When electricity points were put in, it was possible to have an electric cooker and kettle which could be rented, (the latter at sixpence a week). Wires and poles straddled the village and surrounding countryside and blackouts were common, particularly during the war years and in bad weather. Later the company was nationalised and taken over by the South Western Electricity Board.

In 1958, few women had the use of modern machines in their homes. At Manor Farm, there was a vacuum cleaner, a washing and ironing machine and an electric dishwasher. Some other farmers' wives owned a washing machine but the majority of women still did the weekly wash by hand, boiling the clothes in a copper, fired by wood, situated in the lean-to, or a separate stone outhouse. Many women used soda in the washing-up water. (Not so kind to the hands!)

Newly married couples were satisfied with second-hand furniture and carpeting was unheard of; rugs and mats were still the accepted covering over linoleum, or plastic tiles, if the house was newly built. In the grander houses, quality rugs and mats looked well and were warmer, on the wooden or flagstone floors. For the bride, of the late 1950s, were gifts of Pyrex ware.

As soon as the worst of the winter was over, the women would do an annual house-clean. This meant turning out every room and washing the walls, paintwork, curtains and beating the dust out of the upholstery. Blankets were washed, pillows and eiderdowns hung out to air. Spring cleaning was a long and laborious job.

Whilst 1958, brought an electric cooker to replace the oil stove and kitchen range, there was much preparation of food to be done and many hours were spent over a hot stove or a steamy washtub. Mangles were still in use, in some homes and the washing was put through the rollers to squeeze out the water. Wringing sheets by hand was done by two women turning in opposite directions. No women needed to attend "Keep Fit" classes or go jogging!

Gone were the days when a village woman delivered the babies. By the 1950s, women gave birth at the Bridport Maternity Hospital, particularly for the firstborn. Those who could afford the expense, went to private nursing homes. There were still some who stayed at home and were attended by the district nurse; either way, there was a long convalescence period and this natural event was still considered as a kind of illness. Childbirth still had its uncertainties and women could die, although young Mrs Sylvia Elsworth, née Mitchell, chose to have home confinements.

Prior to the nationalisation of the Health Service, women, who could afford the fees, paid a registered midwife to attend their home confinements, rather than have a village nurse. Training before or after the birth of their baby was unheard of but first-

hand experience and advice was forthcoming from their mothers, mothers-in-law and grandmothers, who were usually living nearby.

Many women had been born into large families and were familiar with how babies and children were raised. The family units were still very close. Illegitimacy happened, as it had always done and was frowned upon.

34. The women were the backbone of the community. Back row (L to R): Winifred Holly, ?, -Gale, Marion Booth, Dorothy Codrington, ? Gertrude Cammell, Daisy Panten, Minnie Nethercott, Elizabeth [Annie] Shipp
Seated (L to R): Mabel Burton, -Gudge, May Legge, Mary Bickford, Beatrice Mercer, Florence Partridge, Miss Chitty.

Most families rallied and the child was brought up in the same household, or by a close relative, as their own, sometimes given the father's surname as a middle name.

35. WI Ladies, circa 1950. (L to R): Annie Williams, Mary Churchill, Queenie Darby, May Williams, Kathleen Cammell, Gertrude Cammell, Caroline Greenham, May Northover, May Legge, - Hyde, Florence Thorner, Lilian Mullins, Caroline Cammell.

Others sent the girl away, until after the child was born, when it was handed over for adoption and the incident was never mentioned again. Divorce, particularly amongst

36. A group of friends on The Pound, circa 1945. (L to R) Elizabeth Walbrin, Gillian Legge, Florence Partridge, - Gudge, May Legge, Daphne Bartlett, Nellie Walbrin, Maud Mitchell, Sylvia Mitchell. (Cottages R burnt down in 1951)

the working class, was extremely rare.

Until a National Health Scheme was introduced, most of the working community contributed to "The Hospital League Fund". A collector, from the village, received the payments of sixpence a week. Should the contributor, or his family fall ill and require a doctor or hospital treatment, then all, or some of the fees, would be met by this means of insurance. Many families had to resort to using home-made medicines, many of which appeared to cure the illnesses. Cold tea served as an eye-balm, a bread poultice was ideal to 'draw' boils and poisonous swellings and charcoal arrested some stomach disorders. There were many other recipes for remedies that the villagers used which had been handed down through the generations. Some people were wary of 'going to the doctor', as those were the days when some conditions were incurable and the doctor took the blame.

In the 1950s, a number of the Burton Bradstock women belonged to the Mothers' Union, the church choir, the Women's Section of the British Legion, or the Women's Institute. They dressed their hair with home-perms and older women still used hot tongs, which were heated in the fire. The contents of everyone's wardrobe, (often a corner space curtained off in the bedroom), were modest. A best outfit was kept for Sundays and special occasions. There was not the desire or finances to buy much and everything was looked after carefully, as it had to last a long time.

No respectable woman would dye or bleach her hair, or be seen in a public house on her own, or even with other females but would venture in, if accompanied by a male, usually using the lounge bar. Women drank very self-consciously and would request a lemonade or the newly marketed "Baby Cham". Few women had learnt to drive by 1958. The men who owned cars, mostly farmers, businessmen and the gentry, drove their wives to the town, or on outings, whilst those without their own transport, relied on bicycles or the bus service. Pre-war there had been a village carrier/bus, run by Bill Smith who had gone over to motorisation in the 1930s. Parcels, small livestock and people travelled together.

Post-war, a National Bus service, (averaging six buses a day), plied to and from Bridport, via West Bay. Once a week, the women, many with children at heel, journeyed to town for goods that were not produced in the village and often bought some commodities at Jeff's pannier market, in Gundry Lane. The weekly shopping expedition was also a social outing. Wednesdays and Saturdays were market days, in Bridport, when the women could enjoy a quick cup of tea

37. The Shipp family. (C) Sidney Shipp DSM and his wife Marion, circa 1950 and his parents, (L) Elizabeth, [Annie], (R) Albert Shipp, DCM.

and chat at the West End Dairy, whilst waiting for the bus.

Some village girls had married servicemen, either those who were stationed in the district during the war, or men they had met whilst serving in the forces themselves. They had made their home in Burton Bradstock, bringing in some new blood. After the war, displaced persons from Estonia, Latvia and other Balkan countries, had found resettlement and were working on farms or in the factories in Bridport. Originally, many of them had been housed in the old Nissen huts at Common Knapp. Some married local girls, others had brought their wives from their homeland, as had an Estonian man and his beautiful, blonde wife and two little girls, who took rooms with the Derryman family, in Shipton Lane. Betty Mullins, whose father kept a village shop emigrated, having married a soldier and sailed with other GI brides, to live in the United States of America.

From time to time, in the winter, there were evening classes run by the Dorset County Education Committee, in dressmaking, music, history and art. Women who wished to further their education, attended these classes. Women working on the farms in 1958, were few, except some farmers' wives and daughters helping out at busy times or tending the poultry. A former Land Girl, Jean Harris, was employed by Mrs Daphne Cooper, at Wych Bungalow, near Marsh Barn. She had stayed on after the war, becoming one of the community. Vera Smith was head dairywoman at Manor Farm and female students sometimes came there to undertake a year of practical work and stable girls worked at the Bishop's equestrian establishment.

One thing had not changed at all over hundreds of years; in 1958, women could still be found braiding at the kitchen tables or, in summertime, standing at their doors - some adorned in a cotton bonnet that they had made themselves or that had been passed down through the family. With the wooden needles in-hand, as they braided, they could socialise, exchange news and gossip, on their thresholds, with their young children, playing at their feet, in complete safety.

Preserving food was very much part of the woman's work. She salted runner beans, sprats and herrings, pickled onions and eggs and made pounds of jam, jellies and other preserves. Salting pork and utilising every bit of a pig, came easily to the farmers' wives. A good housewife made as much of the family food as possible, frowning on buying anything that might be tinned or artificial, when she could cook fresh ingredients. Most women were fortunate to have husbands who took a pride in their fruit and vegetable gardens and allotments, producing potatoes which were gathered in and stored in clamps and apples picked and spread out in lofts, or sheds and stored for the winter.

****

The food, totally 'organic', that the women prepared for their working husbands and families was plain and nourishing. Every kind of fish - fried, soused or baked, stews, (usually rabbit or mutton), offal prepared in numerous, nutritious ways and vegetables and potatoes formed the main diet. Bread, butter, or margarine, cheese, milk, jams, dripping, (often as a spread), apples and other fruits, in season, could all be easily obtained and varied, to make good meals. Moores's knob biscuits were a locally acquired taste. The old folk soaked them in tea which gave them a good start to the day.

Milk puddings, apples in all their cooked form, were put on the table, much of it topped with homemade custard. Rhubarb, which grew in clumps in every garden, was both nutritional and medicinal. Those who could afford it, made fruit and sponge cakes and everyone could make an apple cake. The secret being, that it had to have plenty of apples in it so that it was more like a pudding. The farmers were able to feed their families, on joints of meat and poultry but the best commodities were sold at market and they ate what was second quality.

Practically all the cottagers kept a few chickens at the bottom of the garden which were fed on household scraps and some barley meal. This provided the family with eggs for most of the year. Old hens were killed and cooked with an assortment of vegetables, by slow boiling. Hens were allowed to go "broody" and sit on fertile eggs, (sometimes duck and goose eggs were used), otherwise day-old chicks could be bought in Jeff's Market and put with a broody hen, or reared on, in artificial, warm conditions which were provided by means of paraffin oil lamps that were liable to smoke and catch on fire.

★★★★★★★★★★

Christmas was a very special time; the highlight of the year. A feast was prepared; the best that they could afford. The last Sunday in November, or first in December was "stir up Sunday", so named from the Collect on the twenty-fifth Sunday after Trinity, 'Stir up we beseech thee…', when the pudding was made and wrapped in a cloth awaiting the great boiling, often in the copper. Stout was usually added to make the pudding really dark coloured and was a permitted tipple for the women of the household. It had medicinal values!

Knitting, sewing, darning and patching took up a great deal of the women's time. (Children held the skeins of wool for winding and filled the braiding needles with twine, for their mothers). Through the wars years it had been instilled into the women 'to make do and mend'. Darns and patches adorned most everyday garments. Sheets were turned 'sides to middle', shirt collars reversed and blankets were patched and re-hemmed. (The girls learnt blanket stitch at school). Nearly all outer woollen clothing, such as jumpers, cardigans and pullovers were hand knitted, as were socks, scarves and gloves. Women made their own frocks, blouses and skirts; all this essential craftwork took up many an evening. The wealthier ladies had clothes made for them. Mrs Brown, a professional dressmaker, was kept busy sewing afternoon and evening wear, as well as making bridal dresses, remodelling or undertaking alterations.

Elderly people were not put into residential homes when they could no longer cope alone but lived with their offspring and saw out their days in familiar surroundings. The working-class people, with no relatives, were destined to go to the former workhouse, in Bridport, or Stoke Abbott, which catered for those who had no other means of support and it still carried the stigma of a hundred years before.

When the village was 'sold up', three generations of one family might be found living under the same roof; an undisturbed pattern of life.

THE FARMS IN 1958

Following the recent war, farmers were encouraged, with subsidies, to produce food for the home market rather than the country should rely on imports, for which there was little money available. Machines were taking over from men and the number employed on farms was declining. Yet at Manor Farm fifteen or more workers queued outside the back-door each Friday, in the late afternoon to collect their wages. The men(and

38. Stan Parsons the dairyman, driving Rob Gale's Ayrshire cows to the milking shed, past Lot 3, The White House. (Beyond) Lot 48 The Red House, and Lots 68 and 69 Sunnyside.

a few women) were called in, individually, by the farmer, to sign the wages' book and receive a small brown envelope containing the cash that had been earned that week, from which, National Insurance and "pay as you earn" deductions had been made. The regular workers were entitled to a quart of milk a day, as a perquisite and they arrived for the afternoon shift carrying the milk cans, which were left in the dairy, to collect on their way home.

Nationally, there had been a decline in the use of working horses on farms but at Manor Farm a couple of the heavier horses were still in use. David Legg, born in 1886, who left school at twelve years of age, had retired in 1956, from a lifetime working at

74

Manor Farm. With him and his older brother, Fred, passed an era in the old crafts and farming methods and a way of life. Working horses were retained for general use at Manor Farm, because Bunny Lenthall was reluctant to see the old traditions die out and heavy horses could work in sticky clay and difficult areas, where a tractor would be useless. Yet, Lenthall had the most progressive farm in the village and the latest machinery was used alongside the traditional methods.

Farmers Bailey, Bishop and Hawkins, had still retained a working horse but had begun to mechanise their holdings and had become familiar with a combine harvester or baler coming in to sweep through the crops, utilising only a couple of men, where a dozen had once been employed. No more the pooks of hay or sheaves of corn standing proudly in the fields. In addition, Edgar Hawkins and his two sons, Bob and Dennis, continued to deliver milk in the village. Geoff Derryman had a much more widespread round and bought-in additional milk.

In addition to the larger farms in Burton, four smallholders rented under Pitt-Rivers and kept cattle, pigs and poultry, grew some crops and made hay. For the farmers producing milk, a lorry collected the churns from the stands, at the farm entrances, every morning. No dairyman dared be late, as the lorry called at a regular time and would not wait.

A tragedy had altered the lives of the Bishop family. Frank Bishop had died, following an accident, in 1957 leaving his son, Tony, to manage the farm. Frank had been a fine horseman and had run a high-class riding establishment. Like his father, Tony was at home on a horse, breeding race horses, riding point-to-point and in flat races, with a number of successes. During the 1957/8 season he had won the Malvers Novices' Hurdle Race, at Cheltenham, on his own horse, Crossways, by four lengths, at 25-1. This was an exciting day for the Bishop family and any locals who had placed a bet.

At Cogden Farm, AF Bailey and his son Frank, who were classed as "gentlemen farmers", oversaw a vast expanse of land which stretched down to the shore, along the coast to Swyre and northwards to Berwick. In 1958, AF Bailey still rode around his land on a good, strong grey cob. When he ventured into the village on business, his horse might be seen, over the lunch hour, tethered to the iron ring, outside The Anchor.

All the farmers and their families had led an ordered, steady life. A regular round of seedtime and harvest geared the years. Now, in the spring of 1958, they were being forced to make a great decision. A huge and ominous cloud was hanging over them.

THE FISHING AT THE TIME OF THE SALE

On the Chesil Beach, in 1958, a few men owned fishing boats, as their forefathers had done. None was fishing as a full-time occupation. Other men formed the crews and spent most of their spare time earning some extra cash and enjoying a healthy and invigorating way of life. The camaraderie that was established, could be witnessed in the local pubs in the evenings and on pay-out night. The proportion of the takings varied but generally, the captain of the boat, being the owner of the boat and net, took three shares of the catch, (or two shares if he was generous) and the rest was divided amongst the crew. An extra hand, who was not a regular crew member, would be given a string of mackerel, [usually six or a dozen fish, threaded through the gills, with twine, for easy carrying]. As soon as the beach had been reopened in 1943, when it was considered that the threat of an invasion was over, the fisherman took to the water once again.

At the time of the Sale, there were at least four fishing crews at The Hive. Skippers were Joe Thorner, the very last of the older fishermen in the village, Alfie Hutchings, Louis Brown and Dennis Bullock. Keen crew members were Ted Hitt and Bert Thorner. AE (Bert) Williams was now a village sage and Fred Copp, although seiners as well, spent a great deal of time "hooking"[catching fish on hooked long lines]. All the men, fished to supplement

39. Fishing off Burton Beach 1950s. (L to R), Philip Hutchings, Brian Bettison, Alfie Hutchings and Dennis Bullock. Inset 39a 1983, Philip Hutchings holds the family heirloom [cow horn] used to call the fishermen to the beach.

their incomes but mainly for the age-old thrill of waiting, sighting and catching fish, particularly mackerel.

Some enterprising fishermen took visitors out on trips, mainly feathering for mackerel. This innovation was discovered soon after the second war when Dicker Thorner on holiday in Cornwall, saw the fishermen bringing in mackerel by the dozens on lines, the hooks decorated with coloured feathers. Astounded by this, he brought a line back to Burton, only to be scoffed at by the local fishermen. When he demonstrated the procedure, with amazing success, Bertie Williams and Fred Copp dashed off down to Cornwall to purchase more of these feathering lines, not only getting good catches themselves but making a fair profit by selling on. Ivor Guyatt concentrated on this popular new method. John Eastwood, had latched on to the way of life and had his own fishing boat, whilst of the younger generation, in 1958, were Burton boy, Bobby Cammell and Desmond Gape, originally from Puncknowle, who kept their boat at Bexington.

There were still fine strong men who could row these, fishing boats, known as "lerts" [lerrets], which were sixteen to seventeen feet and even up to twenty feet in length, with a beam of five or six feet. Cyril Toms, from an old Abbotsbury fishing family, wrote that they were called "double enders", having a bow at either end, exclusively for use on the

Chesil Beach. Coming ashore could be very difficult, even treacherous and it was no easy task to manoeuvre the clinker-clad craft [one plank lapping over the other], up and down the beach, launch it successfully and take it out into the swell and cope with the various tides, that beset the waters of the Chesil. The boats were dragged up and down the crub [ridge or rudge of the beach], the stretch and ridge of shingle between the sea and safety of high tide, often steep, as at Abbotsbury, on flat boards, or poles which were greased with lard or old engine grease. The old sailors would stroll down to the beach and cast their eye over the proceedings and could be seen sitting on the seat outside The Three Horseshoes, or the wall, in the village street. They smoked their pipes and discussed the world of 1958, and reminisced.

THE WORKING VILLAGE

When Captain Pitt-Rivers decided to sell the Burton Estate, those not employed in the village, walked, cycled or caught buses to West Bay and Bridport, where there was work to be found in the netting factories, shops and for the more academic, in offices. At West Bay there was employment at Good's gravel works, or with companies such as Burt, Boulton and Hayward and Bradfords and at one time Ralls and Son, who were timber, fertiliser, coal and cattle-feed importers.

The rest of the inhabitants, of Burton Bradstock, were made up of 'the gentry', retired service officers and professional people. A number of elderly spinsters lived alone, as the 1914-18 war had taken its toll on the eligible bachelors as was noted in 1921, when, there were fifty more females in the village than males.

Law and order was attended to by a resident village policeman who pedalled around his beat, on a heavy-weight bicycle. Originally, the police constable had lived in a cottage in the High Street. As Beach Road became residential, a Police House was built at the bottom of the road; its blue light there for all to see.

There was practically every basic requirement available, (few working people had a telephone), the two general stores delivered groceries and newspapers

40. *Steve Northover putting bread to bake in the oven at the Grove Mill.*

throughout the valley and bread could be either bought, straight out of the oven, at the Grove Mill bakery, run by brothers-in-law, John Panten and Robert Gobbett, or delivered three times a week. Albert Stevens, was the delivery man, travelling around in a three-wheeled van, for Burton Mill Limited. When he gave up, Charlie Day took over. Competition came from a bakery in Puncknowle, owned by Alphonso Bartlett, a Burton man. From 1938, until his death in 1971, he made bread and delivered it throughout the

Bride Valley and Shipton Gorge. As well, milk was delivered daily to the doorstep and the butcher's man would call twice a week.

There were a few women, out in the country, who did not have electricity in the home, who were still cooking on oil stoves and most households had heaters that required paraffin. Stanley Williams sold and delivered paraffin and it was common for it to be delivered alongside the grocery orders, in his van. Charlie Major, from Bridport, had a round, visiting the village and outlying hamlets, bringing in oil and hardware goods.

The four main Bridport clothing shops of Reynolds, Fenwick, Brailey and Day, sent a man out with orders and carriers visited, with goods that were not produced on the spot. Nearly all commodities could be found locally, at the time the village came under the hammer. No one had to venture far for their everyday needs.

THE BURTON TENANTS OF THE PITT-RIVERS ESTATE

Surviving Estate Books of 1905/06, record repairs and requests at Sturminster Newton, another part of the Pitt-Rivers Estate, as attention to: thatch, privies, windows, drains, walls, fencing, fronts falling out, gates, painting and door locks. The concerns for Burton Bradstock would have been similar. Right up to 1958, the rents paid by the tenants were extremely small and there was a limit to the expenditure that the Estate could stand. On the other hand, wages in the district were lower than other parts of the country and the tenants struggled to find the money. It was from Dorset that the Tolpuddle Martyrs, who were agricultural labourers, took a stand, forming a group, in 1834, demanding more money, for which they were transported. Descendants of Martyr, James Brine, were living in Burton at the time of the Sale and the brother of George Loveless, the Martyrs' Leader, had worked at the flax mill, at the time of their persecution.

For the farmers the twice yearly outlay, was a major liability, usually dependent on the milk cheque. The businessmen needed regular payment to remain solvent. Tradesmen usually sent out their accounts annually to the farmers and gentry and that meant a long wait to recoup outlay. Other payments were in cash, weekly or monthly. The milk money would be put out with the empty milk bottles on the doorstep and any change was left with the freshly delivered milk. A similar procedure was done for newspapers. Stanley Williams presented a monthly bill for the goods which he delivered.

The Estate provided a steady repairing system and from 1953 to 1957 almost £1,000 had been spent on the commercial premises and more than £5,000 on the farms, in the village, as well as a hefty expenditure on maintaining the cottages and larger houses. In 1956 Captain Pitt-Rivers had written to his tenants to inform them, that due to ill-health, the Agent, Mr Frank Cowley, was retiring. Cowley had worked himself up 'from the ranks' and had been in the Estate employment for over forty years. Through Senior and Godwin of Sturminster Newton, Mr MD Taunton had been appointed as resident Agent, in the management of the Rushmore and Burton Bradstock blocks.

In the same letter, the Captain recalled retrospectively, the events from 1880 to the present time. "I am hopeful that the long connection between the farming and other tenants in Dorset and Wiltshire which has been handed down over so many generations of the Pitt and Pitt-Rivers families may still continue to bring some measure of prosperity to our agricultural interests in these difficult times, " he wrote. This letter had the measure of a landlord, conscious of his loyalty to the tenants, with a burden on his shoulders, regarding the regular upkeep of the Estate and the constant problems in agriculture.

The Burton tenants had always saved carefully in order to pay the rent. It was considered a great disgrace to fall behind, or fail to pay. When a serious fire destroyed a row of cottages in Southover, in 1898, Mrs Hussey said, "We have lost our drifting nets and thirty shillings saved up for the rent. " The Landlord was entitled to evict anyone who could not meet the payment until the Rent Acts were in place. By 1958, an Act covered some of the problems that arose with housing.

The Estate was careful as to whom they sanctioned a tenancy and bad payers or those of dubious character were excluded. Henry Whittle, the village carpenter and undertaker,

No. 300

Rivers Estate Office,
Hinton St. Mary,
Sturminster Newton,
Dorset,

September, 1947.

Exors of Mrs E Buckler

RIVERS ESTATE.

The collection of the Rent due by you to the Rivers Estate, for the half year ending 29th SEPTEMBER, will be held at THE ANCHOR HOTEL, BURTON BRADSTOCK, on TUESDAY, 7th OCTOBER (from 10.15 a.m. to 12.45 p.m.)

Cheques should be made payable to the Rivers Estate

F. COWLEY.

	£	s.	d.
Arrears		:	:
Allotments		:	:
Arrears		:	:
House or Lands	15	10	:
	£ 15 "	10	0

P.S.—Please Bring this Notice.

Note.—All communications must be addressed to the Agent at the Estate Office.

41. *Pitt-Rivers Estate Rent Notice, September 1947.*

who was a local representative for the Estate, warned that an applicant for John Steel's house 'will not be a desirable tenant'. They had had a great deal of trouble with her. John Steel had lost his sight and was unable to work and Whittle enquired what he was to do about the arrears. Steel was going to ' be on the parish. '

H Tucker objected to a proposed scullery that was to be built on his home in 1888. He wanted another bedroom but if he was not to have that then he would like the scullery across the front to shut out the view from the cottage windows at the bottom of the row! A[lfred?] Churchouse was interested in securing a plot or two when Cousins, a farmer, was moving to Askerswell. Gush (presumed at West Bay), was not in a position to pay any part of laying on water to his closet. How fortunate he was to have a flushing closet! Similar problems and requests were continually directed to the Agents of the Estate, over the years.

Brian Galpin recalled that the rent, in the 1950s, was paid half-yearly at The Anchor Hotel and the tenants were given a voucher, which could be 'spent' in the pub. Barbara Bishop had similar memories of Rent Day, in the years immediately prior to the Sale.

When the working day was over and the fishing or gardening was finished, there was recreation to be found with a visit, by the men to the local pubs. They played, darts, skittles and card games. The youngsters could play football, cricket and tennis. The playing field, off the main street, served as a sports ground and there was a private tennis court at Gages House.

Further away, there were public tennis courts, in the old Shipyard, at West Bay. For League football matches, farmers had lent fields. Those along Bredy Road were preferred, as these were level, though wet. Whist Drives, with some good prizes, were held regularly, in all the villages and the keen players got up parties and travelled around the district. Saturday evenings at the cinema, or the "pictures" as everybody called it, was one of the most popular pastimes. There would be long queues in Bridport, outside The Palace, in South Street and at The Lyric, in Barrack Street. Going to the cinema, each week, was a social habit. The seats at The Palace ranged in price from 1/- to 2/9d, the latter being up in the balcony and in the year of the Burton Sale *"Carousel" and " The Spirit of St Louis",* (starring James Stewart) were showing at The Palace.

Between the wars, there was a concert party, which was revived after 1945. The village could boast a lot of musical and theatrical talent which, Mrs Gladys Gale, the butcher's wife, channelled into variety shows and pantomimes. In the late 1940s and during the 1950s, pantomimes were staged in the WI Hall, where the performances were soon sold out. Everyone had the opportunity to be involved.

For the retired gentry and professionals in the village, their social life consisted of tea, cocktail and bridge parties, musical evenings in their homes, a few rounds of golf, a trip in a motor or sailing boat and following the local fox and otter hounds, usually as foot followers. Burton Bradstock came within the Cattistock Hunt and it was known as "Friday Country". Some of the farmers met up for supper parties where they ended the evening with games of cards. They were prominent members of the Melplash Agricultural Society and played in skittles and dart competitions.

Walking was a necessity. Many people walked to and fro to work, to the beach to fish, to the allotments and to West Bay and Bridport. For everyone, walks along the beach or over the fields and cliffs was a recreation, even after walking, (or for some, cycling), several miles in conjunction with their work, each day. All this contributed to a healthy and leisurely pace of life. No one seemed in a hurry, yet they managed to be on time for work or appointments.

Families, or just the children, looked after by their elder brothers and sisters, spent a great deal of time, on summer days and in the autumn, gathering wild flowers and produce that grew freely in the hedgerows and fields, such as mushrooms, blackberries, hazel nuts and elderberries. The farmers never seemed to prevent people crossing their tenanted land and anyway most fields were intersected with footpaths. Many people owned dogs which would soon catch a rabbit, until Myximatosis had swept through the whole country in the 1950s, when this disease killed off the majority of rabbits.

Those who had been reared on rabbit stew, became sickened by the sight of these stupefied, dying and dead animals and never ate a rabbit again, bringing a halt to catching rabbits for profit and the skins, too, became worthless. There was a time during the war, when a lorry came around collecting rabbits and skins on a Ministry of Agriculture scheme and men could earn a living as rabbit catchers.

The indigenous villagers were law-abiding folk, distinguished by their smooth, rhythmic brogue. Whether worker or employer, the village people used a certain amount of the Dorset dialect when speaking. They all understood the various colloquial words and phrases. As for their appearance, there were two main types. Some families were of medium height, dark and swarthy. Others were taller, fair headed or dark. All were weathered by years in the open air. Mostly, their disposition was that of a retiring, shrewd but gentle nature and it is this that may have, from time to time, annoyed the new, more outgoing residents.

There were no 'territorial' areas except perhaps rivalry between villages, mainly over sport or fishing. Captain Pitt-Rivers's tenants were never idle. There was always a busy atmosphere predominant in and around the village and the streets and lanes were never empty. People were out and about and everyone had to be an early riser. No one ever passed anyone, whether they knew them or not, in the street or wherever, without greeting them.

HAPPY TIMES

The teenagers of the 1950s, joined the Youth Club, organised and run by Nancy Wratislaw. They rode their bicycles around the streets and from village to village. The older boys still cut an ash pole from the hedge and vaulted across the river. Discipline was good and it was only the occasional scrumping, [stealing], of apples that gave rise for reprimand. Finding birds' eggs was legal and the young lads had extensive collections. The bicycle was the main mode of transport and as they got older, the youngsters thought nothing of cycling to school and work in Bridport, or ten miles to a dance or social. Most weeks, nearer home, there was a village 'hop', which was held in the Women's Institute Hall or the School.

42. The village band, Victory in Europe Day 1945, led by Fred Mullins on the kettle drum, Fred White on base drum, Stanley Williams piccolo. The jubilant conductor is one of the crowd!

The Swyre Bull Thrift Club, the British Legion, the Askerswell Young Farmers' Club, and the Burton Bradstock Youth Club, organised the dances and the hall and the pubs would be packed-out that evening.

By 1958, the melodies of the 1940s had begun to give way to skiffle and Rock and Roll dancing, never quite replacing the sedate waltzes, quicksteps and much enjoyed polkas and the Gay Gordons, (or the jitterbug, that had been introduced by the American troops when stationed in the area), all rounded off with the "Hokey Kokey". From America the "Jute Box" had arrived and 'put a nickel (or sixpence) in' to get the latest tune played in the pubs was a novelty.

Local bands, or a man with a radiogram, were engaged to provide the music. One local band was Ada [Brinson] and her Rhythm Boys. Such was the popularity of the Swyre Bull Thrift Club dances, held in Burton, that a coach was chartered to pick-up people throughout the Bride Valley.

There had always been a football team in the village, since RB Howarth set one up in the early part of the century and the Canaries, as they called themselves, had taken part in all the local competitions, with great success. It was young Douglas Hawkins who had been responsible for choosing the black and yellow shirts in 1907, when the schoolboys were asked to give their preferred colour combination.

Soon after the Second World War had ended, a new team was formed and began playing matches again, on a regular basis, coached by Ted Hitt and Bill [Ginger] Jarman. A team was formed which won the West Dorset Youth League trophy in the 1948/49

43. Burton Youth Football Team 1949 winners of the West Dorset Youth League.
Back row (L to R): Peter Canterbury, Bob Miller, Bill Ives, Ray Tompkins, Tom Foot
Seated (L to R): Fred Kerley, Bob Cammell, Roy Nethercott (Captain), Johnny Giles-Townsend, Edwin Aylott and Stuart Crabbe.

season. Burton boys Roy Nethercott (Captain), Edwin Aylott, Bobby Cammell and young Fred Kerley as well as Johnny Giles-Townsend, from Bradpole, (who later married a Burton girl in 1958 and came to live in Burton), were playing. The rest of the team were recruited from nearby villages and Bridport, such was the draw to play for Burton Bradstock.

Most youngsters taught themselves to swim in the sea, or in some cases, in the deep pools of the River Bride. In good weather, any spare time was spent swimming off the Chesil Beach or at West Bay. Wherever they swam, the youngsters were very conscious of the dangers of the Chesil coast knowing that the beach shelved and the undertow could be fatal.

Young men saved up and acquired motor-bikes but they were not required to wear protective helmets. Accidents were rare, even though, the muddy, wet roads, presented a hazard. The three village pubs had regular customers. Some of the young men would try to imitate their elders, get a little merry but rarely with unpleasant consequences. The majority of men smoked as did a few of the women. There were darts, card and board games to play, table and alley skittles and teams were formed to play matches. Eating out was a long way off!

A mobile film unit occasionally came to the village. The younger ones were saving-up to buy record players that were replacing their parents' old wind-up gramophones. After 1945, Guy Fawkes's Night was celebrated with bonfires, (a communal one on the cliff) and boys let off rockets and bangers around the village, completely forgetting about the thatched roofs. (Only once, in the early 1900s, had a rocket landed on a thatched roof, with dire consequences).

Twice a year, in April and October, 'everyone' went to the Fair in Bridport, where swing-boats, roundabouts, dodgem cars, shooting galleries, hoop-la, boxing booths and numerous side-shows could be enjoyed. Those who went to the Fair brought back a gift for those who could not attend. A fairling [gift] was a keep-sake and was treasured by the recipient. It might be a china ornament or a bag of gingerbread. Over the centuries, the Fair had moved around the outskirts of the town but its final home was at the bottom of South Street, opposite the gas works. In earlier days the children had been given a half-day holiday, from school, as they would have absented themselves, anyway. Everyone looked forward to the Fair Days which were exciting highlights of the year.

★★★★★★★★★★

The old customs provided entertainment and continuity in Burton Bradstock. Apart from the paying-out of the Thrift club, Christmas did not begin until Christmas Eve when the simple decorations went up in the home, as it was considered unlucky to trim the house, or bring in holly beforehand. (When the twelve days of Christmas were over it was essential to take down the decorations and discard the withered holly immediately. It must never be burnt). Carol singers ventured out on Christmas Eve and maybe a few evenings previous but most people had to work until the last minute, some on Christmas

44. *The Concert Party, WI Hall, 1950s. (L to R) Alfie Hutchings, Arthur Bartlett, Stanley Williams, Albert Shipp and John Panten. Inset 44a Shirley Hutchings dances with (L) to (R) Violet Bull, Albert Shipp (seated at table) and Audrey Welch, Elvina Wilkins, Edwin Aylott and Janet Spier.*

Day, depending on whether their occupation was connected with the festivities. There was a time when the post was delivered on the Bank Holidays as well as milk and even last minute groceries or paraffin. The animals were milked, fed and bedded down, in time for the farmer and his men to be home in time for the Christmas Dinner. Others may have managed to get to church and/or the pub where both would be decorated simply with holly and ivy and a few trimmings, often home-made. Boxing day was similar. The hounds met in Bridport and there might be an afternoon football match. The evening concluded with a social or dance and it was back to full-time work the next day. New Year's Eve was festive, with yet another dance, or sing-song in the pubs but seeing in the New Year and First Footing, when it was considered lucky to have a dark man cross the threshold, bringing a piece of coal, were followed all too soon by work on New Year's Day, which until more recent times, was another working day.

LAYING TO REST

Until the death of Frank Marsh, in 1958, the village carpenter had doubled as an undertaker. Previously, the Burton/Shipton based builder, Bartlett, who lived at The Retreat and had his yard and two carpenters' shops, behind the house, had been called in to deal with funerals. The body was placed in the front room for relatives and friends to view, prior to the funeral and the coffin was screwed down at the last minute. The windows were thrown open during the funeral to freshen-up the room ready for when the mourners returned to hold the Wake, (a feasting held after the funeral, in Burton Bradstock).

In bowler hats and dark suits or fishermen's caps and Jerseys, the mourners would gather at the home of the deceased and family members, or close friends, acted as the bearers. Often the coffin had to be brought down from upstairs or out through narrow doorways and passages. This could necessitate tipping the coffin on end or cutting a hole in the bedroom floorboards or taking it out through a window. No refridgerators housed the body in the interim period and in hot summers, acting as a bearer, could often be unpleasant but such matters did not bother them. They were the sort of folk, who, literally, took all in their stride and got on with the task.

With the undertaker, wearing his black suit and bowler hat, (in Burton, not a top hat) and preceding the cortège, the coffin was pushed on the village bier. A subscription had been raised to obtain funds to purchase a bier, when the new burial ground was opened but it seems that it was not until 1925 before one was in use. Close mourners, which could include the women who had decided to attend, walked immediately behind. Some families hired a funeral car for the women, when motor vehicles became more common. In times gone by, shops and other business premises would shut and the blinds of all the properties, along the route, were drawn, or the shutters closed. Frederick Kerley, a farmer, died in 1954 and his coffin was borne on the farm wagon.

Until 1907, burials had taken place in St Mary's Churchyard but after several hundreds of years, a cemetery was consecrated in Shipton Lane, which was being used in 1958. The first person to be buried there had been a coastguard. A volley of shots was fired over his grave. Others at rest in the cemetery, were sailors who had been washed up on the beach after the sinking, off Lyme Regis, of HMS Formidable, in 1914, Brian Swaffield who fell in action on June 11th 1942 and Alfred Cammell, killed in the same war. Members of the Stephens family, from Haddon House, West Bay, which was within the Estate, were interred in a family vault, just inside the entrance gates. Captain Pitt-Rivers had given a site for St John's Church at West Bay, which was consecrated in 1939 but there was no burial ground there.

When there was no longer a resident undertaker, in Burton, funeral directors from Bridport took over. The older people always prepared for their demise, although they rarely had much to leave and a will was unnecessary. They made sure that they had saved enough cash, secreted somewhere in the house, for their funeral expenses and many had put aside the "coffin clothes"[clothing], in which they wished to be buried. The men were buried in their best suits, fisherman's gear or naval uniforms and the women in a best, clean nightgown and stockings. Their families sacrificed a lot, in some cases, to erect a headstone. Cremation was rare amongst the villagers.

The people of Burton Bradstock had lived and gone to their rest in the same age-old fashion for generations. At least, the impending Sale would not alter this.

WHAT THE LOCAL PAPER SAID IN 1958

A local newspaper first came out in 1855, later known as *The Bridport News*. Not everyone could read in those days. By the late 1870s, Lord Rivers had rented out a cottage to the parish, for use as a Reading Room. It was a very small building; a 'one up one down' cottage, in the main street where the villagers could go to read the national and local newspapers, in which the latter, also carried a great deal of world news. The Reading Room became a place where meetings could be held, a social venue for concerts, lectures and lantern-slides.

In 1958 *The Bridport News* led with the reports of the disposal of the West Dorset block of the Pitt-Rivers Estate and the views of those concerned. It was full, too, with other local news. The weather always featured in the columns. In January it was very cold, followed by a wet spring, whilst Whitsuntide was sunny, bringing visitors flocking to the district. This influx was short-lived, as the numbers of holiday makers coming to West Bay, that summer, dropped. Officials thought that there was not enough to interest them. The lack of publicity and strikes, resulting in a shortage of money, were deemed another cause and to add to an already depressing holiday season, the weather, in early August, was bad and yachts capsized.

However, that summer, the fishing along the coast was abundant. In June, there was a huge catch of sprats in the harbour basin; the shoals had been chased in by the mackerel. The sprat glut was so heavy, that by July, the surplus was being sent to a fertiliser factory, at Newbury. The mackerel catches were good but sharks, usually a sign of plenty of fish, were damaging the nets. One was caught, near Abbotsbury, by Walter Thorner, of Burton and it was put on display later, at Gluning's fish shop. (In the baking hot summer of 1955, thirty men, led by Bert Williams and Alfie Hutchings, were needed to pull a dead, fourteen feet long, basking shark ashore, that had been caught in an oil discharge. Previous attempts to haul it in proved dangerous, as the boat nearly sank).

The Bridport Laundry, that summer of the Burton Sale, was offering a dry-cleaning service and advertised for two girls to learn the work, in pleasant, modern conditions. There was an outbreak of Foot and Mouth disease in Beaminster and forty animals were shot and at the same time, the Ministry of Agriculture and Fisheries encouraged farmers to arrange shoots of rooks, although it was doubtful if there was anyone left who still ate rook pie. Experts were saying that farming must be capable of rapid expansion. Also reported in *The Bridport News* that summer, was that eighty rail enthusiasts had chartered a passenger train for a nostalgic excursion to West Bay, with large crowds turning out to witness the scene.

Bridport Borough Council whilst endeavouring to purchase specific properties in West Bay, from the Pitt-Rivers Estate, decided that it was too costly to set-up a new cattle market. Councillor Miss Frances Reynolds was concerned about the over extraction of gravel-dredging between the piers. "If five hundred tons were removed who could say what would happen," she said. Councillor Lambert, Vice Chairman of the harbour committee, did not want to take the chance. He thought that Nature would win every time. A Bristol company was offering sixpence a ton. "What a cost to the Council if the piers did collapse," concluded Lambert.

The paper reported that there was a serious fire in the thatched roof of the Burton post office and the fire brigade remained on the scene for several hours. Off the beach, a holiday maker, from Yeovil, was caught in the swell. A bus conductor, alerted by a woman, hailed a doctor and ambulance, using the nearest telephone, at Cheney's garage. For saving the man's life, PC Peach, the village policeman, received a certificate from the Humane Society.

In the "Burton" column was an account of the church fête where £151 was raised. Pony rides were an attraction and there was a dance in the evening. A Conservative Association meeting was hosted at The Rookery, with Mrs Ryan presiding. Two well respected men of the village died; William Marsh, aged 75, the carpenter and undertaker and Albert Bull, 79, Vice Chairman of the Parish Council, a member of the British Legion for twenty-two years, captain of the bell-ringers and retired head gardener at The Rookery.

The Bridport News of 25th July 1958, had as its headline, **'BURTON WAITS'**. The village was living **'under a shadow'**.

THE SALE IS ANNOUNCED

It was the clanging of the auctioneers' bell that brought the large crowd, to attention. The marquee, the largest, that a number of the people assembled had ever seen, had been erected a couple of days before, in the field, adjacent to the Recreation Ground. This field lay beside the main road that wound, through the village of Burton Bradstock, to Weymouth, shown on ancient maps as *"Corn Croft"* and known to the older villagers as *"Corn Crack"*. Until the mill closed, the field was rented from the Estate as part of the mill holding.

The element *"cweorn"* was an old English word and was associated with water mills and mill stones and the 'cracking' [grinding] of the corn. However, here it was, that in times gone by, the Corn Crake had nested and reared its young. Over the years, Corn Croft had been associated with the Corn Crake and the two, inter-changeable meanings were appropriate. The dampness of the meadow and the grass that grew there was an ideal habitat for the bird but with advanced farming methods, it had disappeared as had the proper use of the mill. Only the older residents had caught a glimpse of the Corn Crake and knew the sound of its call. It seemed like an omen. The Estate, as they knew it, was about to disappear too but their roots were deep. It was going to take a lot to get them 'out' of Burton.

The atmosphere that prevailed in the marquee was one of excitement and great apprehension. At the sound of the bell, the mood changed to anticipation. The unknown had brought an air of foreboding to many of the tenants whose families had lived and departed in Burton Bradstock for generations. Strangers had stalked about with the Sale particulars in-hand and measuring tapes at the ready. The rumours were rife. Few had heard of such a complete sale of an estate and the decision of Captain George Lane-Fox Pitt-Rivers, to auction off the greater part of the properties, land and the shoreline, in West Dorset, had dismayed everyone. Had the church tower fallen down there would not have been a greater shock and subsequent concern.

All the tenants had received a letter from their Landlord, informing them that, apart from economic considerations and his profound regret at having to sever a connection with the Burton Bradstock and West Bay tenantry which had existed for many generations, he no longer felt justified in retaining the Estate at considerable personal sacrifice, 'without the prospect, as I had originally planned, of any happy succession in my family. ' He intended to sell, what amounted to one thousand, six hundred and eighty-two acres, in this most attractive village with over three miles of coastline of unsurpassed beauty along the Chesil Bank, from Cogden, to the harbour at West Bay.

Captain Pitt-Rivers had three sons; Michael Augustus, born in 1917 and Julian Alfred [later Professor], born 1919, from his first marriage to Rachel Forster and George Anthony, still a relatively young man, at the time of the Sale, by his second marriage, to Rosalind, daughter of Brigadier the Honorable Anthony Henley.

The Captain's letter continued, "I sincerely hope if you wish to become the freeholder of the property you occupy, you will be able to do so." Rumours circulated as to the family reason for the Captain's decision to part with the Burton Estate. In the letter, dated the seventeenth of March 1958, Captain Pitt-Rivers stated that he wanted them, the tenants, to be the first to know.

Senior and Godwin, Auctioneers and Surveyors, of Sturminster Newton, had been appointed to sell the Burton Estate and they would be calling to draw up the particulars. Captain Pitt-Rivers was prepared to assist tenants and informed them that a substantial part of the purchase price could be left on mortgage. The smallholding, Cliff Farm, which had a licence for twenty-five caravans, had been offered to enquirers, around the same time as the announcement but the asking price of £4,000 had not been forthcoming and it was, subsequently, included in the August Sale.

When all was accounted, the Sale Catalogue listed nearly *two thousand acres of land, five farms, additional accommodation and building land, three caravan camps, one with vacant possession, three unique private beaches, which had only 'been developed to a limited extent on exclusive lines', the West Dorset Golf Course and two licensed free houses, one of which would be vacated at the end of the year. There were seven other good houses, fifty cottages, a petrol station cum garage, a shop and the old flax spinning mill, together with other property, warehouses and land at West Bay.*

The impressive Sale catalogue, costing ten shillings, gave the particulars of a total of one hundred and forty-four lots in Burton Bradstock and West Bay. It had been planned to hold the Sale in the Women's Institute Hall but interest was so great that the auctioneers decided, at the last minute, to erect a marquee, as the hall would not accommodate anything like the number of people expected to attend. It appeared that there had been careful consideration given to the proposed disposal of the Estate, as so many of the Lots were to be sold with vacant possession. As the leases had expired, the Vendor had not sought to offer them up again.

A minority of the cottagers did not understand anything about buying and selling property and the terms, "mortgage" or "freehold" were ones that they had never come across. Only having been witness to the occasional sale of boats and nets on the beach, a furniture sale, or transactions in the sale-room at Jeff's weekly pannier market in Bridport, did not prepare them sufficiently.

A number of the tenants had never had to write a formal letter. The main concern of everyone involved in the decision as to whether to buy, was the fact that they did not borrow. The farmers may have had overdrafts with their banks but borrowing money was not done. If you could not pay for something, you did not have it! The tenants had little idea how to set about purchasing a property and the Vendor's solicitors, Payne, Hicks Beach and Co. , of Lincoln's Inn, London and legal teams in Bridport, became involved in the procedures. The tenancies were often held on a verbal agreement, such was the trust between landlord and tenant.

Either this lack of knowledge and/or insufficient money for a deposit, were instrumental, in some tenants not even considering to purchase. Borrowing money was extremely difficult and there would be a long period of repayment. Several properties needed patching, re-thatching, or major work carried out on them. The worried tenants felt that they needed to possess 'a fortune', to put all in good order.

The uncertainty, even amongst the more enlightened tenants, such as the farmers and business people, generated much speculation and a great deal of concern for their futures.

NOT A HAPPY DAY

It was eleven o' clock on Thursday July 31st 1958. The morning was bright and fair and just a little sultry. It was to be a summer's day that none of them would forget. Silence fell. Five hundred people had crowded into the marquee. Where the Corn Crake had squawked its throaty call, in that field, there was now a buzz of excitement mixed with great apprehension, even fear. Partners in the firm of Senior and Godwin were Messrs EC Ingram and AW Richards, who had been instructed with the Sale and they and their clerks had spent the previous months calling on all the tenants, to draw up the details of the properties, farms and individual plots of land.

One elderly man, who lived in a cottage, in the village, had expressed his fears to a journalist from *The Bridport News* . He was not in a position to buy his home, having only his pension to live on. He could never afford the weekly payments. The old fellow, whose family had lived in Burton for several generations, was afraid that a new landlord would make improvements to the cottage and charge him a higher rent. If a new owner put up his rent, "I would pack up and leave, " he declared.

Some of the tenant farmers had been concerned about the manner in which the buildings and land had been divided up. Breaking-up of the farmland would obviously generate higher prices. Bunny Lenthall was worried that his famous flock of Dorset Horn sheep might have to go, if the land that was suitable for their grazing, was sold off in separate lots.

The particulars when they were drawn-up referred to boundaries, rights with regard to drainage, water, electricity, cables and poles, private roads and public rights of way. The Vendor would be exonerated from any problems associated with a tenant not leaving where there was to be vacant possession. Tenants' fixtures were presumed to be stated and care had been taken over this but a purchaser was deemed to have satisfied himself as to what was and what was not a tenant's fixture or improvement.

Very detailed, accurate descriptions and measurements of each cottage, house and farm left nothing out. Everything that was outside was listed. Lavatories were given as either Elsan closet or EC (earth closet) but some buckets had been installed by the tenants. The services that were available were given for each Lot and the present manner in which water was obtained was described.

The Estate was to be sold with certain tree preservation orders, Town Planning Schemes, Development Plans and various restrictions. Orders by local, county and public authorities were to be complied with, whether mentioned or not and the cultivations referred to the current state of the land. The Vendor reserved the right to sell in any order and to withdraw Lots. Everyone had resented the carefree and inquisitive attitude of strangers who had swarmed into the village, since the Sale had been announced. The whole village had been under siege.

The auctioneers, had written to *The Dorset Evening Echo*, shortly before the Sale date,

45. *The auctioneers and clerks on the rostrum ready to start the Sale.*

46. *The crowd in the Sale marquee, summer 1958.*

'to rectify the erroneous impression'. An article had appeared in the paper, without information being obtained from the Vendor's agents. It had not portrayed Captain Pitt-Rivers in a favourable light. Senior and Godwin pointed out that the majority of the tenants were covered by the Rent Acts and that their position would not be affected by any change of ownership.

Their client was not in a position to sell privately before the auction and that many of the tenants would therefore be afforded the chance to purchase their properties at the Sale. No prior negotiations had been made with the tenant farmers by the Vendor and the National Farmers' Union had been informed of the allocation of the Lots and expressed themselves 'satisfied with the arrangements made'. A representative from the planning authority would be at the Sale, as so many enquiries had been received.

On the morning of the Sale, the whole village was up even earlier than usual. The cows were soon milked, pigs and chickens fed, papers delivered, boats, gardens and allotments checked and the tenants dressed themselves up, as if it were a Sunday, many women adorned themselves with hats; all were ready for the unknown. R B Howarth and the Rector were abroad, in the village, from an early hour. Both had missions of a different kind.

In the marquee, as the sound of the auctioneer's bell faded away, Mr Ingram rose from his seat, on the rostrum and broke the silence that had fallen, by saying how sorry Captain Pitt-Rivers was not to be present but he was away in London. The Captain regretted the Sale but had no alternative. It was due to circumstances beyond his control. Ingram went on to say that it had been considered to sell the Estate as a whole but it was preferred that the tenants should have the opportunity to purchase the freehold of their homes and land. Private negotiation was not possible and hence they found themselves there, on this particular day, to offer the Burton Bradstock Estate for sale.

He continued, "It has been acknowledged, or has to be acknowledged, that the tenants have had a very benevolent landlord. The majority of the rents are what one would call pre-war; in fact there has been very little alteration for many years. I hope this is appreciated. " He raised the question of 'development', indicating that it would surely come. Bournemouth had sprung, a century before, from a small village. The possibilities were immense. "Seldom does such an opportunity come one's way, " he concluded.

Then, the auctioneer announced that Captain Pitt-Rivers had generously donated the Reading Room to the parish. Replying on behalf of the Parish Council, the Chairman, RB Howarth, who also held the office of Chairman of the Bridport Rural District Council and formerly, Head Master at Burton Bradstock village school, for some thirty-five years, expressed thanks for this gesture. " It is not a happy day for the people of Burton Bradstock, " said Howarth. "A long association with the Pitt-Rivers Estate is being broken up, " he told the audience. RB Howarth, the forthright, north countryman, said that he did not share Mr Ingram's opinion about the possibility that the village could become another Bournemouth. He was adamant that measures had been taken to ensure that uncontrolled development would not take place. This would apply, in particular, to the coastal area, he added.

Loud and prolonged applause greeted this statement, although most gathered there remained ignorant as to exactly what the measures were that 'had been taken'.

THE FIRST LOT

The silence was such that the assembled people could hear each other breathing. A tense atmosphere had built up in the marquee. The tenants and their families huddled together, unknown speculators sat separately, with an air of hope of obtaining a good bargain. The Rector, [Canon Arthur Dittmer], representatives from the Parish and Rural District Councils, solicitors, a representative from the National Union of Teachers, builders, architects, agents, auctioneers' clerks, photographers, the Press and others, with either a vested or curious interest, waited......and so it began......Lot One was called!

Lot 1 Number 51 Church Street, a picturesque, rose-covered cottage, situated opposite the church, in the centre of the village was let on an oral tenancy of £36 per annum to Cecilia Brown who was a neat and reserved person, a dressmaker by profession and widow of Alfred Brown. This property was announced as the first Lot.

47. Lot 1.

★★★★★★★★★★

One of the outstanding memories of this cottage was that a German prisoner of war, who had been recruited into the Hitler Youth had lodged there after the war. He was a handsome young man who worked at Manor Farm and was well liked. No one knew the 'going' of him.

★★★★★★★★★★

Cecilia Brown's cottage was a well maintained property and one of the best and prettiest on offer. The rateable value was £11 and outside there was a concreted yard, a stone and slated wash-house, fuel store, small garden and an Elsan closet. Mains water was connected. The sewer was nearby but neither a flush lavatory or bathroom was installed. The auctioneers, conscious of an uproar if the first Lot went 'out of the village', rattled on the bidding, which hastened the drop of the hammer, at £750 to the tenant.

It was a good move on the part of the auctioneers to let the first Lot fall to the tenant and not be 'sold away'. There was a huge cheer and clapping, tempered with a sigh of relief, as the first of the locals had secured her home, if at a high price.

Mrs Brown stayed on there for some years and was having the property modernised when she died. It stayed empty for a while and since around 1976 it has been in the ownership of a true Burton born and bred person who has preserved and enhanced its charm.

THE WESLEYAN CHAPEL.

Lot 2 In the early part of the nineteenth century Methodism was strong in the West Country. In 1818, an unfinished house, in Burton, had been taken on lease and converted to a chapel. By 1825 it had been abandoned for a more suitable place in the centre of the village, which at that time was in the occupation of Farmer Brown, father-in-law of Giles Lawrence Roberts, later known as the "Poor Man's Friend". Roberts had been born at The Sloop, renamed the Bridport Arms Hotel, Bridport Harbour, where his father, a mariner, invalided out of the navy, was the harbour pilot and host at the inn. His mother, Mary, the daughter of John Lawrence, a gentleman, came from a prominent Burton family, whilst Giles Roberts's great-great-grandfather, Solomon Lawrence, had shares in ships at the harbour.

★★★★★★★★★★

After a unsettled youth, not knowing what he wanted to do in life, Giles Roberts qualified as a doctor. He married Phoebe Brown, a farmer's daughter and began preaching in the district in 1803, becoming instrumental in setting up Wesleyan chapels, one of which was in Burton Bradstock. He set-up a pharmacy in Bridport and administered to the poor by using an ointment that was reputed to cure most ailments. The chemical basis of the potion is questionable but Roberts was renowned and well respected. His empathy with Gypsies may well have been both social and professional, as they are noted for their ability to cure humans and animals with simple, natural remedies.

★★★★★★★★★★

For well over a century, the Chapel in Burton had attracted a large congregation. A beautifully illuminated text, "O Worship ye the Lord in the Beauty of Holiness", had adorned the wall above the altar. The pews and screen, in an imported rich red wood, gave the interior a welcoming feature. Continuously, from 1828, a wall-mounted clock had ticked the hours away. This clock, with its Roman numerals, had been presented by two prominent members of the congregation, Doctor Robinson and George Brown.

Renovations had been carried out in the 1870s at a cost of just over £30, of which half was still outstanding by October 1874. At a re-opening service, the Burton Bradstock Temperance Society's banner was displayed; "Deliver us from Evil". A further £9 was raised with the tea that followed.

★★★★★★★★★★

At the Sale, the handing-over of the Chapel, was to be a generous gesture by Captain Pitt-Rivers, who had gifted it to the Trustees. Whilst reflecting on one hundred and thirty years, there was no way that the Trustees could have afforded to buy the property. The Reverend Stanley Willson, Chairman of the Trustees, on behalf of the Methodists of Burton Bradstock and the whole Circuit, said how grateful they were to receive the gift of the Chapel. "A bright relief to me and my people, " he concluded.

The building continued as a Methodist chapel, with dwindling congregations until 1972. The Dorset County Council then saw the possibility of turning it into a library, which, with the increasing population, was well received.

Today, it serves as a welcome facility as a Dorset County Library and is open on a part-time basis, all year around. It is furnished with numerous reference books, local information and the most up-to-date technological equipment, from which, all corners of the world, can be reached from the heart of Burton Bradstock.

Presently, threats to close the library hang over the village. It is a lifeline and even with less use than is officially required, closure will put yet another nail in the coffin of community unity.

THE WHITE HOUSE

Lot 3 *'An attractive small residence of character.'* This property produced immense interest. Here was a premier house, albeit with a tenant, also in the centre of the village. It was built in 1635, by Simon Bowring, who owned Down Farm, in Shipton Gorge, which included St Catherine's Chapel, that lay between the two villages. Bowring had married Jane Ridgeway, a wealthy woman, who owned the 'mansion and lands' at Graston, a hamlet about a mile from the village.

The date-stone, embedded in the front wall of The White House was a permanent reminder of those times and the battles of the Parliamentarians and the Royalists, when the families were caught up in the disputes. The house was an ideal gentleman's residence. It was extremely well constructed of stone, with a slate roof. The mullioned windows confirmed its date. Inside, the drawing room, 16 feet 3 inches by 15 feet by 7 feet 10 inches high, had an original moulded ceiling beam and elsewhere were period fireplaces. The stairs were of exceptional quality and design. There were five rooms on the ground floor and four bedrooms, with a bathroom on the second floor. In addition, two attic rooms made it very spacious, yet it was compact. The gardens and courtyard, with its iron pump and the fish pool, (into which Andrew Collins had tumbled as a child), added yet more features. The whole was sold subject to *'the joint use of a drain'*.

★★★★★★★★★★

Major John Marc Wratislaw and his wife, Nancy, a retired, upper-class, childless couple, had lived there since the 1920s. The Major was a portly, fatherly looking gentleman, with a military air, who greeted everyone by their surname. His cheerful nature and significant dress of corduroy breeches, thick knee stockings, tweed jacket and a green plush, trilby hat, endeared him to everyone. He claimed to be a descendant of Good King Wenceslas.

The chatelaine, Nancy Burrow Wratislaw, was a Founder Member of the Dorset Floral Decoration Society, which was the forerunner of these societies in the whole country and spent a great deal of time in her garden. During the last war she had served in the Civil

Defence and Women's Royal Voluntary Service, generally, playing a prominent part in the war effort. She was also a school governor and a leading Women's Institute member, started the Pooh Club for the smaller children and organised the Youth Club. Keen on theatricals, she encouraged the children, of all ages, to take part in tableaux, plays and pantomimes.

Nancy Wratislaw surrounded herself with village children, providing interests and fun for them and at the same time, instilling morals and discipline into her charges. The Wratislaws took in evacuees during 1939-1945. Notably, were Stanley and Barbara Moon, from the East End of London. Nothing could have been more of a contrast for those children, as they enjoyed and benefited from their happy, if sometimes eventful, evacuation to The White House.

Local people were employed by the Wratislaws. Kathy Cammell, had been with them, in domestic service, since leaving school and Colin Hodgskins, the gardener, regularly came from Shipton Gorge, arriving on his bicycle. During the more recent war, the Major served as an air raid warden and was to the forefront in the "Dig for Victory" campaign. The whole household and the way of life practised at The White House, epitomised the life of gentry retired to the country. Their presence was an asset to the village.

★★★★★★★★★★

Wratislaw purchased Lot 3 for £3,500 .

> Major and Mrs Wratislaw lived on at The White House until 1963 when he was killed in a road accident. Nancy, at the wheel, was seriously injured. She remained as a semi-invalid, until her death in 1984. The church was packed for her memorial service. The house was sold again, a building site siphoned off and with the going of the Wratislaws, went another anchor in the old village.
>
> Of necessity, vehicular access has been cleverly made.

BEULAH COTTAGE

Lot 4 Beulah Cottage, was situated in Middle Street, although few locals needed to refer to the street as such. The name of this cottage had some significance which had long gone into disuse. *Beulah,* it was reputed, was given to properties which were rented out to widows and spinsters of good character. The cottage had an unusually large window that faced south, in one of the upper rooms. Eliza Clark Hoskins, a needlewoman, had married Edwin Buckler, a fisherman, around 1860 and was widowed in 1871 and to aid her, as she was forced to earn a living, the Court Leet had sanctioned this window, to provide her with better light, upstairs, where she had her sewing room.

The custom of the specialised tenantry lapsed and the Aves family had taken Beaulah Cottage. Tom Aves, a former Dorchester prison officer, took work as an Estate carpenter. Mrs Doris Klopper, née Williams, remembered the pride that Mrs Aves, from a Portland/

Burton family, had taken in the flower-knots that adorned the outside of the cottage which were still blooming in 1958.

Their son, Henry, known locally as "Sonny", employed by Bests of Bridport, was living at home with his father. Henry was a radio and television genius and had installed a television set in the cottage. His old father, Tom, would stand at the door, as the boys came out of school and boast, "American film at four o' clock. " Some of the lucky ones, who lived handy, were invited in to enjoy an hour's viewing, which was often Wild West excitement. One of the fortunate boys was Brian Galpin, who marvelled at the apparatus which was a 'small affair, housed in a an open frame, with a small greenish screen. The reception was fairly faint, picking up the signal from the transmitting station, at Wenvoe,' often interrupted by the "test card".

★★★★★★★★★★

Who was this Mr Macey of Sandbanks, whose bid of £290 made him the new owner of Beulah Cottage? He was a complete stranger in the village.

INGRAM HOUSE

Lot 5 Ingram House, once the home of Admiral Ingram, from whom it took its name, a contemporary of Captain (later Admiral) Thomas Masterman Hardy, of Portesham, who sailed with Nelson, was sold to a speculator, at the knockdown price of £900 to a Mr Hayward of Sherborne.

In 1802 an old record stated :- *'dwelling house lately repaired by Nicholas Ingram. '*

The Estate documents recorded a lease, which was signed by Nicholas Ingram, of a dwelling house. Nicholas Ingram, *'a captain in His Majesty's Royal Navy'* was *'recently deceased'* in 1815, aged 60. Elizabeth, his wife, aged 41 and Jane Bishop, his daughter, were the other two 'lives' named in the lease.

★★★★★★★★★★

Ingram House, a charming property, in the heart of the village, was the home of the Collins family. The Captain, a Master Mariner, under sail and Hilda Collins, had moved to Burton Bradstock, in 1926, with their children, Elsie, Marjorie and Frank. The younger children, Dorothy, James, Audrey, Amy, Andrew, Geoffrey and Barry, (who had died as a little child), were either born in the village, or Bridport.

What had brought the Captain and his wife to Burton Bradstock, with their three firstborn seemed to be his connection with old naval colleagues from his South China days. One was Captain Harry Trowbridge, who knew Charles Stride, the Agent, at the time, for the Pitt-Rivers Estate.

At first, it had been considered that the Collins family would move into The White House but it appears that Ingram House, (which was at the time the "School House", headmaster Milburne having resided there), became vacant first, when the then, school headmaster, RB Howarth, moved into the Magnolias. Invalided out of the Navy, the

Captain, now equipped with a wooden leg, was encouraged to move to the south-west of England. Captain Trowbridge obviously had an influence in putting forward his name.

★★★★★★★★★★

Captain Collins, had a shortened but distinguished career in the Merchant Navy. He was employed by the China Navigation Company, working out of the South China seas. His Master's certificate was dated May 1918 but much earlier documents survive of his service on the steam yacht " Cavalier". He had voyaged to and from Australia, via the Amazon River and the United States of America where he was in charge of the watch, 'to the complete satisfaction of the ship's master. ' His career was cut short in 1917, losing his right foot, when his ship was blown up, off Alexandria.

The Captain maintained his sea-going discipline and ran Ingram House like a ship. His children were the crew. The boys were assigned duties, one of which was to weed the cobbled path, outside the house, (with a broken kitchen knife). Mrs Collins, on occasions, took herself off to the cinema, on a Saturday afternoon, as relaxation from her huge task of raising such a large family, that were such a credit to her and Captain Collins.

This family lived quietly, the older members, who had left home, were using it as their base at the time of the Sale. During the Second World War, the offspring who were of age, served their country. Frank brought an element of pride to his parents and siblings and to the village, as a whole, when he was awarded the Distinguished Flying Cross, for devotion to duty, in 1944.

A Pilot Officer and as a Rear Gunner, he had flown forty-three sorties, clocking up over two hundred and twenty-one hours' flying time. He had flown on missions over Berlin, Turin, Genoa, Hamburg and the industrial Ruhr of Germany. On one occasion, as Rear Gunner, he had endured six hours of intense cold, after the turret had been damaged and rendered unserviceable, with the Perspex smashed.

He stuck to his post and by accurate judgement, enabled his captain to avoid the enemy and successfully complete the mission. Another time, far from base, when the aircraft was attacked, in clear visibility, by his cool courage and skill he scored many hits, whilst the captain executed 'violent manoeuvres' to avoid enemy aircraft. Frank was noted for his modesty, cheerfulness, level head and cool attitude.

★★★★★★★★★★

At the time of the Sale, in 1958, Mrs Collins, now a widow, was elderly and although they all considered it their home, some of the family were working away or not sufficiently established, to be in a position to make what was then a large commitment to purchase. Jim, who was a qualified and highly respected mechanical and marine engineer, having trained at the Brit Engineering Works, Bridport and his wife Sheila, née Turner, were still living there, on the look-out for a house of their own, away from a houseful of people. Jim, who was self-employed, had his workshop behind the house, where there were useful buildings and ample space.

The house had many interesting features and was situated in an idyllic location. It had five bedrooms, (the largest being 16 feet 6 inches by 14 feet 3 inches, with a high Georgian type ceiling) a bathroom with bath and hand-basin, four large rooms downstairs, (one measuring 15 feet by 7 feet 6 inches and the fireplace having a marble mantel) and a scullery. The house required renovation and was suffering from woodworm and damp, as did practically all of the properties in Burton, that lay in the path of excessive rain/flood water. Useful outbuildings needed to be made good but they enhanced the value of the property. The outside lavatory was situated in a cold, north-west facing part of the garden, housing various species of spiders and creepy crawlies. ("All this did not encourage long visits there," recalls Andrew.) The large, productive garden, had always been cultivated by Captain Collins and Jim and any other brothers, who were available.

The yard and garden of the property lay secluded behind the high perimeter wall,

48. The Collins family of Ingram House Lot 5. (L to R), Marjorie, Captain John Collins, Frank (holding toddler Geoffrey), James, Dorothy, Mrs Collins (holding baby Barry) and (in front L to R): Amy, Andrew and Audrey, circa 1938. Elsie is absent. Inset 48a Frank Collins, DFC.

which prevented intrusion from passers-by and the cattle that wended their way to the milking sheds. A redundant cottage served as a potato and coal store. Once, this fine residence had stabling, which had been used later as a Boy Scout meeting place. The Collins children were constantly reminded of the scouting motto, "Be prepared," on the broken plaster walls of the family wood-store.

Almost fifty years on, Andrew Collins revealed mixed feelings about the loss of Ingram House. He questioned what sum it had cost to bring it up to present standards but looked back on it with very happy memories.

"The frustrating aspect of the whole affair was the fact that each one of us loved the village and would have done anything to secure the property as a family home. There had been some sort of open dialogue between us; collectively we might have found a way through all the difficulties and secured the house as an investment in which we could all take a share. Obviously, there was the fear of treading on each other's toes, especially, concerning the costs. If one of our large family decided to purchase, then he or she might have an upper-hand over the others and in the end, none of us decided to buy, " recounted Andrew.

★★★★★★★★★★

Incidents and time have taken most of the family in the intervening years. In 2007, only three of that charming, large family survive. Audrey is living in South Africa, Andrew, retired from teaching, in England and Geoffrey is in Australia.

Jim and his wife and two little daughters moved to another property in the village and he continued to regale his customers and others with his 'long headed' philosophy on so many subjects. He had relocated his engineering business to a workshop in Bridport, still enjoying his work, during his latter years, when he and his family moved into town. Until his death, Jim came back, as often as he could, to drink with the locals in the village pub and to walk his dog over the fields, that he had known, all his life. Jim Collins was the only member of the family who stayed, (apart from his war service), in the locality.

Today, Ingram House remains a prominent property in Burton Bradstock, standing serenely in its new cream and dove-grey livery.

DICK GALPIN'S

Lot 6 *'A well situated semi-detached house, in an important position close to the centre of the village.'* Galpin's home stood back from the green at Shadrach and was very picturesque. With a thatched roof, three good sized bedrooms and a large downstairs area it was *'suitable for development and modernisation.'* An earth closet was outside. The tenant had erected garden sheds.

★★★★★★★★★★

Henry Richard Galpin, known as "Dick", was a stone mason and general builder, employed by the Pitt-Rivers Estate. He had moved into number 18 around the time of his marriage to Agnes Mary Gale, from Powerstock, in 1930 and continued working for the Estate until his retirement in 1954. At the time of the Sale he was working in a private capacity, in and around the village and this still included jobs that the Estate required. He was widowed a number of years previously, when he had been left with an eight year old son, Brian, following the untimely death of his wife.

Help came with Mrs Grace MacDermott, herself widowed in Ireland, when her son, David was six years old. She returned, during the blitz to her family in Bermondsey and through taking various work as a housekeeper, eventually found herself and young son in Burton Bradstock.

★★★★★★★★★★

Lot 7 let with the house, was a valuable garden amounting to 12 perches, [a perch is a land measure of 5½ yards]. Galpin paid £28 a year rent on an oral tenancy and £8 rates, for the whole. The purchaser was obliged to erect and maintain a chainlink fence within three months of purchase, between Lots 6 and 7. The garden was in very good order and with a frontage to the street of 50 feet and running back some 100 feet, it would make a perfect building site.

£650 was a large sum for Galpin to pay for his home and together with his housekeeper, who purchased the property with Galpin as a sitting tenant, ensured that all of them had a home. The garden, which was sold separately, went to the speculator, SC Macey of Sandbanks, for £250.

Dick Galpin died in 1959. He was a popular man around the village. Over the years he had worked on all the Pitt-Rivers Estate properties and his son, Brian, relates that he was known to have to walk to Pitfold Farm and West Bay, shouldering his tools, to carry out work for the Estate. This meant setting off in the very early hours of the morning and not returning until nightfall.

Mrs MacDermott, lived on at number 18, until her death in 1979. Her son, David and his wife, Alison, contacted Mrs Macey, as the garden site had been neglected. They purchased it from her and were able to built a bungalow for themselves.

David MacDermott, a trained plumber and conversant with building skills, was kept busy working around the village, being involved in the many jobs connected with the developments. He found that every new occupant wanted the kitchen and bathroom renewed and with the continuous change-over of properties, there was always plenty of work. From the garden of number 18, the MacDermotts moved to Annings Lane and even when David and Alison moved out of Burton, to build themselves yet another home, he continued to work in the village. There was no

---

need to work anywhere else, such was the demand.

Brian Galpin, a qualified engineer, moved to Bridport, on his marriage but has maintained his interest in Burton Bradstock, as have the MacDermotts.

EPHRAIM'S HOME

Lot 8 Numbers 19 and 20 Shadrach, the latter with vacant possession, had a large garden of 29 perches, where an earth closet was situated. In the corner cottage had lived Ephraim Hussey, a part-time fisherman, who had taken work as a gardener at the White Ladies, the community centred above the Mere. By the time of the Sale, he was too frail to care for himself and his quaint cottage had become vacant.

★★★★★★★★★★

49. Lot 8 1930s. Inset 49a Ephraim Hussey, sailor, fisherman and part-time gardener.

His sister, Mabel, had pre-deceased him, long before. She was a knowledgeable fisherwoman who could row a boat and make and repair the fishing gear, as well as any man, spending a great deal of her time on the beach, assisting Tommy Swaffield to repair his nets, as well as being one of the crew when the seine was cast. Mabel was rarely seen without her cotton, sun bonnet.

★★★★★★★★★★

103

In 1958, the whole of Lot 8 was in need of renovation. Number 20 Shadrach had two bedrooms. The remainder of the cottage consisted of a living room and pantry. Water was taken from an outside standpipe, in the front of the cottages. This was the first place to be offered with vacant possession.

Frederick Northover and his widowed mother, Florence, had lived in the adjoining cottage, number 19, where several generations had reared large families, in this small tenement.

After his mother's death, Fred, with his wife, Olive and young son, had stayed. Northover paid £12 a year rent, as well as settling the costs of the rates of £4 per annum. At the back of the cottages the good sized, long garden, was bordered on the roadside, by the same high stone wall that continued to Ingram House. This garden, which ran north/south, was sheltered and grew early vegetables. Its length lent it to having once been suitable for growing flax and hemp and as a rope [making] walk.

Previously the Pitt-Rivers Estate's Agent had offered the corner cottage, number 20, to a young couple, who declined it, at £100. The whole realised £750, a good sum at the time and was bought by Macey, of Sandbanks.

Ephraim was cared for away from the village, living to be eighty. He died in 1964.

Fred Northover and his family had moved into Bridport, by 1963, to be near his work. He did not enjoy good health and died prematurely.

In due course, the two semi-detached cottages were 'knocked' into one, having been sold on to Mrs Peggy Kastell, one of the early property developers, with an eye for restoring. The architect she engaged, was from Stroud, in Gloustershire.

However, Arthur Watson, the present owner, believes that she ran out of money, when the job turned out to be more involved than expected. This was a familiar story throughout the district when developers expected the cost of the work to match the original estimate. By 1960, when the Watsons moved in, most of the alterations had been done. They have added an extension and had the thatch renewed.

Peter Symonds, a local thatcher from Chideock, noted that the old thatch was extremely thick and under the top coat, it was as good as the day it was done, some two hundred and fifty years previously. The spars, (wooden twisted hazel-'sticks', used to hold the thatch in place) and rafters were in good condition, as well.

The house blends in magnificently with its surroundings. Its outward appearance is little changed from a century previous and is a credit to all who have been involved in modernisation and converting the cottages into one dwelling.

DISCOVERING THE NEW INN

Lot 9 Mrs Partridge's substantial, detached cottage, with three ground floor areas, a large landing and three *'good'* bedrooms, backed on to the boundary of some allotments, sited on a very ancient burial ground. It was secured, on her behalf, by her son for £350. She had provided a stove and garden shed. An earth closet was outside and a standpipe and drainage gully were shared with Lot 10. A right-of-way existed with next door.

★★★★★★★★★★

Florence Partridge's story was fascinating and more involved than was apparent, to all but the older villagers, on the day of the Sale. She was a war widow of the Great War, having married Henry William Wells Mitchell, a local man, who served in the Horse Guards. He had enlisted at the outbreak of the war and died in August 1916 from the effects of gassing.

Florence, was a London girl and had come to Burton Bradstock, in domestic service, working for the butcher, William Gale, who hired out riding hacks, as well as owning a horse and trap which conveyed visitors to and from the railway stations. She married Henry Mitchell after they met in London. At the time he was working for Northover and Gilbert, a Bridport furnishing company, who also undertook removals. In 1905 their son, Archibald, was born.

Around 1920, after being widowed, she married a former Merchant Navy man, who was then aged about fifty. William [Bill] Partridge's family had lived at 14 Shadrach for several generations and were carriers by trade. The records did not appear to refer to the New Inn but the family had recollections of mention of the Partridge family being landlords of a public house. Maurice Ouseley's survey in the 1930s, stated that the older villagers could calculate that there were once thirteen inns and beer houses in Burton, which included the Partridge's. There were many places in the eighteenth and nineteenth centuries that were licensed to sell only beer. The New Inn could have been one of these.

Number 14 High Street, was converted into a private dwelling, its origins lost in the mists of time. Partridge had taken up the family employment as a carrier after leaving the Merchant Navy and was well known in the locality with his horse, Polly and governess cart, which was often hired to take the ladies of Burton out for drives.

Florence Partridge was a prominent member of the village organisations and was a Founder Member of the Burton Bradstock Women's Institute. She died only a few months after the Sale and the property was then modernised. The old flagstones, which ran the length of the passage, were lifted and a well was uncovered. The family had often questioned the reason for the dampness in that part of the house! The well was void of water but was half-full of broken beer bottles; the glass inscribed, "New Inn". When the rendering on the front of the property was renewed in 1959, the words, "The New Inn", were clearly visible.

Archie Mitchell sold the house in 1994 but with the proviso that it was always to remain a lived-in home and not to become holiday accommodation. This was a very unselfish gesture.

Mrs Partridge's granddaughter, Sylvia, [Mrs Elsworth], still lives in the village and has passed on to her son all the documents relating to the sales of the family home. She has a great love for the village and her heritage but regrets the changes that followed after 1958.

THE OLD BAKERY

<u>**Lot 10**</u> Only the older residents remembered that number 13 High Street had once been a bakery. They could recall taking the family Sunday and Christmas dinners there to be cooked. Such meals were impossible to cook on open grates. Only the larger homes had (black-leaded) kitchen ranges and the open fire was a common means of cooking, until after the First World War.

A standpipe and gully were shared with Lot 9. Electricity was connected. A plot at the back was used for growing vegetables and a small patch of ground formed a little front yard. This detached cottage had two rooms downstairs, a scullery and tiny lobby. The fact that it ran back from the road tended to mask that it had three reasonably sized bedrooms. The tenant had created the third bedroom by putting up a partition and had separated a scullery area from one of the sitting-rooms, in a similar manner. Outside was a lean-to shed and earth closet. The cottage was rented by Frederick White, at an annual sum of £21.18/-. He paid the rates of £7.

★★★★★★★★★★

White had once been employed at the Grove Mill. He started there as an apprentice miller and baker in 1897. The conditions of the apprenticeship stated that he had to maintain a sober lifestyle and do nothing to bring his master's name into disrepute. When he had completed the term and became a journeyman baker he was able to ask his sweetheart, Alice Bugler, to marry him.

Alice lived in Southover and walked to church, on Boxing Day, (one of the few holidays for the working class), in her gown of grey silk and wide brimmed hat decorated with ostrich feathers. The newly weds first lived in number 57, for which they paid £2 a year rent, with an additional 1/3d a year for an allotment. Later, they moved to number 13, paying £8 a year to the Pitt-Rivers Estate.

★★★★★★★★★★

It had long been the family home but White had decided not to attempt to purchase and the sale at £310, went to a stranger, SW Wyatt of Hampton-on-Thames.

Such is still the tie with home that Freda Moore, only child of Fred and Alice White, who had lived away for most of her adult life and who died in 2006, expressed the wish that her ashes be brought back to the village.

VINE HOUSE

Lot 11 was described as _'a substantial dwelling-house.'_ Two sitting rooms measured 12 feet square, with a pantry almost as big and four bedrooms, the largest being 15 feet by 13 feet 9 inches. Two wooden chalets, used for the over-flow of guests, an earth closet and good stone and slated wash-house with the unusual and useful addition of a loft were outside. This stone building was probably part of the remains of cottages that had stood in that old part of the village.

Vine House was an imposing late Georgian property, standing just off The Pound, to the east of The Anchor Hotel. The front sash windows had wooden shutters and the main rooms were tastefully furnished and comfortable, with a piano prominent in the front room.

Since the railway had come to West Bay, guest houses had sprung up in West Dorset. Vine House was one, run by the tenant, Kate Hutchings, née Tucker, whose family had been established in the village for a considerable time. As a girl she had gone into service and by the time she was sixteen she was at the Yetman's home. This was where she learnt how a good establishment should be run. She married her cousin, Simeon Hutchings, from a sea-faring Burton family. He was a house painter and ardent fisherman.

Mrs Hutchings was one of the first to offer accommodation, in the village, for visitors,

50. August 1958. (L to R) Harold and Ada Spiller, Ron and Pamela Fry, John Spiller (bridegroom), Shirley Hutchings (bride), Gillian Legge, Alfred, Philip, Winifred and Christopher Hutchings. Inset 50a (L) Lot 23, Hill House, (C facing) Lot 9, formerly the New Inn, (R) Lot 11 Vine House and Shadrach Stores, (converted from Lot 12) Inset 50b Kate Hutchings in 1958, aged 82.

who would have been good class families, business or professional people, with sufficient means and free time to visit the area. Having raised a family and long established the business, by 1939, in *Kelly's Directory*, Vine House was listed as a boarding house, which meant a lot of hard work, particularly as there was no bathroom or flush toilet. Improvisation had taken place and the Sale particulars noted that there was an Elsan lavatory, in a small room upstairs. This meant that someone was obliged to empty and maintain the facility.

Kate Hutchings was a renowned cook and guests returned annually to savour her local specialities, cooked on the kitchen range. There was considerable laundering of the table and bed linen to do in a copper in the wash-house and she had to organise plenty of hot water, which would be carried to the bedrooms in large jugs. Before the 'upstairs facility' was installed there were chamber pots in every bedroom. Mrs Hutchings was assisted with the immense amount of laundering by her daughter-in-law, Winifred and grandson, Christopher, who put the linen through a mangle. This required a lot of effort and arm-ache. Until electricity came to the village, in the late 1930s, the lighting was by oil lamps and candles.

Hundreds of visitors had come to Vine House during the Hutchings's time. The hammer fell at £1,150 but not to the tenant. The Edens of Bristol took over.

Mrs Hutchings had become too frail to continue the arduous tasks connected with taking guests but friends and visitors still called to enjoy a delicious tea at Vine House. The Sale left little alternative but for her to live out her days in a new property built from the ruins of a fire, opposite The Anchor, on the main highway. It was there that she had lived as a child.

Her attractive, only daughter, Kathleen, had given her and the villagers something to be proud of, when she sailed to India, as governess to the two Scofield boys, whose father was an army officer. A great adventure for a young girl in the 1940s. In due course, Kathy married an army officer, herself. Her rare visits back to Burton caused much interest and excitement. The Proctors retired back to the Old Country, to Devon, where Kathy died in recent years. She always retained a great love for her family and birthplace. Her daughter had pre-deceased her but her son, Michael, continues his links with the family and village.

THE ESTATE YARD AND WORKSHOP

Lot 12 The Pitt-Rivers Estate had employed a number of men from Burton to maintain the Estate, particularly the properties, walls and gates. This carpenters' workshop, with a sawpit, was situated adjacent to Vine House, on the road to Shipton, with a sloping roof and 30 feet frontage to the street and was let to Charles Galpin, an architect, (brother of Dick), at one time employed at the Pitt-Rivers Estate Office, in Sturminster Newton. Near retirement, he had come to Burton to oversee work, with the Sale in mind. He paid

£19 a year rent on an oral tenancy for the workshop. Rates were £12 per annum. The Sale catalogue suggested that it would make a good store or garage.

The Burton Estate workforce had over the more recent years been Bill Nethercott and Reg Webb, (Pat Pattinson followed him, they acted as labourers for Dick Galpin, the builder), Wilf Gale, the painter and Tom Aves, the carpenter - an expert at making farm gates. Self-employed thatchers, brothers, Felix and Harry Legg from Loders, were brought in to undertake the considerable amount of thatching required in the village. The brothers, cycled in all winds and weathers, carrying their tools and lunch in a "nammet" bag [a woven straw bag, measuring about 30 inches across by 24 inches deep] on their backs.

Lot 12, was in use up to the time of the Sale. This valuable commercial snip was sold to AG [Joe] Linee, an up-and-coming local builder, for £200.

Joe Linee bought this useful and valuable commercial premises and used it as his builder's store, as his business expanded, particularly in the 1960s when he undertook building new properties in Annings Lane and Norburton. When he moved out of the village, he sold to Mark Bell, who, almost alone, converted it into living accommodation and a general shop. It was a clever move to set-up a shop nearer to the new developments, on the northern end of Burton Bradstock. It, too, was the victim of difficult parking in a fairly narrow road with the increase in passing traffic. During conversion the duplicate keys, for the Burton properties, which had been kept in the workshop, were retrieved for safe keeping.

Janet and Geoffrey Guppy, on one of their regular visits to her home village, bought the shop, on a whim and ran it successfully for several years. The business went through a lean time after they gave it up and finally the property was turned into living accommodation, its pretty bow windows, a reminder of its conversion days.

A GIFT

Lot 13 a lucky Lot for the Burton Bradstock parishioners was the Reading Room which Captain Pitt-Rivers had generously given to the parish. The announcement came at the start of the Sale which was intended to soften the blow that had recently fallen. The Reading Room lay in a very prominent position, with a frontage of 24 feet to the High Street. It was well built in 1879, with a slate roof and a small garden, 12 feet square, behind. In all probability, it had been fashioned from a derelict or a burnt-out cottage. The lower level of the slated roof, below the coping stones, pointed to the fact that it had once been thatched.

The main portion of the Lot had been let on a 21 year lease to the Bride Valley Branch of the British Legion, at £2 a year, as from 1948. The organisation paid the rates of £5 and undertook the repairs. The lease was valid until 1969. The garden was let to Sid Jones at a peppercorn rent of 1/- a year. Water and electricity were connected with the main sewer nearby.

> It took some time, following the Sale, for the responsibilities to be sorted out when the Reading Room was taken over by the Parish Council and modernised. A safe upper floor inserted, with cloakroom facilities. Downstairs, a partitioned off kitchen, with an *inside* tap, made the room suitable for present day use. It has computer facilities and is now used, predominately by the Parish Council and the Royal British Legion for meetings and is a very useful building for small exhibitions. Its problem, like all the properties along the highway, is that the front door opens straight on to the street and the fast moving traffic presents hazards. Difficulty can arise when trying to load or unload equipment.
>
> The Reading Room holds a fascinating history and one wonders how the room ever held so many people gathered for socials and lantern slides!

BURTON MANOR FARM

Lot 14 caused a great deal of interest and apprehension. It was one of the main Lots in the whole sale; Manor Farm was rented by Martin [Bunny] Lenthall. Although this was the only type of house that lent itself to being the Manor, the Lord of the Manor was termed 'an absent landlord'.

The farm consisted of 385 acres, with further accommodation land in Shipton Gorge and West Bay (sold separately), covering a triangle, from Southover, in the south, to North Hill and down to Marsh Barn, which lay to the west. Accommodation land appeared in a number of the lots, indicating that this land, usually on the periphery of a farm, was used to 'accommodate' stock. The stone and slated homestead, standing back from the main street, in its own grounds, dated back to the seventeenth century, the existing house having been built on the site where the Burton Manor farmhouse must have stood for hundreds of years.

The Sale particulars called the house, *'an attractive old Manor House, in stone and slate, in a secluded position'*. It had been updated in the Georgian period and the main rooms had sash windows. This design was apparent in most of the larger houses in the auction. Parts of the old bell system, when there were numerous servants, several living-in, were still visible. The accommodation was made up of three large reception rooms, the largest measuring 19 feet by 16 feet, a breakfast room, 12 feet by 11 feet and a very generous kitchen, as well as an office and spacious storeroom. The older rooms had flagstone floors.

The storeroom was once a cool room where the farmer's wife had made butter, kept her perishable food, preserves and salted meats, game and poultry, fish and vegetables, separated the cream and stored truckles of cheese. On the second floor, there were six fine bedrooms, the largest, 20 feet by 16 feet 6 inches, a bathroom with WC and two attic rooms. The windows looked out, across the village, in all directions . Outside, an old derelict cottage served as an egg-washing and grading depôt, using the latest machine. Young chicks were reared in the shelter of its rooms. Outbuildings, two garages and an outdoor WC were included. The property was surrounded by a paved path and a courtyard flanked the back of the house. The walled kitchen garden, with many productive fruit trees and bushes, completed the immediate homestead. A garage had been concocted, rather as an afterthought, when John [Jack] Lenthall had first acquired a motor-car. It was set in the wall, off the main street, beside the Horse Chestnut tree, beloved by the children who crept in to gather the nuts and played "conkers".

The type of farm buildings, which lay handy to the house, could still be found on most of the larger farms but this was one of the finest range, not only in Burton but for many miles around. The complex consisted of cart sheds and stabling for up to a dozen working horses and hunters, with a harness room. The farmyard comprised a number of

51. Martin [Bunny] Lenthall at the Melplash Show 1956, with brothers (L) Dave Legg and (R) Fred Legg, who had been awarded medals for Long service, totalling 125 years.

assorted buildings. There were pig sties, a cattle yard, (partially covered on the perimeter), a tractor house, an animal-feed store and a bull pen. Central to it all, was a magnificent barn that had seen years of the results of the corn harvest, as well as harvest homes. A report in *The Bridport News*, earlier in the century, related that Mr Henry Lenthall provided a meal at a harvest gathering, for his employees. He was not well enough to attend but watched from his bedroom window, as his son, Jack, supervised the festivities. The barn was also used for some of the more fortunate farm workers to do the inside 'wet weather' jobs.

A modern, milking parlour and adjoining dairy, for around eighty Lincoln Red cattle, had been built south-facing, near to the water meadows. Here, in 1958, each day, hundreds of gallons of milk were produced. The new stall, with its cluster-type milking machine and up-to-date dairy, replaced an old cow-stall, which may once have been nearer the main entrance, where a dairy and cheese room, used as an apple store at the time of the Sale, had been. Lenthall had done away with the favoured West Country breeds of Devons and Shorthorn cattle, so popular in pre-war Dorset. Additional loose boxes, for isolation purposes, calf-rearing houses, an implement shed, an elevator store and a new asbestos and concrete young-stock house, plied the old with the new.

★★★★★★★★★★

Near the mouth of the River Bride, at Freshwater, were Nissen huts that had been used by the army in the war and converted to battery-chicken houses. Lenthall had led the farming world by installing some of the first battery cages in the whole of the United Kingdom, after a visit to the Royal Agricultural Show in the 1950s, where the latest in everything, in farming, was on display.

Pupils came to Manor Farm to learn husbandry and to take advantage of Lenthall's knowledge of agriculture. One of these was Captain Pitt-Rivers's youngest son, Anthony, who spent three months at Manor Farm, living-in with the Lenthall family, in 1952.

With the number of students that passed through, many incidents occurred, some which were kept from Lenthall's ears and eyes. When he decided to bring in the first battery hens, the chosen breed was "Leghorn". These chickens were good egg layers but were easily frightened by sudden movements or strangers in their midst. There were numerous occasions when a farm worker would walk into the Nissen hut and the birds would lift off in unison, from the floors of their cages, which ran the length of the building, dislodging the mesh roof of the battery and enabling most of the top layer of birds, to escape. The students had a hard task in catching-up the identical chickens (but ringed with numbers) and trying to put them back into the correct cages, essential for egg recording!

★★★★★★★★★★

With the farm, went five farm workers' homes with a sixth at Marsh Barn. Some improvements had been made to the cottages in the High Street by the Estate. Mains water was installed, with drainage from the sinks and electricity was connected. The mains sewer was available. All was there for an entrepreneur, to negotiate, modernise and to sell off the cottages, at a profit, or impose a higher rent.

These picturesque cottages, mostly thatched, still with Elsan closets, were essential to the working of the farm. At Marsh Barn, the stout cottage, recently modernised under a

Housing Act grant, had the benefit of a bathroom and WC. It had housed shepherds and their families and latterly, for a period had accommodated farm students, who were cared for by a housekeeper. The cottage lay at the junction with the road to Bridport Harbour, where once a gate had stood across the road. The junction was known as "Marsh Barn Gate". The cottage, probably originally two, was adjacent to another fine old, thatched barn where the Dorset Horn flock of sheep were brought for the annual shearing. Inside the barn, cruck-trusses were visible in the roof. Faded cards and rosettes, won at local and national agricultural shows, for prize sheep, hung alongside the cobwebs. A century before, the Melplash Agricultural Society had awarded prizes to *'the shepherd who had reared the greatest number of live lambs and to the farm labourer who had raised the most legitimate children without parish relief'*.

★★★★★★★★★★

Manor Farm was on an annual tenancy at £460. The Estate had expended £5,784 on the farm in the past two years. Under the Rent Act, anyone contemplating buying the farm was obliged to buy the Lot as a whole and continue to rent to the sitting tenant, (or try to buy him out). The latter would have taken some doing, as Lenthall was not a man to be trifled with or easily persuaded. This was his home and his farm workers and their families were his responsibility. He was a hard task-master but strong ties bound him there.

The land on Manor Farm was suitable for mixed farming and varied from dry, sandy stone-brash on the cliff tops and sidlings [hill slopes], to lush meadows beside the River Bride. When the river flooded, the old water channels soon filled up in these fields, as in the days when they were purposely flooded to bring on the early grass. Besides this, elsewhere, the heavy clay soil lent itself to growing good cereal crops and rearing beef cattle. The slopes were ideal for grazing the famous flock of Bradstock Dorset Horn sheep. A great asset was that the main road dissected the farm, giving easy access to much of the land, some of which offered valuable shooting and fishing rights.

★★★★★★★★★★

As a young man, Lenthall had sailed to Australia and worked as a "jackaroo", on a cattle station, driving cattle hundreds of miles to the marketing centres at the ports. He had a great respect for the Aborigines and admired their affinity with and knowledge of their land and Nature. Their understanding of animals, "Was second to none, " he said.

Back in the village he and his wife had taken part in the village pantomimes and it was hilarious to see the well proportioned fellow, who usually carried such responsibilities on his shoulders, acting the fool. His wife, Miriam known as "Copper" for the colour of her beautiful hair, made a stunning principal boy or princess. At the annual Farmers' Ball, at the Drill Hall, Bridport, they stopped the 'show' with their dancing and Bunny's enthusiasm in "The Lancers", had to be seen to be believed. There was a tale, in Burton, that in his heyday, he could hold two struggling bullocks under his arms. He was no less

113

strong when he whirled the ladies around in the dance routines!

Like his father and grandfather before him, Lenthall was a progressive farmer. There were a number of labour saving, modern innovations around the farm buildings. Many up-to-date gadgets had been added in the house, too, where he and Copper entertained friends and business associates, besides having students who lived-in. Not given to tolerating any form of authoritariasim, he was well known for taking a stance when challenged. This may have been the reason which led to an unexpected happening in the Sale marquee.

★★★★★★★★★★

Lenthall, in his mid forties and his wife, sat amongst the other tenants. Unusually, he remained quiet, as the Lot was announced. "Goo on Bunny, " the local crowd yelled out. The bidding soared. To the astonished audience, the whole of Lot 14 was knocked down to a Mr Jeffery, for £19,500.

Dismay and disappointment, from those assembled, was very apparent. A popular local character and one of the main tenants of the Pitt-Rivers Estate, had not bought his home and farm. Neither had he saved his farm workers' cottages. Already their fears were materialising. Who was this stranger in their midst who had just secured the core of the village? However, some people did know what this person's business was there, that day.

It had been some eight years since the Sale had taken place. Lenthall was under a new landlord and a new tenancy agreement. There was absolutely no guarantee that his son, Harry, (then aged around ten), could ever take on the farm and this was of great concern to Bunny Lenthall. His ancestors were renowned farmers and he had great hopes of red-haired Harry following the line.

Lenthall set about having discussions with the new owner of Manor Farm but he got nowhere with regard to obtaining a surety that the tenancy could be handed-on. Disillusioned, Lenthall and his wife travelled to Australia to look at the possibility of buying and emigrating. He had had enough, too, of the red tape and beaurocracy that swamped farmers, throughout the kingdom. He did not relish the prospect of remaining a tenant farmer for the rest of his life and felt that there would be more opportunity for his family, in Australia.

As often as possible, he had returned to the other side of the world to see old friends and to judge sheep, at major agricultural shows. Rams exported from the Burton Bradstock flock of Dorset Horn sheep had been successfully crossed with the native Merinos and Lenthall enjoyed a good name amongst the sheep breeders in Australia.

In September 1966, with Copper and three younger children, Susan, Dorothy and Harry, Bunny emigrated to Australia, taking his sheep and several of his workers with him and set up a new farm, in Albany, Perth, naming it "Bradstock Downs".

114

They farmed and lived the life there that he had envisaged, until Mrs Lenthall became seriously ill and returned to London, for a major operation, in 1977. Bunny never managed to regain his enthusiasm for life, after her premature death and his health deteriorated, although Dorothy and Harry stayed with him on the farm in Perth and Susan lived handy. Bunny Lenthall made one last journey back to his old home, in 1982, to see his elder daughter, Beverley and her family and to judge at the Melplash Show and meet old friends. He died in 1986.

★★★★★★★★★★

One eighteen year old, young man, from the village, who emigrated with him was Alan Jarman who had come into farming, through his friend, Rob Churley, who was the shepherd and living at Marsh Barn [the centre of sheep husbandry at Manor Farm]. Jarman was descended from an old West Dorset family, the Northovers, some of whom were fishermen. Having trained as a chef, he found helping with the lambing and year-round shepherding, appealed to him. The opportunity for a promising life in Australia was a chance that might never come his way again and with the Lenthalls and three other young men, he left Burton.

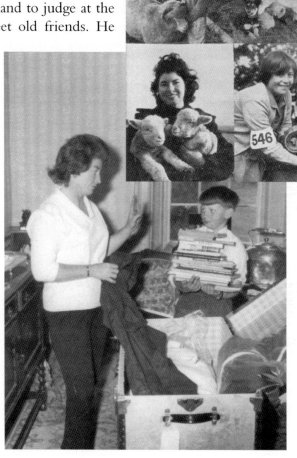

52. Miriam [Copper] Lenthall, with son Harry, packing for the family move to Australia in 1966. Inset 52a, the Lenthall children around the time of the Sale. (Clockwise L to R), Harry, Dorothy, Susan and Beverley.

In Australia, he joined a shearing gang and travelled the territory, which led him, in 1973, to meet his future wife, Pamela, a farmer's daughter. They set-up their home in Redmond, Albany, where they became noted farmers. They raised two daughters, one who was to marry in the autumn of 1999 but tragedy struck, just two weeks prior, when Jarman was killed in a motoring accident. His sister, Rita and brother, Brian flew out to comfort his family and attend a much subdued wedding celebration for their niece. His mother, Marjorie Jarman, née Northover, by now an elderly widow, chose not to make the long journey. The happier side to this was, that Marjorie and her husband, Bill, had, previously visited their family, in Australia and spent some time with the Lenthalls, as well.

Just before his death, Jarman had come out of farming and was involved in starting the Q Lamb, low meat-fat company, one of the first of its kind. A scholarship has been established in his name in the country where he had found great happiness and a new life. Over the years, he had returned to Burton, to meet old acquaintances and having become an expert, judge sheep at the Melplash Show. Other local young folk, Rob Churley and his wife, Chris Murless and girlfriend with Roger Harrison and his sister, Sue, emigrated with the Lenthalls, eventually going their own ways in Australia.

★★★★★★★★★★

Sue, Dorothy and Harry Lenthall have stayed on and raised families in Australia. Harry did not go into farming, as his father had hoped and planned but made his mark in medicine. They all live about five miles from each other and their elder sister, has travelled out to join them on numerous occasions. In more recent years, they all came back to the home country for a family wedding and with Beverley, paid a nostalgic visit to Burton. For Beverley, seeing flowers flourishing, that her mother had planted in the garden of Manor Farm, was too much.

★★★★★★★★★★

Jack Burt, with seven daughters, a well established Evershot farmer, whose family were originally from Somerset, purchased Manor Farm in 1967. Burt arrived in Burton with his wife, Olive, who, besides raising seven daughters, threw herself into village activities and did much for the community. Burt soon found himself on the Parish Council and the support that he gave to Burton and the youth of the village, in particular, endeared him to everyone.

He had served as Chairman of Burton Parish Council for ten years and was also a Churchwarden. Olive Burt became a popular, active member of the Women's Institute and the Young Wives Group, besides running tea rooms at the farm, (the old calf-rearing house had been converted into a restaurant), with the help of daughters and local staff. She did this from the mid-seventies until her death. A new house was erected, in 1983, in the old kitchen garden but Mrs Burt, died before she could enjoy complete retirement and Jack Burt was only there eighteen months before his death in 1985. A memorial seat to them stands adjacent to the gateway at Manor Farm.

★★★★★★★★★★

During building work, behind the kitchen, at Manor Farm, a second well was discovered, with a depth of around twelve feet. When it was cleared out, several superb water pitchers, of stone ware were found. These were dated by experts to be from the thirteenth century.

★★★★★★★★★★

The land at Marsh Barn was split off to form another farm [Brynvella], some more land was sold to the Freshwater Camp proprietor, the cottages released from the agricultural tie and some of the farm buildings, near to the homestead, were put to other uses. A calf-house, from the old Manor Farm days, had been converted into a superb restaurant. It overlooked the garden and provided a pleasurable experience for the many visitors who used it. The cream teas were especially delicious. After Mrs Burt's death, her daughter, Heather, [Mrs Thomson], continued the facility until 1990. On occasions organisations in Burton were granted the free run of the premises, to serve teas for their fund-raising.

Heather and her husband bought-out the rest of the family and introduced caravan camping rallies for recognised Caravan and Camping Clubs. The meadows along the River Bride are used and enjoyed, by a number of campers, throughout the season. Where the cows once grazed, holiday makers now reap the benefit of the beauty and tranquillity that can be found there.

The old barn appears to be 'sleeping' with pretty shrubs growing up around it and a small acreage of land is still retained, with Manor Farm, for agricultural purposes. Whilst there are some small businesses operating, in particular a substantial bakery housed in the former milking parlour, as well as the West Dorset Research Centre, in what was formerly the restaurant, within the immediate old farm area, the other empty buildings cry out for development, in some form or other.

If that time ever comes, it will once again divide the village but it could put some life back into Burton, in the form of shops, a doctor's surgery, visitor centre, galleries for local artists and craftsmen and a host of much needed amenities and no doubt some further residential development. The access is good, as there is now a through-road.

When the Lenthall family quit Burton, the heart went out of the village but the Burts have done much to fill the gap.

BARROW FIELD

Lot 15 adjoined Barr Road. It consisted of 13 acres of good pasture, with the advantage of a frontage to the main road of 460 feet. With a south facing aspect and magnificent outlook over Freshwater Bay, it was suitable for development, subject to outline planning permission. All the services were available nearby. Lenthall paid £30 a year rent.

This land rolled down from North Hill, where higher up a barrow protruded against the skyline. It was one of three known ancient burial sites around Burton Bradstock, unfortunately much disturbed in the previous century and it was from this that the land took its name.

With the fact, in mind, that this land, following on from the Barr Road council housing development and leading to pre-war (1939), privately owned properties on the crest of the hill, would be in the forefront for further building, Lenthall paid double the going agricultural rate for the Lot, at £1,300.

A WALLED GARDEN

Lot 16 also rented by Lenthall, at £2 a year, was an area of 22 perches in the High Street. It had 66 feet frontage to the main road, a depth of 92 feet and outline approval for residential development. Electricity and drainage were in the road nearby and a standpipe was already installed. There had been a right-of-way over the adjacent allotment, to Lot 16 but that was not included. On the Tithe Map of around 1840, cottages were sited in that area and what was probably an earth closet, is marked at the far end of the garden.

John Panten, a former partner in the Grove Mill acquired this plot for £480.

> The walled garden was developed by Panten and his wife, for their retirement, where they had a Woolaway bungalow built.

(Lot 17 was to be offered after Lot 26).

ON WITH THE AUCTION

Lot 18 A cottage, number 6 High Street, to the west of The Anchor Hotel, fetched £320. A large kitchen, 15 feet by 13 feet 6 inches was the dominant room and an Inglenook fireplace could be found in one of the two sitting rooms. The simple, plain row of cottages was built in the 1700s, from local stone.

★★★★★★★★★★

Many of the village properties had what were 'open' fireplaces. A recess housed the grate, with niches either side where small items could be stored. The chimney was open to the sky and hooks dangled down from a fixture embedded inside the chimney, from which cooking pots, kettles and a spit could be hung. In some of the homes this open space had been partially filled-in later with a kitchen range and the chimney sealed around.

The second sitting room was usually called the parlour and was only used at certain times, such as Christmas and for funerals and christenings. If 'important people' or the Rector called, then they would be invited into the cold, often damp, front room. The fire was only ever lit on the morning of the event, (if it was wintertime). Otherwise, the dusty, bare grate was left empty except, sometimes, for an embroidered fire-screen, proudly displayed. As the room was usually cold and damp and the chimney out of regular use, a fire would have little heating effect in such a short time. The atmosphere was of little value either, for a piano which some of the better off tenants could afford.

****

Mrs Marsh, widow of the tenant, who had been the village carpenter and undertaker, did not buy her cottage. Alfred Allen, from Kenton in Middlesex, took a chance and bought it without seeing it, recalls Mrs Marsh's great-nephew, Allan Rodway. When the auctioneers' clerks had called to measure up the property they did not bother to go into the roof space, as it had caved in.

Allen, made it his home, after repairs and re-thatching and in due course, he became part of the village community when he married a local spinster, Barbara Cheney and subsequently purchased Bridge Cottage Stores, moving in there to improve and run the business.

Lot 18 has changed hands a number of times. Its quaintness is only marred by the rush of traffic that thunders past.

HIGH STREET COTTAGES

Lots 19 and 20 were two cottages, in the same row, which ran along the main Bridport Road, in a westerly direction. At Number 7, lived Miss Symes, known as "Dolly Sims", (the surname Symes often became corrupted into Sims). Miss Symes came from a West Dorset family which was widely spread; her branch well settled in Burton. The living room was a reasonable size for a cottage and there was a sitting room, scullery and two bedrooms, both 14 feet in length. Miss Symes had a telephone connected! There was no mention of the lavatory arrangements, which may have been shared with the neighbours.

Outside was a small back yard and a stand pipe. The garden was let to Mrs Webb at an apportioned charge of £1 a year.

Number 8, High Street, was tenanted by Phyllis Webb, née Foot, whose father had held a smallholding in Shipton Gorge but may have once been the tenant of the property. Mrs Webb's husband, Reg, was employed by the Estate. Similar in design to the property next door, number 7 High Street, had three bedrooms. Outside was an Elsan closet and a lean-to shed and a coal-house. The rent was £19 and the tenant paid the rates.

A narrow cobbled path fronted the cottages with the front doors leading straight into the living rooms/kitchen. The area of the whole amounted to 35 perches. Another outsider, Mrs Knight of Bournemouth, paid £220 for each of the cottages.

Today the traffic and dangers from stepping out straight into the roadway, give the new occupants much cause for concern. The young boys of Burton, who had helped to push the very first motor-cars, in the early 1900s, up the steep hill at Common Knapp, could never have imagined the volume of high-speed traffic through the village, a century later. These modernised cottages have retained their façade as the only means of extension is at the rear. Number 8 has recently (2007) gone on the market for £175,000.

An unofficial record was made over the Easter period 2004. From 9am on Maundy Thursday morning to 5pm the following Tuesday, it was estimated, that 21, 000 vehicles passed through the main street of Burton Bradstock.

THE ANCHOR

Lot 21 The Anchor Hotel, recently modernised, was sold with vacant possession. *'The very valuable and well situated fully licensed free-house',* was the description in the catalogue. The rateable value was £121 a year. (A rent book of 1904 had listed an orchard with the property).

A prime hostelry, with good rooms and proper facilities, it lay in an excellent position at the entrance to the village. The purchase price to Bristol Brewers, Georges Ltd. , was £10,500. There was one draw-back to the property and that was that there was no off-road parking. Ponies, with traps, had stood or been tied up out-side in the road; a tie-ring was still visible. Later lorries and a few cars had circled the pub, causing little concern.

Herbert Allen, the landlord, a Canadian, with a rich accent, married to a Bridport woman, who had been the host there since Alfred Churchouse had vacated in the 1930s, had given notice to quit on the following 29th of December. The way was open for a major refurbishment. The old inn that had stood there for about two hundred years had been refashioned earlier, in Art Déco style, and given an fashionable front but not at all in-keeping with the surroundings.

At The Anchor, a smart lounge bar had accommodated those who wished for more decorum, whilst the public bar continued to serve the working men. This latter bar, with its blackened, wooden floor, scraped bare in places by hob-nail boots, was furnished with sawdust spittoons. The little bar at the back, was approached by a side entrance and was used by the Thrift Club, where the weekly savings deposits were taken and recorded. The yearly pay-out was about ten days before Christmas. Much of the savings went straight back in to the host's coffers!

There was a table-skittle set and men played cards in the Snug Bar. Local organisations held committee meetings there and it had been used by the Agent on the rent days. Here, too was the jug and bottle serving hatch. Customers could slip in unnoticed, to buy bottled drink or have a jug filled with cider, or buy cigarettes, to take away. The lounge bar was smart and clean but rather uninviting. By leaning over the counter, each side could view the other!

There were packets of Smith's crisps, (plain, with the salt in a blue screw of paper) and nothing else available to eat. By ancient law, a traveller could demand food and drink, which could not be refused but no one had appeared to exercised these rights for a considerable time.

In the public bar, the men had met and argued, discussed and joked together for

53. (R)Lot 21 The Anchor Hotel, (C) The Retreat, Lots 18,19 and 20, with Lot 16 beyond.

decades. The walls had been party to conversations that spanned the time from the Battle of Trafalgar and every other war since, politics, the fishing, the bosses, the visitors, the Veäst days, the football and darts matches, even argument about the suitability of 'the passon', [the parson] and all manner of topics that were part of village life through the generations.

The Anchor had been frequented during the last war by British and American troops and local men, home on leave. It was also a place for business transactions and many deals were struck in the bars with just a shake of hands. Most important was the talk about the weather, by which so many of their lives were governed. In the past four months, there had been great discussion, speculation and argument about the forthcoming Sale.

The incoming hosts in 1959, were Peter and Dorothy Barnett. They brought a different life to the hotel. The Barnetts offered summer accommodation, with full board and later vacated their private rooms for further letting, having purchased a flat in the newly built Rosamond Court.

Since their departure, after fifteen years, the subsequent hoteliers, (one being Christopher Thorner, a local young man), have concentrated on the restaurant and closed down the accommodation, although the latest owners are again offering bed and breakfast.

Andrew Spiller, a Bridport writer of detective yarns, who featured Burton Bradstock and local characters in his numerous novels, renamed The Anchor as "The Grapnel Inn". A grapnel-iron was used by fishermen and smugglers to retrieve sunken pots or barrels.

Today the connection with the sea, is prominently displayed. A car park at the rear, has cleared the street and The Anchor is a popular and welcoming hotel. There are some thirty main course dishes on the menu and fish, in all forms, is abundant. There is "The catch of the Day" and skate done Oriental style and plenty of prawn sauce to top it all. The old Burton fishermen's wives would have "tut tutted" !

JIMMER'S

Lot 22 was the home of bachelor James [Jimmer] Norris, who was the village postman, working part-time, and had been so, as long as most people could remember. He had lived there for most of his life and hailed from an old village family and was well respected but was not expected to attempt to buy the cottage. For a very long period, probably man and boy, he had been gardener and general outdoor assistant to the Mercer family, in Shipton Lane. In 1956, the two maiden daughters who were still living there, made a presentation, as well as giving him an inscribed photograph of the family, taken around the turn of the century. He had only been absent to serve in the First World War.

★★★★★★★★★★

Number 10 High Street, stood on the top of The Pound, and opposite the east side of The Anchor, had a large garden of 11 perches to the front. It was a typical 'one down and two up', with a wash house, store and an outside lavatory. Norris paid the Estate a rent of £12 and the rates were £4 a year.

Reg Buckler considered trying to secure the property, as he could foresee the need for a car park for the hotel and Jimmer's garden would, in time, be just right. However, as his own land had not yet come up in the Sale, he held back and Lot 22 went to RB Howarth for £175, who no doubt had the same idea, in mind.

HILL VIEW

Lot 23 with its explicit name, was a substantial detached house on the north side of The Anchor, from which the property commanded a good view of the hills beyond. All the rooms were generous in size and a large, landing led to five bedrooms. In the roof space was a huge attic measuring 33 feet by 15 feet 6 inches.

The tenants of this stout house were content to still use an old-style lavatory. Apart from that, a wash-house, large walled garden, with a side access and a long road frontage, made this desirable to any speculator. The sewer was in the road and mains drainage could easily be installed.

William Rogers, held the tenancy although he was reputed to have first come to lodge there. Rogers and the Holly family were all staunch Methodists and of Liberal political persuasion. The property was rented on an oral tenancy of £35, (a higher sum than the majority), increasing to £36 a year, to take effect from the following December. The rateable value was £11. An electric water heater, Alnite fire, back porch, store sheds, greenhouses and fowl houses had been provided. There was side access to the superbly tended garden, where beautiful tomatoes and other vegetables grew which were the envy of the other villagers. No one was concerned that chicken were being kept within clucking and crowing sound of other properties! It was at Hill View that villagers could take the accumulators, used to power wirelesses, to be recharged. A bit of pocket money for Will Rogers. The whole of Lot 23 measured 24 perches. If it had a drawback, it was that the front rooms, which faced the road, were dark.

A speculator, named Knight, bid to £760 for Hill View. There were no cheers forthcoming at the fall of the auctioneer's gavel.

TWO GOOD FAMILY PROPERTIES

Lots 24 and 25 Somercotes, Lot 24, *'a semi-detached modern building',* stood back from the road, in the Shadrach area, where the road led on to Shipton Lane. The accommodation consisted of two large living rooms of 14 feet in width, a lobby, scullery and larder. There was a landing from which three bedrooms, of reasonable size, led off. Somercotes was occupied by the Hutchings family. The name given to the house had originated from Mrs Hutchings's home town, in the Midlands. It could be described as a modern, family house, with a good sized vegetable garden, at the back and a pretty front garden and it was one of the few smaller houses that had its own garage. With the similar neighbouring property, *'both draining to a common septic tank',* it had been built following a fire, in 1926.

★★★★★★★★★★

Prior to 1926, a row of cottages and a stable had stood on the site and one was used as a shop. The shop-keeper, Mrs Baggs, was making toffee apples, when the cooking pan had boiled over and the kitchen caught on fire. On that hot, summer's day, the dry thatched roof stood no chance of being saved. The fire spread rapidly to the two adjacent properties. All the men were down at the beach at a sale of boats and nets, or out working on the farms and it had taken too long to raise the alarm and for assistance to arrive. The parish owned a hand-pumped fire appliance but it was of little use by the time that it had been extracted from its shed and the men reached the blaze.

★★★★★★★★★★

Winifred Hutchings, a very pretty Derbyshire lass, had moved, to The Rectory, from the Midlands with the Reverend Harrison and his family. It was there that she met her future husband, Alfred Hutchings, when he called and noticed her through the kitchen window. Later she was employed as a barmaid, at The Anchor Inn. Alfred and Winifred Hutchings had three children, Shirley, Christopher and Philip, who were raised in the village and attended the school. Fortunately, for her family, Winifred Hutchings was gifted with a canny business-head.

In 1958, the tenancy of Somercotes, was in Alfred Hutchings's name whose family, was well rooted in Burton Bradstock and had made their living mostly from fishing, or at sea.

★★★★★★★★★★

He could trace his family back to his great-great-great grandfather, Thomas Hutchings, a carpenter, born in Burton in 1765.

Simeon and Joseph Gerrard (who were brothers-in-law), with two other close family members, had been lost at sea, together with another Burton sailor, William Gear, in the freezing winter of 1881.

★★★★★★★★★★

Alfred Hutchings started his working life, learning the trade of carpenter with the Pitt-Rivers Estate but later joined the local builders Bartletts of Burton and Shipton. After a motor cycle accident he changed his trade to painter and decorator (not known if that was with the Estate). At one time, in partnership with Jim Churchill, they ran a grocery store at the top of the High Street, on the Bridport Road but they were too lenient with some of their customers and allowed them to run-up accounts. Not given the heart to call-in money owed to them, the business had to fold and was taken over by Freddie Mullins who had another shop in Burton.

Both Hutchings and Churchill had always taken part in the village activities, particularly seine fishing and the concert party and pantomimes where they would bring the house down, with their slapstick and amusing singing. Hutchings's two sons learnt fishing at his heels, joining him on the beach as soon as they could walk. Christopher was given the job of "knocker-up" when he was a teenager. His brief was to go around the village at crack of dawn and wake his father's fishing crew. This entailed pulling on a stick, which was attached to a string, hanging out of the window, with the end tied to the fisherman's arm or toe! Alfie Hutchings made his own seine nets and trot lines as well as supplying other fishermen and the fishing and braiding were done in all hours, either side of going to his 'proper job'.

★★★★★★★★★★

On the Sale day, Hutchings had seemed little concerned about buying the property. The atmosphere around the village, on this unusual day was like the old Burton annual Feast Day. For those not affected, it seemed like a holiday. Many people had downed tools to be part of the occasion. There was a relaxed feel in the air for those who had either decided against purchasing or were not involved. Hutchings, preferred to go to the beach to check his boat and nets and round it off with a visit to the pub, with others who were unconcerned. On turning homewards, Alfie Hutchings had been confronted by Stanley Williams, who enquired about the purchase of Somercotes. This unexpected news, that his wife had bought Somercotes, spurred him to pedal his bicycle on home with much alacrity!

Unbeknown to Alfie, his wife had investigated the possibility of buying Somercotes, arranged a private mortgage with a solicitor and armed with instructions, went along to the Sale and came out the proud owner; the price - £800, which included, she maintained, £50 extra for the garage.

The house, next door, "New Cottage", which did not have a garage, Lot 25, was secured for £750, by Alan Bennett, on behalf of his mother, the tenant, Bessie Thorner, formerly Bennett, the second wife of coal merchant and fish dealer, Walter Thorner.

Mrs Mary Ward, née Legge, was a very small child when the row of cottages was burnt down. Her father was away serving in the Royal Navy and her mother was living with Mary's grandparents, in one of the cottages in that row, adjacent to Girt House. After the devastating fire, her parents then set-up home, opposite The Anchor Inn, in another cottage that was to burn down, in the early 1950s, although the family had moved elsewhere by then.

★★★★★★★★★★

Alfie Hutchings died in 1963 and his wife lived on at Somercotes until she was unable to care for herself. The sons maintained their interest in fishing from Burton Beach and in due course, Christopher, moved out of Burton, as did Shirley who had married, in 1958. Philip, a builder, later moved out of the village too but visits Burton, with his wife, Patricia, née Gape and family, to revive memories but they find that they rarely meet anyone they know and that the streets, in the centre of Burton, are void of people, whilst the pubs, where they once enjoyed many happy hours, are patronised by strangers.

Christopher, still holds happy memories of life in the village and is a delight to listen to when he recounts, in his smooth and fast-disappearing accent, the tales of fishing at Burton.

Today, Somercotes is undergoing a remake, with fashionable doors and trimmings. In the back garden are new lobster pots. Some things never change!

THE GREAT HOUSE

Lot 26 Queen Anne in design, Girt House, was an outstanding property. The recent survey for The Royal Commission on Historical Monuments had listed the Venetian window above the door and interesting sash windows. It was one of the gems on sale. *'With a pleasant hall, drawing room, 16 feet by 15 feet 6 inches and 8 feet 10 inches high'*, together with a dining room, kitchen (13 feet by 12 feet 10 inches and 7 feet 3 inches high), with a water softener, a scullery, *'with hot and cold water to the sink'*, a Redfyre Independent boiler, a boot room, cool larder, back lobby and three well appointed bedrooms with fitted wardrobes and hot and cold in the main bedroom. The bathroom had a panelled bath, with hand-basin. In addition, this grand, house had an airing cupboard, fitted immersion heater, which appeared to be 'hired', a large store room, as well as good attics and a secondary staircase. This was a modernised substantial house. It was of particular architectural interest in that it was brick faced with gabled ends. Adjoining was a cottage that escaped the fire in 1926. The stone and brick façade was attractive and imposing and had been carefully looked after. The house was ready for immediate occupation, being sold with vacant possession.

A very attractive feature, outside was a mature garden, *'which will appeal to the discriminating purchaser, with walled pleasure garden and kitchen garden with fruit trees.'* A large fruit cage housed the soft fruit bushes and a good tool and potting shed were there.

Viewing for this fine house had been *'by appointment, preferably in the afternoon.'* The Dennings had made a stand to avoid disturbance and time-wasters.

★★★★★★★★★★

In recent years, Girt House had been the home of an elderly couple, Mr and Mrs Denning, who had retired to Burton and were about to move to a smaller property. Girt House was, some said, built, by, Admiral Ingram, a contemporary of Captain, [later Admiral] Thomas Hardy of Portesham, or commissioned by one of the other local naval officers. It was known to have been lived in by members of the Roberts family.

★★★★★★★★★★

From Ross-on-Wye, came the purchaser, Charles Harvey, who prior to the last war had been a professional actor on the London stage. He had been brought up in Margate and by 1958, found himself, with his wife, running a guest house in Hereford. Wanting to get back to be near the sea he had lighted on the Pitt-Rivers Estate Sale, through a friend from Dorset and set about to attempt to make Girt House the family business residence and continue to take paying guests. Harvey paid £4,000 for the privilege of owing this elegant house with its history of distinguished tenants and soon moved in

126

with his family.

Girt House was so named because the villagers referred to it in the Dorset dialect as "the girt" [great] house.

Lot 17 was offered next, with three cart sheds, a garage and an open-fronted implement shed, in all amounting to about 1 acre. Once used as allotments, it backed on to Girt House and would make an additional area for a larger holding. Country houses with a paddock were preferred. Lenthall, paid £8 rent. The buildings were a great advantage to him, for use in conjunction with the running of Manor Farm. It was a potential building site as it adjoined the Barr Lane council houses.

★★★★★★★★★★

This plot was cultivated by Lenthall, as a "home close", ideal in which to grow maize or kale, that the dairyman would cut fresh every morning and cart back to the farmyard for the dairy cattle. During his year as President of the Askerswell Young Farmers' Club and with Alan Musgrove, the Club Leader, who was working at Graston Farm, he had encouraged the members to cultivate, grow and harvest an acre of potatoes on this same patch.

The open-sided wooden shed served as an ideal machinery store and had the advantage of being handy to the road, as well as easily accessible to many of the fields where the machines were deployed. Prior to the early 1940s, it had served as a base for Charlie Moore, who was a fish merchant and lived across the road. Then the shed would be stacked high with fish boxes and bushel baskets, a boat or two laid-up out of season and a lorry was kept under cover there.

★★★★★★★★★★

The auctioneer announced that the main sewer butted into the land and water and electricity were handy. With 60 feet of road frontage, this was a Lot for which there was competitive bidding.

Lot 17 was not bought by Harvey but the mystery buyer secured it for £450. It was a great asset to Manor Farm, which he had just purchased but it had all the makings of a building site.

Nigel and Julian Harvey became fully involved in local activities and married into well established Bridport families. For many years, Julian was a right-hand-man at Shadrach Dairy Farm.

TWO USEFUL 'GARDENS'

Lot 27 was a plot of land, of 36 perches, with a road frontage of 90 feet and running back for 120 feet, known as "The Retreat Garden". The Retreat was now a privately owned house adjacent to The Anchor Hotel and this second garden, had been tenanted by the new owners and lay opposite. It measured 90 feet by 120 feet and was let to the Lowes at £3, on a lease which would terminate in December 1958. Previously, General Bickford, had rented the garden with the house. Lot 27 was well cultivated, possibly the site of a ruined or burnt-out cottage and was to be sold with vacant possession.

A new, strange bidder, Mrs MS Coward of Worcester Park decided that £450 was a reasonable price to pay for this good, main road site.

Lot 28 already had outline planning permission for residential development. It was tenanted by Florence Symes at £1 a year. With all the main services in the road, it lay directly opposite her cottage and formed a good parcel of land, next to Lot 27. The Pitt-Rivers Estate had been very prudent to obtain the outline permission on several plots of land, with a view to realising a larger sum. Miss Symes's garden was one of these.

Mrs Coward stepped in again and bought the site for £280.

> These two gardens formed the site for Rosamond Court. Here, in 1963, builders found ancient skeletons and ware buried. This site, on the village perimeter, must have been used as a cemetery around the time of the Romans, or even earlier.

A GROUP OF COTTAGES.

Lots 29, 30 and 31 represented a row of three quaint little cottages, on the western end of the village, facing north, standing up off the High Street, with a stone wall to the road. With slightly differing arrangements on the ground floor, each had two bedrooms. A lean-to kitchen had been added to numbers 4 and 5.

Electricity was connected to all of them and water was taken from a standpipe out on the highway. The tap was set into the wall, with a pleasant feature of a stone canopy which surrounded it and a slab on which to stand the water bucket. The householder could stand quite safely to draw the water without fear of being knocked down by passing traffic.

Only Lot 29 had an Elsan closet, (the others had buckets or earth vaults) and the tenant had provided the garden sheds. The rents of the three High Street cottages, varied from £8 to £16. The gardens of numbers 4 and 5, averaged 10 perches and number 3, measured only 4½ perches.

At number 3, at the Bridport end of the row, lived Frederick Legg. He was an old retainer at Manor Farm, where he had served five masters during his long life working on the farm. His cottage went with the job and the outgoings were paid by Bunny Lenthall. A short-cut, through a door in the wall, beside the cottage, led straight down to the farm, across the field and Fred Legg must have used that route to and from Manor Farm, hundreds of times.

★★★★★★★★★★

Fred's life had been what could be described as that of a traditional farm worker and knowledgeable countryman, renowned as a skilled hedger. He had worked on Manor Farm from the age of thirteen, commencing on a wage of 2/6d a week, as a shepherd boy, starting on October 1st 1894, his birthday. He then branched out into general farm work and although he was supposed to be retired, at the time of the Sale, he still worked part-time at Manor Farm, doing 'a bit of gardening'.

He could tell of going out at dawn, on summer mornings, with a gang of mowers [men] with a scythe over his shoulder, to cut the grass at haymaking time and of the long trek, taking several days, there and back, to drive sheep from Burton to Martinstown, near Dorchester, to the annual sheep fair. He recalled the excitement at harvest time of catching the rabbits as the last swathes of corn were cut and the continuous rhythm of the workforce at thrashing time, when the sheaves of corn were passed from the ricks to the men on the machine. The ensuing dust and sweat as the crop was shot into the huge West of England sacks and taken by wagon to be stored, made the work uncomfortable and arduous. The process was not without its excitement as the terriers snapped and killed the rats that escaped from the base of the ricks.

54. *Sheep washing on Manor Farm, circa 1958. (R) Fred Legg.*

Fred always dressed in traditional farm workers' clothes and was rarely seen without a hat, wide leather belt, thick waistcoat and leggings. In wet weather like all the farm workers he draped a West of England Hessian sack over his head and wore another around his waist. In this manner practically all of the body was protected.

In 1956 he and his younger brother David, had been awarded the Melplash Agricultural Society's Long Service certificates. At the time, Fred had completed sixty-nine years and Dave, the carter, fifty-six years, on the same farm. They had been born and raised at number 1 High Street, just a stone's throw from where Fred was enjoying his remaining years.

Fred had worried as soon as the Sale was muted, as he did not have sufficient reserves to buy and was concerned that he might lose his home. Lenthall, had a soft spot for Fred and Dave, as he had been raised with them. He was not going to let anyone else get hold of number 3 but it appeared that he had instructed one of his younger farm workers, Fred Sibley, to do the bidding, as Lenthall remarked, "They won't charge you as much." The cottage was secured for £280 where Fred lived out his days.

★★★★★★★★★★

At number 4, the Bullock family bought their cottage for £200. Charles Bullock had met his wife, Florence, who came from the old Burton family of Thorners, when he was serving in the Royal Navy. Bullock had been born in Taunton but found himself at Portland during his service days. Some of the Burton girls would cycle to Weymouth,

via the Coast Road, to see the shops and stroll along the promenade, where they would sometimes meet sailors, ashore on leave. This was how Charles and Florence were to meet!

Ernest Thorne paid a little less for his cottage, Lot 29, at £180, His wife, Queenie, daughter of Charles Moore, [the fish and coal merchant, who had once been the tenant of the store sheds, opposite], had lived there all her life.

Lots 32 and 33 The vending followed on with other nearby farm workers' cottages that went with the Manor Farm tenancy, numbers 1 and 2 High Street. At the time of the Sale, these two cottages were not required for farm workers and were sub-let by Lenthall, who paid the Estate £8 a year for each of them, to Mrs Jones and Leslie Gale, (who had provided an Elsan closet). The properties had three bedrooms and lay at right angles to the roadway. A right-of-way through the door in the wall and over one property was declared. There was a shared standpipe.

The cottage 'nearest the sea', Lot 32, with an earth closet and small garden, was secured by Lenthall's in-

55. Charles and Florence Bullock, circa 1914. Inset 55a around the time of the Sale.

laws, Mr and Mrs Ryder, from Birmingham, for £250. The cottage adjacent, number 2, Lot 33, also with a small garden, at the rear, was sold to R Faulkner, of Sunbury-on-Thames, considered as another speculator and realised £170.

CHENEY'S GARAGE

<u>Lot 34</u> The auctioneers then switched their efforts to the southern end of the village, to Cheney's Garage, offering the first of the ground rents.

★★★★★★★★★★

In the 1920s, Albert Cheney, a clever mechanic, had come from Weymouth to Burton. His connection with the village is uncertain but at sometime he was servicing and repairing, Edward Sturdy's motor-car. Cheney's future wife and her sisters often visited the area, on holiday from London and when he and Lilian married, they set up home in Barr Lane, in one of the new council houses. These houses were meant for village families but the rent of one guinea a week was far more than many of them could afford.

56. 1935 Cheney's garage. (L) Edward Sturdy's car. (R) Steps lead up to the footpath.

For some reason, a double drive existed between the Cheney's, number 13 and number 12. This may have been where there was originally a field gate. Leslie Maddocks, from Lancashire, was the Bridport Borough Surveyor and in due course came to live at number 12. (Maddocks later survived the Battle of Dunkirk, recalling how he was dragged into a waiting boat, expecting the enemy to fire on him and other retreating soldiers, at any minute.) This was the only driveway to any of the council properties. Cheney had a workshop leading off from the drive and a commercial hand-operated petrol pump, which generated a quarter of a gallon, each time it was wound up.

In 1931 he moved the business to a corner site in the village where a farmhouse and old barn had stood, adjacent to a row of allotments. The barn was the out-building to the dairy-house, mentioned in the 1841 Census Return. It was once, the hide-out for smuggled contraband, providing quick and easy access from the beach. Here, after erecting a wooden building, used as an office, Cheney developed his business.

★★★★★★★★★★

Edward Sturdy, a gentleman, a traveller, philosopher and converted Buddist, lived at Norburton, in Shipton Lane. The Sturdy family seat, lay at Trigon, near Wareham. He had come to Burton Bradstock at the turn of the century and built a beautiful house, Edwardian in style with some Eastern features, on the site of the old North Hill Farmhouse, (which featured in Eden Phillpott's romantic novel, *The Spinners*) and lived into his nineties. He was a very tall, upright, highly educated and charming gentleman, unimpressed by some modern inventions, in particular, electric lighting. Norburton was lit by candles and oil-lamps until his death. His daughter, had died in childbirth and there was a family connection with "Scott of the Antarctic". In the 1920s, he drove his new motorised vehicle around the countryside at high speed, heedless of any dangers or approaching cross-roads. Alfred Scudamore, from Shipton Gorge, a friend, rode with him and told of the hair-raising sorties.

A pioneer in motoring, Edward Sturdy, had found Albert Cheney to be just the man to do repairs and maintenance. Whether he was instrumental in encouraging Cheney to move to larger and more prominent premises and/or contributed to financial backing, is uncertain. It was about the same time that the Cheney family moved into the Red House, owned by the Pitt-Rivers Estate. From a very modest beginning, sprang a busy garage, where repairs were carried out and later, the accompanying three petrol pumps were installed. When the spinning mill, off Mill Street, closed, the company took that over, using the premises for a repair workshop and store.

★★★★★★★★★★

Sturdy also, had a tale to tell, of smuggling in Burton and how three prominent men were involved in a deal together, one of them living at North Hill Farm. They were caught and two of them turned "King's Evidence" and according to Sturdy, the families of those who had betrayed the third man, never prospered again. Cheney's garage premises stood on the very site of the former dairy house and barn, reputed to be used in these smuggling activities. At Norburton, Sturdy took pride in showing visitors, broken wine bottles in a cellar, which he said were left from those days. The connections with Norburton and Cheney's garage premises were a strange coincidence.

★★★★★★★★★★

Ted Cheney, the elder son, volunteered for the Royal Air Force and found himself stationed in Suffolk during the Second World War. The garage in Burton was requisitioned by the army, as a petrol supply base and Albert Cheney and others in the village, with their issue of petrol coupons, during rationing, had to journey to Bridport for their allocation. Gordon Cheney, the younger son, had a haulage business, taking tons of shingle from the beach, by lorry, to be used in the construction of war-time aerodromes.

Ted Cheney was sent to Kenya during his service, where he met his Polish born wife, Gen. She was serving in the Free Polish Air Force, having escaped from Poland. Her father was never seen again but after the war, when prisoners were finally being released, her mother was the first to be freed, generating wide publicity on television and the radio but died shortly afterwards. The Cheneys were married in Nairobi Cathedral. When he returned from the war, Ted decided to set up a separate garage on the outskirts of

Bridport.

★★★★★★★★★★

In 1945, the Burton garage came back into the family's hands, with Albert and Gordon re-establishing, what was to be, a great asset in the area. The senior partner of the business, Albert Cheney, died, following a short illness, in July 1956. His nephew, Basil Dent, then joined the staff, taking responsibility for the sales. They soon acquired an Austin franchise and the garage became a very competitive enterprise.

With the advertising of the ground rent, in 1958, there were a number of speculators who were interested. The garage frontage, which ran along the main Weymouth Road, measured some 265 feet. The whole, was set in a prime position at a crossroads. The garage had three, electric petrol pumps with a total capacity of over one thousand gallons. The ground rent amounted to £30 a year and the tenant paid the rates. The Vendor was selling the ground and not the buildings, (some of which were wooden and temporary).

Gordon Cheney was bidding on behalf of his mother and finally the hammer was brought down in favour of Mrs Lilian Cheney, at £1,500. This was a great relief to the members of the family, opening up the way to build an extension and repair vehicles and stock spare parts on the premises.

Around 1960, the garage was extended by the construction of a workshop behind the forecourt. The company continued to utilise the old flax spinning mill as a secondary premises.

Gordon Cheney and his wife, Brenda, née Pike, worked hard to expand the business and in due course ran other garages at Litton Cheney and Beaminster. He died suddenly on August Bank Holiday Monday 1984, aged fifty-eight. Brenda and Basil Dent, with a large work-force, continued the business until it was sold in 1988, when it was taken over by two young enthusiasts. Crippling interest rates ruined their intentions and not long after, the bank foreclosed. The garage stayed idle for two years when it was sold again, reopened and revitalised.

Dent retired in 1988. One of his outstanding memories of his time at the garage, is of a flood, when the water rose to forecourt height. This was the same week as Albert Cheney died and the funeral was postponed, because no one could get out of the village to the crematorium.

Cheneys' garage has changed hands, several times and expansion, way beyond a small village garage has taken place. It stands incongruesly at the end of Burton Bradstock, where thousands of vehicles pass by on a regular basis. The former flax spinning mill remained in the Cheney family until 2006.

The present proprietors of the Burton Bradstock garage, (which over recent years has been extended considerably), incorporated a small shop, where extras for a journey, could be purchased at the same time as fuel. Now a Spar mini-supermarket, has been opened. This is not only an asset to motorists but will benefit the community. The local population's needs are similar to a town and with the hundreds of visitors it should flourish. All that is needed now is a safe means to cross the very busy road! Any new enterprise attracts comment but Sajiv Vij and his enterprising family are continuing the welcome and courteous service that stretches back some eighty years.

GREENWICH COTTAGE

Lot 35 stood opposite the garage, a pretty thatched property, known as Greenwich Cottage, approached over a wooden bridge, across a deep ditch. The Manorial Records of the sixteenth century, referred to the field in which stood two cottages, as "Venis Plot". The cottages were probably built by the Venis brothers.

On the day of the Sale, this was the home of William [Bill] and Kathleen Cammell, let on an oral tenancy of £16 per annum. The Cammells had previously swapped cottages with Ivor Guyatt who worked at Cogden Farm. The living room, *'with a sink'*, was in constant use. With the parlour and two bedrooms, about 14 feet 6 inches by 10 and 13 feet respectively, there was ample room for a family. A wash-house, store shed, Elsan closet and a good vegetable garden, which Bill and his wife, Kathy, had tended to an extreme, made it an attractive prospect that day.

Allan Rodway remembers Bill Cammell, son of Jack Cammell and of an old village family, rising to his feet when Lot 35 was called and informing the assembled gathering that the place flooded. The locals were all too aware of the flooding at Greenwich Cottage. Whenever there was a flood, the river water would rise up over the bridge, rapidly filling the ditch and rushing into the cottage and outbuildings. Water would seep up through the ground, too, as the water-table was high, on the flood-plain, where the cottage had been built. Extremely severe flooding, which was said by the old inhabitants, to occur twice in a lifetime, had left the cottage almost submerged, on many occasions. In November 1824, there was a night of terrible storms at sea and exceptional floods which had gone down as the worst one. Dozens of vessels were lost at sea and Fleet Church was demolished.

★★★★★★★★★★

The Bridport News of December 1874 revealed a bad flood in Burton, after tons of snow had melted, filling the river and pouring off the hills, bringing dirty water down Shipton Lane and off Parson's Hill(above Gage's lane). At "Rookery Farm", Mr Chaffey had his milk-house filled with water and seed potatoes were washed around the floor. At Shadrach Dairy Farm, workers pulled down a wall to get the pigs out and Mr Hawkins, licensee of The Three Horseshoes, had never known a flood like it, having been the landlord there for thirty-one years. Water in Mill Street was up to the third stair of the cottages and Messrs. Buckler's business premises at "The Back o' November" was flooded, as well. James Hutchin[g]s kept his pigs beside the river and wading, up to his armpits, saved them 'from a watery grave'. The corner house that 'stood high' (was this where the garage now stands?) on the Litton Road, had three feet of water in and the family 'beat a hasty retreat to the loft'. Greenwich Cottage, must have been almost submerged! The village policeman, PC Mansell, waded around, up to his waist, assisting people. Brand new machinery, at the recently rebuilt spinning and cordage factory, off Mill Street, was badly damaged and quantities of flax and hemp, stored ready for processing, were 'immersed'. After the devastation, Lord Rivers sent £10 for 'the poor and needy' to receive blankets and sheets.

★★★★★★★★★★

The older residents, at the Sale, recalled that in 1886, the Symes family who were living in Greenwich Cottage, were in dire straits on the night of 26th December, when blizzard conditions caused the sea to burst through at Freshwater and to meet the River Bride in full flood. A wall of water hit the cottage and the family found themselves marooned. The flood water had risen to bedroom window height, causing the walls to start to crumble.

An attempt was made to rescue the family by boat, by the fishermen, who lived above the flood level, in Southover, who 'shouldered', a boat, in atrocious weather, from the beach. When the boat was launched, in the pitch dark, into the flood water, Charles Bugler who had volunteered to row, was swept overboard. He was miraculously saved by Jesse Hitchcock, George Hussey, John Cammell, William Thorner, Edwin Buckler, Joseph Buckler, the younger and William Sponsford, who were helping in the attempt to rescue the Symes family.

It took all of the strength of those tough fishermen to hold the boat against the fast flow of the freezing water. Eventually, they saved Bugler, who had grabbed a branch of an elm tree and was clinging to it, in peril of his life. All the men had their clothes frozen to them and were taken to The Dove Inn to thaw out and recover. No doubt some strong spirits were found to revive them, even though The Dove Inn was only referred to as 'a beer house'. Because of their great courage, they were acclaimed as local heroes. The family survived and were rescued next day.

★★★★★★★★★★

The Cammells had seen many floods since they had come to live in Greenwich Cottage, evolving a system whereby, as soon as word reached them that the River Bride was in flood further up the valley and Freshwater was bayed-up [choked], they lifted all their furniture and mats up off the floor, usually with the help of the garage staff and neighbours, retreating to the upstairs rooms, where they could watch the water rising, and invading their home.

The worst flood that they had experienced had been only a few years previously, on July 18th 1955 when the Bridport area was deluged by a record fall of rain, in twelve hours, (11 inches of rain were recorded at Martinstown in 24 hours), falling during severe thunderstorms which had followed unbroken sunshine over the previous few weeks, when the temperature had risen to 95 degrees Fahrenheit and 84 degrees in the shade. The main of the storm hit Bridport, West Bay and Burton Bradstock and thousands of acres of land were under at least three feet of water.

At 10. 30 pm the campers were moved out of Freshwater and RB Howarth declared a state of emergency in the village. The Women's Institute Hall was opened up and members of the Civil Defence unit and ladies of Burton, took over organising relief and sleeping arrangements. The river burst its banks and the village was cut in half, water spreading half-a-mile across. The Rural District Council put all its resources at the disposal of Burton Bradstock.

Six hundred meals were served over a period of thirty-four hours, using half a hundredweight of potatoes, twenty pounds of meat which were served with vegetables, suet dumplings (in July), and followed by puddings. Thirteen gallons of milk were given to the children and cigarettes were requisisioned for the adults. The next day, milk churns from Shadrach Dairy Farm, were seen to be floating around and the furnishings in all the low lying houses and cottages had been destroyed. At the village shops the stock was deemed useless.

A relief fund (1886) already existed and an appeal was launched by the Town Mayor of Bridport, Alderman JB Edwards, who donated five guineas and a total of £47. 10/6d was raised on the first day.

★★★★★★★★★★

In that serious flood of July 1955, Richard Wylde, a young man, living at The Dove Inn, had been resting in bed, looking at the light on the landing of Manor Farm, across the meadows, when he heard a loud rushing noise and realised that the familiar light was reflecting in flood water. He quickly got downstairs and went along to the end of Southover, to see a similar sight to that witnessed by the rescuers of 1886.

Water surrounded Greenwich Cottage. It was pouring in from the back of the cottage and rushing out through the front. An animal lover, Wylde, saw the Cammell's cat stranded on the wall and without any thought for his own safety, he manoeuvred his way along the top rail of the bridge, with the water washing over him and grabbed the cat, clasping and pulling it to safety, whereupon he received numerous scratches.

That flood brought havoc to Bill and Kathy Cammell's home and reached four feet high on the telephone kiosk, opposite The Three Horseshoes Inn. It was up to the ground floor windows of the "Shoes" and Wylde recalled that the stock in Williams's and Mullins's shops was ruined.

It was estimated that 1, 600 telephones were out of order in West Dorset after the violent storm. A week after the flood, a water shortage was declared, with the influx of 100,000 holiday makers to the area and the Bridport Water Company cut off the supply for long periods. It was reported that 500 cars had parked, that week, on and around The Mound at West Bay.

The Sunday following the 1955 flood, local girls, Jacquiline Cammell, Jennifer

Churchill, Judith Grigg, Ruth Kerley, Marion Wakely, Barbara Widger and Madeleine Williams were Confirmed at St Mary's Church.

★★★★★★★★★★

Waiting for the water to subside depended on the amount of rain, the state of the tide, the strength of the wind and the height of the flood water. Once the water had gone down, the Cammells were left to clear up the stinking mud which had been left behind, dry out the cottage and eventually put everything back in its place. This could take several days. Depending on the time of year, the drying-out process was a problem. Stains on the walls indicated the heights to which the flood water had risen over the years.

The Cammells and other families, whose properties were flooded, always coped with the situation, taking the inconvenient event, as an inevitable hazard. Friends and neighbours always rallied to assist. Families were always on the alert for the next flood which for those in the lower reaches of the Bride River that was Christmas 1956.

★★★★★★★★★★

Bill Cammell's stand in the Saleroom, informing the audience that the cottage was very prone to flooding, was all the more gallant because he suffered from a speech impediment and it took some effort for him to challenge would-be purchasers.

Greenwich Cottage was quickly knocked-down to him at £240. A loud cheer resounded in the Sale marquee.

Bill and Kathy Cammell continued to live at Greenwich Cottage. He served the village in many ways, particularly as a bell-ringer and member of a fishing crew. When Kathy's sister died leaving five small boys, the Cammells helped their father to care for them and the youngest, Christopher, knew no other mother than Kathy. These boys did their parents and Bill and Kathy proud as they all made good in life. Between them they saw service in the Merchant Navy, as prison warders and a governor on the Isle of Wight, the army, the RAF and Christopher later became the licensee of The Anchor Hotel.

Kathy stayed on, after Bill's death, still keeping a look-out for rising flood water. She enjoyed her lovely garden and plied her braiding skills to the last. In the passage of the 'unlisted' cottage she had hung numerous photographs, of her home standing in flood waters, which she delighted in showing to surprised visitors.

When she died, the cottage was put on the market again at around £150,00. It had lost its thatched roof, as she preferred a more modern look to the place and extensions had been added but it still had no means of parking on site. The advantage was, that flooding was supposed to be a thing of the past, with the flood-alleviation scheme having included Greenwich Cottage, although the older residents believe that serious flooding will still occur, from time to time. A wooden bridge was no longer the means of entrance. The surplus water was piped underground, the ditch concreted over and the occupants approached the cottage, straight off the roadway.

The present owners, of Greenwich cottage, had long admired the property, in spite of some of its disadvantages and are most worthy custodians for the immediate future.

★★★★★★★★★★

Richard Wylde, fifty years on from the flood, in which he rescued the cat, realises how lucky he was not to have been swept away. The day after the 1955 flood, with another newspaper boy, John Perrin and Fred Northover, who could not get to work, he helped Fred and Lil Mullins to clear out their shop. Richard chuckles now, at what they found; old biscuit tins crammed with copper coins, from the newspaper sales, five pound notes rolled up in a Bourneville cocoa tin and tons of soaked, old newspapers. Fred seemed to stock-pile the old papers for which, his only means of disposal would be to burn them, at the back of the thatched premises. It took two days to clear the debris from the shop premises and two lorries came to cart it away and it was said that live trout were found in Mill Street.

THE SMITHY

Lot 36 was a village focal point and *'an important commercial site'*. A village smith had practised his trade there for at least fifty years. In the Estate records, the Knight family were blacksmiths, in Burton Bradstock, followed by the Kerleys. An old rent book gives the smithy as being adjacent to The Three Horseshoes Inn, in the late eighteenth century. Another blacksmith appears to have worked in the Shadrach area, at the bottom of Shipton Lane. The present site had been used as a blacksmith's workshop, by the Kerley family, who preceded Benjamin Burton, born in Chideock, a third generation blacksmith. The premises had a 200 feet frontage to the main road, with a depth of 50 feet.

The smithy was rented with the adjoining allotment, part of which was to be included in the Lot and a small piece of garden on the west side, let to Frank Ward, on an oral tenancy of 5/- a year. Dennis Burton, the village blacksmith, was an enthusiastic gardener and his allotment, which was visible to all who passed by, was always productive and tidy. The whole area had a 100 feet frontage to the River Bride.

An interesting stone and slated building was used as the workshop. Inside was the forge and alongside was a wooden shed, measuring 20 feet by 18 feet with a lean-to store, used by the farrier/blacksmith as stabling. The horses, (cart horses used on the farms and for hauling shingle off the beach and Bishop's racehorses) and riding ponies were shod there, undercover.

★★★★★★★★★★

Old Benny Burton, had become famous across the Atlantic Ocean, when in 1944, soldiers serving in the American army were stationed in the village and some of them

138

57. Dennis Burton, village blacksmith and farrier at his forge, Lot 36.

were photographed watching him shoeing a grey horse. These photographs were sent back to appear in the newspapers in the United States of America, to show the 'folks back home' that the boys were fitting into life in England. Benjamin Burton died in 1948.

★★★★★★★★★★

In 1958, his widow, Mabel Burton, held the property with her son, Dennis, known as "Young Benny". Dennis had completed an apprenticeship at the Brit Engineering Works, in Bridport, before doing his National Service in Germany in the early 1950s. With the premature death of his father, he took over the business and was the youngest shoeing smith for miles around. Throughout the years leading up to the Sale, he was keeping a record, in his ledger, which included work undertaken for the Estate. Mending farm gates, repairing metal structures and supplying nails, nuts and bolts featured amongst the myriad of other work he did and materials that he supplied. Besides shoeing, he acted as a wheelwright, made and repaired many implements, as well as, turning his hand to crafting more domestic items, such as iron railings and garden gates.

The plot, to be sold with Lot 36 had already been at the centre of discussions between the Parish Council and the Pitt-Rivers Estate. The smith's workshop, situated on a prime, corner site, along the main street of the village, was well worth considering, by any speculator. The crowd assembled in the marquee was anxious. Surely, no one would dare to snatch Dennis's livelihood away? He was a well liked, local young fellow and a skilled craftsman. So many people relied on his work and availability.

The auctioneers showed sympathy and Lot 36 was soon knocked-down at £150 to the Burton family.

Dennis Burton held the monopoly throughout West Dorset, as the number of equines grew. By the 1970s he had become a mobile farrier and travelled around to the stables and farms, with a portable forge, shoeing on the spot.

The workshop forge was then electrically powered and the original bellows disused but still in place. This was exceptionally hard work and the pressures of keeping up with the demand for all the shoeing and modern farm machinery repairs, undermined his health. Breathing in the smoke and fumes, when shoeing and working the metal, was contributory. It was a sad day for the village when Dennis Burton died, aged sixty-two, in 1991.

Somehow he had found time to serve the community as the Royal British Legion Bride Valley Branch Standard Bearer for years, twice winning the county and South West area competitions and runner-up on three other occasions. Burton attended the Royal Albert Hall, for the Royal British Legion Memorial Service, as Standard Bearer and was the local Branch Secretary for many years, also serving on the Dorset County committee. Most memorable, for him, had been two pilgrimages he made, escorting war widows and family members to cemeteries, in Normandy and Belgium.

As a Verger, Sidesman and Sacristan, for over twenty-five years, he was a devoted member of St Mary's Church. There was one occasion when Dennis and Kathy went to prepare the church for a service, when they came across a wayfarer, in a state of inebriation, who had passed-out under the Altar. After much persuasion and difficulty they were able to extricate him and send him off for some earthly attention.

The Burtons considered applying to build a bungalow in the garden adjoining the smithy but their idea was immediately thwarted, when they sought advice, as there was a strong possibility that a by-pass, Route 7, would skirt Shipton Gorge, come behind Freshwater and join the main Bridport – Weymouth Road, where the proposed bungalow would be sited. The Burton family, gave up their dream-home plan and stayed on at number 2 Mill Terrace.

Forced by ill health to give up his work, Dennis sold the smithy and its grounds, lock, stock and barrel; his leather apron hanging where he left it. Today, in a state of gradual decay, there are few who are left, who can recall, the days of standing, gazing at the blacksmith at work, skilfully forging horseshoes and many other functional objects from metal. On winter days, the warmth of the forge was a sanctuary. Dennis Burton's "Pom, pom, pom," muttered under his breath, as he went about his daily tasks is silent. As for the smithy's building, recently sold on again, it awaits its destiny. The triangular bit of land to the west, now has maturing trees which hold the river bank and have replaced other trees lost to disease.

★★★★★★★★★★

Mrs Kathleen Burton, took on the position of Verger, at the church, and for many years her cat, Leo, who became well known to the congregation, accompanied her to the church, or went on alone to check it out, in her absence. She continued to serve Burton and its people, putting-up with the church's ancient vacuum cleaner, until moving, in 2006, to be nearer her son John and his family. The problem Kathy had always encountered of being "Burton" from Burton, was behind her but the happy memories of half a century in Burton Bradstock still linger on.

Lot 37 it was announced, would follow the sale of The Dove Inn.

STANLEY'S

Lot 38 Much emotion was shown when Stanley Williams proceeded to bid for the family home and his shop premises, which consisted of two large cottages, numbers 90 and 91, The Bridges. The tenancy of number 91 was complicated, in-so-much as it was let to Miss May Williams, Stanley's elder sister but she sub-let a front room for use as a shop. (The cupboard, under the stairs, formed a good sized store). Many village shops had started in the front room.

Stanley Williams held the tenancy, taken on after Tom Ward died, of number 90, which had a living room and a parlour, *'scullery with a sink and water laid on, a point for an electric cooker'* in a kitchenette and three bedrooms, of which the largest was 14 feet 6 inches by 9 feet 6 inches and about 7 feet high. Here, there was ample accommodation for Stanley's immediate family - wife Annie, née Hitt and daughter, Madeleine, known to everyone as "Toots".

May Williams, her sister, Eva, with youngest brother, Bert, still had a great deal of room, at number 91, having three additional bedrooms. She had given over her parlour to Stanley to use as the shop, following the difficult days after the spinning mill closed in the early 1930s. The

58. Stanley Williams relaxes beside his grocery delivery van in the yard of Lot 38, The Bridges. Inset 58a his wife, Annie Williams, putting out vegetables on the stand outside the shop, 1955.

catalogue described the whole of the property as *'in a good position on the main road with about 85 feet frontage, midway between the beach and the village centre'*. Knocked into one, The Bridges would have made a good sized family house or guest house, situated on the main thoroughfare, with so much storage and parking space behind it.

The river flowed beside the southern side of the property where, across the yard, at the back, Stanley had a thatched barn, used as a store. On many occasions the flood water had invaded the whole area. In a garden beyond, Stanley had a large greenhouse where he raised plants and early vegetables for the shop. It was there, too, that he and his brother, Bert, decided to build a fishing boat. This they did with no trouble, knowing all there was to know about the boats launched from the Chesil Beach. The one thing they overlooked, was getting the boat out of the greenhouse! It transpired that they had to take down one of the sides but Stanley was the first to laugh at it all.

★★★★★★★★★★

Helen Allingham, 1848 – 1926, who was born in Derbyshire, a famous nineteenth century artist, specialising in cottages, visited Burton Bradstock in 1896 and painted the scene from Venis Plot across to the group of cottages beyond the bridge. One painting depicted two of Stanley's siblings, in the field and was entitled "Duke's Cottage". At the time, the artist was in Burton, part of the property, now up for sale, had been tenanted by the autocratic Symes, known for his habit of dictating to the villagers who nicknamed him "The Duke".

Marcus B Huish in his illustrated book *The Happy England of Helen Allingham,* concluded that many of the Dorsetshire cottages were not far removed from Irish cabins, at the time.

★★★★★★★★★★

In fine weather, vegetables and fruit were displayed on a stand outside the shop, in the main road. Not much traffic went past, except for the bovine kind that would grab the odd cauliflower or bunch of carrots, as they meandered through the village. Stanley and Annie never seemed too perturbed by this. It was an occupational hazard and Annie would come out shooing the cows away, rather like Betsy Trotwood, getting the donkeys off her lawn, in Dickens's novel.

The arrangement, of the family 'sharing' the two properties, worked well. They had all been born and raised there with their elder brother, Jim, the only one to make his home away from Burton. They had been left motherless, as small children. The family was so well liked and the shop was a Mecca for village life. The property was always known as "Stanley's". Everyone knew Stanley.

When their mother died, May, had raised her siblings, at great expense to her personal life. Forced to leave school at twelve, she worked, for many years, at the spinning mill and knitted, sewed and braided to supplement the family income. Their father, who served in the Royal Navy at some time, was away working in the Portland quarries all week.

(Men from the village walked, along the track behind the beach on Monday mornings to Portland and back again on Saturday afternoons, sleeping rough, in sheds around the quarries, during the week.) Throughout their lives, May and Eva were prominent in the village organisations. When Stanley and Annie were busy running the shop, the aunts cared for Toots as if she was their own. It was one strongly united and loving family.

★★★★★★★★★★

The youngest brother, AE[Bert] Williams, who at the time of the Sale was in his fifties, was another village character who had served an engineering apprenticeship at the mill. He was conversant with everything mechanical, knowledgeable on most other things; particularly market gardening and fishing. Following the closure of the mill, he had set up a horticultural business at West Road, in Bridport and specialised in growing anemones but the war halted the import of bulbs from Holland and he had to resort to earning a living, as best he could, by other means. Whatever happened, he regularly returned to number 91 for Sunday and Christmas Dinners.

As a boy, on the beach, Bert had learnt his fishing skills from the old fishermen. When the 1939 war shattered his market gardening enterprise, he spent much time as an assistant to his brother, Stanley, growing vegetables for the shop and serving as an air raid warden.

By 1943, after the access restrictions, to the beach, were lifted, Bert, with Stanley, devoted most of his time and energies to fishing, later becoming a fish retailer. His horticultural skills gave him another income from making bouquets and wreaths. He was a great raconteur and could be found in the local pubs, which he frequented on his travels, telling the tale of his eventful life, as well as yarns about the characters that he had encountered. He was a great mimic and could illustrate his stories with the voices and actions of those that he had come across.

★★★★★★★★★★

As for Stanley, who was standing in the Sale marquee apprehensively awaiting the outcome of their home and business premises, he was a God-fearing, honest and most likeable character that the village had ever spawned. He, too, had worked at Rendall and Coombs's spinning mill, where he had met his future wife, Annie, a village girl. At one time he had a horse and cart and with Bert, went around the district, selling fruit. All his life he had sung in the church choir and been a bell-ringer. In the 1914 war, he served in the Royal Navy, aboard HMS Burham. On his return home, he became a voluntary fire-fighter, manning the hand-pumped appliance that was wheeled out whenever there was a fire. As a Civil Defence volunteer, in 1939, he took part in the watches and events of those war years.

Stanley Williams delivered groceries throughout the area, from Burton to Puncknowle, making his last call of the week, at Kennon Knapp, about eight o' clock on a Saturday evening. With an indelible pencil, which he kept stuck behind his ear, order-book in

59. The Williams family's last reunion in 1970 outside number 90 The Bridges. (L to R) Bert, Stanley, May, Eva and Jim. Inset 59a Stanley was a man of many parts including the village chimney sweep.

hand, he would write down the requirements for the following week.

After a couple of glasses of cider, having related the news from the village, he would retire to one of the pubs, play a game of cards, sing a few songs, particularly his favourite one, *"Cockles and Mussels"* and enjoy a pint or two. On Sunday morning he would be up early, checking his garden and greenhouses, perhaps fishing, first thing, at the beach, off to ring the bells, then into church to sing in the choir and afterwards, a quick pint at one of the pubs, before going home to a roast meal with all the family.

Stanley was a leading-light in all village activities. He played the comic in the village pantomimes and concert group, singing solos in his fine tenor voice. He led the village band and became a keen member of the Greenfingers Club, based at The Dove Inn. Nothing was too much trouble for Stanley and supported by his wife, he could be found helping at the fêtes, doing an odd job connected with his various activities, or running an errand for some elderly person.

His many enterprises combined the grocery business with being the village chimney sweep. No one seemed to suffer from the combination! He was a dedicated fisherman and in any spare time, he could be found on the beach casting the seine net or hauling in the catches. On cold November nights, he rowed, often single-handed, herring drifting. The only contact was a lone man, with a lantern, holding the line, on shore.

★★★★★★★★★★

The Sale particulars gave the full details of the two cottages, the large thatched barn with a loft, the garden where Stanley had greenhouses and the yard, common to both properties. One cottage without the other would have caused considerable problems and fractured a close-knit family unit. Stanley's sisters did not attend the Sale. It was far too much of an emotional strain for them to contemplate the outcome and anyway, business matters were always left to Stanley. They had known nothing else all their lives but the steady pace of a life - landlord and tenant, Stanley and shop, home and livelihoods.

The marquee fell silent again as The Bridges was offered for sale. There were speculators in the audience. The bidding rose rapidly to £600. This was a large sum for Stanley and Annie to find. "Gone to the tenant !", declared the auctioneer. Stanley Williams breathed a sigh of great relief. Lot 38 was his! Another enormous cheer went up.

> Stanley and Annie Williams were only to have another ten years together, as she died in 1968. Stanley lost a 'part' of his being but carried on for a while running the business. He moved in with his sisters who cared for Stanley's needs and Bert continued to join them all on Sunday. Madeleine had married, George Wakely, whose work lay in farming.
>
> There was to be one last get-together when Stanley, May, Eva and Bert Williams were joined by their elder brother Jim, on his last visit to his home village.
>
> Burton Bradstock lost another of its great characters when Stanley died, aged eighty and the premises were put on the market and sold in 1971. May, Eva and Bert moved into sheltered accommodation, next door to one another and lived to a great age.
>
> At Stanley's funeral, when St Mary's Church was packed, his signature tune, "Cockles and Mussels, Alive, Alive Oh", brought even the hardened fishermen to tears.
>
> Only old photographs are left to remind of what had been.

SHADRACH DAIRY FARM

Lot 39 The lands were *'well farmed, all easily accessible from good roads'* and the soil varied from strong loam on clay subsoil, to sandy stone-brash, on limestone. Lot 39 was the epitome of a Dorset dairy farm. It could have come straight out of a Thomas Hardy novel. The old homestead lay at the hub of village activity and the meadows, bisected by the River Bride, skirted Burton.

★★★★★★★★★★

A trailing footpath ran all along the river bank from the recreation field to Timber Bridge and on to Arch Bridge. Another path joined it and led to Larkfield. Each stile was formed from magnificent blocks of local grey-coloured stones. Originally, these paths were short-cuts to and from work, or to and from the beach, for fishing. They had also been frequented by the villagers and later the visitors for a pleasant stroll or to exercise dogs.

★★★★★★★★★★

In the early 1900s, when the sons, at Townsend Farm, reached maturity, their father, Joseph Hawkins, encouraged them to go their own ways. One stayed on at the family farm and Edgar took over the tenancy of Shadrach. This was the dairy farm, in Mill Street, not to be confused with Shadrach Farm, at the bottom of Shipton Lane. Both farms may once have been held by the Stone family, of Portland, of whom the majority bore the Christian name of Shadrach, buying or renting land and property in the village, from the proceeds of smuggling.

Edgar Hawkins and his sons, Dennis and Robert, devoted their lives to good husbandry. Both played village football, Dennis served on the Parish Council and Bob interested himself in various local agricultural organisations.

There had been a family milk-round, started by Joseph Hawkins, who delivered the milk with a pony and trap as did his son, Edgar, for many years. The fresh, almost warm, milk was laddled into jugs at the doorsteps. Over the years, the Hawkins family had added to the acreage that they farmed, as it fell vacant and used suitable land, on the cliff top, for a camp site. Edgar Hawkins was well into his middle years and had involved himself with the Parish Council and at the time of the Sale was the Vice Chairman.

★★★★★★★★★★

Behind the farmhouse were the ancient buildings, alongside up-to-date, covered yards. The original cow-stalls were built to accommodate fourteen and eight milking cows respectively and the milking had been done outside in the yard but with modernising the equipment, the Hawkins men and their employees were able to put through, under cover, eighty cattle. When Shorthorn cattle went out of fashion, they chose the Guernsey breed. These were ideal, with golden, rich milk, popular with housewives. The improvements such as a concrete yard, four calf boxes and a five-bay Dutch barn, had been made by the tenant. Set in the wall, along Mill Street, was a wooden door. It was here, in a bad flood, during the Great War, that a hole was breached, to allow the cattle to escape to safety.

Seventeenth century in construction, the house faced onto Mill Street and a high wall opposite. Its main features were a Tudor fireplace and Tudor beams. A sitting-room, 18 feet by 13 feet, with 10 feet to the ceiling and a dining room of similar proportion, gave the place an air of antiquity. The kitchen was smaller than would be expected for a farmhouse but there was plenty of utility space. The master-bedroom was extremely large, being 17 feet by 13 feet, with a ceiling at 7 feet 2 inches. All of the three bedrooms were in a raised slated roof, with temporary divisions, after a serious fire, in the earlier part of the century, (the roof had been thatched when a branch of the Gale family rented from the Estate) and a bathroom, completed the living accommodation. The tenant had put in some fixtures and could claim a boiler, hot-water system, linen cupboard, bath, sink and draining boards, a door and side porch and an Elsan closet and shed. Outside he had provided a water-bowl installation for the cattle, galvanized sheeting in the stalls, steel fittings and a milking machine. Mains electricity, water and a telephone were connected. The main sewer was nearby, in Mill Street. A small garden and the two spacious yards, added to the property.

146

Few outsiders ever noticed the cylindrical, concrete blocks in Mill Street by the entrance, to the farmyard. These had been placed there during the war, in case of an invasion, when they would have been manoeuvred to block the road. Hawkins used these as a milk-stand. By the farm entrance, stretched across the road, was a line of holes, covered with iron lids that were tank traps. Had an invasion happened, huge metal zigzag bars were to be inserted, as well, to prevent the enemy tanks penetrating into the heart of the village. The Mill Street blockade and a similar one at the entrance to Manor Farm, would have certainly held-up the invaders.

★★★★★★★★★★

A farm-worker's cottage, number 44 Burton Bradstock situated in Darby Lane, was included with Lot 39. At the time, the Sibley family were living there. Hawkins had installed electric wiring, a sink and Elsan lavatory. Built of local stone and thatched, with two bedrooms and the usual downstairs facilities, set in a charming, secluded position, it would make ideal holiday accommodation. There were only a few holiday homes, in the village, although as far back at the 1880s there were some places that were used as such. Second homes were nothing new. The arrival to the area, of the visitors, who were named, was posted in the local newspaper.

60. Halcyon days in Mill Street, all flowers and no traffic, circa 1918. Tank traps were put across where the women are standing, in 1940.

★★★★★★★★★★

The farm of 91 acres, was offered, including the very field, Corn Croft, (or Corn Crack), where the Sale was being held. Larkfield, as well as Green Cliff, Broad Meadow and Sows Close, were other fields that formed part of the farmlands. With the large herd of dairy cows, a good supply of clean, fresh water was essential. Drinking troughs had been installed in the fields, mainly by a gravitation system from a spring in Hanging Holwell. Some of the land was bordered by the river, from which the cows drank at shallow pools, that had formed, over the years. The pasture known as Weagemore, received water from a stream at Cogden.

There was permission, under the Town and Country Planning and Public Health Acts, for forty caravan sites, on a annual basis, in the fields on the cliff. The licence expired at the end of September 1958. The Vendor received an additional £90 a year for the consideration. Lots 89 and 93, formed the caravan site and were included in the Shadrach Farm tenancy and were to be sold separately .

The annual rent for Lot 39 was £230. The rateable value was £9 for the farmhouse, £4 for the cottage and a proportion of the whole allocated to the caravan camp. One condition was that the purchaser of Lot 39 should erect a good cattle and pig-proof fence on the expiration of Mrs Ackerman's tenancy, where she was renting a small garden and orchard, adjoining the homestead at 10/- p. a.

£427 had been expended, by the Estate, in the previous five years on the farm. At the 1958 Sale, £7,250 was the sum paid by Edgar Hawkins for the family home and livelihood.

The Hawkins family continued to farm at Shadrach Dairy Farm for the rest of their lives. They improved the buildings and extended the caravan camp, which was moved to Larkfield. In 1974, Edgar and his wife, Catherine [Kitty], died on the same day, both aged 79. Sons, Dennis and Bob, took charge of the business, sharing the many duties that a modern, busy farm generated. They taught their cousin's son, John Heal, the rudiments of farming and he spent many long days working on the farm, alongside others, who were employed as farm workers, particularly loyal and knowledgeable, Julian Harvey who worked for about thirty-five years as a right-hand-man on the farm.

Many years later, when the manual work began to take its toll, the sons sold off Larkfield Camp and some other parts of the farm. Near the end of their lives, the old orchard, opposite The Three Horseshoes, was sold for building, (not to everyone's approval, as well as the high water table presented difficulties) and imposing, luxury homes, sprang up in the centre of the village. It is believed that the site changed hands for £250,000. The Parish Council would have welcomed the old orchard as an open area for the village but the sum required was way beyond the funds that were available.

Fate dealt another of her peculiar hands in the summer of 2000, when Bob died and was followed three weeks later by his brother, Dennis, both in their seventies, leaving Julian Harvey to attend to the farm in the aftermath of the unexpected.

With their deaths, went the last of the working farms, in the heart of Burton and a century of family, farming endeavour, ground to a halt.

A CAR PARK FOR THE THREE HORSESHOES

Lots 40 and 41 had received outline planning permission for commercial development. The road frontages were extremely good.

Consideration had already been given to making some of the area of 23 perches into a much needed car park for the pub. One patch of ground, the old garden of the ruined

61. *The Three Horseshoes Inn just after the Sale in 1958, with the wall of the new car park opposite. (R) Lot 3, Shadrach Dairy Farmhouse, the roof tiled and altered after a serious fire in the early part of the century. Inset 61a Customers sitting outside in 1964, prior to the refurbishment.*

cottages, beside the leat, was let to Edgar Hawkins and the other to the licensee, of The Three Horseshoes, Harold Greenham, at £1. 4/- and 5/- per annum respectively. Palmers, the local brewers, succeeded in purchasing Lot 40 at £640 but Mrs Coward claimed Lot 41 for £420.

TERRACED COTTAGES IN MILL STREET

Lot 42 Numbers 79 and 80 Mill Street lay opposite Shadrach Dairy Farm and number 79 was let to farmer Edgar Hawkins who sub-let to Frederick Hyde. There was a small living room, approached straight off the street, a scullery and a main bedroom 11 feet 6 inches by 10 feet and another bedroom formed on the landing. (No size was given for this in the catalogue). Water was from a shared standpipe behind the cottages and a little, narrow garden, backed, onto the property.

Hawkins paid the Estate £8 a year, the occupier met the rates of £4. Number 80, which mirrored its neighbour, was on a monthly tenancy, between Jack Cammell and the Estate, at £14 yearly, with rates amounting to £4 a year.

★★★★★★★★★★

Down the road, a passage led to the rear of the Mill Street cottages. A right-of-way, on foot, existed for numbers 75, 76, 77 and 78. AS Knight, paid £280 for Lot 42. Annie

Cammell had been concerned, prior to the Sale, that there were speculators interested in their cottage and she had fears of being evicted.

★★★★★★★★★★

Jack Cammell had been born and bred in Burton Bradstock. He and his brother, Robert, who both served in the Royal Navy in the First World War, had married the two Sponsford sisters, Annie and Gertrude. Jack had worked at various jobs in Civvy Street, including shingle hauling at Bridport Harbour and as a gardener at Wych. Amongst his attributes, was his contribution to the village, as a good footballer, playing for the Canaries and his fishing skills. During his war service he was a stoker in the navy and witnessed the sinking of the ships at Scapa Flow, a story he once related to his grandson, Roger Saint.

Jack and Annie's son, twenty-eight year old, Alfred, a L/Sergeant in the 17th/21st Lancers, Royal Armoured Corps. had been killed in 1942, aged twenty-eight and the family still felt the loss and regularly attended to his grave, at the cemetery, in Shipton Lane; his body having been brought home.

> Annie Cammell lived out her long life in the cottage and on her death, Jack moved to Lower Townsend, to be with one of his daughters for another five years.
> On the death of their parents, the Hyde family moved elsewhere in the district.
> In due course the cottages were purchased for council housing.

ADJOINING PROPERTIES

Lot 43 was another pair of similar cottages, in the row, with two bedrooms. Number 81 was let to Mrs Florence Northover, (the same family names often caused confusion) and number 82 to Mrs EM Northover at £14 a year. The yearly rates were £4 each. The inspectors for The Royal Commission of Historical Monuments had estimated that these properties were built around 1700. There was water to a stand pipe and an earth closet. The whole area amounting to 14 perches. Lot 43 was purchased by VJ Houghton of Abbingdon for £300. The worry of these strangers coming into their midst was unsettling for all the elderly tenants.

> Mrs Eva Hope, [known as Josie], recalled how her mother, Florence, had been widowed and left with a young family. Josie, the baby, was only six weeks old and Mrs Northover, worked at the factory and undertook braiding at home, to keep the family together. She lost a son in the 1939 – 1945 war. Josie had been employed, at some time, at Shadrach Dairy Farm as a domestic and had married a soldier, Leonard Hope, who was stationed locally. They set-up home in Burton and Len became involved in numerous local organisations, particularly as Parish Council Clerk and the Royal British Legion, of which Josie was a long-serving member,

too.

Cyril Northover who was serving with the Dorsetshire Regiment in Normandy, was killed at Tilly sur Seulles, France, in 1944 and is buried in a war cemetery there. In 1987, Josie, her husband, Len and her brother Steve, visited the grave for the first time. Steve took some sand from Burton beach and scattered it on his young brother's grave. "A bit of Burton, " he said.

MILL CORNER GARDEN

<u>Lot 44</u> was a large walled-in garden, adjoining the main Rectory garden, amounting to 20 perches. There was a frontage of 55 feet and the widest part of the garden measured 80 feet. A septic tank drainage system was installed but not in use, which would form a good start, to obtaining planning permission, for a dwelling.

A passage ran from The Rectory towards this part. It was said that a former rector had built it to save himself the embarrassment of seeing his servants going to visit the privy. Or was that a cover-up and the passage was really used as a get-away for smugglers? A peppercorn rent of £1 a year was charged for the garden.

Canon Arthur Dittmer, secured Lot 44 for £300 on behalf of the Church Commissioners.

62. The Cammell family, outside their cottage, Lot 42, in Mill Street. Circa 1930 (L) to (R): William, Annie (mother), daughters Caroline and little Annie, Jack (father) and (R) other son, Alfred who was later killed in action. Inset 62a Annie, née Sponsford, circa 1918.

The part of the garden sold off was approved for a building site. Uncovered recently, in the remainder, is a "Treacle Mine", not as ridiculous as it seems. David Edelstan, and other references explain that the liquid which exudes from the rocks was recognised by the Royal College of Physicians in 1665, when the Great Plague of London had spread like wildfire. It was used as a medicinal aid known as "Theriaca" or (tryacle or treacle).

Similar to coal, it is a natural material found underground, lying in beds rich in fossil remains of early forms of sugar cane. These were trapped in rock layers from the

Jurassic period. The Romans were known to mine it and extracting the material could date back to the Iron Age.

THE OLD POST OFFICE

Lot 45 The sub-post office and stores, with a room, 16 feet by 15 feet, a long thin living room, 23 feet by 9 feet 6 inches and 6 feet 8 inches high and three bedrooms, of a very good size, was bid for by Albion Wylde, a Bridport solicitor, to the value of £1,000, acting on behalf of Palmers Brewery. Securing this corner property, which was vacant, adjoining The Three Horseshoes, would enable the brewers to extend and refurbish the old inn, which they already owned.

★★★★★★★★★★

Just as the Sale was announced, in March 1958, the Post Mistress, Miss Clara Swaffield, had given notice that she was retiring. Her two sisters, Lilian and Bessie had assisted and served in the shop. Clara Swaffield had taken over from her mother, Mary Swaffield, formerly of Shipton Gorge, at the turn of the century, when she had been left to fend for herself and children.

Throughout the fifty years, the post office had been an asset to the village and a great meeting place. Originally, when a post office first came to Burton, it was run by the licensee of The Three Horseshoes, Joseph Hawkins.

★★★★★★★★★★

The Three Horseshoes Inn, situated in a busy part of Burton, lying on the main road, was once called "The Ship Inn", (very appropriate for a sea-faring village), in the Estate records. It may have gleaned its new name when a blacksmith/farrier had his workshop adjacent. Old records listed other past hosts, at the inn, as Samways, followed by Churchill, who was succeeded by Walter Cliff and the last landlord, at the time of the Sale, was Harold Greenham. A survey in the early 1950s referred to some original windows of the seventeenth century.

Before visitors came in any great numbers to Burton, it had been difficult for the licensee to earn a living from just the pub takings, alone. Most of them had a second occupation and/or rented a piece of land on which to raise cattle, pigs and sheep. In some other Dorset villages a field often went with the tenancy of the inn.

To those assembled in the Sale marquee, Harold Greenham was a familiar figure in the district. He had earned his living as a fish, fruit and vegetable retailer, in Bridport, before taking on the pub, in the early 1940s but kept his fishing interests. Greenham was a great character. He wore his slippers most of the time when serving in the bars. This was undoubtedly for comfort, being on his feet so long but it also proved safer on the flagstone floors which when wet, could be very slippery. The passage-way of The Three Horseshoes was well worn with the tread of feet, over several centuries. Greenham spoke

152

with an attractive Dorset brogue which was filtered through the pipe that he constantly chewed.

His wife, Caroline, known as Carrie, née Cammell, was a Burton woman. Her family could be traced back in the village to the earliest Parish Registers. She was a perfect landlady, decisive, smart, fashionable and decorative. Being local, she knew everyone and was able to soon make acquaintance with any newcomers, or the soldiers who had been stationed around the village during the war and later the holiday makers, all of whom found a convivial Dorset welcome.

With the proposal to incorporate the old post office in The Three Horseshoes and a complete rebuilding and refurbishment, in1963, competition was keen for new licensees for The Three Horseshoes Inn, on the retirement of the Greenhams. Alan and Joan Gillett were interviewed by the brewer. They were catapulted into running a pub, after holding the fort for Joan's brother, Bernard Brooks, popular licensee of the Bridport Arms Hotel, in West Bay, whilst he and his wife went on holiday for a fortnight. The Gilletts enjoyed the challenge for the brief spell at West Bay and gave some thought to trying their hand at it for themselves, even looking at a few of Palmer's inns in the area, that became vacant.

★★★★★★★★★★

Alan Gillett's life had been far removed from that of a country pub landlord. In 1938 he had joined the Auxiliary Air Force and found himself in Flying Training Command, ending his service in the Middle East. He met Joan in 1941, when she was making components for Spitfires. In civilian life, he was a buyer for Windsmoor, a fashion house, in London. When the Gilletts got word that "The Shoes" at Burton was coming up, they successfully applied to run it.

★★★★★★★★★★

The inn was completely refurbished and extended. The old bow window of the former post office became a feature of the new lounge bar. The overall design changed the place and two thatched porches were added to give it a quaint look. Newcomers would never have any idea of the modest hostelry, originally dark cottages, with low ceilings. When "The Shoes" was re-thatched, in 1965, by Guy Gale, a master thatcher, from Stoke Abbott, who undertook all the work for Palmers Brewery, ash poles, cut straight from the hedges, and ship's masts used as rafters, were exposed. In the past it had been thatched with local water-reed from Cogden. For this large project, the reed used had been grown in Norfolk.

The Gilletts were landlords of The Three Horseshoes for sixteen years. Their very hard work was well rewarded by their acceptance into the community and success in the business. Joan was a pioneer in providing food in pubs. She served pasties, known as "Tiddy Oggies" and could not make enough! It was calculated that in the sixteen years, she made, cooked and served 22, 000 Tiddy Oggies!

Whilst "The Shoes" was being refurbished and extended the hosts managed with the old place for eighteen months. There was no water upstairs and the bathroom was only an afterthought on the side of the old kitchen bar. In due course, six local girls were employed and guests were taken on a bed and breakfast arrangement. Starting with five guests a night, the enterprise ended with a dozen at a time being accommodated, which included famous actors, television stars and dignitaries from around the world. Joan often provided an evening meal as part of the hospitality on offer.

Alan and Joan loved every minute of the job and only took one week's holiday all the time they were there. They were too busy always to bother that they had little privacy and did not have a sitting-room of their own. Originally, the customers frequenting the bars were from the village but as Burton expanded, business people, workmen on the new developments and visitors crowded into the hostelry.

★★★★★★★★★★

Mrs Gillett, now widowed, is a prominent member of several high profile committees in the village but she still considers herself a Londoner!

The Three Horseshoes is a popular eating house. Music is an important part of what's on offer there and local groups hold suppers and tea parties throughout the year. The welcome is as warm as ever, though the accents are not local. 2007 heralded another refurbishment for "The Shoes" and it has once again been brought up-to-date.

Visitors to the village will always sit outside the pub, on warm days, savouring the atmosphere, in Mill Street, just as countless numbers of Burton men have sat, whilst the ghosts of those fishermen, sailors, farm and factory workers will hang around for evermore.

★★★★★★★★★★

and the Post Office…. With the post mistress retired and the premises gone, a new post office was set-up, by the Maddocks family, nearby, in Mill Street. When the notice of Clara Swaffield's retirement was posted in the main Bridport office, a young couple had made enquiries from RB Howarth, about the possibility of locating the new post office in the Shadrach area, at number 20 Burton Bradstock. This cottage, with vacant possession, has been offered to them, by the Pitt-Rivers Estate's Agent. RB Howarth did say in an interview that there were two vacant cottages in Mill Street for which the Estate was asking £700. It was revealed later that, at the same time, Leslie Maddocks was investigating installing his son, Bobby, as post master, there.

The cottage was converted and for a number of years, Bobby and his wife, ran a more modern establishment. Half-a-century on, Mill Street is a congested thoroughfare, with the majority of householders living in the northern area of the village. The new post office in the Shadrach cottage, might, with hindsight, have been ideal.

When Bobby Maddocks left the village, a retired army officer and his wife, a charming, well liked couple, Mr and Mrs Constance, took it on from 1965 to 1969, followed by Joe Wyatt, whose journey to Burton Bradstock was fascinating. After surviving his war service, in 1945, which involved flying gliders and having seen most of his pals killed, he came to live in Bridport where his parents, formerly Sussex farmers, were running boarding kennels.

Joe Wyatt married Barbara, a Queen Alexandra nursing sister.

****

In 1946, Wyatt, with the rank of Captain, was at a loss what to do, as were so many men who had just been demobbed and with his charisma and strong personality, he

63. (L) Gertie Cammell, ? and (R) Jack Norris, in the 1930s, outside the cottage, which was later converted to the post office. Inset 63a Jonathan Wyatt, Post Master from 1979-2002 and Thelma Aylott, assistant from 1965-2002, celebrate 20 years at Burton post office in 1999.

landed a prime position as managing director of Woolaway Construction, with the branch that had recently set-up in West Bay. By the mid 1960s it was bought by Peter de Savery and after a number of successful years, the factory, which had employed a considerable number of local men, closed. Wyatt joined the Taunton branch which made sectional bungalows, much needed at that time. As their surveyor until 1966, he travelled the country. In time, he was made redundant, the bungalows had served their stop-gap purpose when people were demanding brick and stone properties.

Faced again, with what occupation to follow, Wyatt stumbled on the vacancy for a post master at Burton. By coincidence the cottage, next door came up for sale at the same time and he and Barbara took on the lot. They endeared themselves to the village, Barbara continuing to work as a nursing sister in Bridport and helping out at the post office, entering into the spirit of the village and stayed on after 1979 when they retired and son, Jonathan, took over.

Jonathan, had left the district to attend university and was working in publishing and as a journalist for a magazine. With a young family, he felt that a better life could be had for his children in the country and West Dorset, in particular and he broached the subject to his father that he would like to take over. This was duly agreed and for a further twenty-three years, Jonathan Wyatt ran the Burton Bradstock post office. Leaving his parents to stay on in their cottage, in Mill Street, he set-up home in Bridport and commuted to the village. Throughout the whole of this period, the post office was also an information bureau and provided a social service.

When Jonathan Wyatt changed tack in 2002, in order to save the village being without the facility, the Parish Council bought the premises, partly with a large sum, left by a benefactor and managers were installed. The price of the property is believed to have been £80,000. Jonathan Wyatt and his assistant, Mrs Thelma Aylott, (who had worked there from 1965 until 2002), were given a good send-off by the villagers. They had done a splendid job!

★★★★★★★★★★

The first of these managers decided to relinquish the post in 2006. Others were appointed. With their knowledge of the area they have already taken on the mantle of operating the headquarters. The post office is a hub of activity, all day long but not necessarily a 'gold mine'. Definitely, it is a vital asset to the village and visitors, yet the shadow of its closure must surely hang over the village.

THE BACK O'NOVEMBER

Lot 46 "The Gardens", originally two properties, lay behind The Three Horseshoes, approached by a path in Donkey Lane. The old residents had named it the "The Back o' November" because it faced north, in a dark situation and was tucked-in behind. A very narrow drain could be used to cut through from the main street. The property, with four bedrooms, was rented from the Pitt-Rivers Estate, by Sidney Jones.

The large garden was sub-let to RB Howarth and FM Brown, at a rateable value of £8 per annum. Jones had provided cupboards in the living room, a cooker panel in the kitchen and a greenhouse in his bit of the garden. Sid Jones's cottage fell swiftly, at £400, to RB Howarth, whose own, fine garden, of Manor Farm Cottage, ran down over the slope and joined Lot 46.

This was a good investment on RB Howarth's part to secure the house, then reverting to its original name, (Jones not wishing to buy).

Later Howarth's son, another Robert [Bob] retired to The Back o' November and was well liked in the village and the pubs where he joined the camaraderie.

After Bob Howarth's death, Clive Taylor, a journalist and Elsa, his wife, an actress, came to live there with their small daughter. They, too, soon fitted into life in Burton, working from home and mixing with the locals. They had a great respect for the Burton Bradstock traditions and mode of living.

Changing hands again, it has been modernised, enhanced by its age-old view to the church and the addition of a garage and parking space, after a wider approach had been cut. In June of 1999 it was on the market again at £238,000. The chimney breast, deep sills and a vaulted beamed ceiling were featured. The particulars referred to a 'dining hall, guest suite, master bedroom, dressing room or study and breakfast room'. When the property was constructed, some three hundred years previously, the families housed there would have had little requirement for such grandeur and what in 1999 was a spacious house would have been filled with the large number of children and the everyday accoutrements of living.

TWO GOOD HOUSES

Lots 47 and 48 had brought a large amount of speculative interest. Two good village houses were to be offered. Rock House, in the main street and the Red House, beside the village green, were sold in quick succession to the tenants, although each received bids from outsiders. Both properties were equipped with modern plumbing.

★★★★★★★★★★

Elvina Wilkins, née Wrixton, known as Viney, from another old village family, had been renting Rock House, Lot 47, from the Estate, after swapping places with elderly Mr Samways, who moved into the Wrixton cottage, number 64. Her parents, Alfred and Elizabeth, had brought up a large family who travelled to all corners of the world, especially the Wrixton sons, five of whom had served in the Royal Navy in the 1914-1918 war. All returned to Burton, except Fred, who gave his life for his country. A sixth brother, Roy, had died in infancy.

★★★★★★★★★★

Charles [Charlie] Wrixton was mentioned in Dispatches and received The Royal Commendation, by the King, gazetted on the 6th April, 1918.

★★★★★★★★★★

As a young woman, Viney had been employed at Norburton and later at Haddon House, in West Bay. It was through this move that she met her husband, George Wilkins, who was serving in the Royal Navy. His father was a coastguard, stationed at West Bay. The family were originally from Cornwall and on

64. Elvina [Viney] Wilkins, née Wrixton.

a visit, George met up with Viney, a very pretty, smart young woman.

Wilkins was due to be posted to Malta, where Viney would accompany him but the outbreak of war in 1939 put paid to that and she found herself and her little daughter, Valerie, spending the war years, in married quarters, around the British Isles. They finally settled in the village at the Wrixtons' family cottage, 64, High Street and later moved to Rock House, around 1945.

★★★★★★★★★★

Rock House was double fronted, with sitting rooms on either side of the large hall. A breakfast room, kitchen, 15 feet 6 inches by 6 feet 3 inches, with a sink and adjoining larder, formed the ground floor accommodation. There was a landing, from which, four, generously sized, bedrooms led off, together with a bathroom, *'with bath and hand-basin'*. This Lot was a good prospect for any speculator.

★★★★★★★★★★

At the turn of the century, Rock House had been the home of Walter Ouseley, a Captain in the Church Army, and his family. As a Preacher, he ministered in the surrounding villages and particularly, at Bridport Harbour, to the fishermen and the ships' crews. His son, Maurice, an Oxford undergraduate, had the foresight to photograph the village scenes and its people in the 1930s, leaving a permanent record.

★★★★★★★★★★

Outside Rock House, the main highway was peaceful and safe, causing no question about disturbance from traffic. The busiest activity in the street, during the day, was the parade of the dairy cattle to and from Manor Farm and the cart horses and tractors, going back and forth to the fields but this was never troublesome. The house was advertised, in the Sale catalogue, as having 100 feet of frontage and a nice, walled garden with the prospect of its use for commercial purposes.

Elvina Wilkins was able to obtain Rock House for £650.

★★★★★★★★★★

Lot 48, The Red House was a substantial gentleman's residence and sold for £1,200. This property lay in the heart of the village, overlooking the central green [Parish Pump]. Being brick-faced, it stood out against the mellow stone properties. The bricks were made locally and would have come from one of the works, in Bothenhampton, or Bridport.

A hall, sitting, dining room, 12 feet by 10 feet, breakfast room and office, four bedrooms, of a good size, a bathroom, with an indoor flush lavatory, also *'with bath, hand-basin and H and C'*, were topped by two good attics. The tenant had installed an Aga cooker in the kitchen. Outside, a walled garden gave valuable privacy and a garage and outside WC were included.

Mrs Lilian Cheney, had lived there for about thirty years. Her son, Gordon, did the bidding on her behalf and secured their home.

Rock House has changed hands, several times. Elvina and her husband, Chief Petty Officer George Wilkins, moved to a modern bungalow, called "The Nook", (Lot 16). She died in 1975 but her connection with Burton lives on in her daughter, Valerie, (Mrs Alec Aylott), four grandchildren, seven great-grandchildren and at the time of writing, four great-great-grandchildren. Some of this extended family live in the village but recently Valerie has decided to move away from Burton to be near one of her sons.

In the new millennium, Rock House featured in a television relocation programme, which failed to point out the problems with the constant flow of passing traffic. The purchasers, thrilled with every other aspect of their find, seemed unperturbed by this disadvantage.

★★★★★★★★★★

Mrs Cheney moved to Bridge Cottage Stores to live with her daughter and The Red House was sold on and is still in that same ownership.

NUMBER 42 DARBY LANE

Lot 49 lay in an old part of the village. Darby Lane had obtained its name from the Darby family who had a long association with Burton. William Derby, (the name was spelt in various ways), had been Rector in 1564 – 1567 and the family had farmed at Sturthill. The Broadmayne Charity was set-up by a family member to provide money to apprentice Burton boys to a trade.

★★★★★★★★★★

Frederick Buglar (spelt with an 'a' in the catalogue), with a safeguarded tenancy, rented Lot 49 but the tenancy was complicated, by part of the garden at the rear, being let to the school managers. Len Starkey, the schoolmaster, cultivated this garden and had erected a shed on it. Buglar paid a high rent of £19 and the rates of £6 a year for the converted three bed-roomed, double fronted cottage, having two doors opening on to Darby Lane. The two sitting rooms, a scullery, and wash house were small and dark, with the customary low ceilings. An earth closet was still in use. The whole amounted to 16 perches.

Secured by Doctor Philip Shemilt, of Salisbury, number 42 Darby Lane realised £400, this was one of the most expensive, of the cottages, for sale that day. Doctor Shemilt would have preferred to have bought The Rookery. This was a rather modest compensation! The unknown purchasers were gathering up too much for the villagers' liking. The marquee seemed remarkably quiet.

With Buglar and his son, Jack, as sitting tenants, under the Housing Act, it was a decade before Doctor Shemilt was able to take possession. In the mean-time his architect obtained permission to convert the property into one house. It was soon discovered that the timbers were rotten and the walls had to be taken down to the base. Doctor Shemilt visited one December whilst the work was going on. The depth of winter is the best time to view but Doctor Shemilt had already bought number 42!

A damp-proof course had to be put in and the roof re-thatched. Eventually, it became a bright, airy house and the entrance moved to the side, rather than opening directly onto the ever busier Darby Lane, the cost, no doubt, far outweighing the purchase price of The Rookery. Saving the property was an expensive business. Doctor Shemilt, recalls his interesting 'encounter' with the Sale.

His family is still able to enjoy the charm of this tucked-away cottage.

A SITE FOR DEVELOPMENT

Lot 50 fronted onto Darby Lane for 32 feet and its extensive depth was 110 feet. This was Fred Buglar's other garden on which he had erected some sheds, paying £1 a year as rent. All the services were to hand.

With his house and butcher's shop, old slaughter house and newly built bungalow, in close proximity, butcher Rob Gale bought the garden site for £160.

THE MAGNOLIAS, 'the school house'

Lot 51 The Magnolias, was another of the attractive houses in the Sale, standing opposite the church, in the old part of Burton. The accommodation consisted of a sitting and dining room, a kitchen, with an Ideal boiler, scullery, 'with sink', larder. WC, three main bedrooms, (the largest 15 feet by 13 feet by 7 feet 2 inches), a nice bathroom and two 'good' attics. The Magnolias was so named because two, impressive, Magnolia Grandiflora trees framed the front porch. Dating from 1795 and probably built from the ruins of very ancient cottages, it had a fascinating history. Lieutenant William Hansford, RN, who during his distinguished career, served with Nelson, had resided at The Rookery and married, Mary Adney, a widow, in 1762. Her family had lived at Berwick and Chilcombe. (The date stone, on The Magnolias bore the initials AH).

At the time of the Sale, the well appointed house was the home of the headmaster, Leonard Starkey and his family, although the tenancy was held by the managers of Burton Bradstock School, on a yearly basis, at £43. 6s. 8d.

The first the Starkeys knew of the Sale, was late one evening, when clerks from the auctioneers called to inform them of Captain Pitt-Rivers's decision. Unlike others in Burton, they had not received a letter from him, as they were not the actual tenants, the property being sub-let to them by the school managers, RB Howarth and Mrs Wratislaw.

Outside, an early producing, walled garden, running north/south and store sheds were an attraction for enthusiastic gardeners, offering seclusion, on the far side, away from the main thoroughfare of Church Lane. The sound of the church bells ringing and the church clock chiming, so close, might have been considered a disadvantage, by some. This house had featured in Eden Phillpotts's book, *The Spinners*. In the novel, he used a combination of The Magnolias and Magnolia Farmhouse, which also sported a Magnolia Grandiflora, as the residence of one of the principal characters, "Mr Churchouse".

In 1952, Leonard Starkey and his wife, Elizabeth [Betty], had moved there on his appointment as headmaster of the village school. By 1958, with their three young daughters, they were well at home.

As the Sale date approached, officials from Dorset County Council visited to survey the property, with a view to purchasing. The managers had informed Mr and Mrs Starkey that they had no intention of bidding at the Sale and the matter was left with the County Council Education Department. It seemed that all was in-hand for the attempt to buy, although the Starkeys were left in a state of limbo, as to their future accommodation, if the County Council was unsuccessful.

★★★★★★★★★★

What had brought Len and Betty to Burton in the first place was very co-incidental. On Friday the first of September, 1939, Betty, a young, single teacher, was on holiday with family and teaching friends, staying at Cliff Villa guest house. News came through from their home, in Surrey, where Betty and the other friends were teaching, that war was imminent and that they were to report back, to assist with the evacuation of children. Her brother, who was one of the party, was already serving in the Territorial Army and was recalled immediately. They all thought that the war would not last long and made a pact to return to Burton Bradstock the following year.

★★★★★★★★★★

It was to be some twelve years before Betty would set foot in the village again when Starkey took up the headship of the school. He had been sitting his teaching examinations, in 1939, at the same time as Betty and the others were enjoying their visit to this quaint, peaceful part of Dorset. The invigilator, told the gentlemen to put down their pens. A war was about to be declared. In these extraordinary circumstances, Len Starkey was granted a teaching certificate without completing the examinations. As yet, he and Betty were not acquainted and it was not until after the hostilities had ended, that they met, when teaching in Surrey. He had served in the Royal Air Force during the war and commenced teaching on being demobbed.

Starkey wanted to rise further up the ladder and kept a look-out for better positions. With Betty, he considered several moves but she was happy where they were and no offers seemed to tempt her. One day he came home with a copy of *The Times* and asked her how she would fancy a move to a place called Burton Bradstock. She jumped at the idea, much to his amazement, as he had no idea that she had ever heard of the place. Their move to Burton was very successful and it was an ideal place in which the Starkey girls could grow up.

In the Sale marquee, the auctioneers settled for a lunch break following Lot 50. Betty's brother and his wife were on holiday in the village and her sister-in-law had taken the girls off their hands, in order that they could attend the Sale. Len and Betty Starkey had gone to the marquee, "Like lambs to the slaughter, " (the whole procedure being 'foreign' to them), as they did not know if by the end of the day they would have a roof over their heads. If the County Council did not buy and someone else became the owner of The Magnolias, they could be in real trouble, particularly with three children, of which the youngest was five years old. RB Howarth had given them some reassurance, that should they be made homeless, they would be in the running for a council house! Even in the position as the occupying schoolmaster, Starkey did not have tenant's rights.

Mr Guest, a Bridport solicitor, had accompanied them to the Sale, as he was the local representative of the National Union of Teachers and went along to see that they were fairly treated. As the hammer fell on Lot 50 and the lunch break was announced, Starkey looked around for the County Council official who he expected to take part in the bidding for their house, which was scheduled to be the next Lot in the Sale. The official was nowhere to be seen and he raced home to telephone the Dorchester office, only to be told that the Dorset County Council had decided not to try to buy The Magnolias!

65. *The Starkey Family off to a wedding in the 1960s.*

An extremely quick decision had to be made, as the Sale recommenced and encouraged by Guest, there was no alternative but for Starkey to enter into the competition.

The Starkeys faced with the low salary Dorset teachers received, which was below that paid in some other counties and a growing family, they knew that they did not have the necessary reserves. As the rent of The Magnolias was due to be increased, anyway, by the Estate, Betty had decided to return to teaching, which would commence, the following autumn term and she had secured a post at the Alfred Colfox School, in Bridport.

As the hammer was raised, the main contestant for the purchase of The Magnolias, was Mary Beavis, a teacher, who had grown up at The Magnolias. Several strangers were competing for Lot 51, too. With Mrs Beavis's determination and others in the competition, the bidding went way-up beyond the amount expected. Starkey remained his usual calm self and eventually The Magnolias was knocked down to him, by a sympathetic auctioneer, for £2,150, as it reached the high reserved price.

Betty was led away, to the tea 'room' where she was in a state of shock and trembling, wondering where on earth they would get the deposit from, let alone pay off the large amount. Her brother, from the north of England, who had an appreciable amount of "brass", came immediately to the rescue. With his financial help and some friends and Betty's return to teaching, the couple weathered the very unexpected, storm and became the freehold owners of their charming home.

Those who were bidding for The Magnolias were none too pleased that as it reached the reserve price it was quickly knocked down to Starkey. The auctioneer was not 'selling away' again. It was a prize well deserved by the Starkey family.

Len and Betty Starkey stayed on in the village, raising their girls, who attended the village school and later the Alfred Colfox School. Mary, the eldest daughter gained a place and went up to Oxford University. Anne specialised in languages and Susan took up teaching. The family has remained close.

Starkey retired from teaching in 1977, continuing as a Lay Reader. He was the pioneer of the Bridport Twinning Association with St Vaast La Hougue, in France and encouraged local junior schools to include French in the curriculum.

Mrs Starkey continued to teach for some twenty years. As she so openly said, "My teaching paid for the house. " She became a valued member of the Burton Bradstock Parish Council and other organisations.

Almost fifty years on, the house remains in the Starkey family; one, of only a very small number, which has not changed hands since the Sale. The Magnolia trees, with their delicate lemon scented flowers, still flourish.

★★★★★★★★★★

Memorials to the Hansford family can be found in the church.

THE ROOKERY

<u>Lot 52</u> '*a long term investment, free of maintenance cost*', was how the auctioneers had described The Rookery. Situated below the church, over the stone bridge, the largest and another of the beautiful places for sale, in Burton, also lay in the old, picturesque and secluded part of the village. Its name had been formulated, in more recent times, from the gathering of rooks that had nested in the elm trees. Their calling and chattering was familiar to all who passed along the track to Timber Bridge.

Most of the building dated from Tudor times, with very interesting period features. In particular the doors, stone-mullioned windows, staircase, a seventeenth century decorated plaster ceiling, the fireplaces and a portion of plank and muntin partition were of great architectural interest. No one knew, how legend arose, that it was once the home of monks, or that it was reputed to have a secret passage to the church. In all probability it was a farmhouse and had come within the ownership of the Church. All records of what The Rookery actually was had been lost in the mists of time; its more recent records were destroyed in the blitz on Exeter.

★★★★★★★★★★

By 1871, termed a farmhouse, the property appeared to be divided up, (maybe as a result of a Will). The heads of the four households there were a farmer, a tailor, Greenwich Pensioner and the foreman of the mills. It is known that The Rookery changed hands in 1875 to Mrs Mina Legge of the Court House, Litton Cheney for £1,050 and on her death it was sold, by the Trustees, to the Pitt-Rivers Estate. General Pitt-Rivers evicted some tenants, on occasions and in 1897 he ordered that Mrs Gillett, seventy-five years old and ailing, had to come out of The Rookery, against her wishes.

Subsequent families were Travers, Wallers, and Robinsons. The latter, in the 1940s, were important clients at Bishop's Riding School and Mrs Robinson, attired in her black habit, would be seen, riding side-saddle, through the village. [Dame] Peggy Ashcroft, the actress, was one of many notable guests at the Rookery.

In 1943 Jennifer Robinson was married from the house, walking on the arm of her father, of Harley Street, to the church, attended by two small bridesmaids. The bridegroom, Lieutenant Bulmer, of the Bulmer cider-making family, from Herefordshire, was killed soon after, whilst on active service.

★★★★★★★★★★

Now as the hammer was raised, all was up to Doctor Ryan. The auctioneers presented The Rookery as one of the most attractive houses in the district to be offered for sale; *'the attractive and well appointed period residence of distinction'*. In very nice condition, with four main rooms downstairs and service accommodation, together with seven bedrooms, two with hand-basins, the master bedroom, with a Tudor fireplace and ancient beams, measured 17 feet 9 inches by 16 feet. There were two bathrooms, *'both with bath and WC and good heated linen cupboards'*. The loft was reached by means of a hatch. The drawing room was 23 feet 6 inches by 15 feet, having panelled walls, with a fine decorative plaster ceiling and open Tudor hearth. All the principal rooms were centrally heated and with an impressive staircase, cloakroom and workroom, it was above every other house in the Sale. The whole formed an extremely well appointed, family house; a residence for entertaining. The speculators, gathered in the marquee, knew that it would make a fine country hotel.

Adjoining it was a large studio, giving a secondary residence, which had been converted from the original stables and the overhead loft. A garage, outside WC, boiler house and garden stores complemented the whole place. With the advance in motoring and the use of larger cars, the narrow main gateway, made for horse-drawn vehicles, presented some difficulties.

The immaculate gardens, intersected by the leat, which wended its way between the two mills, were a particular feature. Here, over many years, fêtes, garden parties and meetings had been held on a regular basis, as well as musical soirées. Prior to 1939, gymkhanas had taken place in the fields beyond the house.

Included with The Rookery, were an orchard and meadows. Although sometimes wet, these were ideal pony paddocks, totalling six acres. The house always seemed full of family and guests, whilst villagers were constantly calling there, for one reason or another. A septic tank was in use, with a drain across Magnolia Farmhouse land, and out of use, was an ice house, (or pit), which had been covered over, left from the days when the big houses bought ice.

****

Doctor Ryan, a doctor of medicine, had served in the Royal Navy during the Second World War and at the time of the Sale had a practice nearer London. The Ryans had lived at The Rookery for a number of years. They had two day-bungalows overlooking The Hive Beach and had originally visited the village years before the Sale. They were well respected and always supported local activities. Frances Ryan was known for her generosity and also her elegance and charming manner. Their three daughters had spent a great deal of their growing-up years in Burton Bradstock, regular patrons of Frank Bishop's riding establishment and as they went their own ways in life, returned, as often as they could, to their country home.

Staff were engaged at The Rookery and long retained had been Mr and Mrs Albert [Bert] Bull, as Head Gardener and Housekeeper, who, on their retirement, around 1948, moved to St Laurence's Cottage, (now called "Jackdaws").

The Ryans were sitting tenants, in 1958 but that did not prevent speculators considering the chance to secure such a fine investment. The tenants had purchased a repairing lease on the property which would run until December 1971. The rateable value was £92 and the annual rent £270.

Doctor Ryan successfully secured The Rookery for £5,000.

Extensive research by Michael Hansford, of Marnhull, has taken The Rookery's history back to around the middle of the eighteenth century. In March 1762, William Hansford, a blacksmith's son, born in Loders in 1719, joined the Royal Navy and had built up a substantial fortune from prize money, obtained from the capture of enemy vessels and successful battles at sea. He married Mary Adney, a widow, née Hansford, (a cousin?), of Chilcombe and settled with her into a pleasant house, which was The Rookery, although not always known as such. At this time he was on half-pay and a third Lieutenant, having recently served on HMS Kingston, a sixty gun vessel. By the time of his death, in 1799, Hansford had risen to the rank of commander.

Commander Hansford's codicil to his Will in 1793, stated, at great length, his wishes concerning the property in Burton Bradstock: *'I did not mention my dwelling house in my last will and fearing that my wife and children may not agree to live together, in that case if my wife comply with the particulars of my last will then the house may be parted in the following manner. My wife to have the best parlour as there is a door to go to it without going through the little parlour with the chamber that is over the said best parlour which is called the best chamber and the chamber the servant now sleeps in and the sheppard's house which may serve as a pantry and kitchen, with a little alterations in making a door through the sheppard's pantry and that part of the Court on the west side of the house, that is before the parlour windows. This is for her during her life and at her death my three children but if she do not comply with my last will or if she will be so imprudent to marry again then this is to be void and of no effect. The above is fearing that my wife and children may not agree but it is my earnest wish that they may continue to live together and that there be no occasion of any such parting'.*

★★★★★★★★★★

Doctor Philip Shemilt had trained, pre-war, at St Thomas's Hospital in London where Doctor Ryan was a consultant and had got to know him and his family and their holiday resort of Burton Bradstock.

Years later, in 1958, recalls Doctor Shemilt, when the village was up for sale, he drove down to Burton to discuss the purchase of The Rookery with Doctor and Mrs Ryan. As the Ryans had a twelve year lease still to run and considered their tenure was safe, it was agreed that Doctor Shemilt would bid for the property.

On his arrival in Burton on the morning of the Sale, Doctor Shemilt sat next to Doctor and Mrs Ryan, in the marquee but was dismayed to find that they had 'been up all night' and had decided to bid themselves. Doctor Shemilt had to content himself with the purchase of the Rookery Cottage and number 42 Darby Lane, both with sitting tenants and was unable to obtain possession of either for some ten years.

★★★★★★★★★★

Greta Heal recalled that the day of the gymkhana, which was held in The Rookery meadows, was an exciting one, for the village. *The Bridport News* of July 31st, 1936 advertised the Bride Valley Mounted Gymkhana and Annual Show at Burton Bradstock, when the gates, in the meadows beyond The Rookery, would open at 12.30 p.m. Ringside parking was 2/6d, admission 6d and there was to be open jumping, skittles, teas and refreshments. The day was to conclude with dancing in the Women's Institute Hall, to Reg Inkpen and his band.

★★★★★★★★★★

Rooks nested there and every spring, their shrieks and squabbling could be constantly heard by the passer-by, until Dutch Elm disease wiped out the trees, during the 1970s. Around this time, a row of huge conifers which had grown to a great height and girth, were felled. During the eighty years since they were planted, these had spread their roots right across the lane below the school. A slab, from one of those conifers, now forms a coffee table and a memory of the past.

After the death of Doctor and Mrs Ryan, the whole family has continued to retain a love of the place. The construction of a bridge across the mill stream, from the part of The Rookery, now known as "Swaffield", to Grove Road has caused division in the village, whilst a wild rabbit has been seen, sitting on the base of the bridge, contemplating a trip to nearby gardens across the stream.

Change is imminent with the proposed sale of The Rookery with an asking price of £1,750,000 (June 2007).

ROOKERY COTTAGE

<u>Lot 53</u> the Rookery Cottage, in Church Street, lay opposite the school.

On the front wall, of the cottage, were two buttresses which propped it up. This was common practice with older properties, when the walls bulged, rather than pull down the wall and rebuild as it would have 'disturbed' the property. Cottages had stood for several hundreds of years and would last a few more, it was reasoned. The Rookery Cottage had been divided into two sections, at one time.

The property consisted of a hall, living room, dining room, kitchen and a bathroom and three good sized bedrooms. Outside was a small courtyard and another flush lavatory. The main services were all connected. It was the modern conveniences that had lured Albert Bull and his wife, when they came with their employers to The Rookery, from the Home Counties and were allocated the cottage as their home.

This was the part of Burton Bradstock that had been most favoured by artists. Numerous paintings abounded looking, to and from Magnolia Farm, which showed the cottage, the bridge, with the path leading to Timber Bridge, beyond. The Rookery Cottage had been let, to the Ryans, on a full repairing lease until 1971, at a rent of £26 a year.

Doctor Shemilt, an acquaintance of Doctor Ryan, purchased Lot 53 for £700, after losing his chance to bid for The Rookery.

Ten years after the Sale, Doctor Shemilt was able to obtain possession. On paper and from a quick viewing it looked like a sturdy stone built place but the rear walls were made of cob [a mixture of clay and straw] and these were in a bad condition. A major rebuilding would be required and Doctor Shemilt reluctantly, decided, when the tenant vacated, to sell.

It came into the hands of Burton born and bred, Ronald Guyatt and his wife, Ruby, who lovingly renovated it, in keeping with the Victorian period. When the renovations were being carried out, a stone staircase and stone carvings, as well as "priest holes" were discovered. Did monks really live in this old part of Burton Bradstock and were ordered out at the time of the dissolution of the monasteries in 1539? Did it have some other religious connections? Who was it who fashioned those stairs and carved those walls? Uncovered, too, were the signatures of Charles Hitchcock and his young brother, Percy, apprenticed to him. They had worked on the property three-quarters of a century before in 1906.

Guyatt sealed the board, on which they had inscribed their names, back in to the wall. When all was finished inside, he set about outside pruning the overgrown old–fashioned, fragrant roses that adorned the cottage. The Guyatts lived out their days there, visited by their two daughters and their families and Ruby's sister, Beryl.

The Rookery Cottage changed hands again when an elderly owner was burgled, whilst in hospital. Today it is as picturesque as ever.

MAGNOLIA (FARM) COTTAGE

Lot 54 *'An attractive detached property, in a secluded position, substantially built in stone and thatched'.* The auctioneer read out the particulars. This had been the home of Miss Elfrida Buckler since 1891. Her father, Joseph Buckler, was well respected in Burton Bradstock, for his local knowledge and participation in all village activities. He was the last of the farmers, fishermen and flax spinners, who combined the enterprises.

The property was called Magnolia Cottage in the Sale catalogue but it was far too big for that reference. At one time, it was listed as a school for young ladies, under a Miss Gammis. In 1765 it had been reconstructed from the ruins of several cottages and outbuildings that ran along the ancient track towards Timber Bridge. Around 1830, it had again been refurbished by a bachelor sea-captain who lived there with his valet. The lid of the Captain's sea-chest formed the door to the back-stairs. Later the house served as the residence of a sail-cloth manufacturer, John Burt and by 1881 it was the home of Edward Rendall, aged twenty-eight, a twine manufacturer, when it was further linked with the spinning mill. It subsequently was rented to the Bucklers in 1891. Until the closure of the flax spinning mill, in the early 1930s, a path was constantly in use from Magnolia Farmhouse, over a wooden bridge, from the orchard, across the stream.

★★★★★★★★★★★

Joseph Buckler was born in the village of an ancient Burton line. His wife Elizabeth [Bessie], née Wrixon, was born at South Poorton, near Powerstock. The Bucklers had moved from their temporary home at Sunnyside, soon after the birth of their son, Reginald, when Elfrida, [known as Freda], was eighteen months old.

The house had six bedrooms, the main one measuring 16 feet 9 inches by 10 feet 6 inches, a good sized hall, 11 feet by 6 feet 6 inches, two generous reception rooms, 16 feet in breadth, Georgian in style, with high ceilings and wide doors. The kitchen was equipped with a Victorian, traditional coal-fired range, the original means for cooking. A bell-system connected all the rooms to the servants' quarters. The kitchen floor was covered with blue flagstones, where a secondary, narrow, winding staircase ran up from the kitchen to what was originally the servants' sleeping quarters.

All the front windows had, casement shutters and were fixed in place by a large iron hook which stretched right across the whole of the window. When not in use, the shutters folded back into the window recess. The front door could be secured by another large, heavy iron hook that spanned the width of the door and hooked into the door jamb. It would have been very difficult to break-into the front hall! In renovating, the sea-captain had done his best to obtain privacy and security.

The back-kitchen, with double doors, had a drain running through it and a floor of blue tiles. At one time, this section had been used as stabling. Across the lawn was a derelict two bed-roomed cottage, which the family had utilised for many years in its heyday and a conservatory, adjoined the drawing room, where a vine grew. A well was covered in but had been used for all the household water necessities, until mains water was connected.

**********.

In 1902, Buckler, had scaled the roof between the cottage and the other adjoining three, to make a break in the thatch, when a spark from the factory chimney caught one of them on fire. Magnolia Farm Cottage was all that was left of that cluster of dwellings, below the school.

Freda's mother, an experienced cook and housekeeper, had set-up one of the first guest houses in the area, in the 1890s, taking in professional and business families. At that time, the working-class had only Bank Holidays and Sundays free. The families who came to visit, would stay for a month or six weeks, bringing the children with their nursemaid, governess and friends. The man of the family would remain for part of the vacation, returning to business, after a couple of weeks. Full board was provided, with a six course dinner in the evenings. Originally the families arrived by pony and trap, hired to meet them from the railway station at West Bay. Later a motor vehicle would bring them out to the lodgings. Wedding guests were accommodated and receptions were held there. Local girl, Jane Bartlett had a 'grand' wedding when she married into a Liverpool business family. The guests who had travelled south stayed at Magnolia Farm and the photographs of the wedding party were taken on the lawn, with the large fig tree as a backdrop.

Douglas Northover related, that the village boys would creep down over the bridge, to peep in at the dining-room window, at the dinner table, loaded with good food. If Mrs Buckler caught them, she would come out and give each of them a huge hunk of fruit cake. This only encouraged them, all the more!

Until electricity came in the 1930s, lighting was provided by candles and oil lamps, requiring a daily task to clean, trim the wicks and replenish the lamps. Water, originally pumped-up from the outside well, was heated on the kitchen range and in the copper, as was the procedure in all the homes. Wash stands and chamber pots were placed in all of the bedrooms and water carried to and fro. Bed linen and napery were boiled in the copper, with a "blue bag" to accentuate the whiteness and hung to dry on the privet hedges. Ironing was done with flat irons, of various sizes and weights, according to the piece of linen, or garment to be ironed. These irons were lined up on a shelf above the kitchen range, where they were heated on one of the hot-plates and then covered with a shiny metal sheaf to protect the cloth; most of the materials were pure linen, damask or silk, with much lace trimming.

The old lavatory, built around 1830, was intact but had been superseded by an Elsan closet, by 1958, housed in its own, new tin building. The *dunegan*, a Dorset term, as Mrs Buckler called the original lavatory, adjoined the stables and was completely surrounded by privet bushes. The kitchen clothes' line was strung from the wooden facia board to a lilac tree, giving a good excuse to pretend that one had gone to hang out, or bring in the washing, rather than be seen to be visiting the lavatory!

★★★★★★★★★★

Inside this building, which measured about 8 feet square, was a long wooden box with a hole cut in it. There was a wooden cover to go over the lavatory seat. Behind, fixed to the wall, was another box, lined with tin, which spanned the whole length. Into this contraption, a sack of lime would be emptied. A handle protruded from the box. This could be pulled in and out and the 'covering' contents would fall into the pit below. No one ever remembered the lavatory having to be dug out, so effective was the lime that was used and because the house was low lying, near the river, the contents would have easily decomposed and seepage occurred. An old drain ran across the orchard to the river.

66. (L) Elfrida Buckler and her friend Clara Swaffield (former postmistress) 1950s. Inset 66a Elfrida, 1914. Soon after she set-up the first self-catering bungalows.

★★★★★★★★★★

67. Magnolia Farmhouse and the cottages below the school before the fire in 1902.

68. Magnolia Farmhouse 1990. Inset 68a the first holiday chalets were set-up there in the 1920s.

69. Lot 115, The Dove Inn, Southover after the blizzard in 1978. Inset 69a Some of the regulars. (L to R) Tony Legg, Desmond Wylde, Alfie Hutchings, Dennis Bullock, with the hosts, Gus Wylde and Mrs Wylde. 1950s.

70. Mill Terrace as it is today. Inset 70a Dennis and Kathleen Burton 1958.

71. *The River Bride in flood, circa winter 2000.*

72. *Mrs Olive Aylott looks out on surplus rain water flowing through the central streets of Burton Bradstock, May 1979. Inset 72a, The Aylott family in 1954. (L to R) Reuben, Olive and their elder son, Alec.*

73. The old chapel was converted to a Poor House and then a dwelling, Number 9 Burton Bradstock, which was sold by the Pitt-Rivers Estate in 1951, pictured here in 2007.

74. Lot 78, Cogden Farmhouse in 2000. Inset 74a, the fire in 1914.

174

In her younger days, Freda was a clerk to the mill-owner, Henry Rendall, a bachelor, who had asked her to marry him, which she declined. Her fiancé, George Morris, a sergeant in the Royal Marines, died in the influenza outbreak of 1918. She spent some years as an Electoral Roll Enumerator but even with these other jobs, had always assisted her mother in running the house. She had an uncanny sixth (or was it seventh?) sense and had claimed to have seen, a female apparition pass through the dining room, on several occasions. This lady, in a long gown, appeared to go through the wall but many years later, her niece discovered a blocked-up doorway, just where the ghost was supposed to vanish!

With her father, until his death in 1933, Freda reared cattle, pigs and poultry on the plots of land adjoining the property, renting additional fields, in the village, from the Pitt-Rivers Estate. This was when the premises took on the form of a farm and they inserted 'farm', in the property's name, in order to benefit and clarify their business enterprise. Until he acquired land of his own, Reg, too, kept cattle, pigs, poultry and ponies. He gave riding lessons to the visitors, in the paddocks. When war broke out in 1939 rooms and meals had been provided for families, who had been evacuated from London and Southampton.

The whole place became a holiday centre again after 1945. Visitors came back year after year, either accommodated in the house, the chalets, or camping in the paddocks, amongst the apple trees, beside the river.

★★★★★★★★★★

The cooking facilities in the two wooden and asbestos holiday bungalows were oil-stoves and lighting was from paraffin oil-lamps, later connected with a rather home-made electricity supply. The bedrooms each had wash stands. Water was obtained from a standpipe in the orchard. The lavatories had originally been the bucket type but replaced by Elsans. These chalets were some of the first self-catering units in the district. A serious fire had broken-out in one of them in 1931, when Ron Guyatt and Bert Williams, who were the first on the scene, 'rolled out the hoses', (from the village fire-appliance).

On her mother's death, in 1947, Freda took over the running of the holiday complex and continued to rear animals and poultry. Geese were her special interest. With access to the river, they produced large, healthy eggs and strong stock.

★★★★★★★★★★

In 1958, Freda was sixty-seven years old. It had come as a immense shock to her to find that her home was about to be sold and she had worried a great deal about it since the Sale was announced. The Sale particulars stated that Miss Buckler had installed the Elsan closets, a Diana stove, water to the paddocks and two wooden chalets. The rent was £19. 10s a year, which was to be increased on Lady Day 1959 and the rateable value was £12. She paid £8. 10/- a year extra for the paddocks.

Numerous speculators had called to view the property. Beyond the front lawn, was a partly walled garden with old varieties of apple trees and a medlar. In the orchard were more apple and pear trees and bushes bearing a small type of plum, known locally as "Christians". The paddocks amounted to 2½ acres, with river frontage.

Freda's brother, Reg, stood up in the Sale Marquee. A tall and imposing man with a strong voice, he informed the crowd, that Magnolia was liable to serious flooding. This was, indeed, quite accurate.

★★★★★★★★★★

The Bucklers had experienced severe flooding, on many occasions. One of the worst floods had been during the First World War. The flood water at Magnolia was three feet deep in the dining-room, which lay at the higher end of the house. The kitchen, back-kitchen, lawn and grounds had been flooded to a depth of over ten feet. Freda's chicken had been swept, out to sea, at Freshwater and she and her mother, had manoeuvred themselves around the ground floor rooms, as the water receded, by standing on chairs.

Joe Buckler had to give his energies to saving stock and equipment at the mill, which also took the full brunt of the flood. Another bad flood had occurred in 1955. Heavy thunder storms had brought thousands of tons of water racing down the Bride Valley. It was haymaking time and the mowing-grass, lying in the fields, choked the drains and waterways.

★★★★★★★★★★

There was some strong competition in the bidding for Magnolia Farm Cottage. Several speculators were keen to get their hands on the property, including Mrs Beavis, RB Howarth's daughter, who had just missed out on buying The Magnolias, further up the road but although being financially stretched and having to go beyond what she had anticipated, Reg acquired the property, on Freda's behalf, for £1,350. Tears of joy were apparent all around.

A cheer went up from the villagers, when the gavel came down in Freda's favour, as she was very well liked and was so much part of the old establishment.

For another twenty years, Freda Buckler lived on at Magnolia, surrounded by her dogs, letting out rooms in the house and the two chalets in the old orchard, (these were originally in the cliff fields. Freda had bought them and they were dismantled and re-erected in the orchard, in the 1920s). She saw to the administration, without the aid of a telephone. On the change-over days, she was assisted by women from the village and from time to time, by her friend, Bert Williams, who regaled the visitors with his tales of the locality. She became well known for her success in rearing goslings and passers-by in the lane and the visitors, enjoyed chatting to her as she had so much local knowledge to reveal to them. She entertained friends and family and gave help to many less fortunate than herself, besides giving practical jobs to Jack Way.

Floods still swamped the property, on occasions but Freda was used to putting up the flood boards, which were not always sufficiently high or strong enough to hold the water back. The cleaning up afterwards was just routine.

During the night of 17th January 1977, Elfrida Buckler was found dead in the house. She had always had an empathy with the number seven, all her life, being born on the 7th (which was a Sunday) of the 7th month. She had passed away, peacefully in her home aged eighty-seven years. Her niece, Elizabeth, modernised the house, (it still had wash-stands in all the bedrooms) and continued to run it as a holiday centre. When renovations were carried out in 1977, a George III penny, dated 1756, embedded in the sitting-room hearth, was discovered, by Frank Beazer, a local builder.

Two new chalets were built in the old vegetable garden to replace the original wooden ones, which had by then stood for some sixty years. When planning permission was refused for a further two units, to make the enterprise viable, Magnolia had to be sold, an immense wrench for the family. A petition was signed by 'both factions'of the villagers, to oppose the plan. After the sale of Magnolia Farmhouse, in the 1990s, the height stipulation for the existing chalets was waived and the dwelling was raised by the new owner.

****

The Environmental Authority, carried out a flood alleviation scheme for the village. This entailed putting a bank across the centre of the plot, spoiling it for ever. Whilst preventing flood water rising from that direction, it has done little to prevent the river, when in flood, finding its natural way over Timber Bridge, up the footpath and into the Rookery Meadows and the garden of Magnolia Farm, where the water-table is high; the direction in which the water has always risen.

The old servants' quarters has recently been extended, with interesting architecture and the property and grounds have been split into two separate sections. Both are in the hands of couples with a love of Burton and for Magnolia Farm. Geese still graze the paddock beside the river, dogs run freely. People come and go there, enjoying its tranquillity. A Union flag flutters in the garden, as the property enters another phase of its long history.

THE ROOKERY GARDEN

Lot 55 was *'a fertile and secluded garden',* over ½ an acre, lying opposite The Rookery and adjacent to Magnolia Farmhouse, with the mill stream running beside it. This piece of land had become the garden to The Rookery, following a fire that had destroyed several cottages, at the turn of the century. The soil was fertile loam [alluvial] and the whole piece, was virtually enclosed. There was a constant, melodic rush of water over the weir, at the end of the garden, which formed an attractive feature. Doctor Ryan paid the Estate

£4 a year rent. The rates were included in The Rookery payments. Mains electricity and water were nearby. This plot would make an ideal building site. Doctor Ryan was determined to secure this asset to his recently purchased house and paid £225.

> It continued as a garden, producing beautiful vegetables and fruit for the Ryan household, tended by gardeners, Arthur Bartlett, Steve Northover and David Roper, over the years. Eventually, it was sold as a building site in the early 1990s. Poole Brothers, Bridport builders, bought it and built a fine house.

THE OLD FLAX SPINNING MILL

Lot 56 If the walls could only speak! Here Roberts had set up his flax and hemp spinning mill in the 1780s. Hundreds of men, women and young children had laboured in appalling conditions, for very little reward, in this factory. Roberts built the original mill or renovated an existing one, there being numerous references to mills in Burton. The mill listed in the 1958 sale was a comparatively new one, built after the fire in 1874.

★★★★★★★★★★

In *The Spinners,* a novel based on industries, published in 1918, Eden Phillpotts, described the mill as '*a heterogeneous pile of dim, dun colours and irregular roofs, huddled together with silver-bright excrescences of corrugated iron. A steady hum and drone as of some gigantic beehive ascended from the mills.* '

In a letter to Mrs. Thomas Hardy whilst researching for *The Spinners*, Phillpotts wrote, '*Burton Bradstock is a delightful theatre for a story…… . most of the people at the little mill are women and girls.* '

To his daughter he penned, '*This is quite a sleepy hollow where I am working, a gorgeous and friendly little hamlet full of simple beauty. The folk are more articulate than the Devonshire Moor men and very winning and very, very poor. I hate to think how little the eleven girls in the little spinning factory are getting for their labours. They work ten hours a day and only skilled spinners get much more than a penny or two pence an hour. Yet some of their work involves much cleverness and a great deal of physical energy, for those who watch the spindles have to be on their feet dancing about all the time.*'

★★★★★★★★★★

Approached by an unmade private track, the flax spinning mill, consisted of a stone and slated building, 120 feet by 52 feet, 16 feet high, with high double entrance doors. The original water turbine and gear were still there and the occupier was entitled to draw 'tail' water from the sluice at The Grove Mill. Roberts had constructed a leat, which flowed from his swingling [processing the raw materials] mill at The Grove, to this spinning mill, providing a head of water driving the turbine for the looms. In order to do this Roberts had demolished a cottage. By means of hatches, the main river was diverted to flow to The Grove Mill and on to the spinning mill, off Mill Street. The water then found its way behind Shadrach Dairy Farm and on to join the River Bride.

A spacious, partly metalled yard fronted the old mill and a paddock was let to Edgar Hawkins at £5 per annum. The whole area totalled about 1¾ acres. The County Council owned a shed on the premises, used as a fire station, for which a ground rent of 1/- a year was paid. For the rest, the Cheney family, paid £30, on an oral tenancy and rates of £45.

It was an invaluable asset to the business and the family was relieved to buy it for £850.

> The old mill was used as a store until Cheney's garage was sold and has remained in a static state.
>
> A planning application has been sanctioned to build ten residential homes. The spinning mill and its surroundings had been left to Nature and an application to build on the brown-field site has divided the inhabitants. There are few who would, or could afford, to miss the opportunity, although this lies in the over-developed heart of the village but it will save the old building and remind generations to come of a piece of village history. The factory with its ghosts of exploited children, hard-worked and ill-paid flax and hemp processors, spinners and weavers, deserves a new lease of life.

THE MANAGER'S HOUSE

Lot 57 Not far from the old flax spinning mill was the Mill House. Until a quarter of a century before, it had housed the mill manager. He was on the spot to control work at the factory and took in apprentices who paid for the privilege. The warehouse and office, known as the Counting House, lay only a stone's throw away.

★★★★★★★★★★

Mrs Edward Ackerman, (*Acerman* in the Sale catalogue), was a long-standing tenant. Her late husband had been the manager and they had lost their little daughter some years earlier. Then, one day, news was brought to her from the mill that her beloved son, Eddie, had been killed. He was an engineer and was adjusting one of the machines but had failed to shut it down. In those days, there were no safety-guards on the machines and to the horror of other employees, he was caught in a belt and whisked up and fatally injured. Mrs Ackerman, never recovered from these tragedies and seemed a lonely and sad lady. She was always dressed completely in black.

★★★★★★★★★★

This former Mill House, set back off Mill Street, was a handsome property with three bedrooms, a large back-house, flush WC, with drainage to a cesspit and two good attics, for which the tenant paid £23. 10s annual rent; all rated at £7 a year. Mains water and electricity were connected.

It was sold for £675 and according to the newspaper it appears that the purchase was made 'on behalf of the tenant' by a MG Cookman. A separate record quotes that it was purchased by Fred Welch, a Bridport property landlord. He certainly showed an interest.

MILL TERRACE

Lots 58, 59, 60 and 61 formed Mill Terrace. The row of four houses, adjacent to the old flax spinning mill and opposite Mill House, nestling under the south wall of the church, had been built by Roberts, in 1806, as a warehouse and counting house. Many were under the misunderstanding that Mill Terrace had been built as cottages, by Roberts, to house his workers. When the mill closed, the warehouse and office had been converted, by the Estate, to good, well designed homes for local families. An interesting bay-window remained at number 3. Mrs May Legge, née Tucker, remembered that this was the window of the office and the manager had a commanding view of the comings and goings at the mill. Sidney Shipp had memories of attempting to climb up inside the (then lowered) factory chimney with his friend, Ray Ackerman, where there were brick ledges, seemingly designed for that purpose.

At number 1 Mill Terrace, lived Bobby Cammell, a bachelor fisherman. He had taken on the tenancy after the death of his father and lived there with his mother.

Each house was made up of a sitting-room, about 18 feet long, living-room, in the region of 11 feet by 9 feet and 8 feet high, with a kitchen-range. Behind was a scullery. A landing, three bedrooms, two of a good size, with and a bathroom, completed the accommodation. Mill Terrace was modern and much sought after in the Sale.

The back windows opened on to the churchyard. The graves and headstones lay close to the wall of Mill Terrace where those of the Roberts's family and old Burtoners, many who had worked at the mill, were buried. The annual rents were £39. 10/-, for numbers 1 and 2, (to be increased by 10/-) and £35 p. a. , for the others. The tenants paid the rates of £12. All the drainage flowed to a septic tank in the garden of the old Mill House.

Lot 59 was secured by the tenant, the blacksmith's mother, Mrs Burton, for £500. Lot 60 was the home of two widowed sisters, Bessie Thorner and Ermaline [Ermie] Brett, née Swaffield.

Numbers 1 and 3, were bought by speculators, at £500 each. AS Knight, stepped in again, buying number 1 and FRGN Sherrard, of Dorchester, who had speculated in the 1951 sale, secured number 3. Lot 61 had Mrs Parrott living there as tenant and was bought by the outgoing landlord of The Three Horseshoes, Harold Greenham, for £700. This was the best in the row as it was on the end, furthest away from the road, bordering the gardens and the old rope walks.

Owners came and went at Mill Terrace. Gertie Cammell died in 1969 and Bobby, stayed on at number 1, until his untimely death in 1973, following years of suffering from a motor-cycle accident, when he was returning to barracks, as a National Serviceman. He lost the lower part of one of his legs. A horrendous tragedy for a talented footballer.

Bobby Cammell was well known and respected, one of the last seiners, descended from a long line of Burton people. John Eastwood, paid tribute to him, in an obituary in *The Bridport News* . He wrote of Bobby's gentle but sometimes shy, gruff nature, his dedication to the fishing tradition and his enthusiasm to raise money for various charities. Bobby's favourite song was *"Gone Down to Hilo"* and Eastwood concluded, that no more would Bobby's voice be heard in Burton singing, "Oh Wake 'em, Oh Shake 'em", as Bobby had, himself, "Gone down to Hilo".

★★★★★★★★★★

Ermie and Bessie passed on and their home was purchased by relatives of another local family, wanting to settle in the village. When Harold and Carrie Greenham died, number 4 Mill Terrace, was bought by John Eastwood.

New owners have discovered that the numbers of the gardens of Mill Terrace, do not relate to the numbers of the houses. This complication never bothered the original tenants, who chopped and changed according to the circumstances.

In the garden area is a deep man-hole where the water still surges through as it did when the spinning mill was in action, the lowered factory chimney now completely dismantled.

★★★★★★★★★★

Mabel Burton, her son, Dennis and his wife Kathleen and their son, John, remained at number 2 Mill Terrace, their life caught up in the work of the blacksmith's shop and service to the church and community.

After Mrs Dennis [Kathy] Burton moved to Bridport in 2006, the new owners, Mr and Mrs Philip Milner, from Lymington, set about renovating the property. They discovered that the rafters ran horizontally along the whole of Mill Terrace, a style known as "shedding" used in warehouses and workplaces and that the stout floorboards were strengthened with metal binding.

Most interesting and somewhat spooky was the discovery, after the lock on the sitting-room door was removed, on May 22nd 2006, of three names, pencilled underneath. These were "Montague", the Bradpole based builder, who undertook work for the Pitt-Rivers Estate, Hile, an employee and Swaffield, the carpenter and the inscription was dated May 22nd 1936!

SHADRACH FARM

75. *Shadrach Farmhouse circa 1900.*

Lot 62 was catalogued as '*a rich dairy and grazing farm.*' The house and farm buildings were situated at the northern end of the village; the land took in Annings Lane and the meadows beyond. This superb farm, mostly good loam on clay, totalled 112 acres and consisted of a large farmhouse, two cottages and some fine buildings, with the benefit of Annings Lane and Bredy Road providing good access to the lush fields. The river dissected it all. Some of the land was very level and the early growing meadows, along the river, were ideal for milk production. When Frank Bishop's riding establishment was in operation, the soft, flat ground, by Arch Bridge, was ideal for schooling riding pupils and ponies. In the meadows, hemp could still be found growing 'wild' from the days when it was cultivated for making ropes, sacks and other durable articles.

Shadrach Farmhouse, was the most picturesque in the village and had modern conveniences. The Royal Commission for Historical Monuments, in 1952, listed it amongst the outstanding properties in Burton and gathered that the house had been considerably altered over the years.

Mains water had been laid on to the cattle drinking-troughs, by the late tenant, Frank Bishop. The row of pig sties needed re-roofing and Bishop had approached the Estate, on this, some time before. £282 had been spent by the Estate, in 1957, on Shadrach Farm and there was a sum of £160 provisionally allocated for 1959. The farmhouse was mainly stone and tiled, with a hall and two good sized reception rooms, three first floor bedrooms, the attics, previously used as servants' accommodation, as well as a kitchen, 17 feet 6 inches by 10 feet, a storeroom and the traditional backhouse. The advantage of the house was that there was a bathroom. The main sewer was connected to number 21. With the new developments in Annings Lane, springing up, a mains sewer had been laid, in the vicinity of the farm.

The cottages, had been renovated and 22 Burton Bradstock, had been converted into one dwelling, under a Housing Act grant. Numbers 21 and 22 had two and three bedrooms, respectively and were occupied by farm workers and situated handy to the farm, in an idyllic setting, at the foot of Gages Lane.

★★★★★★★★★★

Frank Bishop and his wife had lived there since the mid 1920s. The elder Bishop son, Peter, born in 1923, had been killed in the Second World War, serving in the Royal Air Force. A former Bridport Grammar School pupil, he had volunteered at the outbreak and had trained as a pilot in Canada and the United States of America and at the time of his death on March 16th 1944, he was a Flight Sergeant, assigned to protecting shipping. His plane was brought down over Sicily and he had no known grave.

By a strange coincidence Barbara, (later to marry his brother Tony but not then acquainted with the Bishop family), was working as a clerk in the main Bridport post office. The news of Peter Bishop's death was wired through to Bridport and it was Barbara's job to then inform the post master, or mistress, of the village where the serviceman came from, of the wording of the telegram. At only sixteen years old, Barbara telephoned the grave news through to Clara Swaffield, the Burton Bradstock post mistress who was supposed to transcribe the message, and deliver it to the next of kin.

On hearing the dreadful news, Miss Swaffield and her sisters, who assisted her, broke down and were so distraught that they told Barbara that they could not face having to deliver the telegram to Mr and Mrs Bishop. Barbara immediately assessed the situation and told the Swaffield sisters that she would arrange for a telegram boy to go out to Burton, which she did.

Tony, the younger son, also a Grammar School boy, had volunteered for the services, too, putting his age on a year to get in. He served in the Royal Air Force and trained in Southern Rhodesia. With two sons serving their country, Frank and Muriel Bishop had never considered the possibility of keeping them both, or at least one of them, at home, to help run the farm.

Freddie Mullins, the village newspaper agent, who ran a general store, remarked to Mrs Bishop, who happened to be one of his best customers, that it would be possible to keep her sons out of the services, in a reserved occupation, if they were required for agricultural work. She took great offence at this and never again ventured into the shop or ordered groceries. Mullins may have felt a tinge of guilt as he continued to deliver newspapers to Shadrach Farm. This went on throughout the remainder of the war, right up to the death of Frank Bishop, in 1957, when an account was requested and Tony Bishop received a bill for £700, after he had taken on the tenancy earlier than anticipated, by the tragic death of his father.

★★★★★★★★★★

At the outbreak of the First World War in 1918, Frank had volunteered for service. As a knowledgeable horseman, having hunted and ridden all his life, he found himself in the top cavalry regiment, the Blues and Royals. The war took him to serve in France, in the horrendous conditions that occurred during those battles. No doubt, because of his ability and quick presence of mind, he was eventually given a motor-cycle and became a dispatch-rider, much to his amusement and some dismay. He survived the carnage in France and always maintained that although he had joined the army as a competent horseman, he learnt "equitation", which stood him in good stead, later, in civilian life.

When he returned to West Dorset, he was devastated to find that his brother had sold up the family farm at Melplash and moved to Loders. Frank was granted the tenancy of a small farm, also in Loders and in 1921, he married Muriel Inkpen from Cogden Farm, Burton Bradstock. (Muriel, from a family of seven children, was the daughter of Samuel Inkpen, a gentleman farmer and Elizabeth, née Sims who had moved from Chettle, near Blandford, by horse and cart, driving the livestock on the hoof). Bishop was not too happy with the limitations of the Loders set-up. The tenancy of Shadrach Farm, at Burton, owned by the Pitt-Rivers Estate, came up and without hesitation, he took it on.

The years of an agricultural depression in the 1930s, soon followed and it was then that he turned his energies to establishing a riding school at Shadrach. With his smart, slim stature and good looks which made him stand out, on or off a horse and his perfect seat, together with his scrupulous attention to detail, he made an ideal "Master of Horse". It was a time when the wealthier people were visiting the country and staying at guest houses, hotels, or in their own holiday cottages. There were plenty of the 'smart set' of the day, visiting Burton, who could afford riding lessons and to hire horses for hacking.

Amongst his clients were [Dame] Edith Evans, who was not such a brilliant horse-rider as she was an actress and [Dame] Peggy Ashcroft, who became a friend to Muriel.

★★★★★★★★★★

With his wealth of riding knowledge and skills in handling horses and ponies,

76. Frank Bishop, farmer and Master of Horse, who was tragically killed the year before the Sale. Inset 76a His daughter-in-law, Barbara and granddaughters, Sally and Georgie.

Frank Bishop became extremely well known in the world of equitation. It was ironic that his early death, in 1957, should be caused by mechanical means.

Before, setting off to play a game of snooker, at Portland, one summer's evening, in 1957, he had been rolling a silage pit, in Annings Lane, driving a tractor, to help out on the farm, as his son, Tony, was suffering with chicken-pox and was unwell. News of a terrible accident was brought to Tony and his wife by a young village lad, in tears, who had come across the tragedy. Frank Bishop was pinned under the tractor. They raced to the scene and called an ambulance. Frank Bishop died in hospital, the following day. The village was once more in mourning for a well respected, member of the Bishop family.

★★★★★★★★★★

Picking up the reins, Tony took over Shadrach Farm completely and with Barbara, was working hard, with their farm employees, to make the enterprise viable. The immediate family unit included Tony's widowed mother, Muriel and their young children, Sally and Georgie. At the time of the Sale, their third child was expected, the following October.

At Shadrach Farm, in 1958, a dairyman was employed, to milk some fifty head of cows which took their daily stroll along Annings Lane, a narrow, rough road, which originally was a muddy lane, intersected with gates, that separated the fields between Burton and Bredy. The dairy cows were not too popular with the new residents in Annings Lane and the old track was soon up-graded, with a more suitable approach to the new housing developments.

Following his father's death, Tony Bishop and his mother received a visit from the Agent for the Pitt-Rivers Estate. There had been no written agreement with the late Frank Bishop and there was some question as to whether Mrs Bishop, or her son, could take on the tenancy. This had rambled on since Frank's death and was only finalised shortly before the Sale was published. Only a matter of days prior to the bombshell of the Sale falling on the village, it had been agreed that Tony Bishop could take over on a September 29th [Michaelmas] tenancy.

This was still not a signed contract and was a gentlemen's agreement. The Estate would not sanction Mrs Muriel Bishop as a tenant. However, the Agent did promise to get the pig sty roofs put in order. When the Sale took place, Tony was a sitting tenant but still only on a verbal arrangement.

Like their father, Peter and Tony were fine horseman. Tony and Barbara had married in 1948 and shared the living accommodation at Shadrach Farmhouse. Barbara who could ride horses, already, became fully involved in the farm and in particular the horse management. Following her father-in-law's death she assisted Tony in breeding and running race horses, with much success. One win, in due course, would prove to be of great advantage to them.

★★★★★★★★★★

As the Sale day loomed near, Tony Bishop, who was very popular in the village, Barbara and his mother, could not see their way clear, by any means, to buy the farm. It was going to require thousands of pounds! It was a harrowing time for them all to contemplate a new landlord and the unknown consequences. Prospective purchasers looked over Shadrach Farm and were enamoured with the lovely farmhouse and its setting and the good, easily worked land.

It was the morning of the Sale, that Tony paid a visit to his bank manager, who had persuaded him to attempt to buy the farm. This meant a considerable overdraft as 'lending money', as such, was still a thing of the future. Tony raced home, exclaiming to Barbara that they were off to the Sale marquee. She found it very hot inside even though she was wearing a cotton frock, being seven months' pregnant, at the time.

It was with this quick decision, in a matter of a few hours, that they bought their home and farm, that day, to an arousing cheer from the assembled Burton folk.

and Lot 82 a further 8 acres, was offered with Shadrach Farm and together it sold for £7,250.

Research by a Mr Stone, interested in his Portland ancestors, has revealed that the place got its name from Shadrach Stone, a Portland smuggler. Through the generations of the Stones of Portland, the majority of the firstborn males were christened, Shadrach. In the heyday of smuggling, Stone had used the money, acquired from his illicit activities, to purchase or rent properties and land some distance from where he was well known. In 1861, Mrs Sarah Stone, a lady of independent means, was living in Shadrach House and a field, in the Shadrach Farm particulars, listed in the Sale catalogue, was given as "Stone's Close".

★★★★★★★★★★

During the Second World War, Frank Bishop was an officer in the Burton Home Guard. The company met outside Shadrach Farmhouse on Sunday mornings for drill and rifle practice. A stack of live ammunition was kept in a store adjacent to the house and sometime after the war, a local fisherman was given the task of taking the remaining rounds out to sea and dumping them. This was fortunate as there was a fire at Shadrach in the years following the Sale and had the stock of explosives still been there, the whole place would have blown up.

★★★★★★★★★★

The New Year's Eve following the Sale, Tony Bishop had a bumper win with his racehorse which came just at the right time for the Bishops to pay off some of the huge overdraft incurred in buying the farm.

After he bought the farm, Bishop set-up a milking parlour in the fields in Annings Lane, which later formed the nucleus of a new farm, named Peacehaven. An application by the Bishops to convert the use of the homestead to an hotel was turned down, on the grounds, that there were ancient cruck trusses in the property. Later building took place all around, but the reason for the Bishop's refused application seemed petty, as the beams would have been incorporated as a feature.

Around 1969, the family became aware of impending changes in agriculture and problems looming up. With the scheme for the hotel turned down, they decided to sell. The house and yard were sold separately and Peacehaven Farm sprang up from the outlying land. In 1971, Tony and Barbara moved to Chideock to run the village stores and post office. Their son, Simon, born the October following the Sale, became a keen and successful golfer. He is now well established as a professional, with his own golf course.

Tony Bishop died in 1985. Barbara, still extremely active lived locally, in close proximity to her daughters and their families. Like so many of those in Burton at the time of the Sale, she found it difficult to go past her old home, with its poignant memories.

Another strange coincidence was that pre-war, coming from the London area, as a child, she had spent a holiday in Burton, with her parents, little realising that she would later set-up home in the village. They camped on the cliff and were washed out and were given shelter in a barn by Edgar Hawkins.

★★★★★★★★★★

Barbara had one strange tale to tell of her time at Shadrach, when she was washing-up, standing by the kitchen window, with one of her small daughters. A woman, looking rather Gypsy-like, in appearance, came to the window and vanished as quickly as she had arrived. Barbara looked out to see where she had gone but there was no sign of her. When she related this to her mother-in-law, without hesitation, Mrs Bishop said, "Oh that was Miss ----- . "

The daughter of a previous occupant of Shadrach Farm, in the early part of the 1900s, was known to haunt her home and had been seen on several occasions. Her family had made a hole in one of the bedroom doors for her to 'pass through'. It was known as "Miss ----'s hole" by the Bishops. Her tale was sad, as she had drowned herself in the reservoir on North Hill. Rumours as to the reason, rattled around the village, at the time but most people kept their counsel.

When Shadrach Farmhouse was sold, the new owner, had the house exorcised and the ghost was 'laid to rest' and has never appeared since.

Today, the house exuberates its quality, the yellow Ham stone standing proud against its local neighbours.

★★★★★★★★★★

Mrs Barbara Bishop died during the final stages of the writing of this book in December 2006. She considered it essential that future generations should know how it had been for the Burton people and it is enthusiasm like hers that has made it possible to write this account. In her late seventies, Barbara's vibrant personality and stunning good looks were still apparent and she so enjoyed reminiscing and telling *her* story.

BUTCHER GALE

Lot 63 was known as Lower Townsend, *'ripe for development'*, part of the farm that had given its name to the new council estate.

77. *Robert Gale, butcher and farmer who served in the Great War.*

Rob Gale had followed his father, William, as the local butcher and held a property, Hydrangea House, smallholding and business which had its own slaughter house, adjacent to the shop. In the First World war he had joined the Blues and Royals, serving throughout the duration with Frank Bishop. Although a retiring man he served on the Parish Council and was happy that the concert parties and pantomimes, as well as Young Farmers' variety shows, were planned, rehearsed and 'dressed' in the house. His wife, Gladys, niece Janet [Spier] were of a very gifted musical and theatrical family and the house reverberated with music and singing.

Wedge Cottage beyond the butcher's shop, was originally within the tenancy. Gale, a skilled butcher, supplied meat around the Bride Valley and Charlie Day was employed as the delivery man. Lower Townsend council housing development, had been built in the 1950s, from land owned by the Estate and after Douglas Hawkins's death Gale had taken over the remaining land and enlarged his holding.

Lot 63 amounted to 1½ acres with outline planning permission to build, for residential purposes. There was another ¼ of an acre, behind the barn in Grove Road. Water and electricity were connected and the main block had a frontage of 325 feet on to Annings Lane. The sewer lay nearby. The rent was £25 a year and the tenant had installed a water trough, water-bowls, a milking plant, a dairy, where the milk was cooled and the churns filled, for collection by the milk lorry. In addition, there were two sheds. Gale's cows, a herd of around fifteen Ayrshires, with their elegant, upturned horns, could be seen every day, being brought, through the streets, from outlying fields, driven by the dairyman, Stan Parsons. They sauntered through the main highway, along Mill Street, past the church and the two village greens, for milking.

The purchaser of Lot 63, was required to erect a chain-link fence, four feet high on the boundary of Lots 63 and 66, within six months. The latter was a newly built bungalow. At the time of the Sale, Gale, was far from well and had to vacate his sick bed to attend.

PLANNING PERMISSION FOR DEVELOPMENT IN GROVE ROAD

Lot 64 had outline planning permission for residential development and was to the west of The Grove House. Nearly ¼ acre in size, with a frontage of 70 feet onto Grove Road, it was let to Gale, on a Lady Day oral tenancy, at £2 a year. All the main services adjoined the site. This had been included with Lot 63.

Gale had thereby secured one of the most valuable areas in the village, as it was assured, that he could sell on for building.

Although building permission had been granted for a particular number of properties, when Gale sold on, the developers reapplied and were able to build far more residences than were originally sanctioned.

NUMBER 35, GROVE ROAD

Lot 65 was a pretty corner cottage, at the higher end of Grove Road, [Bull Lane/Duck Street], thatched and south facing. This consisted of a sitting room, 13 feet by 12 feet by 7 feet high, kitchen with a larder and three bedrooms, of average size. Outside was an earth closet, old stable and store shed. A large garden of 51 perches was noted as being *'fertile'*. There was a right-of-way, *'for all purposes'*, for Lots 68 and 69 and sanction for the owners of those properties to lay a drain to the sewer, subject to making good any damage. Rob Gale housed his farm worker there. This was Stanley Parsons, the dairyman, who paid the rates of £10, quite a high sum in comparison with other cottages.

★★★★★★★★★★

Parsons, who was born in Shaftesbury and worked much of his life in Wiltshire, had come to the village in the early 1950s and raised nine children on a farm worker's wage. When he moved to Burton, some of the elder children were off his hands and the family lived in several properties in the village before settling at number 35 Grove Road. One of these moves had been the result of a fire. The verbal rent that the Estate had agreed with Gale, for number 35, was £15.

★★★★★★★★★★

Electricity was connected but the householder shared an outside standpipe for obtaining water with the two other cottages at Sunnyside. Gale paid £350 for this cottage.

Peter Parsons, revealed that Rob Gale had questioned Stan Parsons, his farm worker, as to whether he wished to attempt to buy but had received a negative answer. Parsons and his wife had been living in the cottage as part of the contract.

Stan and his wife finally moved to live with family members, at Lower Townsend. He is immortalised in a photograph which shows him driving milking cows through the village, in the days when Burton Bradstock High Street had little traffic and no one was concerned about the twice daily ritual.

The Parsons family play an important part in local activities, amongst them are John, at Shipton Gorge, and Peter, Burton's builder and decorator and grandson Mark, who serves on the West Dorset District Council, (2007), as well as grandson, Gary Parsons, who keeps the cemetery in immaculate order.

★★★★★★★★★★

Changes ensued, in Grove Road. New properties were built, the old slaughter-house beside it, converted to a garage and the butcher's shop, after another butcher took over for a while, reverted to living quarters. The cottages changed hands.

NEWLY THATCHED

Lot 66 This *'compact modernised bungalow of character'* which stood along the road, in Duck Street [Grove Road], with a single bedroom and thatched roof was let to Freda Elton, née Symes, the widow of Bill Elton, the former Estate toll-gate keeper. It was constructed from a former old thatched cottage and a flat roof extension added. Similar additions would become quite common to many of the older properties.

The bungalow was one of the very few 'cottage type' properties that had a telephone; a new idea for the elderly, living alone. (The working people did not have telephones). The bungalow was let to Freda Elton on a 21 year lease or for life, if the shorter, at £10. 16s a year. This was a more realistic rent from the Landlord's point of view. The Eltons had retired to the old cottage in Grove Road, and the Pitt-Rivers Estate saw that it would be a good move to re-house them there on the spot, in a renovated property.

Mrs Elton did not acquire the bungalow. It was bought by a R Nesbit, of Exmouth, for £500.

Grove Road is attractive and Lot 66, later altered to a house, stands with other properties built since the Sale.

OLD HIGHER WAY

Lot 67 had for convenience, been renamed, Gale's Orchard, once part of Townsend Farm and sat in the heart of the new developments in Annings Lane. The catalogue even suggested that with 70 feet of frontage to Grove Road, with planning permission, it offered scope for development.

All the services were handy in the nearby road and measuring over ¼ acre, it had great prospects. The orchard was part of butcher Gale's holding and lay almost opposite his house and shop, sandwiched in between number 35 Grove Road, Lot 65, which he had just purchased and Freda Elton's bungalow, Lot 66.

Let on an oral, Lady Day tenancy, at £3 a year, Gale secured this Lot for £525.

SUNNYSIDE

Lots 68 and 69 Sunnyside had been well named. The sun was trapped behind the cottages and consequently, had early producing gardens, totalling 35 perches. Each cottage had two bedrooms, averaging 15 feet wide by 13 feet. Lot 69, fronting on to Middle Street, had a second entrance in Grove Road. In these cottages was so much of Burton's history embedded. These cottages and another adjacent in Grove Road, were considered amongst the oldest properties and both tenants' families had played a great part in the life of the village.

Lot 68, number 33 Sunnyside, was let to HG Thorner at an annual rent of £18. The cottage comprised a living room, kitchen, two bedrooms, a wash house and an earth closet. That garden amounted to 18 perches. Water was taken from a shared standpipe with numbers 32 and 35. Both properties had electricity connected and were rated at £5. The mains sewer was out in the road.

Number 33 was listed as '*a building of architectectural interest.* ' An attractive beamed ceiling was a prominent feature. The outside '*wash house*' was a reminder of the arduous tasks the women had performed, to cope with drawing and heating water and then undertaking the weekly wash, as well as bathing a number of children. The tenant, at number 33, an avid gardener, had provided the garden sheds and a greenhouse.

★★★★★★★★★★

Elderly, HG [Joe] Thorner was formerly a foreman at the spinning mill and always a fisherman, as were most of his family. Local legend had it that the swarthy appearance of some of the folk along the Chesil Coast, was inherited from their Spanish ancestors, who had been cast up on the beach from shipwrecks. Whatever the truth in this, the men were dark and handsome and the women were beautiful, black-eyed, with raven coloured hair. The Thorner family fitted this description well.

★★★★★★★★★★

Joe Thorner did not buy number 33, Sunnyside. It was sold to SW Wyatt of Hampton-on-Thames for £200, with Thorner as the sitting tenant. Later Wyatt's relative, Miss Myrtle Wyatt, from old Dorset farming stock, came to live there and carried out some modest modernisation.

★★★★★★★★★★

At, Lot 69, number 32 Burton Bradstock, lived the Aylott family. Olive Aylott, née Hitt, who was born there, by 1958, had inherited the tenancy from her parents. She had an oral agreement with the Estate and paid £16 a year. The cottage was similar in size to its neighbour and the Aylott's garden measured 17 perches. The Hitt family had commenced renting the property around 1891. Grannie Hitt, née Downton, a tall, handsome woman, a self-styled midwife, known as " the Angel" of the village, had delivered scores of babies, in primitive conditions, some with difficult births. Her qualifications came by way of experience.

The Aylotts had originated from Wiltshire and as builders had come to Burton in the 1920s, to work on the Barr Lane council housing project. The family moved into number 8 when the row was completed, later going back to the Hitt family home at Sunnyside, where Aylott, with his carpentry skills, had provided a cooking cubicle in the living room. The Aylotts secured number 32 Sunnyside, for £225.

★★★★★★★★★★

The Aylott sons, Alec and Edwin, his son, Marc, their uncle, Ted Hitt and his son, Gerald, were known for their football prowess and all the family were involved in village activities.

Olive and Reuben Aylott lived on at Sunnyside, enjoying having a number of grandchildren around them. Mrs Aylott continued to live alone there, following her husband's death. Almost twenty years after the Sale, the property was sold. Some of their descendants continue to live in the village.

★★★★★★★★★★

The Thorners and fishing skills and tales of wrecks, faded away and the younger members of the family moved elsewhere in the village, or to Bridport, where their good looks stand out still, amongst the crowd.

The cottages have undergone further modernisation and had extensions added.

Inside, the features have been emphasised and what was once functional for the working families of the past three hundred years are now adornments. Outwardly, that corner of the village is relatively unchanged.

TOWNSEND FARM

<u>Lot 70</u> a 'substantial and extensive property', was situated, in an excellent position, at the bottom of Shipton Lane and near to the recent developments in Annings Lane.

★★★★★★★★★★

It had been the home and farm premises of a branch of the Hawkins family, since the turn of the century. When Joseph Hawkins came out of The Three Horseshoes, where

78. *(Far R) Lot 70 TownsendFarmhouse and (L) Lots 71 and 72 with Archie Mitchell, friend and sister pictured around 1910. Inset 78a Isabelle and Joseph Hawkins. He set up a farming dynasty in Burton Bradstock, that was to last one hundred years. 78b "Margie" Chapman, née Hawkins, shortly after emigrating to Australia in 1959.*

he was the innkeeper, postmaster and baker, he and his family moved into Sunnyside, temporarily. In 1891 he had written to the Pitt-Rivers's Agent saying that (financially) "It has been very dull here (at the inn) of late. " Whilst at Sunnyside, he saw the cart-shed, land and activities associated with Townsend Farm and set about to change his mode of employment. Little did he contemplate that within a hundred years, his descendants would hold one of the largest farming enterprises in West Dorset.

The original acreage of Townsend Farm, was some 45 acres. Hawkins farmed there until too old to carry on, when one of his sons, who was serving in the Royal Navy, Douglas, was called back home. Another son, Conrad, had been killed in the 1914-18 War.

After his death, Conrad's fiancée, Elsie, a Wiltshire girl, (where he was stationed in the army), came to visit the family, in Dorset. They all took a liking to her, especially Douglas, who she eventually married making their home at Townsend Farm.

In 1941, aged 49, Douglas died, prematurely, leaving his wife to carry on the farm, with the help of Henry Pitman, the cowman. She did not enjoy good health and died in

1948. Her daughter, Margaret, known as Margie, had worked in Bridport, having been forced into 'the war effort' at the factory, at the onset of the war, along with many other girls who were too young to serve in the forces. This thwarted her ambition to train in pharmacy. After the war she had married and had her own family. Greta, shouldered much of the caring of their mother preventing her, too, from following a career away from home.

In its productive days, the farm had cattle, pigs and poultry. The cow-stalls and other farm buildings were situated behind the house; beyond lay the land and orchards that went with the farm. Two orchards supplied apples for gallons of cider which were made in the fine old barn, in the yard, behind the house. A cider press, crusher and several forty-gallon hogshead barrels could be seen in the ancient barn which became a gathering centre for the men of the village, where they passed around the cider "loving-cup", whilst 'sorting out the world'. The farm business was wound up on the death of Mrs Hawkins when the land was let to Rob Gale. Greta married, William Heal, from London, in 1949, who had been evacuated to the area, during the war. Greta's marriage, when she was given away by her uncle, Edgar Hawkins, was a very pretty village wedding.

★★★★★★★★★★

Margaret and her husband, Ray Chapman, a Puncknowle man, with their children, Della and Andrew, were living at Townsend Farmhouse at the time of the Sale, sharing the adjoining cottage with Greta and her family. Ray Chapman's parents farmed at Puncknowle and he worked, as an engineer, at the Brit Engineering Company, in St Andrew's Road, Bridport.

Townsend Farmhouse, had four bedrooms. Three of these rooms were about 12 feet 6 inches by 10 feet and the fourth a little smaller. The house had ample reception and utility areas; the latter the former cheese, cream and dairy room. Although this was a fine farmhouse, like the majority of properties in Burton, it had no bathroom and earth closets were used. The farm worker's cottage next door, in all, had three rooms.

Outside, the access was through imposing double gates to the farmyard where there were the magnificent ancient barn, a four-bay milking shed, used as garages, a store and piggeries. The garden and orchard completed a charming homestead.

★★★★★★★★★★

Margie, the elder daughter and Greta were a pretty pair. Greta was a leading lady, starring in the plays that the Pooh Club performed. As she matured she took part in all the musical entertainments, singing solo on many occasions and in the church choir, as well as joining several organisations and holding positions on committees. As well as dedicated to the church, three of the prominent organisations to which she and Bill devoted their energies, were the Parish Council, the Bride Valley Branch of the Royal British Legion and The Children's Society. Greta was one of those treasures, so difficult to come by, spending much of her working life, totally reliable, giving more to her work than would be expected, cleaning and cooking for several households.

★★★★★★★★★★

In the Sale catalogue, Lot 70 was listed as Townsend House and cottage. A good sized garden and still fruiting orchard, gave it a Thomas Hardy atmosphere. It had been a typical Dorset smallholding, in a delightful setting. Margaret Chapman paid £28 a year rental and the rates, which amounted to £7 a year. The old orchard, "Higher Way", was sold separately, as Lot 67. Rob Gale held the tenancy. Speculators sought to get their hands on Townsend House, with its ancient barn and picturesque yard, which had great potential for development. The Rural District Council also had its sights on Lot 70, under the watchful eye of RB Howarth.

The auctioneers swept the bidding along. Everyone waited, with bated breath, as the hammer dropped, leaving Townsend Farmhouse in the possession of the family, at a cost of £800.

Shortly after the Sale, Margie made a surprising announcement that she, Ray and their family were emigrating to Australia and would be selling Townsend House. This came as a dreadful blow to Greta. She and her family moved out and the Chapmans sailed for Australia, on the "Fair Sky", from Southampton at 4 pm., on the 3rd of March, 1959. Greta remembers this awful time with much sadness, as it was the end of her long family connection with Townsend and everything there.

The Chapmans put the sale of the property into the hands of Morey, the Bridport auctioneer. As Townsend House and buildings lay, conveniently adjacent to other council housing in Annings Lane, the RDC purchased it for the South Annings housing development.

Building did not start for some years and in the meantime, Richard [Dick] Ramsden, whose family had been living in the village for many years, rented from the RDC and moved his transport business into the yard. One of his drivers was accommodated in the farmhouse, which brought a new family into the area, in which they have remained.

Dick sold his business in 1962, when it was then moved to Poole and the yard remained empty until the council housing complex was started. All the interesting old buildings were knocked down. The fine old barn did not carry a listing order, as it would have done some years later and was gone for ever.

The Chapmans took time to settle in Australia and considered returning home at one stage. Della, their daughter, did come back for a few months but returned and settled in to the way of life "down under". Mr and Mrs Chapman, and the 'children' (the latter now middle aged), have been back to Burton over the years and Greta and Bill, visited them in Sydney, in 1999; a trip they took to celebrate their Golden Wedding anniversary.

Eventually, Chesil Court and other council accommodation sprang up on this ancient site. The house was sold off and its front aspect made bland, thereby losing its quaint, country charm and it remains a separate, private unit. The old farm gateway now forms the entrance to the council accommodation, some of which is the much needed Magna Housing.

Had Fate not dealt the family a hefty blow and they had been able to continue to farm there, this holding would have generated, for them, the largest area for development in the whole village. Contrary to some opinions, there *were* losers.

Greta Heal and her family have always been part of the life of Burton. The village owes much to their support and efforts, in so many ways. Now nearly fifty years on, Greta's eyes fill with tears, as she remembers the sunny and sometimes sad times, at Townsend Farm and the way life was in the village, before the Sale.

AN ENTREPRENEUR

Lots 71 and 72 In purchasing these Lots, another bidder stepped in. This time, it was someone who was known to the villagers. Jack Norris had been raised in the village and made his way in life in the netting business. The cottages had two bedrooms each and were tenanted by WC Gale, who was employed by the Estate and Mrs Churchill, a widow, from another local family. There was a complicated right-of-way and drainage clause in the details. Water for both cottages was obtained from a shared standpipe. Both had long, thin gardens reminiscent of the cottage industry of growing and processing flax and making ropes.

Norris purchased the two cottages, which adjoined Townsend House, for £200 apiece. As he was a Burton man, the crowd viewed the purchase far more favourably.

DISCUSSIONS in committee

As soon as the Sale of the West Dorset section of the Pitt-Rivers Estate had come to the notice of local officials, discussions had taken place.

RB Howarth was determined to save the village from development. Because of his wide connections, he was the first to know what was going on. He was involved in absolutely everything that happened in the district. His knowledge of what was happening was ahead of everyone else's. Council housing was needed in Burton. There was already a waiting-list and if all the tenants did not purchase their homes, there could be a number who might need re-housing.

This was a matter for the Parish Council and Rural District Council and RB Howarth Chaired both committees. Lots 73 and 74 were *withdrawn* prior to the Sale. The former was a derelict site, of three thatched cottages, following a fire, with one cottage just habitable, in all, 100 feet frontage to Annings Lane. Lot 74, a large site 135 feet along Annings Lane and with a depth of 120 feet was occupied as gardens.

In Bridport, the Borough Council was officially informed of the Sale in May of 1958. The Council rented two small plots from the Pitt-Rivers Estate and there were properties and land at West Bay that were of interest. A small committee was formed to negotiate prior to the Sale.

Plans submitted by Captain Pitt-Rivers for development, opposite Haddon House, in West Bay Road and George Street were refused, although the proposed plan for George Street was later granted, 'with substantial approval' by the West Dorset Planning Committee.

The Borough Council sub-committee met with Arthur Richards, acting for the Estate, to try to agree a price for Lots 136, 138 and 139.

WALTY AND BESSIE LEGG

<u>**Lots 73 and 74**</u> The site of numbers 25 and 27 Shadrach, two derelict cottages and number 26, which was habitable, the latter let on an oral tenancy to Walter and Martha [Bessie]Legg, née Steel, at £7. 2s. 4d, per annum, were *withdrawn* from the Sale and were purchased privately by the Rural District Council.

Outline planning permission had already been obtained, to build residential housing there and Lot 74, a valuable building site was also *withdrawn*. The part was let to RJ Thorner at 15/- a year and WC Gale, cultivated the remainder, rent free. The fire which had swept through in January 1948 had left the whole in a bad state.

★★★★★★★★★★

Walty and Bessie Legg were an unassuming, childless couple. They were good village people, always seeming to be out and about and Walty, could be seen going back and forth to his work, the allotment, or to The Anchor, for a pint. Both their families could be traced back several generations, in Burton. Bessie's brother and his wife had emigrated to Manitoba, Canada and she often spoke proudly of him and his family 'abroad'.

Prior to her visit to Canada, in a letter to Elizabeth Buckler in 1951, Mrs. Steel had written, 'Canada is a big country. You will sure like our country and you will see a big difference to England. The West is sure a lovely place. We left Burton in 1924 and have never been back since. We are hoping to see you for a good long chat about all the folks at Burton.'

It was connections, like that, that enabled the families that they had left in the village, to gain a broader picture of the world beyond. Another Burton woman had emigrated and was living near Toronto in 1951. She was connected to the Hitt family.

THE END OF THE FIRST DAY

<u>**Lot 75**</u> Two cottages had stood alone in Annings Lane for at least two hundred years. The surname Chilcott could be found in the parish registers in the early 1700s. Leslie Chilcott worked for the Water Board and had been orphaned as a baby and had been brought up there by his grandmother. The Chilcott's cottage was large, with four bedrooms, varying in length from 10 to 17 feet, with widths of about 8 feet. The ceilings stood at around 6 feet 6 inches and the sitting room and living rooms were generous, being 16 feet 6 inches by approximately 12 feet. The gardens had a southerly aspect with 125 feet frontage *'and room for garages'*.

★★★★★★★★★★

A Captain Anning is listed as having shares in vessels that sailed from Bridport Harbour and there are indications of him building ships. His early eighteenth century will, referred to his two sons, who travelled far from their native shore. Most notably he gave his name to the lane where he lived. Until the developments in Annings Lane, Lot 75, made up the only dwellings in that part of the quiet and pastoral part of the village, sitting idyllically amidst green fields and fruiting orchards.

Old records indicated that John Anning, a carpenter, (a descendant aged seventy-one was living there in 1871), probably built the property on the outskirts of the village, on land belonging to the Lord of the Manor.

★★★★★★★★★★

The Pattinsons, were tenants at number 24. Dorothy, née Williams, was the daughter of a coastguard. She had one sister and tragically lost her two brothers, Frederick and James Williams in the Second World War. Dorothy's husband, Abel, [known as Pat], from the extreme north of England, had been stationed in the area, during the war. He was popular with everyone and still carried his local accent. There were many amusing times when Pat and his true Dorset pals found it difficult to understand each other! Dot, as she was often known, was a kind and gentle woman and so well liked around Burton. They had two sons, Michael and Peter, who were in their teens.

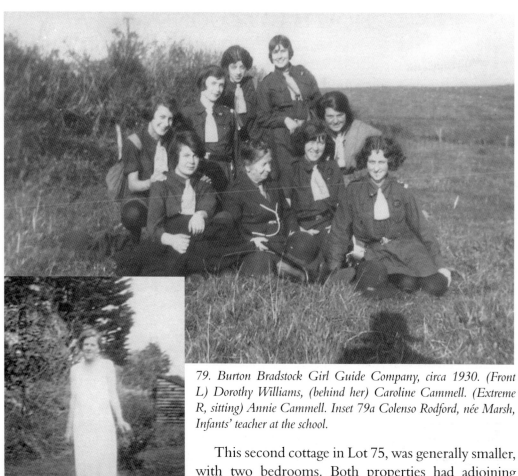

79. *Burton Bradstock Girl Guide Company, circa 1930. (Front L) Dorothy Williams, (behind her) Caroline Cammell. (Extreme R, sitting) Annie Cammell. Inset 79a Colenso Rodford, née Marsh, Infants' teacher at the school.*

This second cottage in Lot 75, was generally smaller, with two bedrooms. Both properties had adjoining gardens, facing south and earth closets. The road frontage along the whole was 125 feet. Mains water was obtained from a shared standpipe, electricity was laid on and the sewer was handy in the lane.

The last Lot of the first day's Sale realised £450, bought presumably by an outsider although *The Western Gazette* omitted the name of the purchaser. Was it yet another pre-planned area for council housing?

Leslie Chillott married later. Both the families lived out their lives there. Their grown children moved to other areas of Burton and West Dorset and finally, this quaint, unique property was demolished around 1967 and council dwellings built.

HOW HAD IT GONE?

Throughout the first day of the Sale, speculators continued to bid for practically every Lot, sending up the price. This was in the interests of the Vendor but caused the tenants to worry, about finding the money, (even if hoping to take up the mortgage offer). Although it was several months after the Sale had been announced, the tenants were all still in a state of shock and disbelief.

As the auction continued, the feeling of uncertainty pervaded. For those whose properties and land were to be sold the following day, no one was sure if they were going to be successful in their bid to save the roof over their head, or the land or premises that provided them with a living. On the first day of the Sale, all of the tenants who intended to purchase, had done so.

Loud cheers went up each time the auctioneer had announced "Sold!", in favour of a tenant. Those bold enough to stand up and point out some detrimental aspect of the Lot that they were interested in buying, spoke out to a hushed audience, which was followed by "Hear, Hear", from others whose fate was still in the balance.

The speed of the auction was unprecedented and the first day's bidding for seventy-five Lots, only took two and a half hours. Some holdings were broken up and parcels of land and gardens were sold separately. This was done to produce more interest, where there was great potential for development. During the first day, some properties and land had been sold to outsiders. What would happen to the tenants involved? The question was on everyone's mind.

In 1958, the village still had a people that kept itself to itself, helping each other as need arose. The 'sons' had gone off across the seas but they were usually drawn back to their home and there were a number of holiday makers marrying into village families and these people were part of the close-knit community. There were families whose ancestors had been living in Burton for generation after generation whose families had inter-married. They shared not only common blood but a common bond which had gone on uninterrupted for several centuries, under the landlord and tenant system. July 31st had been one of the most unsettling days of their lives.

By early afternoon, on the first day, all the Lots had been sold. There was then a considerable melée as the contracts were signed and witnessed. The solicitors, acting for Captain Pitt-Rivers and the new owners, were kept busy. For some of the tenants who had purchased, the formalities were very confusing. It was the first time in their lives that they had had to deal with any legal matter. Deposits had to be put down, contracts and cheques signed, even handfuls of cash counted and receipts given. Some did not have bank accounts and therefore no cheque books, although the more thrifty ones had Post Office or National Savings accounts. The documenting took several hours and lasted well into the early evening. Some men, who had completed their side of the business, or who had not bought their property, retired to the pubs, (which closed at 2 p. m. and reopened at 6 p. m.), to discuss the happenings of the day; the rest went home, quietly, in deep thought.

There was a great deal of talk all around the neighbourhood and for some, a feeling of relief. For others, the balance of the purchase price would have to be found over the next few years - difficult to accomplish as incomes and wages, in West Dorset, were below the national average. In 1958, farm workers could expect around £5 for a forty-four hour week. A dairyman, or overseer, might command six to seven pounds ten shillings, for longer hours and far more responsibility. The farmers had problems. Money was not easily come-by for them. 'On paper', their stock and machinery amounted to a reasonable sum, were they to be sold but without both, they would have no livelihood. Some farmers would continue to be tenants, their holdings bought by the mystery purchaser. An increase in rent seemed inevitable. Only time would tell.

DAY TWO

A full marquee greeted the auctioneers again on the second day of the Sale, August 1st 1958. Fine and dry, it started off much as the day before had done. One of the partners in the firm of Senior and Godwin and other staff had stayed overnight at The Dove Inn. Tenants whose Lots were still to come up, were apprehensive. Those who had already bought wore an air of elation and lent encouragement to the remaining tenants, who had no idea what the outcome of their bids might be. Not had all gone as expected. Bunny Lenthall deemed 'the richest man' in the parish, (because of the amount he tenanted), had lost his farm. There was this 'mystery client' and other outsiders who had bought some of the Lots. Perhaps the speculators, disappointed in not securing everything the day before, might bid excessively and price the tenants right out of the market, on the final day.

LAND AT THE GROVE MILL

<u>**Lot 76**</u> The former flax swingling mill in Grove Road did not come within the Estate in 1958. Presumed to have been bought by the Estate at some time after Richard Roberts died and his sons and grandsons no longer found processing flax and hemp viable, it had turned over to a corn-grinding mill as indicated in the 1851 Census Return which gave John Roberts, aged 19, as a miller, assistant to his father. By 1881 they had relinquished the mill which was in the hands of the Rendall family with Joseph Rendall, aged 54, the miller and baker.

80. (L) Robert Gobbett, partner at The Grove Mill and (R) Albert Stevens, with the three-wheeled delivery van, circa 1950s.

Early in 1958, the Burton Corn Mill had been sold, by private treaty and purchased by a company who continued as "Burton Mill Limited". The property consisted of a four storey mill, still quite intact for grinding corn, a mill house, a manager's flat, five acres of land adjoining and the fishing rights.

The Bridport News did not state the price that this unique property made. The auctioneers were TRG Lawrence and Son, of Bridport, whose office was situated in South Street. Partners and tenants of the Estate, who had been trading there for some years, were brothers-in-law, John Panten and Robert Gobbett who ground corn, sold barley meal for stock and ran a bakery, baking in a fine old bread oven. The newly baked bread was delivered daily, in the village and to outlying areas. It was available, to buy on the premises, as well, where it could be collected, straight out of the oven. The customer often had to wait whilst the baker took the shovel and scooped out the loaves. Steve Northover was employed in the mill. He would emerge covered in white dust but lived to a great age, unaffected.

Charles Day and Jean née Wylde, who had moved to the village from Reading in 1958 were living in the Mill House. Day acted as a delivery man three days a week for the millers and the other three days, he spent working and delivering for butcher Gale.

When Panten and Gobbett retired, the mill was run by Derek Barnes, son of Hamilton Barnes, a miller from Loders. Corn grinding was continued but the bakery closed. Ironically, it was nearing the time when village grinding mills were being superseded by the large animal feed producers.

★★★★★★★★★★

At the Sale later in the year, Lot 76, the remaining acreage, now calculated as 6 acres around The Grove Mill, was let to Burton Mills, [Messrs Barnes], on an oral tenancy of £22. These pastures carried the names, "Hempland Meadow", "Withy Bed" and "Long Meadow", although older maps referred to the meadows as "meads". Burton's history was here, where hemp had once been grown for rope-making, or withies cut for crafting bushel baskets and lobster pots for the fishermen.

In this secluded niche, these lush meadows stretched from the mill towards Arch Bridge, bordering on recent developments, fronting on to Annings Lane. It formed an attractive secluded unit, on the eastern edge of Burton Bradstock, which altogether, made-up a much sought-after holding. The water-wheel was still in operation, as it, (or its predessor), had been for several hundred years.

Bidding was very keen and the Lot fell to the tenant, Hamilton Barnes, for £1,500; treble the price of agricultural land.

> An untimely family bereavement changed matters at Burton Mill and after a few years, the building was sold and converted into apartments, with the mill house and the old bakery and flat as separate units. The water wheel lay forever silent.
>
> Today the fields that were sold in 1958, having changed hands several times, are still grazed by brought-in cattle.

SHIPTON LANE

Lot 77 Since the late 1800s, Shipton Lane had been the exclusive, new residential area of Burton, until the post-war building started in the 1950s. The fields along the lane had come mainly within North Hill Farm, which at some time had passed from the owner, Farmer Brown, to farmer and income tax inspector, George Gale and thence to his son, Richard, the latter given in *Kelly's Directory 1907* as a cow-keeper. Plots had been sold off for building, to private individuals.

Around the turn of the century, John Justinian Robert Whitley Mercer, a gentleman and farmer, (as he termed himself), from Halstock with his wife Lucy Pitfield, had a fine house, groom's accommodation and stables built, calling it "The Mount". They lived somewhere in the village prior to this. One of Mercer's ancestors was a surgeon who had established a lunatic asylum in Halstock.

Mercer lived at The Mount with his wife and three daughters. (One daughter later married Doctor Fraser. The Mercer's only son was killed in the First World War.) The ladies of this household were pillars of the church and held in high regard. They played the organ, ran the Sunday School and organised activities in the village, connected with the church.

Alfred Churchouse, the retiring landlord of The Anchor Hotel had moved to a smart house, in Shipton Lane, with grass tennis court and gardens, naming it "Anchor House". Next door, relatives, William Kiddle Morris and his family, had erected a wooden and asbestos bungalow, which had been purchased from an exhibition. Mrs Morris was reputed to have sung at The Chrystal Palace, in her professional singing days.

Earlier in the century, when the original North Hill Farmhouse, [later Norburton], was sold to Edward Sturdy, Richard Gale, [known as Rajah], who then owned most of the North Hill farmland, had built himself another farmhouse, naming it, North Hill Farm. He subsequently built an identical property, Kennon Farm. Later, Gale and his wife, Minnie and daughters, retired to Vallevue, a large brick house, which lay between the two. Some land was retained and was rented, by William [Bill] Hutchings, a smallholder, of Vine House.

Another large brick house was built, overlooking North Hill Farmhouse and by 1939, two fashionable bungalows occupied sites, opposite Anchor House. Reg Buckler, an Estate tenant, had established his holding, which also took in land rented from another branch of the Gales, at Kennon Knapp.

At the time of the Sale, in 1958, hidden in the trees below North Hill Farmhouse, was Norburton, then a decaying large gentleman's residence, with outbuildings, stables and two cottages, with surrounding land. Sturdy had planted a considerable number of conifers, (the saplings easily obtained from his family estate at Trigon, Wareham). He established formal gardens, as well as a large kitchen garden. In its heyday there were several gardeners and outdoor staff employed, as well as the usual indoor staff.

Mid-way up the lane, at Furzey Corner, a typical 1920s style, wood and asbestos bungalow, had been erected. Here, lived Colenso (so named in 1900 during the Boer War) Rodford, née Marsh, the infants' teacher, at Burton School and her husband, Bob, a baker.

★★★★★★★★★★

The Shipton Lane residences had substantial grounds and everyone enjoyed much privacy. All these properties enjoyed magnificent views across the valley and to the sea beyond. Privately owned, none was included in the Sale.

★★★★★★★★★★

To the south-west of Norburton, lay "The Cot", a brick-built private house, lived in by Billy Williams, (who enjoyed much popularity as he played the "squeeze-box") and his family. Adjoining The Cot, forming part of the Manor of Burton Bradstock, Edgar Hawkins rented 8 acres from the Pitt-Rivers Estate, on a yearly tenancy of £18. This land, ran down to the cemetery and back up towards North Hill that overlooked the village. (Behind lay a field known as "Parson's Hill" and the two reservoirs). Mains water was laid on to a trough. There was a frontage to Shipton Lane of some 370 feet and this formed Lot 77.

With the possibility that this land could eventually be used to 'fill in' with further development along Shipton Lane, Hawkins paid £700 for it, (twice the agricultural value per acre).

Today, Shipton Lane has been completely 'filled in'. Houses and bungalows have been built in every field along the road. A large estate backs and fronts onto Norburton and land that once went with Mercers and North Hill Farm has additional dwellings. Where Bill Hutchings milked his little herd of cows, a row of bungalows covers every trace of his existence.

In 2006, as part of the Hawkins's family holdings, "The Cot" was sold, along with what was Lot 77. Will that field finally succumb to the builders? A planning application to demolish The Cot and erect two dwellings has been recently submitted (2007).

PARISH COUNCIL CONCERNS

In the Parish Council minutes of 21st March 1958, it is recorded that it had been agreed that the Chairman, RB Howarth, would meet with the Pitt-Rivers Estate's Agent, to ascertain the Vendor's intention regarding the playing field. Councillor Bill Jarman enquired about the allotments in view of the Sale. Councillors voted to consider purchasing them. The Parish Council paid the Estate 10/- a year rent for the playing field and this was soon to be increased to £1.

The Chairman reported back on the 28th March. He was negotiating with the Agent and endeavouring to meet with Captain Pitt-Rivers. Councillors Jarman and Hitt were adamant that the Parish Council should be represented at the forthcoming Sale and bid to the limit, which would be set by the District Valuer. The councillors wanted compulsory purchase of the allotments.

81. Receding flood water in the playing field and High Street, 1955.

A resolution was carried to send to the Ministry of Agriculture and Food and Dorset County Council, to seek their assistance. On July 3rd a special meeting was held. The Chairman had met again with the Agent. Certain plots would be offered to the Burton Parish Council, if it agreed to forego others that went with The Dove Inn, the blacksmith's shop, Mr Hitchcock's and Mrs Loving's properties.

Long discussion took place and it was finally agreed to forego all, with the exception of the plot next to the blacksmith's shop. The councillors agreed to proceed with the compulsory purchase of the rest of the allotments. An official notice would be sent by the Parish Clerk, to the Agent. The Parish Councillors, who attended this meeting, were: Jim Churchill, Rob Gale, Edgar Hawkins, Ted Hitt, Len Hope, RB Howarth, Bill Jarman and Fred Mullins. Apologies had been received from Albert Bull who was in failing health.

By July, less than a month before the Sale, a letter was received from the Agent, stating that the Parish Council was being offered Lots 119, 120, 121(this Lot included the Estate yard) and the larger portion of Lot 115, (the ground opposite The Dove Inn). The Pitt-Rivers Estate was not prepared to make any further concessions.

The matter dragged on and after the Sale, in the September, the Estate had agreed to include half of Lot 115. Six months later, the Parish Clerk announced that the price of the allotments still had not been agreed with the District Valuer. The cheque for £40, for the playing field, was sanctioned. The Clerk stated that a small grant would be available from the Playing Field Association.

The Reading Room, Lot 2, which Captain Pitt-Rivers had offered as a gift to the Parish, could not be made use of and had been offered on to a third party, because the land behind presented the Parish Council with a problem. It could only wait on Captain Pitt-Rivers's intentions regarding this. The minutes record that a dispute had taken place within the Pitt-Rivers family and the position of the Reading Room remained unresolved. In the following May, (1959), the Deed of Conveyance of the Reading Room was finally executed.

The negotiations and agreements that had taken place prior, were of extreme importance to both parties. It was some of the prize Lots, ideally suited for development, that had been *withdrawn*. Had speculators got their hands on them, a great deal of council housing could have been lost. The purchases, by the local councils, boded well for the people of the district. The allotment controversy stretched on for a couple more years, before settlement was reached with the Council Valuation Officer and the other two parties.

THE BARTLETTS

The locals recalled when "Tinker" Bartlett had lived at number 35 Grove Road. Bartlett was a stone mason and employed at one time by the Estate. He had raised a family with two of his sons, Ralph and Alphonso, turning out to be fine footballers, as were his grandsons, Roy Nethercott and Adrian Wakely. After Tinker's death, Rob Gale housed his employee at number 35. In a detached cottage opposite lived Minnie Nethercott, one of Tinker Bartlett's daughters.

There had been some private sales, prior to the main auction. When the opportunity arose, the Estate had always made some transactions. Mrs Nethercott, would have hoped that her pretty cottage, was to have been included in the Sale.

★★★★★★★★★★

She had been widowed in 1947 when her husband, Bill, died, at the early age of forty-three. He had served as a submariner, and had been gassed in the First World War. At the time of his death, he was employed by the Estate on the maintenance staff. To his daily activities could be added all he did for village welfare. He was held in high regard, involved in a host of organisations, in particular, the Royal British Legion.

Minnie had first met Bill when she was employed in Plymouth, working for navy personnel. When he came out of the Navy, they married and set up home, in Burton at number 49 Darby Lane, moving into number 54 Grove Road around 1938, with their two young children.

The Bartlett family had great ties with Burton. Having been born and brought up in the village, Mrs Nethercott and her family would have taken up Captain Pitt-Rivers's offer, if it had come their way. Her son, Roy, was in the Royal Navy and learnt of the proposed auction too late. Their home was not included. It had been privately sold.

Minnie Nethercott lived there until her death in 1977. Jeanne had moved away from Burton and Roy, on leaving the Royal Navy, joined the Dorset Constabulary, where he distinguished himself. Although the family was offered a chance to buy the cottage later, things had moved on for them and they declined. Mrs Nethercott's memory is perpetuated in the name, "Minnie's Cottage".

The Bartlett connection faded out when Arthur Bartlett, (another branch of the family who came to Burton to live), former gardener, involved in most village activities and Vera McLean, an actress and variety entertainer, who had married "Ramsbottom", a wartime comedian, died as the century came to a close. Vera's father, was a telephone engineer and had been a newcomer to the district early in the 1900s, marrying Jane Bartlett from Burton. His family were funeral directors in Manchester. There was a grand wedding as the twentieth century dawned - great excitement in the village.

The fading headstones are a last reminder of this and other old local families.

COGDEN FARM

Lot 78 although not the largest farm to be sold, Cogden was, by far, the most prestigious. The house, with its fine architecture, surroundings and seclusion, gave it an air of grandeur. The stylish homestead lay nearly a quarter of a mile off the Coast Road from Burton to Abbotsbury and was central to the land. Cogden was a 'gentleman's' farm.

The house had superb reception rooms, at 18 feet in length by approximately 15 feet wide, five good bedrooms, (three at 18 feet in length or more and varying in width from 8 to 15 feet). There was a generous kitchen and utility areas, a bathroom, with *'bath and hand-basin, H and C'* and a separate flushed lavatory. It included a box-room, invaluable for storage in such a house, where gentry and yeomen farmers had lived for generations.

Cogden House was gutted by fire in 1914, when beautiful moulded ceilings were destroyed. The fire appliance, motorised by then, had to be brought from Bridport and with no telephone, (the service came to Burton in the mid 1930s), by the time it arrived, although some of the contents had been saved by the farm workers, it was too late. The shell of the house remained and was rebuilt. Richard Francis Roberts, solicitor to the London and North West Railway companies and a director of the Bridport Railway, had made it his home, during the late 1800s. In the interim, the farm was rented by farmers Cousins and Inkpen. AF Bailey took over the tenancy, in 1929.

★★★★★★★★★★

Arthur Frank [AF] Bailey, known as Frank, a Wiltshire man, had been training, in Devonshire, in agriculture, when he met his future wife, Edith Stevens, of Eggersford, near Barnstaple, who came from a well established farming family. On their marriage, they began a long association with Burton Bradstock.

★★★★★★★★★★

In the Cogden Farm precincts, there were two good sized farm workers' cottages, each with three bedrooms. The farm buildings and stabling, were very desirable. Mains electricity was installed everywhere and as the house lay so far out of the village, on an almost deserted road, the availability, by then, of the telephone was a great asset. The telephone amenity was prominent in the auctioneer's introduction, as he announced Lot 78.

Water was available by means of a borehole, fitted with a Godwin deep-well pump, in a concrete shed to the east of the buildings. A pipeline, connected from the Bridport Water Company's mains, crossed the land and was fed by gravitation to the homestead, from a 3,000 gallon reservoir, situated in a corner of one of the fields, above the old Coastguard Station. The land was good, being heavy loam on clay with some stone-brash, overlying limestone. The fields which lay in the base of the 'bowl', were sheltered and ideal for out-wintering stock. The landscape surrounding Cogden Farm was of typical

West Dorset fields, of all shapes and sizes, bordered with hedges and stone walls, forming a patchwork, which disappeared into lush valleys, nestling in rolling hills.

The house was well appointed, having two Aga cookers, an Alnite fire in the lounge, as well as a stove in the living room and large enough for the Baileys to have a separate section for their only child, Young Frank, when he married Mary Elliott, a Bridport businessman's daughter, in 1950. With the arrival of Frank and Mary's four children it was a perfect place in which to raise a family. The heating and cookers that were installed were essential in cold winters, when the farm was liable to get cut off, as well as for all the cooking, generated at a large establishment.

82. "Young" Frank Bailey holding a prize-winning Jacob ram.

Out in the farm buildings, there were all the trappings of a busy up-to-date farm. The tenancy was let to AF Bailey at £328. 7s. 5d; an odd sum. Approximately, £582 had been spent on the farm, during the past five years by the Estate. The catalogue stated that the shooting rights were in-hand. The farm had always had a good reputation as an ideal shooting and hunting ground, with plenty of cover. Amongst the improvements, the yard and other buildings had been concreted by the tenant, with the Landlord's permission but Bailey was not liable for the maintenance of the stone wall, that ran along the main road. This wall was a fine example of the use of local materials and local craftsmen's traditional skills. The farmhouse was rated at £24 and the cottages at £4 each.

Old field names were listed in the Sale catalogue as "Rough Ground", "Little Cogden", "Kings Mead", "Middle Hibbs", "Burscombe Knapp". With the main farm, went three more Lots. There were nearly 40 acres of other pastureland, (a small plot being sub-let to Rob Gale). An additional 22½ acres, in Bredy Road, were let direct from the Estate, to Gale, with 17 acres, in the same road, in the tenancy of AF Bailey.

The main of Cogden Farm, which was sold with Lots 80 and 103, (35 acres of pastureland), were purchased by Mr John Jeffery, the same representative who had bought Manor Farm, the day before, 'for a client'. The sum paid for the whole of this splendid farm was £11,000. The auctioneer brought the hammer down twice more, in favour of Mr Jeffery, on Lot 79 at £1,550 and Lot 81 for £1,000. (**Lot 80** had been included with Cogden Farm.)

The identity of the mysterious purchaser was questioned, by those gathered in the marquee. It had been expected that AF Bailey, a seemingly 'well breeched' man, in all respects, would be certain to buy this unique establishment. Bailey was fully aware as to who had acquired the farm but kept his counsel.

Continuing as a tenant at Cogden Farm, AF Bailey, went on farming as he had always done, with Young Frank taking more responsibility but with no security of tenure. Young Frank was an expert sheep judge and was a leader in the Rare Breed movement to save endangered species of farm animals. He kept a flock of Jacob sheep and with Mary, worked tirelessly for the promotion of the Rare Breed Society.

As the years rolled on at Cogden, the family became more and more involved with activities outside the farm. Frank served on the West Dorset District Council and was never afraid to speak his mind for any cause he championed. Along this time, Bunny Lenthall had decided to emigrate and Manor Farm was up for sale and Bailey seized the opportunity to enquire of the mystery buyer of 1958, if Cogden might be for sale, as well.

Young Frank was able to buy Cogden farm in the early 1970s and farmed it in a very progressive and productive way, without damaging the unique land that surrounded the lovely old house and buildings. He sold off the land to the south, to the National Trust but purchased other pasture, that came up for sale, from another holding, (not within the Pitt-Rivers Estate), to the east of the White Ladies. Cogden farmhouse became the venue for many gatherings.

★★★★★★★★★★

One day, as some of the family were assembled, Max, (a Bailey grandson), sidled into the room in a strange manner. Eventually, he recounted that he had been playing a game in the hall, on his own, when a young girl, with long hair, had appeared, dressed in old fashioned clothes. He thought that his mother and grandmother might laugh at him and say that he was imagining the scene but they were convinced that he had seen the apparition. He was able to draw a sketch of her and it transpired that she was dressed in Victorian clothes. He said that she had disappeared 'through the wall'. What he and several other members of the family did not know was that the wall had been boarded up and that the girl had, in fact, gone through, what in Victorian times would have been an opening! Extensive research did not reveal a young girl's death but there could easily have been one who had an unhappy or unfortunate experience and was unable to rest.

This was not the only ghost at Cogden. In one of the out-buildings, which was once a dwelling, was a strange presence. The sheep dogs, who are known for their sensitive nature, would not go in or go past. The Baileys had heard, from villagers, that the unnatural death of a man, had taken place there.

★★★★★★★★★★

AF Bailey died in 1993 and his widow lived on in her part of the house, for a number of years, still taking an interest in everything, well into her nineties.

Mary and Frank celebrated their Golden Wedding Anniversary in 2000, surrounded by their close-knit family. A tragedy was soon to befall the couple when they were involved in a motoring accident, near Freshwater, in 2001, as a result of which Frank died, whilst appearing to be progressing, in hospital. This was a devastating blow for the family and the people of Burton and the whole of Dorset. Frank Bailey was so well known, respected for his work for the community, knowledge on all things agricultural and liked for his charming nature and sense of humour. The village church was packed to overflowing for his Memorial Service.

A great decision had to be made by the family and they reluctantly, decided to sell. In 2003, Mrs Mary Bailey moved down into the village; a complete contrast to all she had known for over half a century. She reveals that she is extremely happy living 'in the city' and is able to walk to the shops, the post office and the many events at which she assists, or attends. From Cogden it was a different undertaking, to even post a letter, which necessitated a walk, pony ride or drive down to the village.

The Bailey family have retained a part of the beach where Young Frank's ashes lie and are reluctant to completely sever the ties. Cogden Farm, now part of a larger farming enterprise, with its ghosts and host of memories goes on, as it must have done, in similar fashion, for several hundreds of years.

★★★★★★★★★★

An account of the death of Richard Francis Roberts, who was living at Cogden in 1883, solicitor and Director of the Bridport Railway, can be found in the book, *Farmers, Fishermen and Flax Spinners*.

SOME GOOD LAND

<u>Lots 79 and 81</u> covered 22½ acres on the outskirts of the village, in Bredy Road, let to Rob Gale, at £84 and 20 acres, at £35, also in Bredy Road, let to AF Bailey. The agent for the mystery buyer paid £1,550 for Lot 79 and £1,000 for Lot 81.

These two Lots consisted of seventeen fields, rich in loam, enclosed with ancient hedges, spread through the valley. All this land, much of which was bordered by the River Bride, was extremely fertile and mostly flat. With easy access from Bredy Road, these fields were useful to both farmers.

Included were "Parsons Meadows", the land from which the tithes were once taken and "Oxhays Willow Bed", where willows grew. The withies were used for making baskets, bonds for tying and put to numerous other uses in the countryside or for fishing. Lot 80 which had been quarried at one time, amounted to 18 acres of good soil, known as "Wolings" [walling]. The land, had the advantage of a water-trough, which was fed by a spring.

Whoever it was buying up the farms and outlying land that went with them, seemed to have a very deep pocket. No one said much as these Lots were disposed of swiftly. There were very few people in the marquee who recognised Mr Jeffery, from Donhead, in north Dorset, who was acting as the agent for the unknown buyer. It provided a double foil. No one had expected this, although most people in the marquee remained ignorant about the purchaser, thinking, in the case of Cogden Farm, that AF Bailey had bought it all.

Lot 82 8 acres in Bredy Road, had been sold with Lot 39. Lots 62 and 82 were first offered up together. Part had been rented by Rob Gale and the other part by Tony Bishop, the purchaser of Lot 62.

BURTON BEACH AND THE HIVE 'an important seaside property'

Lot 83 The Hive [landing place] and a mile of private beach, stretched from Freshwater to the old Coastguard Station, approached by the private drive, 400 yards long, known as Beach Road. It was described as having '*exclusive character* and *the full commercial possibilities have as yet not been exploited*'. From this beach, for centuries, the fishermen of Burton had launched their boats, spread their nets to dry and enjoyed the traditional amenity it provided, by courtesy of the Lord of the Manor.

★★★★★★★★★★

There was an old custom, which had only died out early in the 1940s, that every year, in May, the fisher-folk and their families made garlands from wild flowers. These were mounted on staves and paraded around the village by the children, collecting pennies, as they sang traditional songs at any door where they knew that they would be well received. The garlands were then taken into the church to be blessed. Another service followed in the field behind The Hive, where the Rector then blessed the boats, nets and crews. Finally, the garlands were cast into the sea, on May 12th, as an offering for good, safe fishing. Burton Bradstock used the new date after the calendar was altered in 1751. Originally, this would have been done on May Day, May 1st but due to the change of calendar, when twelve days were lost, Burton opted for the 12th, whilst Abbotsbury chose May 13th, giving some indication as to how long the custom had been observed.

★★★★★★★★★★

This part of the Chesil Beach had witnessed countless shipping tragedies over the hundreds of years and in war-time there had been practices held for the Dieppe Invasion, the Dam Buster Raid and D-Day Landings. Concrete 'dragon's tooth' blocks, barbed wire entanglements, huge inter-locking iron structures and land mines, concrete pill-boxes and gun emplacements, had been a coastal protection against an invasion and separated the beach from the fields beyond. Some of these decaying defences were still visible in 1958.

★★★★★★★★★★

The whole of Lot 83 consisted of 32 acres which amounted to the actual beach, a timber hut which served as a café, public conveniences, with a septic tank, an acre of car park, with room for two hundred cars, an overflow parking area, in an adjacent paddock and the mile of beach. To the locals, the easterly section was known as "Clave End", because of the [blue] clay that formed the cliff. A metalled road led up over the Claves, from the beach car park. It had been laid down, by the Estate, ahead of a proposed chalet scheme, that was halted by the outbreak of the war, in 1939.

In 1958, the old Toll Road, [Beach Road], that led down to The Hive Beach, had no official right-of-way. The National Bus Company paid 22/6d a year for a right to use it and the owners of the new, smart dwellings, that had recently been built in Beach Road, had been granted rights of way. The owners of Grey Stones Bungalow and the Villas, situated to the west, had authorised passage, 'for reasonable enjoyment of the beach'.

To all this, were added the rights to the sand and shingle extraction, used for water purification, pebble-dashing buildings, and path laying. Unwashed, it was not much good for construction work, owing to the salt content. This had, on occasions, been the downfall of some unsuspecting builder, who shovelled himself up some sand into a bag, only to find that it caused the concrete to 'sweat' and not 'go off'. However, the sand, when washed, found in a particular area at Burton was of very special value.

★★★★★★★★★★

The pebbles were pea-sized and formed part of the unique Chesil Beach. This wonder of the world which arose through tides and wind direction, stretched some eighteen miles from West Bay to Portland, the size of the pebbles graduating from the very small ones at West Bay and Burton, to stones, the size of saucers, at the Portland end.

When the merchants wanted to haul the sand and shingle, the foreman would 'smell the air' early in the morning and know where to send the men to dig. It was not just a matter of going out onto the beach with a spade. In 1958, two gravel merchants had the concession to take sand and shingle on a royalty basis of 2/- a ton. Planning permission had to be obtained for this purpose and it had been granted by the local council until December 1966. Jack Gurd of Burton Bradstock and JC Phillips and Sons, of Bridport, had extracted from the beach for many years, first by means of horses and carts and more recently by using a mechanical digger, taking the loads away, by lorry.

★★★★★★★★★★

The land to the east, was let to AF Bailey. Water was laid-on, privately, taken from the Bridport Water Company's main pipe and there were conditions in the Sale relating to rights for the purchaser of Cogden Farm. At The Hive, the main sewer was available, whilst a private connection was installed to the public conveniences. Doctor Ryan rented a store shed at £1 per annum and the local fishermen were permitted to use the Fishermen's Green for storing boats and nets, free of charge.

The income that the Estate had received from The Hive amounted to £767 in 1956 and £754 in 1957, from the shingle extraction, the car park, café and lavatories. In addition, the rent of land and the National Bus Company's toll, realised £22. 2s. 6d. The outgoings in rates had been £101, in 1957.

Lot 83, with its immense potential, was *withdrawn* from the Sale.

It transpired, that the whole of Lot 83 had been *withdrawn* from the Sale, after negotiations had taken place between the Pitt-Rivers Estate, others and RB Howarth. There were to be many twists and turns before the matter was resolved and the beach and its amenities could be administered by the Parish Council.

Howarth had a passion to save Burton from excessive development and could see that it was essential to secure The Hive Beach for the public and not let it fall into the hands of someone who would exploit the area for financial gain, letting it become 'another Bournemouth'.

It could have been the mystery buyer's intention to secure The Hive and he may have discussed 'saving' it with RB Howarth, as a Burton Bradstock Association was soon set-up. Initially, at the start of the auction, Howarth did not seem to be at all assured that Burton, which included The Hive Beach, would be saved from development. Perhaps he was not party to everything concerning the mystery purchaser's proposals, who had secured other land along the coast with the whole forming a vast expanse.

Financial support was needed to form the Burton Bradstock Village Association and shares were sold to selected people and the plan implemented. This was no mean task and the scheme survived for a while. All the land was subject to rights of way. At the 1958 Sale, the initial amount of land/beach at The Hive, amounted to 32 acres. The fishermen continued to exercise their long established right to keep boats on the green and stow their nets in the store shed.

The mystery purchaser of so many important lots at the Sale, was very interested in preservation and tree planting along the coast and in the countryside. By 1966, he had written that 'The Dorset Branch of the Council for the Preservation of Rural England is attempting to interest the County Council and local landowners, (this included himself), in a scheme for improving the landscape on the coastal road from Burton Bradstock to Abbotsbury by planting trees and shelter belts'. He continued:-

'This pilot scheme which they wish eventually to apply to most of the Dorset coast, has made a promising start [at Burton Bradstock]'.

The mystery buyer eventually sold 40 acres to the National Trust in 1967 and the Burton Bradstock Association sold a further 40 acres in 1973 which was conveyed in five parts. (Some shareholders had received their money back, with no interest much earlier). These transactions were followed in 1990 by the sale to the National Trust of 25 acres known as "Burton Cliff" and in 1997, 18 acres of Bind Barrow. This then secured the whole of The Hive Beach and the land that surrounded it on the three 'sides'.

★★★★★★★★★★

Relating to the new development in Beach Road, Basil Dent recalled, half a century later, that the Estate sold off plots in Beach Road in the years leading up to the Sale. (The Buckler family had rented the land for half a century). Some of the early sites were transferred at £50 and by the time he bought one of the remaining four the price was £800. The final plot, at the rear, of the Beach Road development, was valued at £70,000, in the 1980s and sold quickly. The builder split the land, dividing it into two plots. Few of the residents in Beach Road, were aware that one of the properties was standing on the site of an old farm shed where, in the 1930s, a sad and depressed fellow, had chosen to hang himself, from a beam. At the time, this unfortunate happening had shocked the whole of the village.

★★★★★★★★★★

By October 1973, a further 43½ acres of the coastal land had been sold by the Burton Bradstock Association, to the National Trust, conveyed in five parts. 1990 saw Burton Cliff, (25 acres plus), change hands and in 1997, Bind Barrow, (18½ acres), the final portion of this most unique beautiful expanse of coast, came into the safe keeping of the National Trust. These latter sections had been secured by others at the Sale, in 1958.

The National Trust now hold The Hive Beach and adjacent land, amounting to 127 acres [51 hectares]. The foreshore, to high water mark and the cliffs are designated as a Special Site of Scientific Interest. A length of the foreshore, from the east point of The Hive Beach to Cogden, is separately owned.

The car-park, at Burton, is open, at a charge, to visitors. A well-run café serves them. Although owned by the National Trust, (2007) this is contracted out to the Parish Council, on a fifty-fifty basis. The Parish Council rents out the rights to sell food and drink and administers the parking. This entails quite an amount of expense, particularly in wages and negotiations are due to take place for a renewed contract with the National Trust.

The whole of the beach and surrounding land is there for all to enjoy. The road to the beach was in a bad state but will be resurfaced and a splendid, glass fronted extension to the café would do justice to the beautiful surroundings and the excellent cuisine offered by the present proprietors. The Hive Beach has to pay its way and has therefore has to be exploited to a certain extent.

★★★★★★★★★★

Extracting sand and shingle from the beach was halted in the mid 1980s as a precaution against coastal erosion. Years later, [around 2005] it was proved that Burton Bradstock sand had been used in the construction of Abbotsbury Monastery, confirming that the removal of materials had been carried out for at least eight hundred years.

The promontory on the cliff, known as "Look Out", where sentries had watched for invaders, coastguards and customs' officers scanned the sea and where generations of the Burton fishermen had stood, eyeing the approaching shoals of fish, is fast falling into the sea. Most of the track where folk have plodded homeward from the beach for centuries, along the cliff top, has gone with it. Soon, only those who read our writings will know of the days when shipping and fishing along this stretch of the Chesil coast were so important.

Tons of sand and shingle were hauled by horse and cart up over the cliff track and down into Burton village. Nowadays, the "lights on the sea", as they were termed, (from those enjoying a barbeque on the beach), no longer signal to waiting smuggling vessels off-shore or are lights from fishermen's lanterns, on a cold November night drifting for herrings.

The sea will always have its moods and can be fierce, cruel and unforgiving, ferociously beating against the cliffs and at other times it is so still and calm that it is difficult to imagine its possible anger and dangers. Whilst hundreds of visitors can enjoy the beauty of the beach and the sea air, many of them are unaware of the dangers that lurk just inches from the shore. The beach shelves and the currents are strong. The old fishermen and sailors knew only too well this hazard, referred to as – "the undertow". The shingle can suck a person into its clasp within seconds and getting back on dry land has often been impossible with fatal results.

Those who promote our unique coastline and the amenities must take the responsibility to warn the unsuspecting of these dangers.

TWO BUNGALOWS ON THE BEACH

<u>**Lot 84 The Green Bungalow**</u> Over the years there had been a number of wooden bungalows close to The Hive Beach. By 1958, most had been dismantled.

An amazed audience, in the Sale marquee, listened to the price of the right to the ownership of the ground, on which the wooden, Green Bungalow stood, soar to over £1,000, a considerable sum at the time. TJ Lee of Andover, repeatedly bid against Wally Kitzerow, who was a tenant, with the Estate's approval and some sort of agreement with the Executors of the late Mrs EK(given as ER in the catalogue) Golledge, who had owned the actual bungalow. Mrs Golledge had a license from the Pitt-Rivers Estate to erect the bungalow on their land, paying a "ground rent", with a right of access to the sea. Part of the land, to the fore, was "in-hand" and this is where some of the confusion arose. The whole plot measured 105 feet by 63 feet.

★★★★★★★★★★

Mrs Golledge, from Yeovil, had the Green Bungalow constructed, as a birthday present for her husband, Hedley, in the mid 1930s, at a cost of around £100. He was a doctor of Veterinary Medicine with a practice in Yeovil and worked on 'comparative research', ahead of its time. The Green Bungalow had a veranda facing the sea and was surrounded by a picket fence. The accommodation consisted of a living room, three bedrooms, a kitchen where cooking was done on a Primus stove and an outside bucket lavatory. The chalet was lit by oil lamps and candles and the Golledges, with their three children and friends, spent many happy holidays at Burton. Mr Golledge died in 1942 and the chalet was sub-let, after the invasion defence restrictions were lifted, to the Kitzerows, who owned a chain of shoe shops in Somerset. The Yeovil shop having been bombed, Wally Kitzerow used the bungalow to store a large consignment of shoes.

★★★★★★★★★★

It soon became apparent, to the more business-like people assembled, in the Sale marquee that what was actually up for sale was not properly understood. It was not the land *and* the bungalow for sale, just the ground. The bungalow was separately owned and might have to be removed. On and on the bidding seemed to go, until Kitzerow pulled out and the hammer fell to Lee, for £1,050.

The Kitzerows were devastated. They had spent their holidays and weekends in Burton for many years and had hoped to secure the land on which the holiday bungalow was standing, probably with a view to buying the property from the Executors. They were well known and well liked and the sort of people who fitted easily into village life. Wally Kitzerow was involved with the fishing crews and living, as he did, most of the summer, beside the beach, he was able to keep a watchful eye on the boats and nets. Those who knew the family were saddened that this unfortunate misunderstanding had occurred.

Half a century on, Mrs Betty Fitzpatrick, née Golledge, in her eighties, of Bosham, West Sussex, recalled the happy and invigorating times the family had spent living in the bungalow on Burton Beach. She said that there was no road down from the Coast Road and they drove over the fields to get to there.

As children, the Gollege family played and swam and helped the fishermen pull in the nets. Mrs Fitzpatrick remembered Mabel Hussey, who acted as a crew member and mended the nets for her friend, Tommy Swaffield, an old sailor turned fisherman, as well as Tom Ward, another fisherman, who came and 'did' for the family.

The Hunts, of Yeovil and Sherborne, pioneers in frozen foods, acquired the bungalow, with the land within the picket fence, in due course, using it as a holiday home for their employees. When the head of the Hunt family died, it was sold, completely freehold, around the mid 1980s, for the huge sum of £46,000.

In 2006 it was put on the market, once more, when it was expected to make half a million pounds. Following much publicity to this effect, it was taken off the market and awaited its future, standing invitingly at Burton Beach, (having been re-advertised) a reminder of summers gone, when there were no restrictions or regulations. In the spring of 2007 it realised £364,000 to a buyer 'on the telephone' who had not seen it.

83. *The Hive Beach, Burton Bradstock, between the wars, before Beach Road was constructed, showing at least seven fishing boats. The Villas and Grey Stones bungalow stand prominent. The main route up over the cliff leads off from Lot 85, the Black Bungalow.(Centre front) Lot 84, The Green Bungalow, has a veranda. Inset 83a Jack Gurd with his pair of grey cart horses, in tandem to a Dorset putt, hauling sand and shingle off Burton Beach, circa 1948.*

Lot 85 The Black Bungalow The Black Bungalow, set under the cliff on the west side, was owned by Miss Lilian Swaffield, a former nurse, whose family originated from Shipton Gorge. It was said that she had once been a nursemaid in the Tsar of Russia's household. She used the bungalow as a retreat, where she could peacefully spend time knitting and enjoying the superb position that the bungalow commanded, just above the beach. It was made of wood, as were so many dwellings of that period, which were mainly used as day-bungalows, although families had been known to stay in them the whole summer. No regulations dictated when such a property had to be occupied. Neither was there any reason to stop anyone sticking-it-out there, all through the winter. Some owners let the bungalows for holiday accommodation. Lily Swaffield worked alongside her two sisters, in the village post office. She paid the Estate yearly £1. 5s for the ground rent. Being a 'well-healed' spinster, it was surprising that she decided not to try to buy the land.

At the price of some cottages, the ground was secured by Mrs Coward, of Worcester, for £400.

Old post cards show the two bungalows and a number of other attractive summer chalets, that sprung up beside the beach, from the dawn of the twentieth century. They were battered by the strong, south westerly winds in rough weather. Often, the sea came over the Green Bungalow, into the car park and the spin-drift engulfed the whole of The Hive Beach area. These wooden bungalows were well built and stood up to all manner of weather conditions.

Lilian Swaffield had her bungalow taken down and re-erected near Loders along a quiet lane and in due course, she moved to Bradpole, in a modern property, where she lived out her days, far away from the beauty of The Hive and Burton Bradstock. The beach site remains unoccupied.

WITH VIEWS

Lot 86 *'An exceptional residence',* was how Grey Stones Bungalow, positioned on the cliff, to the west of The Hive, was described. It was being sold with vacant possession and commanded a magnificent view of the Chesil Beach and the English Channel beyond. In rough weather it was impossible to venture outside, for fear of being blown over, so strong was the wind off the sea!

The grounds amounted to approximately ½ an acre. Built, for the Pitt-Rivers Estate, 1930s in design, the main feature was the conservatory, which measured 22¾ feet by 4 feet 6 inches, with a beautiful southerly aspect. Since the bungalow had been erected, the locally based overseer for the Estate, Cecil Bailey of Long Bredy, was one who had enjoyed it as his home.

Swift bidding to £3,000, the going rate at the time, (for a prime site and the costs to build), was paid by SR Dodge, of Chippenham.

Until the Sale, there had never been competition to secure a place in Burton, that would markedly increase the purchase price. By the 1980s, the demand to buy a property in the village was intense. A pleasant bungalow in the Burton Bradstock vicinity could realise £20,000 more than one elsewhere. If Grey Stones Bungalow came under the hammer now, it could be expected to sell in excess of £600,000.

BAY VIEW.

Lot 87 had dominated the village scene since the 1880s, when the Pitt-Rivers family had built two impressive villas on the top of the cliff, naming them "Alpha" and "Omega". These towering buildings formed significant land-marks. At the time many grand houses in town and seaside were referred to as "villas".

The houses, of three storeys, with large cellars, had been used by the family as their summer residences. Numerous people from the village had been employed there as additional servants, since the family and friends had first visited and enjoyed the bracing air and magnificent view from the windows and gardens. To the back of the villas the view was equally fantastic. Between the wars, Lot 87 was let as a guest house.

During the Second World War, the villa had been requisitioned by the army and used as barracks. Renamed Bay View it had housed Polish escapees who joined the Royal Air Force, resulting in the area surrounding the properties, being out-of-bounds, to all but those with official passes. Many of these airmen took part in raids on the enemy, showing excessive bravery.

Now in 1958, the villa to the west, was up for sale. The present tenant was using it as a guest house. The rent was £100 and the tenant was responsible for the internal repairs and outside decorations. The latter could be a continuous task, as the property faced the sea, with the prevalent, salt-laden, south-westerly winds, coming straight at it. The second 'matching' villa, renamed "Barton Olivers", had been sold off, privately, some years before.

★★★★★★★★★★

At Bay View, there was a hall, 24 feet wide, four other ground floor rooms, seven bedrooms, on two floors, all fitted with hand-basins, a kitchen equipped for hotel use, pantry and other utility stores and bathroom. It was in excellent order and well appointed and included a porch, hall, morning room, dining room, living room, a garage and workshop. The guest house could boast two flush lavatories and mains water. A telephone and electricity were connected. Outside, were store sheds and a garage. The grounds totalled about ¾ of an acre. The rateable value was £80 and there was an annual licence granted for one caravan.

Recently, Mr and Mrs Wheatley had come to live in Burton Bradstock, to take up a completely different line of employment.

Wheatley purchased Bay View for £2,800.

> Today it is a pleasant hotel, rumoured to be changing hands again, standing a little nearer the cliff edge than fifty years ago but safe for another century.

A PASTURE FIELD

Lot 88 a piece of pastureland, dry, level, of loam and stone-brash soil, to the east of the villas, had a frontage of 420 feet onto the private Beach Road and lay within 100 yards of The Hive Beach. It was wedged between the newly erected bungalow, to the north of the field and the sea. The water-main ran right across the land. A buyer was entitled to take a supply of water from the pipe passing through the field, subject to making good any damage and making arrangements with the Bridport Water Company regarding charges. For the past two years it had been grazed by ponies and was in a tidy state, although the pre-war Estate wire fencing was in need of replacement.

The Lot was *withdrawn*. This was part of the plan to preserve the beach and its immediate hinterland.

VILLA CLIFF

Lot 89 amounted to nearly 9 acres, in two fields, surrounded by impressive walls, built of locally hewn stone. It was rented from the Estate by Edgar Hawkins. This stretch of open land, at the top of the cliff, behind the villas, was managed as part of the annual agricultural system on Shadrach <u>Dairy</u> Farm but in the season, formed a licensed caravan site for forty vans, regulated under the Town and Country and Public Health Act.

★★★★★★★★★★

Those who had camped there from the turn of the century, had been pioneers and were able to enjoy camping unhampered by rules and too many regulations. The total experience could be termed 'natural living'. Admittedly, the wind could blow strongly up there and in hot weather the site became parched, a disadvantage as the whole camp was completely open to the elements with there being no shade or shelter.

Caravans did not have refrigerators. Outside, were wooden cupboards, covered in the front with zinc gauze like rabbit hutches, that served as larders. Most campers had their own Elsan toilet tent, a modern amenity, replacing the old trench latrines. The camp was considered as being well run, proving popular, with so many campers returning year after year. The vans were positioned around the perimeter of the field, giving the campers greater privacy and an open recreational space in the centre of the field and not in rows, as was the custom for caravan camps, later on.

The field immediately behind the villas was used,

84. The Hawkins family in 1971. (L) to (R): Kitty and Edgar with (L) their son Dennis, nephew Christopher Shepperd and other son, (R) Bob.

on occasions, for sports and tea parties, as for the Coronation of Edward VII in 1902.

> With the caravans removed, in the 1960s, a gymkhana was held there. It was an ideal venue, being level with easy access. Now it forms part of The National Trust land and is grazed off by cattle.

★★★★★★★★★★

This prime site had a frontage of 350 feet to the Cliff Road - excellent access. Hawkins paid the Estate, £20 a year general rent(included in his tenancy of Lot 39) and an additional £90 a year for the camping arrangement, which was proportioned for the purposes of the Sale at £54 for Lot 89 (24 sites) and £36 for Lot 93 (16 sites). There was a total rateable value of £60. The licence expired at the end of that September and the land was being sold with vacant possession. There was some sort of scheme afoot, for its future use but that was only known to a few of those immediately involved.

The tenant bought the land for £2,000. This amounted to treble the going rate for agricultural land, sold with vacant possession.

> It was not long after the Sale that the Villa Cliff caravan enterprise was relocated to Larkfield, another of Edgar Hawkins's fields. At that time, the law was not so adamant about the positioning of camps. Years later it would never have been sanctioned. Sited on a fork in the roads, the proximity to a busy main road, with another winding road below which often flooded, would be considered unsuitable. The field was dotted with hollows where there were disused quarries. These were filled in with waste soil taken from Cheney's garage improvements.
>
> Now the fields at Villa Cliff form part of a beautiful, unspoilt stretch of hinterland, managed by the National Trust. The camp site at Larkfield continued to be administered by Dennis Hawkins who enjoyed chatting to the visitors. He rarely ventured out of the village and the tales the campers brought gave him an insight into the outside world. The camp was sold off a few years before the brothers' deaths and became part of a larger complex of good sites along the coast.
>
> In 2007, caravans are being replaced by the excellent, latest idea, of wooden chalets, the very same type of holiday dwelling that would have been turned down by the planning authority, a couple of decades before.
>
> Hundreds of visitors are able to enjoy the relative tranquillity of Larkfield, where amenities, such as shower blocks, wash-rooms or recreation halls are left to other camp sites.

THE JUBILEE ALLOTMENTS

Lot 90 Little Holwell, a 7 acre piece of land, between the main village and the area of recent development, with a frontage on to the Weymouth Road of 500 feet, had been chosen as allotments. The soil was dry and easy to work, consisting of loam and stonebrash. It was let to the Burton Village Produce Association on an oral tenancy of £10, who sub-let allotments to various keen vegetable growers. When the Second World War broke out, this land was put to good use, producing crops to complement the war-time rations. RB Howarth headed the local Produce Association and encouraged adults and school children, alike, to "Dig For Victory".

★★★★★★★★★★

Tony Legg recalls the name, "Jubilee Allotments". He also remembered a day around 1942, when seconded to the school gardening class, he saw tanks and military manoeuvres across on North Hill. When he got back to the village at lunchtime, he met his pal, Bill Allen. That was the end of Tony's day, as the boys skived off, to watch what turned out to be, Canadian troops on a practice run for the ill-fated raid on Dieppe. Elizabeth Buckler, as a small child, remembered the troops, holed-up in the ditches at the bottom of Kennon, early morning, cooking their breakfasts and eating out of their mess tins. For many years afterwards, the debris from that camp could still be found.

★★★★★★★★★★

The ¾ of an acre of land in proximity to the building sites in Beach Road, with the mains water, drainage and electricity in the road, made it a valuable proposition for building.

Lot 90, too, was *withdrawn* at the Sale.

In 1886, landowners were making areas available for allotments that the working people could rent, Earl Sandwich, speaking on an allotment question, said that at least one labourer in three, in the kingdom, had an allotment. There were about twenty acres for allotments rented out by the Pitt-Rivers Estate around Burton Bradstock. Some of the earliest allotments had been sited at the bottom of Common Knapp.

In 2007, the field is still in the hands of the Pitt-Rivers Estate [Rushmore] and is left as "fallow ground".

THE TOLL HOUSE

Lot 91 with vacant possession, this was an attractive but most unusual property, to come on the market. North Lodge lay on the Bridport to Weymouth Road, at the junction of the private road to Burton Beach, built between the wars, by Charlie Hitchcock, to serve as the Toll House, as it was known locally. It was of pleasing and unusual design, with some wooden cladding on the outside and had been built when a private road to the beach was put-in by Captain Pitt-Rivers in the 1930s and a toll charged on the vehicles that used it. At the same time, the long stone wall that stretched over from the cliffs down to The Hive Beach and onwards to Cogden, was broken to allow access to the beach. Development was planned for Clave End but was halted by the outbreak of war.

Inside North Lodge, there was ample space with three bedrooms. A sitting room, 13 feet by 12 feet with ceiling at 8 feet had a block floor and tiled fireplace. The kitchen, with sink and *hot and cold water* and a Rayburn cooker was very modern. At the back porch, were double coal bunkers. The house had a flush lavatory as the mains sewer, to the new houses in Beach Road, passed through the garden.

The Estate had put in Bill Elton, as the toll-keeper, although Cecil Legge, a regular in the Royal Navy, had considered applying for the post. (Legge was one of Burton's seafaring sons but soon found himself caught up in the war that followed, eventually retiring after thirty years' service).

By the time of the Sale, Elton had retired and moved to another Estate property in the village. The present toll-keeper, Charles Galpin, recorded the tolls from the sand and shingle lorries and kept the Estate workforce together. The actual toll on vehicles using the public road had been dropped and it was only the National Bus Company who paid a small concession. Galpin would be vacating the property on the 30th November, 1958.

The Lot did not reach the asking price, (around £2,500) and was sold privately at some later date.

COMMON LANE COTTAGE

Lot 92 *'a very charming cottage'* was the very sort that could be found pictured on a chocolate box. It had been a farm worker's cottage, within the Cogden Farm tenancy, for a considerable number of years and at the time of the Sale, was sub-let to Mrs Alice Guyatt, then a widow, who had brought up four sons. AF Bailey, of Cogden, held the cottage at £10 a year. She had provided an Alnite fire and a greenhouse.

★★★★★★★★★★

Situated about half-a-mile out of Burton, in Common Lane, it stood entirely alone, although there had been several other cottages, in that lane, recorded in the 1841 Census Return. These could have been destroyed by fire, or allowed to fall into ruin and may have been situated where Guyatt had tended his immaculate garden, opposite the cottage where there was a vacant plot. Such overgrown plots usually pointed to sites where cottages had once stood.

★★★★★★★★★★

In the Feudal period, enterprising serfs could build cottages on the common land, on the edge of a village, providing they were erected in a day and smoke was rising by sunset. These cottages fell to the landowner after three lives had expired. Usually, several men would club together to get the place up in the required time, using materials which could be found nearby, such as stone, wrack from the beach and reed for thatching. In the case of cottages in Common Lane, finding the materials was comparatively easy. Within living memory, stone had been extracted, for commercial purposes, from the quarries, just behind Common Lane Cottage, as had the reed, for thatching, at Cogden Mere.

★★★★★★★★★★

William Henry Guyatt had only recently died, at the age of eighty-one. He was a regular soldier and started his career in the 2ⁿᵈ Battalion of the Dorset Regiment. He had fought at Ladysmith and Tugela Heights, during the Boer War and in Turkey and Greece, in the Great War. Guyatt had been mentioned in dispatches and been decorated, by the French Government with the Medal of Honour and awarded the Queen's South Africa Medal and clasps, (Orange Free State, Transvaal, Tugela Heights, Relief of Ladysmith and Laings Nek) and the King's South Africa Medal.

During fierce fighting in the First World War, a retreating Russian, to escape identification, had handed him an inscribed gold cigarette case and his other equipment, which was said to include a sword. When Guyatt retired from the army, in 1920, and came to live in Burton, few were aware of his distinguished service record.

★★★★★★★★★★

Alice Guyatt was a fascinating person. She dressed in colourful outfits, often wearing a pretty scarf tied around her head, in Gypsy fashion. She claimed to be a fortune teller and many villagers had consulted her about their future. She was an avid Whist player, with her friends, May Northover and Gertie Cammell and was seen at many of the village functions. A skilled net-maker, she could always be found, at the cottage door, if the weather was fine, twisting her braiding needle in and out of the net that she was creating, glancing up at the intermittent traffic along the Coast Road and chatting to everyone who walked by, as well as cyclists and motorists who would draw to a halt to watch.

A memorable scene, had been captured by an American army photographer, of soldiers, who were stationed at the US army camp at Common Knapp, standing, talking to her at the cottage door, in 1944. She was also a clever wreath-maker and the beautiful paper flowers she fashioned, could have sold in any London West End store. Did she have some Romany blood in her, as many supposed?

★★★★★★★★★★

The picturesque cottage was thatched, with two bedrooms and the traditional sitting room, kitchen, scullery and larder. Lying in a bit of a hollow, family members considered it rather dark, due to the sombre colours and smoky atmosphere in those days. Pre-war, the road to Weymouth had a very rough surface and was almost void of traffic and one could stand outside the cottage, in the middle of the road, without fear!

A good sized, secluded garden surrounded the cottage, backing on to farm land and the footpath to Timber Bridge. On being demobbed, one of the Guyatt sons, Ron, had

85. US soldiers watch Alice Guyatt as she braids at her cottage door, Lot 92 in 1944. Inset 85a Mrs Guyatt, still braiding in the 1960s.

inherited his parents' gardening and floral skills and had set-up a florist's shop in Bridport. He had made good in life as a horticulturalist, passing numerous examinations and during the war had been employed by the Royal Air Force, visiting the air-stations and advising on growing crops for food production. On his discharge, he was in a sound, financial position, to purchase the Common Lane Cottage, for £400.

Mrs Guyatt lived on there until her death, when her son, Ron, let the cottage as holiday accommodation. An extension was added and the use of light coloured paints brightened the cottage considerably. All who went there were thrilled with its unspoilt charm and the delightful garden, secreted away from passers by. No one complained about the ghost that is supposed to appear, from time to time.

In 1990 it was sold again. Guyatt was determined that only a Burton person would live there. His wishes have been fulfilled and the quaint cottage is being preserved by a true Burton born and bred person who seems to have no trouble from the unsolicited visitor.

The Coast Road now has a continuous stream of vehicles travelling along it. The vast majority are driven by holiday makers or are large lorries, taking a picturesque short-cut.

Common Lane Cottage remains much as it always was, a reminder of the skills of the local inhabitants and unspoilt by modern renovation enthusiasm. Old fashioned roses surround its walls, adding to its charm.

It is one of Burton's best gems.

A PARCEL OF VALUABLE BUILDING LAND

Lot 93 was a 4½ acre field, on high ground, that butted on to the Coast Road and backed on to the new dwellings in Beach Road. A track-way, off Beach Road, afforded another useful entrance. Outline planning permission had been granted to develop the land for residential use. The adjacent field, to the east, had already been secured by the Rural District Council and the building in Beach Road, was well underway. 'Grand', expensive residences, the envy of many, were springing up. All was ripe for a large building project. There was a right-of-way sold with the Lot, for all purposes, over the north part of Beach Road, with the advantage of water laid on.

The field was still pasture which was handy for the heavy horses used on the beach. In recent years, Jack Gurd, a local man living in the village who was a gravel merchant, had grazed his working horses there. When he died, at the early age of fifty-three in 1949, his business was bought by Norman Good of West Bay and the land handed over at £15 a year, on a September Agricultural Tenancy.

Gurd's grey, cart horses had continued to be worked by Len Downton, from Burton, who had taken them on, when Tony Legg declined the offer. Legg was sought-after by the foreman of Goods, who persuaded him that he could be better employed at West Bay. When mechanical diggers were implemented for the sand and gravel extraction, at the beach, the grass keep of Lot 93, had been sanctioned for grazing riding-school ponies, on a temporary arrangement, free of charge, until the time of the Sale.

Lot 93, was sold to Dukes auctioneers of Dorchester. Whether this was for themselves, or they were acting as agents for a third party is speculative.

The price was £300.

BIND BARROW *the ancient tumulus*

Lot 94 Bind Barrow was a landmark, visible for miles around. This earthwork was an ancient tumulus which could be presumed was the burial place of a chieftain, who was settled in Burton, or who had over-run the village. There was an eerie feeling when one looked at the mound on the summit of the hill. It symbolised that the present generation took up only a minute span in time since the tumulus had first been built. It did not appear to have been excavated, although it was officially recorded as an ancient monument. It lay on a ley line, along which the ancient peoples, erected their worshipping places and burial sites. All led to Stonehenge. Bind Barrow field was used, in the 1900s, as a recreation venue for special events. On occasions the harmonium was carried on a cart to the base of the hill and vigorously vamped, to accompany the lusty communal singing.

There were two fields that made up the whole of Lot 94. Almost 10 acres lay on top of the eastern clay cliffs and became, in summer, easily parched by the sun. The whole of the 18 acres had recently been reclaimed [reseeded] by the tenant, AF Bailey, by arrangement with the Landlord. The soil was strong loam on clay, like the exposed part of the cliffs on the east of Burton Bradstock. AF Bailey paid £18 a year rent, payable on

September 29th, annually.

The crowd in the marquee was astonished to realise that neither AF Bailey, nor his son, bought this valuable Lot. TJ Lee of Andover, came in yet again and secured Bind Barrow for £1,300. This very special place in the hearts of Burton people had 'gone away'.

THE COMMON

Lot 95 Common land, in a village, often caused misunderstandings. Certain Common Rights gave the inhabitants licence to walk, collect firewood and particularly, in Burton Bradstock gorse [fuzz]. Fuzz had been gathered in the past, to heat bread ovens and for fuel in open grates. It was also used as bedding for livestock and "staddle" for corn ricks, [a bed of gorse to raise the rick up off the ground to keep out vermin]. Less than two hundred years before, fuzz had been scattered on the earth floors of the cottages. Commoners had various rights to graze cattle and sheep, or take pannage, [grubbing for acorns in areas where oaks grew] for pigs. The land still belonged to the Landlord and these rights were executed by his goodwill.

★★★★★★★★★★

A fire occurred at The Grove (House), in 1814 when it was stated that faggots of fuzz had been left too close to the hearth and had ignited.

★★★★★★★★★★

There were various rights of way over the Burton Common which covered over 200 acres. The western area of some 50 acres, sloped down to the beach and fronted on to the Coast Road. At the time of the Sale, it was all very neglected and was only fit as rough grazing. A government grant was available, if the land was cleared and put into a better order, for agricultural purposes. This would not be easy as the gorse, if left untended, for any length of time, would soon reinstate itself.

★★★★★★★★★★

The west part of Burton Common formed a spectacular section of the coastal strip and part of it, which included the former coastguard cottages, had been siphoned off. The Dowager Mrs Pitt-Rivers, (widow of Alexander), had moved to the old Coastguard Station and converted the cottages into a home for herself. Cynthia Stevens, who worked there, recalled that a long passage ran through the whole, from the kitchen at one end, to the dining room at the other.

A bungalow was built to house the chauffeur and his wife. It was named "Tollard Royal" after a village, within the Estate. Mrs Pitt-Rivers kept pure-bred chickens on a large scale; the methods way ahead of the time. She named the main poultry building, "The Palace".

In these modern laying-houses, the flock had individual nesting boxes and when a hen, carrying a numbered tag, went in to lay her egg, a shutter came down, trapping her inside until she was released by the person collecting the eggs, who was obliged to record each hen's efforts. The breed was predominately White Leghorns although Mrs Stevens had memories of a fierce Rhode Island Red cockerel. Other chicken houses and arks could be seen from the Coast Road. Mrs Stevens could remember collecting the eggs and having to record them individually. Young chicks were killed at a few weeks old, for the dining table, an uncommon practice at that time.

In 1936, Mrs Pitt-Rivers celebrated her seventieth birthday and invited some forty guests, including old servants and their families and friends from her days as the chatelaine at Rushmore House.

She presented her housekeeper, Mrs Emily Case with the deeds of Tollard Royal Bungalow. This gave Mrs Case a life interest in the property, in recognition of her many years of faithful service and devoted friendship.

★★★★★★★★★★

By 1958, the coastguard cottages had come into the ownership of Captain Forth and were let as holiday accommodation. An adjacent piece of land, was used as a caravan site. The cottages were first let as holiday homes from 1907, when the station was closed. In the early 1900s, a man had been employed as a caretaker. A shortage of water meant that he had to carry buckets, from the village, suspended from yokes, on his shoulders.

★★★★★★★★★★

£1,600 was the price realised for Lot 97, the west part of the Burton Common, beyond The Hive Beach, which fell into the hands, of EC Hine, of Shaftesbury.

Lot 96 the eastern end of Burton Common was described as *'a noted beauty spot'*, consisting of over 150 acres of unspoilt, uncultivated wild land. It was bordered by the Coast Road and stretched half-a-mile, down to the sea.

Its great feature was that it included the Mere which was an expanse of wild space and of a wet marshland with a prolific reed-bed, a haven for wildlife. Migratory birds flew in and out and thousands of starlings congregated there to roost, each evening.

The reed beds had been neglected during the war as the coastal defences prevented the thatchers and farmers from cutting the crops. After the war, it had sprung into use again for that purpose, to thatch hay and corn ricks and the roofs of the properties. Local inhabitants had gone there to cut reed for their own use, when they were responsible for the repairs of their homes under the Court Leet. This might have been once part of the Commoners' Rights, although not mentioned in the Sale catalogue.

In very cold winters, the village boys had skated, at the Mere. Once one had drowned when the ice broke. The whole area was wild and bleak. Gorse and rough grass predominated and poachers, who found good seclusion, as well as authorised men, had shot all manner of wild-fowl there, whilst newts, frogs and toads, spawned in the rather brackish water.

Foxes, badgers, rabbits, stoats, weasels and other smaller mammals, found ideal cover in the gorse and rough grass. These wild animals had for decades, been considered as vermin and in the Churchwardens' Accounts, of the nineteenth century, men and boys, were recorded as having received payment, at so much per carcase, head or tail. At the time of the Sale, some of these creatures would be snared or shot, as well as hunted by dogs and hounds. Roe deer found cover at the Mere but were rarely seen.

Amongst the gorse, grass snakes and adders abounded. The latter, were poisonous, never tolerated and were killed at every opportunity. Beautiful wild flowers that enjoyed poor soil, grew in abundance, such as wild purple orchids, known locally as a "Granfie Griggles", cowslips and mauve flowered, wild irises, the latter producing magnificent vermilion berries, in the autumn. Teasels could be found, which although growing wild, had been cultivated for carding in the woollen industry, prior to the advent of the flax and hemp mills. The prickly plants grew in the hedgerows of most of the Burton fields. At the Mere, they stuck their spiky heads up, amongst the fuzz.

The flocks of starlings flew in every evening, in thousands and at dusk, the sky over Freshwater and the cliffs, was black with these little birds. The loud noise they made was comparable to rushes of wind. Their cavorting, was a marvellous spectacle, although it passed unnoticed by most people, who saw it every day. As the flocks appeared to 'break ranks' and then reform, they flew into the Mere; a marvel of Nature.

★★★★★★★★★★

Above the Mere, was the White Ladies' establishment, consisting of a chapel and main building, with numerous little wooden bungalows, dotted amongst the gorse. The White Ladies, an Order of Christian Contemplatives, had been founded at the turn of the century, by Miss Adela Curtis, 1864 – 1960 who was an aristocratic lady, with private means. She called herself "the warden". Others of a similar persuasion joined her, by invitation.

These ladies had a regulated day of prayer and devotion and were self-sufficient. They were vegetarians, grew their own fruit and vegetables and made their own off-white habits from the wool they had spun. This was how they were given the local name of "White Ladies". They were often seen walking or bicycling in the village and later, as they aged, one of them learnt to drive. The outlook from their separate abodes was stupendous. Before them lay the rolling acres of the Common, the Chesil Beach below and beyond that, the vast expanse of the English Channel. On clear days, to the east, Portland Bill and looking westward, the chain of Devon cliffs, were visible.

At one time, their self-sufficiency caused discussion between them, the Rural District Council and Captain Pitt-Rivers, when it was contemplated that drainage should be installed. They were adamant that their "night soil" was best used on their vegetables and rumoured in the village, was the fact that from time to time, food hampers arrived from a well known London store.

A young man from the village, Ron Guyatt, had cut his horticultural teeth at The

White Ladies' establishment, in the 1930s, as the gardener, when he went there with his bride. They lived in the walled cottage and were involved with the day to day happenings. Ruby Guyatt's sister, Beryl Hyde, recalled listening to Miss Curtis's Saturday afternoon lectures which seemed, for a schoolgirl, to droll on and on. She remembered the nuts and lentils put out on the table and the wonderful freedom felt from running straight down to the beach to bathe.

The eastern part of the Common, on the Pitt-Rivers Estate, had been neglected following the agricultural depression in the 1920s/30s. The Second World War years had held-up any further restoration when the whole area had been requisitioned by the government. It was used by the army, in particular the United States' troops and the British and American Navies, for rehearsals for the Normandy landings and other military purposes. Fenced off and partly mined, it had been a no-go area for the people of Burton for a long time. Originally, it had formed a recreational place and had begun to become so again in the 1950s.

★★★★★★★★★★

Behind the beach, from Burton to Portland, was a shingle track, used over the centuries, as a quicker, if hard-going route. Cogden, Bexington, Abbotsbury, The Fleet, Langdon Herring and Wyke Regis lay along the way. What formed the main coastal road in 1958, had been rough and unmade, dangerous and exposed, as well as extremely hilly, especially near Abbotsbury. Men had walked from Burton village to work in the quarries at Portland, using the track along the back of the beach. They would set off very early, on foot, before first-light, on Monday morning, returning back to the village on the Saturday evening. The track was frequented by the fishermen and smugglers, too, being passable with donkeys and sure-footed ponies; all hidden from view.

★★★★★★★★★★

The Bailey family had rented this part of the Common and whilst Mary Bailey, was aware that her father-in-law did not intend to purchase Cogden Farm, she decided that, at least, they should come away from the Sale, owning something. This part of their tenanted land was beautiful, if somewhat unproductive, in a farmer's eyes. It had the benefit of the shingle extraction rights and the unique reed bed. Mrs Bailey, used a legacy of her own, to purchase this area of outstanding natural beauty. The bidding for this expanse of land was high.

By securing this Lot, the family then owned the loveliest stretch along the Coast. The fascinating Mere area and tons of shingle which could be extracted, by agreement, until 1973, by Woolaway Constructions Limited was then in their hands.

★★★★★★★★★★

Woolways had a base at West Bay and manufactured concrete structures. The Woolaway Company also made sectional bungalows. These pre-fabricated buildings, known as "pre-fabs", were in great demand after the war, to accommodate bombed-out families and newly married service people. Later, the construction of more spacious, permanent, Woolaway bungalows, mushroomed whilst, in contrast, Woolaways supplied concrete structures for the rebuilding of Coventry Cathedral.

Young Frank Bailey encouraged the production of the reed bed and was able to market it to local thatchers. Now, apart from a small area retained as a private beach, it is owned by the National Trust and managed by the Dorset Naturalist Trust.

★★★★★★★★★★

John Riggs, recalling, in 2004, his days of evacuation to Burton, that he had seen bodies being brought in at Cogden. This was following the disaster in the Channel, when ships carrying United States' army personnel, practising for landing on D-Day, had been attacked by German E-Boats and hundreds of soldiers lost their lives. This was hushed-up, until some forty years later.

THE SAND AND SHINGLE RIGHTS ON COGDEN BEACH

Lot 97 A complicated issue of the reversion of the right to extract sand and shingle, which at the time was held under contract with the Pitt-Rivers Estate, by Woolaway Constructions Limited, was sold with *Lots 95 and 96,* (the whole of the Common). Woolaways paid the Estate 1/6d a ton royalty, with a minimum payment of £150 a year. In 1956, 1, 917 tons had been taken out and in 1957 there had been 2, 226 tons of sand and shingle removed.

★★★★★★★★★★

When mechanisation superseded horses for extracting sand and shingle, from the Chesil Beach in the 1950s, a reporter from *The Bridport News* interviewed one of the main contractors, Ernest Phillips, of Bridport who had seen army surplus amphibious cargo carriers for sale and immediately thought of the use to which they could be put in his business. A third generation of his family to be in the sand and shingle business, he had tried various types of lorry with no success and his father had been adamant that nothing would ever be as successful, at doing the work, as the horse. After adapting the ex-army vehicles, Phillips said travelling along the beach at 30 miles per hour was possible and a ton and a half could be loaded in record time.

Burton and Freshwater beaches were unique in providing a particular quality of sand which was deposited as it came in with the tide. The merchant and his workers were wholly dependant on the wind and tide and if the conditions were not just right, they would have to wait for another tide, before work might be possible.

At the time of the 1958 Sale, the medium class sand, which would come in on a south-westerly wind, would be sent to Portland, where it was used in the stone-cutting industry. The south winds brought the finer quality sand that was required for the marble industry and a south-easter would carry in the small pebbles, often used in grinding paints and medicine. Men walked the beach picking [selecting] the right sort of pebbles, as all that were deposited on the beach, were not suitable for the various processes.

Phillips went on to explain, that pre-war, the Japanese had competed in the market but now the local materials were in great demand. The Burton sand had been proved to be the only kind in the country suitable for marble cutting. When the stone or marble was being cut, a wire had to be positioned on the surface and the sand fed on to it by water and the actual cutting was by the sand and not the wire. He concluded, "Burton Bradstock sand is still sought-after, the world over. "

★★★★★★★★★★

So it was that extraction at Cogden, was of prime importance and the bidding soared to £1,700 for the rights at Cogden Beach, until 1973 but the Lot was *withdrawn*.

Eventually, Frank Bailey, son of AF Bailey, purchased the shingle rights from the Estate and then, in due course, together with some land, sold on to Trevor Richards in 1973. Tony Legg, a Burton man, who had previously worked at West Bay for Goods, the sand and gravel merchants, later employed by Trevor Richards, recalled the uncertainty, in 1984, when the West Dorset District Council ordered that the shingle and sand extraction business had to close down, within six months.

Richards had upset the apple-cart by applying for planning permission to erect lavatories at Cogden Beach, which had fast become a popular tourist retreat and rod-fishermen's paradise, with competing angling clubs and visitors frequenting that part of the Chesil coast.

A report as to whether extracting the sand and shingle was detrimental to Chesil Beach was inconclusive. The Department of the Environment argued that the extraction was inappropriate in an area of such natural beauty, yet, the very same process had been practised for hundreds of years. Richards was determined to take his appeal to the highest level.

The matter wrangled on until 1986 when he was ordered to put back hundreds of tons of shingle that he had removed from Cogden Beach. Aware of a pending order, he had already extracted and stock-piled huge amounts, in the lead-up to the ban. Lorries had been leaving the beach in a constant flow, through the day and night.

Advice as to the replacing of the sand and shingle was given by the Wessex Water Authority and the Nature Conservancy Council. With the winter storms approaching, these official bodies were anxious to get the beach protected. Fed up with the red-tape Richards put the beach, car park and 20 acres, back on the market.

It is now owned and very effectively managed by the National Trust.

LARKFIELD

Lot 98 Where the lark had risen was marked on the old Estate maps as "Larkfield" and it sat in the fork of Bredy Road and the Coast Road, about ½ a mile from the village. This was an undulating piece of ground, about 5 acres in size, full of hollows, in two fields of 3. 7 and 1. 2 acres respectively. A footpath off the Coast Road ran through the field closest to the fork, to join Bredy Road. The stiles were of great blocks of locally hewn stone and stone steps led down from the path into Bredy Road. All the land was of good loam soil over limestone. Water was laid on and the mains electricity and sewer were handy. Edgar Hawkins was the tenant, paying £15 yearly, with a licence to keep one caravan. The tenant had claimed a water trough, which he had installed. The field was dotted with hollows from the days of quarrying.

Negotiations had taken place and this was another Lot that was _withdrawn_.

BOW MEADOW

Lot 99 had been made up with two other pastures to form the substantial Lot, fronting the Coast Road to Weymouth, on the south side and Bredy Road on the north. The fields, totalling approximately 13½ acres, were easy to work but not particularly level, opposite the development, off Beach Road.

Did Bow Meadow get its name from its shape or was it the field where the village bowmen practised their compulsory shooting, on Sunday mornings, after church? (There is no other name, amongst the many fields in Burton Bradstock, that indicated where the archers tried out their skills).

Its good position put a high price on this Lot which was bought by Tony Bishop, the tenant, for £1,000.

Lot 100 was _withdrawn_ from sale, being 3½ acres, with 300 feet of frontage on to the Coast Road.

An old wooden bungalow, used as a store and a Nissen Hut, were included and let to Edgar Hawkins at £15 per annum. He was responsible for maintaining the hedges, on the roadside and claimed the doors on the Nissen hut.

> It was not until sometime later that the picture began to emerge concerning Lot 100. Eventually, when a camp site was established in (adjoining) Larkfield, it was incorporated within the licensed site and is used for touring caravans.

AND STILL MORE 'VALUABLE' LAND

Lot 101 called "Benditch", 7½ acres, in two fields, was sold with vacant possession. It had a water supply fed by a spring, from other land rented by Edgar Hawkins, who bought Lot 101 for £700.

Lot 102 three fields of just over 7 acres, which lay in Bredy Road, with some good elm trees for timber, went to Hawkins as well, at £450. He had been a tenant of part, (at £7 p. a) and AF Bailey, (at £2 p. a.), tenanted the remainder. This land, too, was sold with vacant possession.

Lot 103 had been sold with Cogden Farm, Lot 78. One 4 acre field was named "Little Kit Whistle". The tenant had been given permission by the Landlord to grub-out a hedge. These were early days for taking out hedges to make the fields larger and consequently, easier to work with machinery. Each hedge took up several yards. Getting rid of hedges, freed more land but in the long term, reduced the habitat for wild life.

THE LONG STANDING TENANT

Lot 104 Reginald Buckler came from a long family line in Burton. He could trace his family back to the earliest parish register of 1614 and surnames of his ancestors appeared as early as 1327 in Lay Subsidy [tax] Rolls. He was now obliged to bid for the land that he had farmed for so long. It amounted to 9 acres of *'valuable accommodation land, fertile loam, intersected by a stream'.* No mention was made of the ghostly cavalcade that was supposed to haunt the bottom of Kennon hill! Perhaps to ward off snoopers, the smugglers of old, had concocted a tale of a carriage and horses, driven by a headless coachman, racing along there.

★★★★★★★★★★

At the age of fourteen, Buckler had taken himself off to join the army, setting out with another lad from Burton, passing themselves off as being seventeen. Buckler was well nourished and 6 feet 2 inches tall but the other boy, who was much smaller, was rejected and split on his mate, who had to return home and fill in the intervening years, before volunteering, when war broke out in August 1914. It was during his service that he saved a Weymouth soldier who was in difficulties and drowning. The unit was ferrying horses and guns across a river in India when Dick Gill got into difficulties. The commanding officer yelled, "Buckler save that man!". He swam out and brought Gill safely to the river bank. They became lifelong friends, Gill going on to become Deputy Chief Constable of Winchester City Police.

Reg Buckler enjoyed army life. He was fortunate to have been posted to India rather than France and stayed on after the First World War but in 1919 took up Prime Minister Lloyd George's offer that ex-servicemen should be entitled to rent land from the large estates.

Prior to his army service, he had kept animals and ponies at Magnolia Farm and he had to decide which career to follow. From the Pitt-Rivers Estate, Buckler decided to rent some 9 acres of land in Shipton Lane, on an oral tenancy, which adjoined another block of land, he rented, from the Hertfordshire branch of the Gale family. He set himself up as a cattle, pig and fish dealer. One field at the northern extremity called "Three Cornered Field", was bordered on the roadside, by a steep bank, where the wild irises and primroses grew and adders basked in the sun. Elm trees grew in profusion.

Buckler had held a tenancy from the Estate the longest in the village and was acclaimed as such by the auctioneers. In fact, his ancestors, some having served on the Court Leet juries, could be traced back as tenants of the first Lord Rivers. On his holding he had erected a 1930s design wood and asbestos bungalow, with the Landlord's sanction. Here, he and his wife Gladys, née Wadham, of Bridport, (although born in Ceylon, where her father was employed as a Government official) and daughter, Elizabeth, lived a life of freedom and peace. During the Second World War he served as a Special Constable.

86. *Reg Buckler 1958.*

★★★★★★★★★★

At Kennon, the water was always a problem. In the 1940s, Buckler had a well dug, about 20 feet deep, down through the blue, 'clingy' clay. It was very hard water but had always yielded a reasonable supply, which he was able to supplement with rain water, caught in huge tanks. The clear spring water, that flowed through the holding, provided drinking water for the animals out in the fields. Buckler was a renowned judge of livestock and a knowledgeable pig breeder and kept one of the largest herds of pigs in Dorset, particularly through the war years. In times of drought, he had to motor down to the village and fill churns from a mains-water tap. He always contended that the advantages of the privacy, beauty and tranquillity of living where he did, far out-weighed any disadvantages.

The holding was situated at the very top of Kennon hill, verging on the northern line of the Pitt-Rivers Estate. The view, extended in all directions to Hardy's Monument in the east, Shipton Hill, looking northwards, westward lay North Hill, with its cider orchards and the ruins of Cowper's Lodge and the magnificent panorama of Burton Bradstock village, with the church in the centre, the villas, cliff and sea beyond, to the south.

No man could have wished for more, he always said. Reg Buckler loved the place and nothing pleased him more than to hear, after a storm, from a mile away, a ground-sea, [the pebbles being drawn back as the waves retreated], or the church clock chiming and the sound of the bells. Although one of the most idyllic spots on the Estate, when a south-westerly wind was blowing, or a cold draught came in from the north or east, it could be the wettest, windiest or the coldest place in the parish. It was certainly one of the healthiest spots! In blizzard conditions it had been cut off, as in 1941 and 1947.

In 1958, the rent was £27 a year on an oral tenancy.

★★★★★★★★★★

After the clapping that had followed the announcement of Reg Buckler's long association with the Estate, he stood up, made a wry comment in appreciation and bid to £900 for his holding.

> Reginald Buckler's daughter, married in the October, following the Sale and a three bed-roomed bungalow, with a magnificent view, was built at the northern end of the holding. When it was completed in 1960, it was named "Buckler's Bid", in consideration. The building site of ¾ acre was valued at £200 and the bungalow cost £2,200 to construct, by Osbourne Brothers, builders, of Bridport.
>
> In 1962, following a blizzard on the night of 29th December, Kennon Knapp was again cut off from the world, with the road to Burton and Shipton impassable. A few days later, it was just negotiable on foot. After several more days had elapsed, a tractor had got through facilitating passage by heavy vehicles, equipped with snow-chains. This situation lasted for seven weeks; the snow remained frozen solid. All water was frozen-up, the stream was iced over and snow had to be melted for the animals. Cans of drinking water were obtained from the farm below, (which lay at about 10° F warmer), after a treacherous scramble over the frozen drifts and icy surface. The summer came lovely, as always and the terrible winter was soon forgotten.
>
> Buckler and his wife enjoyed a few more years at Kennon, before his death in 1964. Mrs Buckler stayed on there another twenty years, roughing it out in all weathers but revelling in the tranquillity, the superb views and gathering her friends and family around her.
>
> The holding was sold and a modern bungalow was built on the crest of the hill in the early 1980s. The architects were unaware that their chosen site, was the most exposed area of ground on the land.
>
> Buckler's Bid, still in the family, was sold in 1989 and a large house was built by Poole Brothers, on the site but it still retains the original, now historical, name. Elizabeth has held on to some land, for sentimental reasons.
>
> The ashes of Reginald and Gladys Buckler were interred, at Kennon, as was their wish, remembering his philosophy in life centred around the old saying that, *'Time and Tide for no Man Bide'*.

SUMMER PASTURES

Lot 105 3¾ acres, known as Lankhams, adjoining Reg Buckler's holding, in Shipton Lane, was tenanted by Geoffrey Derryman, a farmer and milk retailer. He had taken on the tenancy following the death of small-holder, Bill Hutchings. Derryman, rented the major portion of his land, called Kennon Farm, from the Gale family, where he had moved with his wife, pre-war. Their children Colin and Moira grew up there. Originally from Devon, Derryman still carried a lilting accent. He had served in the Home Guard during the war and then was recruited as a Special Constable.

Derryman used these two outlying fields as part of his farming programme. They were of loam and faced south. When the sun shone they basked in its full warmth and the grass grown there was good and lush.

Buckler was interested in buying Lot 105 but when he learnt that his neighbour intended to purchase, if possible, he decided not to bid against him. Being a bit wary of superstitions, this gesture let him off from a fear that he nurtured, that old villagers had always maintained, that the fields were bedevilled and always brought bad luck.

Phyllis Derryman, ran a guest house at Kennon Farm and was a far-seeing business woman. She could visualise building an attractive residence on this land and extend her number of visitors. The fields had access to

87. Geoffrey and Phyllis Derryman, 1967.

the green lane off the main Shipton Gorge to Burton Road, beyond which lay Rowdens, some land belonging to Graston Farm.

A speculator could see potential there, too and when the Derrymans realised that he was determined to outbid them, they dropped out. The bidder was a AT Bargess, from Langport, in Somerset, who paid £225.

Later, Bargess approached the Derrymans, claiming that he was short of ready money and hoped that they wanted the fields so badly that they would pay him on top of the purchase price. Phyllis Derryman is reputed to have said, "That's your bad luck!" In due course Bargess dropped back £50 to £175, selling on to them. The Derrymans built "Barton End", a large chalet type bungalow, commanding spectacular views and a guest house where the family enjoyed entertaining personal friends, as well.

Geoff Derryman served as a Special Constable, in the Bridport district. He became well liked and respected; a policeman, in which one could have every confidence. He served for a considerable time and a presentation was made to him on his retirement.

Colin Derryman ran a milk delivery business and served as Parish Council Chairman. Later he set-up a successful photographic establishment, in which he had nurtured a long-standing interest, in Chard, which has now been taken over by his daughter, Marie.

Geoff and Phyllis Derryman retired to the outskirts of Bridport and Barton End changed hands. He is now (2007) in his nineties and is as kind and considerate as ever.

PITFOLD FARM

Lot 106 '*a compact and mixed farm*', was a traditional holding of 84 acres, situated in the parish of Shipton Gorge, only ¾ of a mile from Bothenhampton. Pitfold Farm had a long and somewhat difficult approach by a public road, along Rudge Lane, past Bennett's Hill Farm and thence by a private road, to the farmstead, or, in the opposite direction from Bothenhampton, along a rough track.

The private road was shared with the tenant and owner of Manor Farm, enabling access to adjacent land, that went with Manor Farm, for which Bunny Lenthall paid 13/2d a year. The Bridport Rural District Council had a right-of-way over part of the road to the council rubbish tip and were responsible for a quarter of the costs of the upkeep. Another condition was that there was a right-of-way, on foot, across some adjoining land which, at the time, was rented by Joseph Barnes.

The field names at Pitfold Farm were fascinating – "Great Fuzey Ground", "Lower New Barn Meadow", "Barret's Coppice" and "Yonder Bennett's Hill". The picturesque farmhouse was set in the hollow, circled by the fields. It consisted of two reception rooms, one measuring 16 feet by 15 feet and 7 feet 4 inches high, a scullery with a sink, large backhouse, cheese-room, storeroom and four bedrooms. Mrs Barnes had been told that once there had been a serious fire at the house.

Outside was a walled-in garden, earth closet and interesting farm buildings. Foremost amongst these was the thatched stall. A cider house remained from the days when all the farmers grew apples and made the local, traditional beverage. Some of it would be sold and the rest consumed by the farm labourers. Another ancient feature, at Pitfold Farm, was an open-fronted wagon house, with its large supporting oak posts.

Day and night a continuous rush of cold, spring water, flowed through a chute into a trough in the yard. This reliable supply, from an underground spring, was fed by gravitation, to a 500 gallon reservoir and then piped to the trough and house.

Barnes paid the Estate a rent of £140, on an oral yearly tenancy, with the rateable value of the farmhouse at £7. In 1954, the Estate had spent £945 on the property. All drainage went to a cesspool and of importance, a telephone was connected.

Lot 107 14 acres of pastureland, were sold with Pitfold Farm and the whole, realised £4,100, being purchased by an unknown lady, Mrs V A Taylor of Stoke-sub-Hamdon, Somerset.

> The purchase of Pitfold Farm caused the auctioneers a problem as Mrs Taylor had bought the farm without seeing it! Mrs Christine Bulger, relates that she was told that when the new owner paid a visit, it was not to her liking and she came to an arrangement with the Estate. The Rushmore Estate office does not appear to have any record of a Mrs Taylor, although she is given as the purchaser in *The Western Gazette* report. The farm was taken back-in by the Estate and was then sold

on to the unknown purchaser who had secured Manor and Cogden Farms and The Hive and Burton Beach.

Barnes retired in 1960 and the farm was then rented to farmer George Bugler, next door at Bennett's Hill, in the first instance and later his sons, Geoffrey and Robert.

Both brothers lived in the farmhouse, at separate times, with their families and they were obliged to paint the outside of the farmhouse in the owner's livery. The new landlord visited the tenants at Pitfold Farm on several occasions and he finally sold the farm. In due course Robert Bugler became the sole owner. Bugler proceeded to extend and restore to a very high standard and he and his wife, Suzanne, (with maternal Burton origins), farmed there for a number of years.

The peace and beauty of the place has been preserved. A hard surfaced, private road connects the farm to Bothenhampton. Updated, Pitfold Farm, it is now a fine working model of a typical old Dorset farmstead.

The summer of 2006 brought tragedy to this happy set-up with the sudden and unexpected death, of Rob but not before he had transmitted his love of Dorset, the old traditions and his wealth of knowledge about the countryside and farming to his children and grandchildren.

BOUGHT BY A SPECULATATOR

Several lots consisted of accommodation land on the outskirts of the Pitt-Rivers Estate, in Shipton Gorge.

Lot 108 an ancient track led over the hills from Bridport to Burton Bradstock, branching off down over the fields into Gages Lane. It was once a pack-horse way. The Ridgeway led on towards Bredy and along the hilltops to Chilcombe.

Ridge [corrupted to Rudge] Lane Ground and Higher Bennett's Hill, 22½ acres, adjacent to Pitfold Farm, were let to Joe Barnes at £22 a year. This was sold to a speculator, FC Fenner of Somerton, for £625. The advantage of this ground was, that it was supplied with water, for part of the year, from a spring there.

THE OLD LIME KILN

Lot 109 was *withdrawn* from the Sale for use by the Bridport Rural District Council.

The old Lime Kiln, at Bennets Hill was conveniently situated well out of Burton, Shipton Gorge and Bothenhampton villages and used by the Rural District Council as the local rubbish dump. The Estate had an arrangement and it was obvious that the authorities could not do without a place to deposit refuse. The area amounted to nearly 3 acres of land and was let, on an oral tenancy, at £10 a year.

There was a narrow public road to nearby Bennett's Hill Farm, over which there was a right-of-way, for all purposes. The owners of Lot 109 were responsible for three-quarters of the cost of maintenance and the entrance gate and post were also their responsibility. If the old Lime Kiln ceased to be used as a rubbish pit, then the owners would be liable for *'a fair proportion of the costs'*. Heavy, loaded lorries went to and fro from Burton and Shipton Gorge, along Rudge Lane, which was narrow and very rough, causing even more damage to the surface.

The amount of waste, for disposal, was growing year on year and the tips that everyone had at the bottom of their garden, for burning and burying household waste, were getting quite inadequate and not to the liking of new neighbours. It was essential that this Lot did not go to an outsider.

Lot 110 stated as accommodation pastureland, in the catalogue, amounting to 7 acres, also at Bennett's Hill, went to, CJ Wakely of Somerton, for £425, who was an acquaintance of Mr Fenner.

JACK WAY.

Lot 111 comprised 12 acres of useful, rough pasture of heavy clay, in Rudge Lane. As the two fields sloped south, it was ideal summer grazing land, affording some good shelter at the bottom, by the stream. Huge, well matured trees, such as elm, ash, sycamore and holly, bordered the sides of the stream, fed by the springs, which abounded. The whole was let to Rob Gale, who grazed his cattle young-stock there in the summer months.

★★★★★★★★★★

Gale had a lodger in the far field. This was Jack Way, a recluse, who had made his home there for about thirty years, in a wooden, shepherd's hut and had set himself up with a galvanised shelter, where he warmed himself by his open fire and worked, in inclement weather, surrounded by his cats, which he had found on the rubbish dump. He made himself slip-on leather shoes and had numerous ways of prolonging the life of his clothing, by sewing leather patches on to his garments.

Jack Way was about sixty years old and was born in Beaminster. A skilled saddler, he had served in the First World War, where he had witnessed appalling suffering to man and beast. One of the main means of transport and haulage were horses, requisitioned at the outbreak of the war, from farmers, who were obliged to bring them into collecting centres. In West Dorset these were at the cattle market in St Michael's Lane, Bridport and Broadwindsor Square.

Way's service in the army, had taken him into France. He was an intelligent and deep thinking man and his time spent in the mud and flooded trenches, with the continuous gunfire, carnage and devastation, had resulted in him being shell-shocked, for which he received no sympathy or treatment.

After the First World War, he had returned to Burton Bradstock, having married into a local family and with his wife, set up their home in the caravan, off Beach Road. It seems they parted company and the Estate required him to move on when the new road to the beach was under construction. This then brought him to Rudge Lane where, in return, he oversaw the cattle for Rob Gale and worked on his farm, on a part-time basis. On occasions, at Christmas, Way would visit his sister, who lived in the Symondsbury area.

Over the years, he worked for most of the local farmers as a 'strapper', [general worker, capable of tackling all the various jobs on a farm], as well as mending harness, saddlery, boots and shoes. His illness never received attention and at certain times, at particular phases of the moon, he was overcome by the pressures within his brain, which made him difficult and confused. Added to this, he did not feed himself properly and often drank too much cider. During one period he had the companionship of a rather fierce dog.

On his way home from Burton, he would often call in at Kennon Farm, the home of the Derryman family and Carolyn Eury, [now Mrs Drewitt], from Guernsey, who worked there, recalled that he smelt of eucalyptus oil. This was Jack's age-old remedy for colds and coughs, to which he easily succumbed, living in such rough conditions. He obtained drinking water,

88. Jack Way.

courtesy of the Buglers, at Bennett's Hill Farm, who were tolerant of his peculiarities.

Some people in the village dismissed him but there were others who gave him work and food and invited him into their home. In his better moods he was a very interesting and well informed person and made good conversation. In his latter years, he rode a bicycle, that he had restored, having salvaged it, as well, from the council rubbish dump, although more often than not, it had no brakes or tyres. In his dark moods, he dragged an axe behind him but to those that knew him, this was as a protection for himself, as he was haunted by his fear that he would be attacked by the old enemy [the Germans].

Way had no time for independent women, although he worked for Miss Marion Rendall, Miss Elfrida Buckler and later her niece, for many years. When he was in a bad mood he would swear at them and mutter about suffragettes!

In the Second World War, he was a member of the Home Guard and when a stray bomb fell on the well, beside Cowper's Lodge, at North Hill, he was convinced that the Germans were after him. Luckily, the bomb fell into the deep, wet clay, surrounding the cattle drinking area; the blast only doing minor damage. Sods of earth flew some two hundred yards, hitting Jack's caravan. This unnerved him, even more and every evening he would dress in his Home Guard uniform, put his belt of cartridges around his waist and armed with his gun, descend on Reg Buckler and his family, who lived nearby. He was given sanctuary for a number of weeks but Mrs Buckler became worried that Jack might lose his senses completely and shoot them in their beds.

When the war was over, he settled down, continuing his reclusive life, just managing to earn enough on which to survive. When he reached sixty-five he was able to obtain a State Pension and he became a regular caller at the post office. From there he travelled around the village, chatting to all he met, ending up in one of the pubs.

★★★★★★★★★★

The land, in Rudge Lane, was bought at the Sale, by speculator, C J Wakely from Somerton, for £550, who was aware that he had acquired a resident with the land. Rob Gale remained as the tenant.

★★★★★★★★★★

Further pasturelands in Rudge Lane and some that led off from the track to Shipton Gorge, from Bennett's Hill Farm, were sold to the tenants, or to the speculators, from Somerton, Somerset, averaging £56 an acre.

Jack Way was allowed to live on there by Rob Gale, who remained the tenant for a further five years, although by then, legally, Way had probably secured "squatters' rights". When the land changed hands again in 1963, he stayed on, living his lonely existence unfettered with rules and regulations. He caused little trouble, except that he was prone to leaving the gates open, allowing stock to roam and he would put his obsession with 'block and tackle' [pulleys], into practice, fixing a rope to the top of good, mature trees, with the aid of a grappling hook and by adjusting the winch, he eventually felled them, to use for firewood.

He did take liberties towards the end of his life when it involved too much effort to go to Bennett's Hill Farm for water and as he was an inventor and certainly, an improviser, he connected a pipe, (salvaged from the dump) to the cattle trough and siphoned the clean water, across the road to his caravan. By means of poles, either side of the lane, the pipe went overhead, except when the 'arrangement' fell down and it lay on the roadway. He had a better water system, (with a type of shower) than many of the tenants in the 1958 Sale!

Jack Way's mental health problems were caused by the trauma that thousands of First World War servicemen had experienced, affecting them for the remainder of their days. He never hurt anyone but his life was ended abruptly, in 1972, when he was struck by a motor car, as he wended his way home from Bridport, one dark night. He was about seventy-nine years old.

His possessions were few. Amongst his belongings were his Confirmation Prayer Book, given to him by his mother and the notice of compulsory requisitioning of horses for the First World War. Shortly after his death, some boys, playing in his old caravan, set it alight, obliterating for ever the strange life of this local character.

★★★★★★★★★★★

In June 2004, Janet Guppy, recalled a day, sixty years before, when she was in the very same fields with her uncle, Rob Gale, at haymaking time. He was on the top of the hayrick and called her up to see a sight that she has never forgotten. Out on the sea, were hundreds of boats, of all sizes and descriptions, awaiting the order, to cross the English Channel, with British and American troops and other allies, on board, for the D-Day invasion of Normandy. Hundreds of U. S. soldiers had been stationed in Burton, Bridport and the surrounding villages. In one fell swoop they had left. Most that set out from Burton found themselves on Omaha Beach on June 6th, with devastating consequences.

A plaque at the village green, commemorates their time in Burton Bradstock.

MORE OUTLYING LAND

More land, belonging to the Pitt-Rivers Estate, lay on the northern extreme of the Estate, in Shipton Gorge and was auctioned.

Lot 112 4½ acres at Greenway, Shipton Gorge was let to the Executors of the late Henry Bartlett, (Bartletts had been builders and were a very old Shipton/Burton family).

AJ Atyeo, a smallholder and agricultural contractor in Shipton, had taken it over. With a frontage of 250 feet, there was a good chance that it would become land for development. Shipton Gorge had seen little movement, for new housing.

Atyeo bought the land for £550, a speculative price.

Lot 113 another 9 acres in Shipton Gorge were let to Bunny Lenthall, at £12 a year on a Michaelmas tenancy, were approached by a rough track and supplied with water, by means of a ram on other adjacent land. The tenant had written consent from Captain Pitt-Rivers to erect a piggery.

This Lot was *withdrawn* at £350.

Lot 114 another field of nearly 4 acres, defined as *'fertile'*, adjoining Bonscombe Lane, on the outskirts of Shipton Gorge, let to Lenthall at £5 a year, made £225 and was purchased by another new bidder, HP West, from Woking.

The auctioneers had done a good job with their advertising. The Sale had been featured in all the newspapers in the south of England and good quality national periodicals. Speculators had come from near and far.

THE DOVE INN

Lot 115 An amendment to the catalogue had been sent out. This revealed that Lot,

115 would include The Dove Inn, built early in the eighteenth century, flat, garden, open ended garage/shed, car park, store and part of the allotments. The new arrangement of this Lot was due to the ongoing discussions between the Parish Council and the Estate. There was to be no Lot 115a as listed in the catalogue which had been given as *'a valuable site at Southover with 45 feet frontage and a depth of 140 feet and long river frontage,'* and intended as a building site.

Augustus [Gus] Wylde paid a yearly, apportioned rent of £95, payable quarterly, for the inn and £4 annually, for the garage, (formerly the stone building) and part of the garden. The amendment to the lotting amalgamated portions of Lot 115 and 115a, a much better arrangement which happened to favour the licensee.

89. *Southover before alterations to The Dove Inn. (R) The 'mortuary' shed. (Front L), Lot 116.*

The Dove Inn, situated in Southover, had long been a hostelry. Very old records called it a 'beer house' and at the time of the Sale it did not have a licence for the sale of spirits.

★★★★★★★★★★

The parish registers recorded many drownings at sea. Often, the bodies that had been washed up, within the parish, had been brought back to the stone shed, opposite The Dove Inn and laid out, awaiting an inquest, which would be held in the village, usually at one of the inns. A foreman and jury, picked from men of the village, were sworn in and were required to bring in a verdict.

On August 1st 1958, this quaint old inn was to come under the hammer. The Sale catalogue referred to it as *'an exceptionally attractive property with great scope and character.'* The 'mortuary' shed was included.

★★★★★★★★★★

William Northover had been the previous landlord and on his retirement, The Dove Inn had been modernised, skilfully re-coated with thatch and front porches added. Almost £1,000 had been expended by the Pitt-Rivers Estate in the previous five years. Gone was the dimly lit public bar, which was divided by a flagstone passage from the cold, stark lounge bar, originally nothing more than the front room of a cottage. 'Out the back', in the beer cellar, 13 feet by 8 feet 10 inches, with a sink and hot and cold water, the landlords of the past had drawn cider and beer from barrels cocked-up on old, wooden trigs. The flagstone passage was worn down with the feet of those who had trodden it for so long. The public bar was scheduled in the Sale catalogue as being *'15 feet 3 inches by 9 feet 6 inches, with brick fireplace and 7 feet long bar table.'* The latter was an historical feature.

The inn had been brought into the twentieth century and bore a chocolate-box cover appearance, attracting the many visitors that frequented the village and camp sites (the gentlemen's lavatory was outside). A number of people came up from Freshwater, by means of a footpath that ran past The Dove. At that time, Freshwater Camp was not self-sufficient. The campers came into the village for the postal facilities, groceries, newspapers, petrol, pony riding and to find a social life and visitors attended St Mary's Church, boosting the size of the congregation, during the summer months.

All the services were connected at The Dove Inn and the mains sewer ran across the nearby allotment. The whole area amounted to around ½ an acre. The tenant was required to undertake the internal repairs of the whole property, pay the rates, a total of £37, and maintain the fences and drains.

There was living accommodation, constructed from an adjoining cottage, where as a little girl, Doris Williams had watched old Brown, sitting across the threshold on the flagstones making sails. Later, the Steel family had taken on the tenancy. The 'flat' had a connecting door to the inn for the landlord and his family. This gave The Dove a total of five, generous sized, bedrooms. Updated, with a bathroom, there was ample scope for letting to holiday makers, on a bed and breakfast system. Inside, the pub oozed an 'olde worlde', pleasant, cosy atmosphere. This was what enticed the holiday maker of the 1950s who had never been inside an ancient, low, thatched, property, with oak beams and thick cob walls.

★★★★★★★★★★

One of the pieces of furniture in the public bar was sold with the premises. This was a plain, rough, wooden table, about seven feet long, which stood on iron legs, made by the blacksmith of the time. The trestle-type table was, in fact, the hatch of a schooner, "The Flirt", that had foundered off Burton, on the Freshwater side, in 1898. Four men jumped overboard, one was rescued by James Gear, who received an award from the Royal Humane Society. Three other men were reported as having been saved by the coastguard rescue team.

It was said that the bodies from shipwrecks were carried back to the building opposite the inn and those from the tragedy of "The Flirt", put on the very hatch that was later made into a table. Henrietta Williams, née Hitchcock, who lived in Southover, recalled, as a child, seeing bodies, from time to time, laid out in the shed. The wreck of the schooner was purchased by Andrew Spiller, of Bridport, for a few pounds.

★★★★★★★★★★

The landlord at The Dove Inn was Augustus Wylde, from a military family who had been a chauffeur to Lady Warrender, in Surrey. During the First World War he had served in India and on his return home, although offered his old position again, declined it to his brother. In the subsequent war, he was a Ministry of Supply driver, based in Reading and in the early 1950s, with his family moved to Burton Bradstock, mainly for the health of his elder son, Desmond, who had a heart condition. He found employment with the Ministry removing the obsolete defences around the coast and later with Woolaway Constructions and Desmond served an apprenticeship as an agricultural and general engineer.

Wylde's association with Burton had been forged pre-war when the family had camped at Villa Cliff site and he was able to experience the thrill of seine fishing with the local men, a recreation he, with Desmond, carried on when he returned to live in the village. His decision to take on as landlord of The Dove Inn was to give Desmond another interest.

The auctioneer called Lot 115 and it appears that Wylde did the bidding, although records indicate that the inn was purchased by regional brewers, Brutton, Mitchell and Toms, Limited, of Yeovil, for £4,250. Speculation, on the family's part, seems to point to an arrangement between Wylde and the brewers. Locals were under the impression that Wylde purchased for himself.

Gus Wylde stayed on as the landlord of The Dove, with his wife, until his retirement in 1965, when they took themselves off to Dawlish, their popular son, Desmond, having died. Their daughter, Jean Day and her husband, Charles, took over as the hosts. They had not intended to follow her parents to Burton but when Charles, a butcher, came out of the forces, they had unfortunate problems with accommodation in Reading. On arrival in Burton he was employed at Manor Farm where his army experience in driving heavy vehicles stood him in good stead and later he worked for butcher Gale.

★★★★★★★★★★

The Dove Inn has had some seven hosts, since 1958 and remained one of the most popular hostelries in West Dorset, particularly as it was the base for the Greenfingers Club where George Hirst, a talented accordionist played and Cynthia Stevens entertained with her beautiful singing, as good as any professionals. The Dove Inn provided employment for villagers and one who speaks highly of the popularity and importance to the village, of The Dove, is Alice Legge, a local woman.

When renovations were made, by Gus Wylde's grandson, Roger Day, to an old stone building opposite, wallpaper fragments were discovered, proving that it had been part of a row of cottages, shown on a very ancient photograph. (One row in Southover burnt down in 1898).

The table was left as a memorial to those who had perished at sea. It was used in the public bar until 2001 when The Dove Inn was closed and the premises split

248

up into separate cottages, much as it must have been three centuries before. For those who used The Dove, on a regular basis, where there was great camaraderie, this was the last straw. What was left of the old Burton Bradstock as they knew it was finished!

By the efforts of David Barnikel, who cherished the old ways and traditions and some other concerned people, the table was secured for all time and donated to the Parish Council and is now safely installed in the Reading Room. In the years to come, those who have to contend with its weight and move it around, may question and hopefully, respect, its origins.

Lot 37 had been delayed until The Dove Inn had been sold. It consisted of three allotments, with 4 perches let annually to Ernest Thorne at 4/-, 6 perches to Leslie Gale at 6/- and 11 perches "in hand". There was an overall frontage to Cliff Road of 60 feet, with a return of 80 feet, an important, prominent corner site. Main water, electricity and drainage were in the road and The Dove sign was erected on allotment number one, by arrangement with the tenant.

Ironically, it was the landlord of The Three Horseshoes, Harold Greenham, (a local man whose wife could boast Burton ancestry), who purchased the whole area for £150.

Greenham's son, Ernest, a popular Bridport footballer, built an attractive bungalow on this valuable, prominent site which is still in the family's hands.

FRED AND ELLEN NORRIS

Lot 116 Frederick Norris and his wife, Ellen had lived in Southover since taken over the tenancy from the Galpin family, whose two sons Henry [Dick] and Charles had been employed by the Pitt-Rivers Estate. Fred Norris had worked as a roadman for the Rural District Council and at the time of the Burton Sale had retired. He was well known and respected in the village and took part in many of the village activities, particularly as a bell-ringer and served his church faithfully as a Sidesman.

The Norris's cottage was situated up on a high bank, off the road and had seen some modest modernisation. It was let on an oral tenancy of £28, a rent which reflected the improvements that had been carried out and rated at £8 a year, the latter found by the tenant. The cottage, like The Dove Inn, next door, was picturesque and consisted of a porch and lobby, sitting-room, 12 feet by 10 feet 6 inches, another living room, called the front room, or parlour, which was a little bigger. There was a "kitchenette", a new term in the 1950s, with a sink and larder.

★★★★★★★★★★

Larders were common to nearly every household. There were few refridgerators and the larder was a cool, large, walk-in cupboard, built into the kitchen area, with a small, unglazed window, covered in zinc gauze. The larder floors, were laid with flagstones and in the grander houses, the shelves were often made from marble or slate. Perishable food could be kept fresh for days, even weeks.

★★★★★★★★★★

There were three bedrooms, in number 99 Burton Bradstock. The main bedroom was 12 feet 6 inches by 8 feet 10 inches and 7 feet 6 inches high. The two smaller bedrooms were 9 feet by 8 feet 9 inches and 6 feet 9 inches, respectively.

Outside, a wash-house still stood, where the women boiled water filled from the nearest tap, in a copper, fuelled by wood and/coal and went through the arduous weekly task of washing the family clothes and linen. In addition, there was a fuel store and stone garden shed. This property was very well cared for and ideal for a speculator and could fall vacant at any time. Both Fred, whose father had been a coastguard and Ellen were from well established village families. Mrs Norris, one of six children, was from the Northover family, and had the largest number of relatives living in different properties, in Burton, at the time of the Sale, than any other family.

★★★★★★★★★★

Fred Norris had served in the Great War, in a medical corps attached to the Dorsets. Edgar Norris, the only son, was employed by the South Western Electricity Board and had served as a paratrooper during the war, landing in the first wave, of airborne troops, in Normandy, in June 1944. He later served in Palestine.

★★★★★★★★★★

90. Fred and Ellen Norris, in their garden at the time of the Sale.

£650 was a fair price for the tenant to find at the time but the cottage was, by far, one of the best in the Sale, having a spacious garden, in all 22 perches, where Norris had erected timber garden sheds and a poultry house. Norris's shrewdness was applauded with the same enthusiasm that had greeted every purchasing tenant when the audience heard him make the final, successful bid.

Fred Norris died in 1966 and *The Bridport News* reporting on his life, wrote of the high respect in which he was held in Burton. He had originally worked at the spinning mill and when that closed he was employed by the Dorset County Council as a lengthsman. This involved undertaking a length of highway, usually a mile, to keep clean and tidy. This Fred did to everyone's satisfaction. The village streets and greens were allocated to him. There was a good deal of grass growing along the roadside and pavements, as well as overhanging trees, in the village, at the time. Weed killer did not come into the situation!

Norris had served on the committee of the Royal British Legion and was a master bell-ringer. He took great satisfaction from teaching the younger men to ring the bells. The paper stated that 'men of his [good] character are rare.'

Their son, Edgar Norris built a bungalow, on a plateau above the garden.

MORE BUILDING SITES

<u>**Lot 117**</u> This was to be one of the numerous building sites that would spring up in Burton Bradstock in the next few years. Although RB Howarth had done his best to prevent certain development, the Estate had realised the potential in Southover and had obtained outline, residential planning permission.

★★★★★★★★★★

Fred Mullins, a village shopkeeper and newspaper agent, who already owned his business premises, had rented the plot, cultivating it as a garden, erected a shed, paying 10/- a year. It formed a possible site, having a road frontage of 30 feet and ran back to over 100 feet.

★★★★★★★★★★

Mullins had moved into the village in the first quarter of the century. He had been the Manager of a shoe-shop in a nearby town and when he married Winifred Buckler, they took over her mother's premises in the High Street. Their happy life together was short-lived, when Winnie died prematurely, leaving three small children, Bob, Betty and Ken. Their neighbour, May Williams, already used to bringing up children who had lost their mother, (she brought up her three brothers and sister when their mother died) was a great help in caring for these youngsters. Fred Mullins never really recovered from his wife's death, although he remarried, some years later, to Lilian Brewer.

A larger than life man, Mullins was a well known character and besides running the village stores, in Burton, supported the football team, dances, Whist Drives, and played in the village band and took part in the concert party. He gave the impression that there was a sad man underneath the clown. Fred Mullins was well liked, particularly for his kind disposition.

★★★★★★★★★★

The speculator, HP West, from Woking, came in on Lot 117 and paid the sum of £200 for it.

THE VILLAGE BUILDER AND CARPENTER

<u>**Lot 118**</u> a substantially built house in stone, with a tiled roof had good accommodation and lay at the western building boundary of Southover, situated at the quiet end of the lane where it petered out into the footpath, across the fields to Freshwater. It was a very pretty and sought-after property.

****

91. Charles Hitchcock, a local builder, Circa 1940.

Charles Hitchcock, another of the tenants from a very old Burton family, lived there with his maiden sister, Kate. He had been born there, one of nine children, five boys and four girls, all of whom made their way, successfully, in life. Their father, Alfred, known as Jesse, (who had served in the Crimean war) was a skilled craftsman, building boats at Bridport Harbour shipyard. He hailed from another nearby village and had married into the Clark family of Burton, whose remarkable story appears in *Farmers, Fishermen and Flax Spinners*. When the shipyard closed in 1879, Jesse Hitchcock, took up employment in Burton, as a builder and carpenter.

Charlie, like his brothers, had moved away. He decided on Maidenhead where he was a foreman in the building trade. He served in the First World War, as a Royal Engineer and was posted to France. During this period, his wife died and after the war he came back to his home village and set up a builder's business.

In the 1920s and 1930s, he built several of the new houses, in Burton. Most notable was Gages House, off Shipton Lane, for two maiden ladies. Dorothy Codrington was a descendant of the Duke of Wellington, (with a connection to Stratfield Saye, which had once belonged to the Pitt family). What brought her and her companion, Alice Fielding, to Burton, is uncertain but the family link may have been contributory. These ladies were the benefactors for the Women's Institute Hall, also built by Hitchcock and opened by Colonel Sir David Williams, of Bridehead, in 1931. He also undertook work for the Estate, in a private capacity and built North Lodge [the Toll House].

****

In 1934, Hitchcock signed a ten year leasing agreement with the Pitt-Rivers Estate for his house and land. This enabled him to make pleasing alterations to the property, particularly putting in an early type of bathroom. His niece, Mrs Doris Klopper, née Williams, had visited as a child. There was cold water connected but the hot water reached the bathroom upstairs, by means of some clever siphoning. With downstairs rooms of 15 feet 6 inches by 9½ and 12½ feet respectively, a kitchen, landing and three nice sized bedrooms, the auctioneers did not hesitate to recommend this fine property. Outside was an earth closet. Beside the house, (too large to be classed as a cottage), Charlie Hitchcock had erected a shed where he kept his tools and materials. When he retired he continued to undertake some work for selected customers.

When the lease expired, the rent was £7. 19s a year and at the time of the Sale, this appeared quite a low sum, having been held over since 1944. It was due to be increased in the following September of 1958, to £13. 6s. 8d. The tenant paid the annual rates of £6 and was responsible for all repairs and insurance. This was the first time insurance seems to have been mentioned at the Sale and could have referred to the Estate's requirements. This was probably because the premises were used for storing timber, paints and other building materials.

★★★★★★★★★★

All the tenants were familiar with the dangers of fire and flood. The Estate had its own policies and only a few cottagers held an insurance against losing possessions, mainly as a result of fire. Insurance policies, rarely existed against flooding and would have been well out of most tenants' reach, because of the extremely high premiums.

★★★★★★★★★★

There were paths on either side of Charlie Hitchcock's house, over which allotment holders had a right-of-way. Mains water and electricity were connected and the sewer crossed the property. Outside there were sheds, (one long lean-to owned by Charles Galpin for which he paid an apportioned rent of 2/6 p. a.) and an outdoor lavatory. The garden was described as *'convenient'*.

Although he was too infirm to attend the Sale, then aged eighty-one, his sisters represented him and successfully purchased his home and business premises for £500. This was another local purchaser; a well established man of the village. The crowd gathered in the sale marquee were jubilant.

> Charlie Hitchcock lived out his days at 107, Burton Bradstock, with his sister, Kate. She, too, stayed on there until nearly her end and her memory has been perpetuated in the name, "Kitty's Cottage", by the present owner, who purchased the property in 1976.

THE SOUTHOVER ALLOTMENTS

Lots 119, 120 and 121 At the request of the Parish Council, who were still negotiating with Captain Pitt-Rivers, these lots were *withdrawn* from the Sale. The area of the Estate yard and villagers' allotments, in Southover, amounted to 136 perches, let at 1/- per perch, per year. Charles Galpin had 8 perches at 2/6d and 17 perches at 17/- per annum, were let to Albert Stevens, who lived in Southover. Various other allotment holders rented the

92. *Albert and Cynthia Stevens in the 1980s. (Mrs Stevens, celebrated her 91st birthday in 2006.)*

remainder and had erected sheds. The total income from the allotments was minimal. In the south-west corner there was a right-of-way through a wicket gate. The allotments were let on a yearly rent at 1/- per perch, which was how the rental had always been calculated.

> The old Estate yard, where once the workers used a handcart to take their tools and materials out on the jobs, is now owned by the parish and rented by a local builder and stone-wall expert, Roger Day. Born in Burton, grandson of Augustus Wylde, the former landlord of the nearby Dove Inn, Day is still maintaining an element of continuity in Burton.
>
> Amongst a collection of vintage vehicles is a United States army tractor he salvaged from the old Spinning Mill; a reminder of the American soldiers' sojourn in the locality.

CORNER COTTAGE

Lot 122 was one of the most prominent cottages for sale. It stood at the foot of Cliff Lane, where the main road from Weymouth swept around the bend into the village. The layout was interesting, as it consisted of the main, thatched cottage, to which was attached another, smaller, slated one, used at the time as a store. Previously, on their marriage, it had been lived in, by the Lovings. Alfred Loving was a driver for the Beaminster milk factory and a Special Constable and his wife, was descended from old Burton families.

★★★★★★★★★★

Ruby Loving's parents, Richard and Sophie Churchouse, had lived in the larger cottage. Her father had been a local Rate Collector and her grandfather had held the ancient office of Relief Officer when money collected from the better off inhabitants was made available to those in need, before the Welfare State. (The old system was that each parish supported its own and to qualify for "Parish Relief", the claimant had to have been born in the parish, resided for a specified time, or worked/apprenticed there for a certain period). The property had been a school in times long-gone but no one living had any recollection of this. Perhaps one cottage was used as the schoolroom, (one of the rooms being unusually large for a cottage) and the other place by the teacher, as living accommodation. It could have been a dame's school, before the National School had opened.

254

In Carner [Dorset dialect for corner] Cottage(s), in the larger of the pair, the kitchen was more spacious than some others in Burton, at 12 feet 8 inches by 9 feet 8 inches and there were two bedrooms with a living room of a typical size. Ruby Loving was always active and kept poultry and tended a neat garden, which was perched above the property, on the Cliff Road. The poultry houses, a kitchen sink and Sadia water heater had been installed by the tenant and were not included in the Sale. The annual rent seemed high at £28 but this amount was for the whole of the property and the rates amounted to £8 a year.

Ruby had always been part of village life and was an active member of several organisations. She was a 'good sport' and could be seen, in her younger days, wearing fancy dress, or dancing, at local events. The football team always received her support, as many of her extended family were footballers. She was very knowledgeable about customs and traditions and who was who.

Having always been thrifty, Ruby Loving was able, to find the £450, to purchase Lot 122.

ANOTHER BUILDING SITE IN SOUTHOVER

Lot 123 West paid £300 for another site of 20 perches, in Southover, which had outline planning permission. This was a valuable acquisision. The front plot was being sold with vacant possession The rear of the site had been let to AE [Bert] Williams at 10/- a year. The frontage amounted to 35 feet, with a return of 75 feet.

THE GARAGES

Lot 124 A wooden and galvanised roofed row of, rather make-shift, garages stood under the hill, on the south side of Southover, where it appeared, from an old photograph, that a row of cottages had once stood. There was a frontage to the road of some 68 feet and a depth of approximately 17 feet.

One of these buildings was rented by Ernest Thorne, at 5/- and the other four by Freddie Mullins, the shopkeeper and newsagent, who paid a yearly rental of 10/- for the lot. He retained a couple of the garages, for his own use and sub-let the rest. A piece of land beside the garages, devoid of buildings, was "in hand".

Mullins bought the whole area for £150.

JUST A BIT OF LAND

Lot 125 was the Loving's garden amounting to 0. 1 acres, with a frontage to Southover of 90 feet and a depth of 150 feet. With a plan to return to Burton, RW Frost and his wife, (who had local connections), could not miss this potential building site.

Frost paid £200 for a very well positioned, large site, albeit Ruby Loving was still the tenant, paying £2 a year.

93. Lot 122, Carner Cottage, Southover, 1955. Elizabeth Buckler in the doorway.

THE RECREATION GROUND

<u>**Lot 126**</u> Burton Bradstock was fortunate to have the Recreation Ground. The field was flat, in a prime position. It was well used as a playing field by the youngsters, as a venue for community activities and as a place to sit quietly, observing life as it passed by, for the older inhabitants. It had been let out to the Parish Council, for many years, at a pepper-corn rent of £1 per annum and the lease for a further 14 years had recently been agreed.

The playing field lay along the main road, with a fine frontage and amounted to around 1¾ acres. Its only equipment was a pair of well used swings, on a concrete base. A couple of slatted, wooden, bench seats, could be found around the perimeter. However, the amenity was one of the few and certainly the best in any village, in the district, at the time, due to the forethought of the Parish Council and the low rental that Captain Pitt-Rivers charged. The only condition, laid down by the Estate, was that the Parish Council was obliged to provide a stock-proof fence.

★★★★★★★★★★

For general purposes, the playing field had been used for large celebrations, such as the Coronations of George VI, in 1937, and Queen Elizabeth II, in 1953, when tug o' war took place across the river. At these events, skittles and the endurance test to hold a greasy pig caused much fun and competition. The pigs, (usually runts, donated by a farmer) were a good prize to win, as it could be kept at the bottom of the garden, fattened up and then slaughtered by the local butcher. There were pig sties at the bottom of several cottage gardens, always built as far from the house as possible.

★★★★★★★★★★

At Parish Council meetings, held just prior to the Sale, councillors had been adamant that the Council should attempt to buy the field. The auctioneers were sensitive to the matter and it was soon knocked down to RB Howarth, the Chairman, for £40, who was bidding on behalf of the Parish Council. Securing the Recreation Ground was well received, by those gathered in the marquee.

Soon after the Sale, Rita Atwooll née Jarman, who was born at The Dove, recalls joining other young children in the village, led by Mrs Georgie Northover, collecting money for new apparatus. With swings, a slide and a see-saw they thought they were in playtime paradise. Over the years, more apparatus has been added and safety measures implemented. About a quarter of the field in now fenced off and utilised as a special safe, fun area. Nearby, a covered underground sump has been built to drain flood water from the surrounding land.

The rest of the field is used regularly by the school as a sports-ground, there being no field attached to the school premises. Additional benches, have been placed there as memorials.

CLIFF FARM AND CARAVAN CAMP

Lot 127 The Sale catalogue described the Cliff Farm and its caravan camp, with twenty-five licensed sites, as *'an important property'*. To speculators it was one of the best business Lots in the Sale. The fact that it was to be sold with vacant possession made it an extremely desirable speculation.

The situation was unique, in that the house lay at the top of Cliff Road and the land almost touched the edge of the cliffs. It was well built, thatched and spacious, having two sitting rooms, a kitchen and three bedrooms. A passage, leading off from an impressive stone porch, divided the downstairs rooms, in a traditional fashion. All the rooms, except the smallest bedroom, were 14 feet 6 inches long, or more. This was originally built as a coastguard's residence. The two houses, built for this purpose, in Cliff Lane, were as solid as the rock on which they stood. An advantage was that main water was piped indoors but only to a tap in the kitchen. The house was lit with electricity. Outside, there were two stores, a wash house and an outdoor earth lavatory. The land amounted to 3½ acres, within which, was a substantially built brick cow-stall, for eight head of cattle and a good sized pig sty. The top field had once been used as a football field.

★★★★★★★★★★

Cliff Farm had been the home of the Kerley family since becoming obsolete as a coastguard dwelling in 1907. The first Frederick Kerley was the village blacksmith and had his workshop at the bottom of Cliff Lane. Their only son, another Frederick, was born in 1905 and reared a family of five children at Cliff Farm, where he worked the smallholding, reviving the camping, after 1945. He died in 1954 and his wife, Annie, had lived another three years. Only Christopher and Ruth were left and not holding the tenancy, had vacated the premises.

Third generation Fred, first worked for the Bridport Electricity Company, on leaving school and subsequently joined the Navy, fulfilling his long-standing wish. David, another son, born in 1934, had spent all his spare time, helping at Shadrach Dairy Farm and was noticed by New Zealand farmer, Bartlett, on one of his visits home to Loders. In the late 1940s, this was a wonderful opportunity for David, to emigrate to the other side of the world. He was later joined by Martin, one of his younger brothers. David married Mrs Bartlett's daughter, by her first marriage.

94. (L) Lot 127, Cliff Farm, prior to closure and (R) Lot 89 Villa Cliff caravan camps, prior to the move to Larkfield, as seen from the air. The caravans are sited around the perimeter of the fields.

★★★★★★★★★★

The great attraction of Cliff Farm, was that it had a licensed site for caravans. The camp was well established, having been in use long before the Second World War, for tenting and caravanning. When the property came up for sale, the Town Planning and Public Health Acts permitted the license to be held on an annual basis only and was therefore only valid until the 30th September, 1958.

Whilst Cliff Farm remained vacant, the Pitt-Rivers Estate had operated the camp during the 1958 season, charging £18 a site and £2 per caravan, for sanitary service. This was provided by the Hampshire Cleansing Company, at a total of £37. 16s, for the season, for a twice weekly arrangement to empty the lavatories.

Most of the clients returned to Cliff Farm year after year. They received preferential bookings and could use their caravans from April to September. Other recent outgoings were the rates at £39 for the camp and £5 for the farm house. There was a right-of-way over the fields, to the road, for the owner of the cottage below, for reasonable repairing purposes, as that dwelling had no vehicular access.

Cliff Farm afforded a magnificent site for the campers, with the most splendid view imaginable. When there was a south-westerly gale, the elements interfered but to ride out a storm, within a few yards of the cliff, in a flimsy tent, or wobbly caravan, could be quite an adventure! As a private holding it was unique.

The successful purchaser was DG Denton of Leighton Buzzard. The Estate's original asking price, in the previous spring, of £4,000, had been reached.

The holding was run much as before, putting a useful extension on the house. At one time large-scale chicken farming was carried on there and in the bitter winter of 1963 water had to be taken from the village to the farm, where everything was frozen solid, due to its high situation. It was realised how much water a chicken can drink! Eventually, 'the powers that be' were able to remove the camping licence, although the Parish Council was not in favour of this.

In the 1980s, "Young" Fred, recalled the happy times that the family had enjoyed there. He joined other village boys, playing baseball and chatting to the American soldiers who were stationed in the surrounding fields. The boys were showered with candy, doughnuts and tins of pineapples. As D-Day approached, Fred witnessed the huge armada of ships which stretched from Portland to Start Point, assembled ready to sail to the Normandy landing beaches. That was the last they heard of any of their US buddies. In his naval days, Fred married and was stationed at Portsmouth and later worked on lighthouses.

Now the farm is in new hands again. It is entirely private, devoid of tents and caravans, which have been accommodated elsewhere in the district but the business they bring is still valued and much needed.

Cliff Farm is beautifully cared for and preserved.

BURTON BANK

Lot 128 At the turn of the twentieth century a roadway, from the bottom of Cliff Lane to almost the cliff top, was blasted out of the rock, to form a hard way to the villas and beach. Altogether, "The Cutting", as the newly constructed road was named, gave excellent access. Previously, a track, across the fields to the cliff top, had been the only route.

The old way was difficult, more suited to donkeys but certainly it was inaccessible for the new fangled motor-cars. Fishermen had brought their catches back over that way for centuries, either in bushel baskets, on their shoulders, or on the backs of donkeys, in pannier baskets. When The Cutting was made, the fish merchants could then drive ponies and traps and later their lorries, up to the cliff top, to await the catches. Loads of sand and shingle could be ferried that way, too and it was still the quickest footpath, even after Beach Road was constructed.

★★★★★★★★★★

Number 97, Burton Bradstock was a stout, sizeable house, perched on the same rock, [inferior oolite, an under layer of stone], that formed the yellow-coloured cliffs. The entrance to Burton Bank had no means of easy approach, except by a set of, almost, perpendicular steps, cut into the rock, each topped with locally hewn, stone slabs.

The accommodation was made-up of a large living room and two bedrooms. A generously sized kitchen was partitioned off to form a larder and scullery. The tenant had installed a hand-basin in the kitchen, as well as other amenities, outside. The whole was let at £16, to Mrs Henrietta Williams, known as Hetty, who paid the rates of £5 a year. The Vendor had obtained vacant possession of an adjacent piece of land, in order that it could be made available to install septic tank drainage.

★★★★★★★★★★

Hetty, one of nine children, was from yet another, well rooted village family, the Hitchcocks, descended, on her maternal side, from the Hoskins Clarks, who were seafarers. She had been born in Burton, in1891 and had witnessed and been told much of the history of the village which she had passed on to her children. She had ancestors who had ventured far beyond Burton Bradstock and been involved in adventures and tragedies at sea. Hetty was an adventurer herself, having joined the Women's Royal Army Corps. in the First World War. Through being in the Services, she had met her husband, who was a Londoner, with a Scottish mother, from a family skilled in clock and watch making. They were married in uniform, during the war.

★★★★★★★★★★

Finding herself in charge of the Sergeants' Mess, Hetty noticed a soldier who was on convalescent leave and they soon struck up a friendship. William Williams, from the London garrison of the Artillery, driving the lead horse, had been wounded at the Battle of the Somme and been left for dead. Hours later, what was thought to be his body had been thrown back over into the British lines. He made a partial recovery only to be sent back and wounded again. For the rest of his life he suffered and always carried shrapnel embedded in his body.

During her service days, Hetty had received praise from one batch of soldiers for organising the preparation and cooking of a barrel of herrings. These were cooked in a traditional Burton method by sousing, (gutted, rolled and baked in vinegar).

Just for a holiday, a lady of strong character and plans and ideas for their future, she brought her husband back to Burton to meet her family and see the home village. He was enamoured with the place and they decided to stay.

During the Second World War, the family took in a very young girl, Betty Mackay, evacuated from London. Betty returned to London after the war but was a stranger there and eventually settled back in Burton where she lives in retirement. The Williams's son, Dick, served in the Combined Forces, working with amphibious craft and crossed the Rhine during the liberation of Europe. Doris, their daughter, joined up as soon as she reached the minimum age of seventeen and a half and served in the Women's Royal Air Force. Her work took her far from Burton, where she learnt to drive heavy vehicles, towing trailers, carrying inspectors and recovery crew, for crashed aircraft.

★★★★★★★★★★

Mrs Williams secured her home for £300. Its unique situation and magnificent views were a great attraction.

CLIFF FIELDS

Lot 129 Two splendid fields, totalling nearly 10 acres, adjoined Cliff Farm and stretched down over towards Freshwater. The entrance was by an Estate five-bar gate, in Southover. The Pitt-Rivers Estate's gates were distinguished with banding on the top rail, of yellow and blue metal strips. The fields bordered the cliffs and were used by Rob Gale, the village butcher cum farmer, as part of his farming plan where he grazed cattle, for most of the year.

Gale paid £35. 10s, on Lady Day, March 25th, on an oral tenancy. The bidding was keen and the tenant was outbid, to the sum of £1,300, by speculators, AT Bargess and CJ Wakely, from Somerset, who had secured some other Lots. This was not too good for the village folk and their peaceful way of life. Their fears that "foreigners" would come in to disrupt the age-old pattern, were materialising.

> These fields now form part of the protected stretch of land belonging to The National Trust.

BATTEN'S GROUND

Lot 130 faced south, at the western end of the village, above Freshwater and was very fertile pasture, being loam soil on clay. In the first parish register of 1614, the surname "Batten" was prominent - an early tenant.

By 1958, Bunny Lenthall had connected mains-water. He paid £30 a year rental for the 14 acres. The mains sewer was nearby and there was easy access on to the Bridport Road. This stretch of land, which bordered the route, used by countless travellers to Bridport, over the centuries, had a long history. Few outsiders knew, that around eleven hundred years previously, the invading Danish Vikings, intending to raid the village, had found their way on to the track to Bridport, from the sea, after landing at Freshwater. (This tale had been passed down verbally, through the generations).

★★★★★★★★★★

When the Vikings raided, there would have been around one hundred inhabitants in Burton Bradstock, who were not deterred by these fierce-looking, fair-headed giants. When news filtered back to the villagers that the enemy was on their shore, the men gathered staves, axes and picks and rushed off to encounter the Danes. In the hollow of the track, leading out of Burton, (bordered on the north side by the field, that was coming up for sale), fierce fighting took place and the enemy was repelled. Ever since, that dip in the roadway, (to the west of Burton), had been known as "Red Bottom", as it had run red with the blood of the invaders.

★★★★★★★★★★

The Lot was put-up as '*valuable accommodation arable land*' and Lenthall paid a high price for it. The speculators were fast running out of possible investments; so much had been knocked down to the tenants and the mystery buyer, Mr Jeffery, '*for a client*'.

Batten's Ground, with its remarkable niche in history, fetched £1,450. Lenthall paid over £100 an acre but as it overlooked Freshwater Camp, not too far from other development and was one of the best agricultural areas in the village, it was worth that sum.

FRESHWATER CAMP 'the money spinner'

<u>Lot 131</u> '*The unique and very valuable property, approached by a metalled road, including half a mile of attractive beach*', was referred to as '*the money spinner of the Sale*'. The site totalled just over 45 acres and included a mile of beach under the beautiful mellow cliffs and handy to the golf course. It was rapidly becoming a large commercial enterprise and in just a few post-war years, a caravan camp had sprung up at Freshwater Bay. It had originally been an open space where the River Bride joined the sea. Eden Phillpotts had described it as, '*where the cliff breaks and there stretches a little strand.* ' He continued, '*the bride flows to one great pool, sinks into the sand and glides unseen to her lover.* '

The lynchets, [a terrace or ridge formed by ploughing a hillside], cut into the hills surrounding Freshwater, were a thing of the past, except as high and dry places to pitch a tent, or graze sheep and cattle. Cultivated, in Mediaeval days, the lynchets were later used to spread flax out to dry and rot, in the rain and dew [dew retting], exposing the inner fibres. The crop was then gathered up, combed and dressed [coaxed into long lengths, separating out the shorted fibres, called tow] in a shed behind the beach by the farm workers, when the weather was unsuitable to do anything on the land. As flax processing advanced, early in the twentieth century, the system at Freshwater was abandoned. Retting ponds, beside the spinning mill, for soaking the flax bundles, had become a better, on-the-spot method.

★★★★★★★★★★

When a rough sea met the River Bride in full spate, the area was prone to flooding. The shingle choked the river mouth and the flood water would be bayed up, [held back]. The rough sea would rise over the whole lot, flow inland, causing flooding in the low lying fields and right into the village, particularly Manor Farm and Mill Street, where it met the river in flood, coming down the Bride Valley.

Nissen huts had been erected during the war. One flood swept over the camp and a soldier was drowned. Throughout that period, few local people ventured there, as wartime defences were in place, curtailing fishermen from launching from Freshwater Beach.

Jack Lenthall, the tenant, at the time, continued to graze the land. It was good summer fattening pasture, with its element of salt. In hot, dry summers the fields could become parched but cattle always seemed to do well in those conditions. For most of the winter the fields were wet and often overlaid with flood and sea water.

95. *Freshwater Camp in its early days, circa 1956*

★★★★★★★★★★

After 1949, on the death of Jack Lenthall, his son took over the tenancy. It was 1951 before Bunny Lenthall took the idea seriously, that Freshwater could provide added income to his farming enterprise at Manor Farm, when the first letting, for a car with tent was agreed, at 1/6d a night .

★★★★★★★★★★

The Sale particulars stated that he had, to some extent, *'developed a popular and select caravan camp.'* The site was licensed for two hundred caravans, which was valid up to September 1960. Permission had been given by the local authorities for the storage of one hundred and fifty caravans on site, through the winter. These vans were packed tightly together and repositioned the following season. The tenant had installed mains water and electricity and a drainage disposal system. A modest hut, with living quarters and a shop had been built, together with two blocks of lavatories.

Many of the campers still journeyed into Burton for their daily needs, making the village busy, every day as they strolled around in a leisurely fashion. None of the original inhabitants of Burton objected to the intrusion of visitors or the camp sites. The revenue generated in the district by the holiday makers was welcomed and the amenities mainly provided to cater for them, improved the lives of the local population. Tourism had long been part of the economy.

From that move, the camp had mushroomed. There was no flood prevention scheme in operation only the knowledge of the old villagers who always sensed when there could be a flood and local men would dig out the accumulated shingle at Freshwater Mouth. Over the years there were floods, even in the summer months when campers, particularly in tents, had to pack up and get off the site. On a couple of occasions, the water had come up to caravan window height.

★★★★★★★★★★

Lenthall, rented Freshwater from the Estate, on a yearly tenancy at £33 but in 1958 was paying an additional £300 a year, as a consideration for the camping rights.

Lot 131 was put up at £5,000 and bidding was strong. Lenthall had set his mind on securing the camp, foreseeing that with a manager, things could work to his advantage. Already working in some sort of partnership with Lenthall was Dick Russell. Whether they both contributed to the cost of purchasing the camp is uncertain. It would seem that Lenthall had decided to invest in the camp, rather than to pay over the odds for the farm and this was, in fact, a point from which there was no turning back, for anyone, or the area.

This money spinner which had yet the better times to come, realised £16,250.

> In an interview with the Press, after the Sale, Lenthall said, "I am still a sitting tenant, at Manor Farm. I have got some good ground [purchased some productive land]. It has been a better day, than yesterday, having bought the Freshwater Camp."
>
> In due course, Russell went his own way, purchasing Norburton and adjoining land, on the death of Edward Sturdy for a sum of around £6,000.
>
> ★★★★★★★★★★
>
> A flood alleviation scheme has made Freshwater Holiday Camp a safer place and it is now one of the most popular and well-run sites in the district. It is a self-sufficient village but the visitors bring money with them which is shared around. There should be no objections to the caravans. No one can begrudge the holiday makers the pleasure of a couple of weeks by the sea and in the beautiful countryside around Burton Bradstock. The income derived from tourism is as essential today as it has ever been.
>
> The current brochure calls it a 'great family seaside holiday park'. It is classed as a private haven for families and sun worshippers, swimmers, wind surfers, walkers and sea fishermen. It is apparent that there is a happy atmosphere and helpful staff at Freshwater. There is so much to do on the site but the proprietors do not shun from advertising the other attractions in the district. The owners take their responsibilities very seriously and provide lifeguards to supervise the swimming activities.
>
> During July and August (2006), a three bed-roomed caravan luxury 'holiday home' at Freshwater Beach Holiday Park, can cost up to £700 a week. The facilities are home from home. For the camping and touring unit the prices are from £15 to £30 per night in high season. It has come a long way from Bunny Lenthall's first venture into letting camp sites for a few pence!

WEST BAY

West Bay made-up a valuable portion of the Pitt-Rivers Estate. Formerly known as Bridport Harbour, the name was changed. It 'sounded' better, when the railway line was extended from Bridport to the harbour, in 1884. Richard Francis Roberts, who lived at Cogden, a relative of the Burton Mill owner, was solicitor to the London and North West Railway and a Director of the Bridport Railway Company. He was instrumental in getting the railway to Bridport, in 1856 and eventually extending the line to Bridport Harbour.

Local dignitaries were directors of the Company and were interested in developing West Bay as a resort. Jackson and Tattershall, railway historians, in their book, *The Bridport Railway,* state that when the line to the harbour was opened on March 31st 1884, shops and businesses in the town closed and the town and stations at East Street and West Bay were decorated. Some five thousand people travelled on the first day, of which, over two thousand were paying passengers. A luncheon was held in a warehouse at West Bay where one hundred and ten people sat down to this special meal. Tickets were 2/6d each.

The names of two of the hostelries were changed, from the "Ship", [or Sloop], to the "Bridport Arms Hotel" and the "Neptune", to the "West Bay Hotel", to give a better impression. The railway connection heralded a great increase in the number of visitors coming to the resort and contributed to the decline in exporting by sea.

It was untimely that Roberts had died suddenly before the line was completed but his memory was recalled in the speeches after the luncheon. Mr Loggin, the secretary to the Company, stated that they hoped in ten years time, the population of West Bay would supersede that of Bridport. This never happened, although in the 1920s, new properties and day-bungalows sprang up everywhere.

★★★★★★★★★★

West Bay lies about 1½ miles from Bridport and has carried various labels over the past two thousand years, such as "creek", "mouth" and "haven". The problem, as a port, had always been the silting-up of its entrance. This barring, to the harbour, had influenced the rise and fall of the prosperity of Bridport and the surrounding area, for centuries.

The River Brit dissects the harbour-based village and formed the division between the land to the east, belonging to the Manor of Burton Bradstock and that on the western side, owned by the Abbot of Cerne and later the Earl of Ilchester. A third area was within the Borough of Bridport. Thousands of years ago, it is thought that a main river went out somewhere between Burton Freshwater and Bridport Harbour, the coast being a mile further out than at present. This river, is thought to have been the River Bride, flowing through the Bride Valley and out through this age-old mouth. This long-held local belief, has been verified recently, by research carried out by Katherine Barker. Thousands of years ago, it seems, the River Brit could have been just a tributary of the River Bride.

The 'modern' River Brit, with its outlet at West Bay, once navigable up to the brewery, meandered its way through the swampy meadows, meeting the sea under the East Cliff, at Bridport Harbour. An early mention of a port at Bridport, was 1272, when the Abbot of Cernel and the Prior of Frampton were entitled to take all the wrecks on their respective side of the weir. A penny toll could be extracted from all vessels on the Burton side.

At one time, a dispute arose between the Prior of Frampton and Bridport Borough over the receiving of tolls and the Borough won the case. Likewise, the right to carry away shingle was questioned and the appointed commissioners found in favour of the Borough against the Abbot of Caen, who held Burton Manor at that time. As early as 1385, John de Huderessfeld began work on constructing a port. In 1445 collectors were appointed to raise funds, with Burton Bradstock contributing 5/3d. By 1541, the port was in decay again. There was a marked decline in its use during the sixteenth century, due to deaths from the plague, when there were not enough men left to dig out the sand-bar and silt that had accumulated.

During the sixteenth and seventeenth centuries, travellers and historians referred to aspects of the harbour. Leland said it was a *'pretie havenet'*, whilst Camden states that *'it was formed by Nature.'* Wainwright told of *'pyrates'* all along the coast and some who were locked up in the town goal, (probably in the present Bucky Doo, where there was an over-night lock-up), before being taken to Dorchester prison, the next day.

96.*Whitsun Fair, Bridport Harbour, [West Bay] 1861.(Far R) The shipyard which closed in 1879.*

The town bailiffs appealed to King James I for permission to collect in the county to repair the haven. In fact, the collectors travelled over half of England and into Wales, with very poor results. The money was insufficient to repair the harbour and was used to support a schoolmaster instead. The coast was extremely dangerous, not only from pirates and invaders, such as a planned raid by the Spanish but the extreme hazard of being shipwrecked. Getting into the safety of the haven was extremely dangerous but once into the shelter at Bridport Harbour, shipping could wait-out the storms.

The Bishop of London, Mr Gibson, in 1722, said that the local inhabitants had attempted to build a harbour but the tides perpetually barred it with sand. Daniel de Foe, in 1721, wrote that *'There was no harbour, although there were numerous boats fishing for mackerel.*' It was obvious to the powers, heading the Borough, that there was great potential for a proper harbour for trade and commerce, particularly the export of locally manufactured lines, nets and ropes. They informed Parliament that if the harbour was restored it would be a great way to revive trade. The Bill received Royal Assent on the 12th February 1721/1722.

In 1740, a total of £3,500, was raised to erect two piers, to turn the course of the river and make a harbour big enough to take vessels of one hundred and fifty tons. A court case between the Bridport Corporation and the owners and occupiers of land at Bridport Harbour caused a hold-up. George Pitt, Esquire, the elder, (an ancestor of Captain Pitt-Rivers) who held the Manor of Burton, had leased out some six acres of land to John Best, Esquire, the tenant of Burton Manor Farm, who would be affected by the new construction work.

Although the meadow in question was referred to as a 'common meadow', the owner was entitled to the after-cut of grass, from the Monday after the first of August to the Monday after the first of February, each year. One quarter of the first cut, of half an acre and five perches, was the inheritance of William Waldron, Esquire but occupied by Henry Davie. The remaining three quarters were the inheritance of John Bragg, Esquire and Elizabeth his daughter. This, too, was occupied by Henry Davie. Others with an interest were two gentlemen, Simon Taylor, and Matthew Hounsell. The whole of the arrangements were extremely complicated. Likewise, on the west side, Thomas Strangways Horner, an ancestor of the Earls of Ilchester, who owned land on that side, had leased to Robert Chilcott, some sandy land worth *'only 3/-'* a year, who had then sub-let to William Lawes. Huts and sheds abounded on the west (working) side of the harbour, some on leases for three lives.

By 1742, all was resolved and compensation granted, allowing the harbour scheme to go ahead and be completed. Keeping the harbour, piers and sluices in good order cost almost as much as any receipts over the following sixty years. It was the ship-building that helped to save the day and finally Bridport Harbour prospered. The export of ropes, nets and many products made from flax and hemp, as well as the extraction of sand and shingle, increased and imports of timber, cattle feed, fertiliser, cement and coal, kept the little port extremely busy.

Imposing stone warehouses were built. One was used by Roberts, of Burton Bradstock, as a store for ropes, nets, sailcloth and other products, manufactured in his factory, as the goods awaited export, *'if the wind stay fair'.* He imported timber, used to repair cottages for his employees, as well as selling-on some of it. He imported cheap dairy products to feed the workers, wine for himself and acquaintances and brought-in French cattle for breeding purposes. In the centre of the harbour village, a large stone building was erected, at the time of the wars with France, some say to house French prisoners, although it was doubtful if it was ever used for that purpose. A more feasible explanation is that French prisoners of war were employed to build the warehouse, as the structure bears a Norman resemblance and the cellars underneath, are similar to those found in France. The building, later, became the store for Goods' sand and gravel business. (Tony Legg recalled the considerable load-bearing strength of the floor boards). This warehouse appears to be the one featured in Eden Phillpott's book *The Spinners,* into which the heroine is lured and where she is ruined.

In 1820, a new road was constructed from Bridport to the harbour, superseding the usual, long, rough and hilly route, via Marsh Barn to the town. It had always been possible to reach the harbour by tracks and footpaths that ran across the fields. From the Ridgeway, over North Hill, a track joined into the Salt Marshes, at the main entrance to the Melplash Agricultural Society's showground.

When the harbour was extended, it became a bonded port in 1828. The trade out of Bridport Harbour with Newfoundland had been long established. Ships laden with nets, twine and ropes sailed to the fisheries, returning with salt cod, furs and seal oil, some of the latter, used for lighting lamps. Another building, on the west of the harbour, was used for storing salt. The ships loaded the salt from the salt-flats in Portugal and parts of France, brought wine and spices back and delivered salt cod to the Roman Catholic community. Cargoes of inferior salt cod were shipped to the Caribbean, to feed the slaves in the plantations and any surplus was for home consumption. In the early 1900s, there were still rope and net manufacturers in Bridport who gave their workers an allocation of salt cod.

Throughout the 1800s, many ships, of all types, were built in the Bools/Good and Cox shipyard, on the west side, of Bridport Harbour, including "The Speedy", a clipper ship, owned by Prowse Brothers of Liverpool, who had a family connection with the Coxes. It was launched at Bridport Harbour in October 1853, having become grounded on the first attempt to launch her, in the previous September. Over 200 feet in length, registered with Lloyds, at 1,031 tons, The Speedy's first voyage was from London to Australia. She drew great admiration from those assembled at Bridport Harbour, for the successful second attempt at launching, although to get her off, it was done at 6. 30 am, on a very high tide, an hour earlier than advertised. Wagers were laid on her completing the first crossing in record time, expected to be seventy days.

The ship-building continued to be a main industry, until the keel of the "Lilian", a ketch, was laid down. She was the last ship to be built at Bridport Harbour, launched in 1879, only to survive a few years before going down with all hands. The First Mate, a member of the Good family, was on board, when she was lost.

Paddle steamers plied between Swanage, Weymouth, Exmouth and Torquay, calling in at the little ports en route. At West Bay, passengers usually boarded off-shore, from the East Beach, the piers being too narrow for easy manoeuvrability. Pleasure boats, together with fishing trips, were popular attractions. The railway was used to transport some dairy products and other farm produce, besides taking surplus fish to the markets up the line and in particular, those in London.

From the mid-nineteenth century, the annual Whitsun Fair was held on the East Beach, when hundreds of local inhabitants came to participate. A photograph depicts the scene as early as 1861. The east side was the smarter side of the harbour and used by most visitors, until the sewer was installed in 1897, which was laid along the old river bed, under the East Cliff. This somewhat unpleasant infrastructure, which was only a few yards long, resulted in sewage floating close to the East Beach, with the incoming tide. Consequently, with that and the closing of the shipyard, the west side of the harbour became the favoured area for visitors and recreation. However, until 1939, a Fair was still held on the East Beach with side-shows, swinging boats and roundabouts.

The Fair was halted for a period but was revived in the early 1900s when it became West Bay Regatta Day. The Regatta was held on the first Thursday (Bridport's early closing day) in August, during Bank Holiday Week and took the form of sailing races in the morning, swimming races and a comic interlude in the afternoon, a polo match in the early evening, followed by the prize-giving and dancing on the promenade, all to be concluded with fireworks.

This was an event that was continued well into the second half of the century. The men's and women's Bridport Swimming Clubs had been prominent for sixty years and besides teaching youngsters to swim, provided great sport. Long distance races in the sea and polo matches in the basin, or river, brought spectators by the hundreds. In the winter months, a dinner and dance kept the club members' social lives buoyant.

In the 1930s, Captain Pitt-Rivers gave a site for the erection of St John's Church at West Bay, having sold some land and property at West Bay, in 1931. The West Bay and George Hotels were sold to JC and RH Palmer, brewers, for £2,600 each, whilst Durbeyfield House went to Sam Gluning, a local fish retailer, for £800. Bradfords purchased the coal yard at £930 and beach sites, where wooden bungalows stood, made £150 each. A warehouse of three floors was withdrawn at £350. Likewise, some years earlier, the Ilchester Estate, on the western side of the harbour, had sold off some land. Four prominent Bridport businessmen, bought a large expanse of the West Cliff and built themselves smart houses.

At the turn of the twentieth century and between the two wars, the railway had brought prosperity to West Bay and holiday accommodation, tea rooms and little business enterprises sprang-up. The passenger line closed in the early 1930s but the goods section remained in operation until 1960. After the Second War, the Municipal Caravan Camp, was acclaimed as being one of the best-run sites in the whole of the United Kingdom. The Bridport Swimming Club boasted a large membership, of all ages and the veterans, back from the war, taught the young club members to swim, in the old polo basin, dangling them from a canvas belt, secured around the beginners' waists by a Bridport rope.

This was a thriving, busy little working harbour, to which hundreds of visitors came. The locals flocked there whenever time allowed, to savour the sea-air and enjoy themselves. Now on August 1st, 1958, the remainder of the Pitt-Rivers Estate, in West Bay, was about to be sold.

THE BRIDPORT AND WEST DORSET GOLF COURSE

Lot 132 The auction was directed now to the part of the Estate which lay in West Bay. *'This course is noted as one of the most beautiful in the South',* so read the catalogue particulars, for Lot 132 the well-known, Bridport and West Dorset Golf Course.

★★★★★★★★★★

The West Dorset Golf Club was the first of its kind to be founded in the county, in 1891. Bridport was added to the title later. The original golf course was on the West Cliff but as membership grew and problems with wet patches occurred, it relocated to the east side of the harbour, in 1911, around the time when the West Cliff was sold off by Lord Ilchester.

Joseph Pearkes Fox Gundry, the head of the rope and twine business in the town, was the Club's Founder and Founder President. The Founder Captain was JT Stephens, Town Mayor in 1897 and 1904, whose residence was at Wanderwell. Other members of his family, who lived at Haddon House and rented from the Estate, in West Bay, were to become keen supporters.

Some thirty enthusiasts paid an annual subscription of £1. Within a year Gundry had died, as the result of an accident, whilst riding with the Cattistock Hunt. The Reverend Templar, Rector of Burton Bradstock, served on the Founding Committee and played in the first match. All the participants, including ladies, were people of substantial means.

The move brought the golf course into the Pitt-Rivers Estate, with the tenant of Manor Farm, having the right to graze the land. As golf became more popular the names on the membership list, over the ensuing years, would be those who were prominent in business and the professions. It was an elite club, with its own professional. In 1909, Ernest Ham, married to a Bridport woman, had laid out the original eighteen hole course and AH Billett, the grounds-man, was well remembered, at the time of the Sale.

Between the wars, the club flourished, adding eminent visitors to its list. It became known for its uniqueness and challenge. The greens were of fine turf but had hazards such as the cliffs, (many a ball went over and was picked up by a misguided seagull), quarry pits, gorse, the old dry stone walls and wet areas. With the charming haven at West Bay and the bracing air on the cliff tops, any difficulties could be overlooked and the Golf Club provided sport and pleasure, in an invigorating environment.

★★★★★★★★★★

By 1950, the annual subscription was £7. 7s and £5. 15s 6d for the ladies. When the Sale catalogue was published, in the summer of 1958, the acreage of the Bridport and West Dorset Golf Course, totalled 58½ acres. There was considerable road frontage and the soil was fertile, being sandy loam on limestone.

Included in Lot 132, which was catalogued as *'the main part'*, was a clubhouse and store, erected on a man-made plateau, on the East Cliff. Depending on who purchased the land, these buildings might have to be removed. Mains water and electricity were connected and an ancient, stone shed, which housed a well and hand-pump, was included in the Lot. This deep well had once served most of West Bay and was used to water the sheep and Good's horses, which grazed on the slopes.

The lease with the Golf Club had been drawn up in 1932 to run to Michaelmas Day 1962. The rent of the whole Lot was £70, of which £46 was apportioned to the main part, with the balance payable for the east part of the golf course. The tenant of Manor Farm paid £29 of the rent for grazing rights, whilst the Golf Club was liable for the rates, of £120, on it all. There was a right-of-way for the farmer over a track, to the east of the clubhouse, for which he paid 5/- a year.

Lot 133 to the east, which adjoined Lot 132, extended from West Bay, as far as Freshwater and amounted to 26 acres. Water was provided by means of a standpipe and the farmer had

97. The East Cliff, West Bay. Lot 133 including the Golf Clubhouse is the land in the background. Inset 97a Lot 136, Haddon House, West Bay, before alterations.

similar rights for grazing, of which £13 was apportioned for that. The Lot was sold subject to the right-of-way over the track to Freshwater, *'for all purposes'*.

Both Lots were not sold to the Golf Club, as most people had expected but were purchased by Mr John Jeffery, *'for a client'*, at £2,600 and £1,900 respectively. The mystery as to who this was, continued to puzzle most of those gathered in the Sale marquee.

The Golf Club committee continued as tenants. Sheep grazed the whole of the course and although supposed to be an asset in cropping the grass and providing manure to produce lush greens, they often proved a total nuisance. Bunny Lenthall upset a few golfers when he declared, that he proposed to plough up the golf course. Fortunately, for the Club, the agreement that he had with the new owner did not run to that.

The Golf Club went through hard times but by the late 1980s, it was in a healthy position, through good management, a rise in subscriptions and a membership of nearly 800. The new landlord curtailed the euphoria that prevailed, by announcing that he wanted a rent of £9,000 a year.

With a substantial number of bank managers and other long-headed financiers, as members, it was decided to investigate offering to purchase the whole. The price, after solicitors' and accountants' fees were settled, was £100,000. With reserves of nearly £50,000 the committee rallied its members and eventually the amount, some in the form of loans, was raised.

Members voted unanimously to purchase 85 acres and to improve the course. In 1989, approximately another 50 acres of land were bought from the mystery purchaser of 1958, who then accepted an invitation to be a Life Member of the Club.

The clubhouse suffered a devastating fire in 1968, when many of the records were destroyed. A new building was built on the same site.

★★★★★★★★★★

The decision to build a luxourious and modern, larger and more impressive clubhouse, above Marsh Barn, extend and improve the course, along part of the World Heritage coastline, with grass mounds, sculptured bunkers and stone walls, at the onset of the new millennium, has been an extremely good and successful one. The new facilities were opened by the Earl and Countess of Wessex in 2002.

Today the Bridport and West Dorset Golf Club boasts that the 6th hole has been voted in the top one hundred holes in the world. It is known as "Port Coombe", a name that appeared as early as 1700 in the Burton Bradstock records.

DOWN MEAD AND THE MARSH MEADOWS

Lot 134 amounted to 10 acres adjoining the golf course, with a road frontage of 700 feet and lying, less than a ¼ of a mile, from the centre of West Bay. Bunny Lenthall, rented this, paying £14 a year. The land was essential to him in order to be able to retain his world famous flock of Dorset Horn sheep.

Lenthall successfully obtained the ownership, by paying £475.

Lot 135 these meadows were '*adjoining the railway*', which was still in use for transporting goods. There were just over 20 acres of Lot 135 in Burton Bradstock parish and 6 acres in the Bridport Borough. In 1958, the River Brit wound its way to the harbour through the flat meadows on the western side of West Bay. Originally, when the river flowed out under the East Cliff, these became known as the Marsh Meadows, according to the old rent books. Ditches and water channels, to drain the land, predominated.

Rushes and water-loving plants grew in the wettest patches. When not under water, the land was productive, being loam on clay soil. Flocks of Lapwings and wading birds frequented the whole area and the ground was only useful for agricultural purposes, in the drier months, although in very dry periods, the soil could become hard and parched; huge cracks appeared. Cattle would do well there in hot summers and Boy Scouts and other organised camps found it a suitable site.

The 26 acres had been recently ploughed by the tenant and reseeded. With the land fronting the road to Burton Bradstock for some 700 yards, it offered potential for development or as a summer sports' ground. In the south-west corner was a plot belonging to the Bridport Municipal Borough Council.

Bidding was swift, as the Bridport Borough Council and others were interested. The Lot reached £1,075, possibly *withdrawn* as an actual buyer was left unclear in any available records.

> A sewerage plant, was subsequently built on the plot after much opposition from residents in West Bay. In the late 1960s the Burton sewer was extended to this plant. Tony Legg recalled that as it was liable to be constantly moving, it was decided to rest the pipe on beach shingle. He remembered carting hundreds of tons of shingle as the work progressed.
>
> The land came up at an auction in 1972 when the Bridport Borough Council were unsuccessful in purchasing it, besides a further 9 acres adjacent to the Golf Club, as it made beyond what was set by the District Valuer. It remains as grazing land and the pasture opposite is now the Golf Club's Mini Golf course. Two acres remain in the Pitt-Rivers Estate.

HADDON HOUSE

Lot 136 This was the best Lot on offer at West Bay. The catalogue stated that it was '*an imposing residential property*', on the outskirts of West Bay, ¼ of a mile from the sea front and substantially built in rendered stone and brick, with a slate roof.

This family residence stood back from the road to Bridport and consisted of a beautiful drawing room with an Adam fireplace, the morning room, 20 feet by 24 feet, with panelled walls and an oak mantel and the dining room, 29. 6 inches by 15 feet. 9 inches, with yet another attractive fireplace, beamed ceiling and French doors leading to the conservatory and garden. The large kitchen at 18 feet square, boasted a range and

Agamatic boiler, pantry, larder and WC. Gas was installed and a fitted dresser was another main feature of this gentleman's fine residence.

On the first floor, six large bedrooms, the largest being 17 feet by 12 feet, two dressing rooms with hand-basins and three bathrooms, (one with the more modern amenity of a shower, another used by the staff), a separate WC and a housemaids' closet, with the secondary staircase for the servants and a third means of getting from the ground floor to the first floor by an electric lift, impressed the audience, in the Sale marquee, as the list was read out. There was huge scope, for a superb family home, or a good class hotel. The latter was much needed in West Bay.

Drainage was connected. All the curtain fittings belonged to the tenant as well as an Otto stove and the gas fires. A garage, measuring 26 feet by 22 feet was equipped with a turntable and inspection pit. The previous tenant, Doctor Stephens was known as an 'inventor' and had a turntable constructed, on to which he drove his car, in order that the vehicle need not be reversed. A rope could be pulled and the whole lot turned around to face West Bay Road! A walled garden, with well kept lawns and a productive kitchen garden, an engine house, boiler room and a store with three loft rooms, completed the particulars of this outstanding property.

The house had served as a family residence and been entirely in the tenancy of the Stephens family, since the late 1800s (and perhaps earlier), many of whom had their final resting place in Burton cemetery. The family had always been prominent in local affairs and one of the last of the local branch, Mrs IM Stephens, was living in Haddon House, at the time of the Sale.

Haddon House was surrounded by lawns. The productive kitchen garden backed on to the house. Opposite, across the West Bay Road, was a paddock, with 190 feet frontage, totalling ½ an acre on the east side of the croquet lawn. The rates were set at £122. Bradfords rented the paddock at £2 a year, over which a right-of-way existed. The whole area of the house and grounds amounted to 1.7 acres. Viewing was by appointment with Mrs Stephens.

The Western Gazette report stated that it had been purchased by the Langport Trust, Bournemouth for £4,000 and in November of the same year, according to minutes, the Bridport Borough Council was offered Haddon House by an estate agent. The Council took no action.

In 1972, the Borough Council received a letter from Bond and Partners regarding the Council's view on demolishing Haddon House and erecting a block of flats there. The Council sought professional advice and were told that a preservation order should be put on the property as it was an attractive Regency house.

Later, the then owners, Presleigh Property Developers Limited stated that they had no proposal to demolish it.

For a while the property was rented out and a license for a club was granted. It lay empty for a number of years, falling into a dilapidated state and in 1978, Bill Loud, a well known publican, took over Haddon House, recalls his son, Paul. The house was purchased from developers, Mid-Star Properties and Gilbert White, (a local builder, who was involved in the refurbishment). A license was obtained and it was turned into an hotel, just as it stood, becoming a great attraction at West Bay. In due course, it was extended, when Loud acquired Burt, Boulton and Hayward's yard, next door. The hotel was completely refitted to a very high standard. Many features were retained and it remains a premier hostelry in West Dorset. Bill Loud retired towards the end of the 1980s and managers were put in until Paul had gained sufficient experience and was able to take-over running this popular establishment.

A WAREHOUSE AND TIMBER YARD

Lot 137 with a frontage to the main Bridport Road of 120 feet and a side depth of 50 feet, was a valuable commercial and industrial premises. It was being used as a warehouse and timber yard by Burt Boulton and Haywood Limited, merchants at the harbour. The tenancy was valid until December 1960, at an annual repairing and decorating rent of £40. 16s 4d, with insurance and rates of £90.

This was one of the warehouses built at the harbour when trade and industry was flourishing. These buildings were substantial and well constructed in local stone and this one was newly roofed in asbestos.

The warehouse consisted of three storeys, each measuring 78 feet by 20 feet with a hand pulley to each floor. Outside there were four asbestos roofed store sheds, the old stables, 47 feet by 22 feet, covered with stone and slate. Included was a three-bay timber store; the whole of this gave a covered storage area of 10, 000 feet. Mains electricity was connected. Water, gas and drainage were nearby.

The Directors of Burt Boulton and Hayward, bought this highly desirable commercial premises for £1,500.

Hotelier Bill Loud, in due course, purchased the premises from the directors, enabling him to extend the Haddon House Hotel facilities. The remainder, today, is divided into business units; the old company no longer trading.

THE CROQUET LAWN

Lots 138 and 139 The Haddon House croquet lawn amounting to ½ an acre was sold with vacant possession. An accommodation field of 2½ acres, adjacent, was let to Bradfords at £12 per annum, Woolaway Constructions rented a small area to the north at £12. 10/-.

Both Lots were *withdrawn*.

It is contemplated that eventually after long negotiations and the threat of compulsory purchase that Lot 138, the Haddon House Croquet Lawn, as well as an adjoining field, of 2½ acres, Lot 139, came into the hands of the local authorities. It was January of 1960 when a confidential report was received by the Bridport Borough Council from the District Valuer.

These paddocks opposite Haddon House Hotel, now form a much used and needed, hard-surfaced public car and coach park, overseen by West Dorset District Council.

WEST BAY ALLOTMENTS

Lot 140 Like many landlords at the turn of the century, General Pitt-Rivers had let out land, at a peppercorn-rent; land for the working class to cultivate, as a ready source of fresh vegetables and to give them a worthwhile interest. At West Bay, an acre of land had been allocated for this purpose. The tenants' annual rent averaged £3. 7s, in total. With a frontage of around 540 feet on to the main road and bounded by the stream, there was further potential for this land to be put to commercial use. The allotments were still being well cultivated, at the time of the Sale.

For £225, FC Fenner, of Broadstone, a speculator, secured 'this valuable parcel of accommodation land'.

SWAINS ROW

Lots 141, 142 and 143 Seven cottages were sold in three lots. Swains Row had obtained its name from a flax, hemp and coal merchant at Bridport Harbour in the nineteenth century. The seven quaint properties, which lay off George Street, at the rear of the harbour, were let separately, at various amounts, averaging £9 per year. The rents had not been increased after the improvements, which had been carried out by the Vendor, with the help of a grant; this was subject to a twenty year Housing Act restriction, unless the grant and interest were repaid to the Bridport Municipal Borough Council. However, accordingly, the rents could be increased to a maximum of £26. The tenants were paying the rates of £8 each, per year.

Lot 141, Number 1 Swain's Row, was being sold with vacant possession, number 2 was occupied by Mrs Hilda Letts, number 3 rented from the Estate by Burt Boulton and Haywood, (on a repairing and decorating lease to correspond with the lease on the warehouse, until December 1960). Number 4, Swains Row, was let to Miss E Green, number 5 to the West Dorset Golf Club, providing a house for staff. Number 6, was rented by Harry Hawkins, retired sailor, now fisherman and pleasure-boat owner and number 7 was occupied by Reg Harvey, respected for his sea-faring knowledge and fishing skills.

Each cottage was similar, recently modernised, brick built, rendered and slated, with two small rooms downstairs and two bedrooms, a larder and the advantage of a bathroom. There were rights-of-way, for each tenant. Drainage had been installed as part of the modernisation, which was by a common drain, from each cottage. The whole area amounted to about 40 perches.

A cobbled path ran along in front and each possessed a long front garden, as well as a second garden, at the back, with a communal coal shed, on the premises. In rough weather, when the tides were high and the river full, with the sea washing over the harbour basin, these cottages had been known to suffer from flooding.

The bidding was interesting, resulting in LM Green of Dagenham purchasing number 1 for £300, Lot 142, Mrs Letts, her home, at £350, and the remaining five properties, Lot 143, at a total of £1,800 by Hugh Lister.

THE FINAL LOT

Lot 144 By now the audience was resigned to the fact that most of the tenants who had wished to buy their home, or land, had been able to do so, by the swift appraisal and understanding of the auctioneers. An immense cheer and clapping had resonated through the marquee on both days, as soon as the hammer fell to one of the tenants; the volume of the applause never lessened, during the whole period. There was an air of mystery pervading over the purchase of several of the larger farms and the Golf Course and various Lots that had been withdrawn from the Sale, particularly The Hive Beach.

There had been a number of purchases, particularly of cottages, potential building sites and accommodation land, made by unknown speculators. The familiar scene in Burton Bradstock, of everyone knowing who was who and who rented what, from the Estate, had been swept away overnight. The second day of the Sale was about to come to an end. The link with the Pitt-Rivers family and their ancestors, as the landlords, that had existed for some three hundred and fifty years, was over.

The paddock to Haddon House, the final Lot in this unique Sale, amounted to an acre, bounded by the stream on the north and west and which formed part of the Haddon House amenity. Included was a timber hut, 50 feet by 14 feet, previously used as a family boat house, part of which was used by the West Bay Women's Institute as a meeting place. There was a right-of-way through the gateway leading to George Street from Haddon House. The paddock, sometimes wet, was level and made up of rich loam on clay. Lot 144 was to conclude the Sale on this unique occasion.

****

In 1952 the West Bay Women's Institute had moved into a hut in George Street, courtesy of Mrs Stephens, the tenant of Haddon House. The building, formerly used by her late husband as a boat house became the WI meeting place. In 1958 the Agent for the Pitt-Rivers Estate had enquired of the committee whether the Institute was in a position to buy the plot and hut. The committee was not able to avail itself of the offer and with consideration, the Estate granted the West Bay Women's Institute the use of the hut, rent free, for as long as the group remained in existence, although they could not have foreseen that fifty years might elapse. The day concluded, on a very generous note with this Lot being *withdrawn*.

****

98. Circa 1950, the leading cattle returning from milking, meandering through the High Street. "Old Salts" sit on the seat and watch the world go by.

As the gavel was stowed away, those who had made purchases during the second day, were required to lay down deposits, complete contracts and sign documents. The whole business had been transacted in record time. The auctioneer said, in concluding the Sale, that when he reported back to Captain Pitt-Rivers, he knew that he would be very pleased that so many of the tenants had been able to purchase.

RB Howarth admitted that he had changed his mind, since the opening of the Sale. Most tenants had bought. The mystery buyer had taken a huge portion of the land and the farmsteads that went with it, although this went unmentioned by Howarth. The occupiers of these Lots had bowed to what, in most cases, eventually turned out to be a sensible outcome. The withdrawal from the Sale of The Hive Beach would, in the end, prove of benefit to everyone.

The Western Gazette, the following week gave the total raised by Captain Pitt-Rivers as £177,775, which excluded Lots that were withdrawn and sold privately. From this, would have been taken a sizeable percentage as expenses and commission fees. A comparison with the cost of earnings in 1958 to the present day would put the receipts from the Sale around £5,000,000. The same land and properties put on the market now, allowing for the gigantic increase in the prices of cottages, houses, building sites and land, might raise around £25,000,000 and the rest.

The paper did not give the name of the mystery purchaser, although *The Dorset Evening Echo* had found out who it was and that he had paid out a total of £37,500, (which at that stage did not include purchasing The Hive Beach or Pitfold Farm). Such prime Lots would be priceless today and could fetch in excess of all the rest put together.

Neither was the mysterious purchaser named in *The Bridport News* . The paper seemed more concerned with reporting individual tenant's reactions and successful purchases. It did state that Mr J Jeffery, of Shaftesbury, had bought Manor Farm. Unintentually, this put many off the scent. The whole issue was confusing. *The Dorset Evening Echo* stated that AF Bailey had purchased Cogden Farm which was incorrect.

Everyone had plenty to get on with and little thought could be given, at first, about these very expensive Lots that had, seemingly, 'gone away'. Those who knew, kept quiet, saving a lot of questions and losing face.

Mr Ingram, for Senior and Godwin, the auctioneers, said, "The general impression in the Sale tent was that Captain Pitt-Rivers had been kind to the tenants. " He continued, "On behalf of the [Pitt-Rivers] Estate, we are glad that those tenants who wished to acquire their own cottage properties were, in the main, able to do so. "

The film showing at the Bridport cinema reflected the attitude of the tenants. It was *"Annie Get Your Gun"*, in which Betty Hutton and Howard Keel were the stars. In similar spirit the majority of the tenants had rallied to their own defence.

AND AFTERWARDS

It was several weeks, following July 31st and August 1st, 1958, before the contracts were finalised. Villagers who had usually discussed their simple business, now wondered how much to tell their neighbours. The village began to wake-up concerning who had bought the prestigious Lots. It was certain that whoever was *'the client'* that Mr Jeffery, had acted as the agent for, must be a very rich man and who were the numerous entrepreneurs who had snapped up some of the cottages, the potential building sites and a lot of outlying land. Butcher Gale had bought a great deal of the land he tenanted and some of that had outline planning permission already. What would be built on it all? What were the purchasers' plans? Questions were asked in hushed tones.

Those who had not been caught up in the 'storm', tried to carry on life in the village, as before but others who had so swiftly become the owners of their homes, businesses, land and farms, now had a weight on their shoulders. Although, time would bring a renewed pattern to their lives, for the majority, there was money for a mortgage or bank overdraft, to find, as well as other overheads. The farmers who had bought, might, on paper, have been comfortably off but they had to generate an income to justify the purchase. Interest rates on the mortgages that had been taken-up, were moderate, as was interest on bank overdrafts but still the money had to be found.

The incomes of the tenants who had bought, whether cottager, businessman or farmer, were modest. Somehow the money had to be earned quicker than in the past. The farmers who were renting, under their new landlord, may have been assured of reasonably secure tenancies but only for the time-being. The inevitability of increased rents troubled them, whilst the chance to be their own master seemed lost.

★★★★★★★★★★

The Parish Councillors' attentions turned away from the Sale, for a while. The steps at Green Cliff needed some improvement. The miller was to be asked to replace the broken timber on the stile at Longmead and Fred Norris was paid 17/6d *for commons preservation'*, [an old term for keeping the public land in good order; in this case the village greens]. There was much that was still the same.

★★★★★★★★★★

The minutes of meetings, give a good indication as to how the land lay. The confusion regarding the Reading Room and allotments, was not settled and eventually a cheque was sanctioned to pay the £40 for the purchase of the Recreation Ground. The land at the back of the Reading Room had been offered to a third party, as the Parish Council had no use for it.

In Bridport, 1958 ended with record Christmas sales in the shops. A Bridport based boat-builder, RH Penny, hoped to secure a contract with the United States of America

99. Harold and Caroline, née Cammell were mine hosts at the Three Horseshoes. Inset 99a During the First World War.

for £50,000 and Burt, Boulton and Hayward held their annual dinner at the Greyhound Hotel. Palmers were selling Scotch Whisky, (although stocks were limited), at 37/6d a bottle and special IPA at 13/- per ½ dozen bottles and much was consumed, when Bridport Industries held their New Year's Eve Ball at the Drill Hall. Dancing was to the Commodore Dance Orchestra, dress was optional and tickets 7/-. Ron Guyatt, a man, from Burton Bradstock and his wife, Ruby, celebrated their Silver Wedding and were living in a bungalow, of unusual design, which he had newly built, on the Dorchester Road. As the year ended, in age-old style, those attending a dance in the village hall, linked arms at midnight and sang "Should Auld Acquaintance be Forgot".

By January of 1959, there had been no further progress regarding the Southover allotments. The District Valuer was unwilling to proceed. There was no grant forthcoming from the Playing Field Association and the Parish Clerk, Leonard Hope, was instructed to 'have one last try'. Stanley Williams and Bert Bull were elected as Parish Councillors, following the death of Bert Bull's father and in place of Jim Churchill, who had moved away.

Up until the time of the Sale, the Parish Council, a follow-on from the days of the Manorial Court Leet, had a simple and limited number of items to consider on the agendas. The state of the roads and greens, flooding, the allocation of allotments, Fishermen's Green and matters relating to the playing field, with just a few planning applications, together with communications concerning the Pitt-Rivers Estate, about repairs and replacements affecting the Parish Council, were all that had been discussed. The councillors, were village men. The advantage was, that they, like their forebears, on the old Court Leet jury, were familiar with the people, places and eventualities.

BURTON BRADSTOCK'S WINDS OF CHANGE

As time went on, the village expanded and became very sought-after for retirement, holiday homes, or a place to put down new roots. Some who now owned sites for development wanted to build places for themselves. Newly elected councillors, came on to the Parish Council, maybe with more experience of larger organisations but little knowledge of the locality. Newcomers were thought of as intruders. There was suspicion and hostility on both sides. Some of the incoming residents were too forceful and outspoken and gave an air of superiority. They tended to think that the locals were dim-witted and had never 'been anywhere'.

100. 1975 Burton Bradstock football team. (Standing L to R) Andrew Bullock, Geoffrey Norris, Terry Lunt, Roger Lewis, Mike Mudford, Peter Stevens, Basil Dent (Coach).
(Front row L to R): Peter Stoodley, Robert Rodway, David Joy, Maurice Youngs, (Captain) Steven Burden. Boy mascot, Mike Mudford, Jnr.

On the contrary, the village had spawned some fine, highly qualified and well respected people. Even those who had perhaps not had the best chances in life, were of a practical disposition and certainly had a 'degree' in common sense. One wealthy new inhabitant caused great offence when he accused the Burton people of being uneducated and ignorant. Another newcomer soon sprang to their defence. Intelligence could not be judged by the job they did. The village people did know what would be best for the parish and there was still RB Howarth, with his quick brain and dominant character, who led them, in practically every move.

The new residents had little idea what happened throughout the year, in a coastal working village. A fortnight's visit in the summer months, was insufficient time to understand that there were certain happenings and conditions that enabled the village to thrive and the inhabitants to make a livelihood, all the year around. Those who had moved into the village, rushed overnight, to smarten up the older properties and attempted to get the gardens, of the old and newly built properties alike, resembling those in glossy magazines. Edward Wilson, an ecologist said that "Whenever people are given a free choice, they move to tree-studded land on prominences overlooking water. "

The new inhabitants had not considered contending with the wet, cold, heavy clay, or the rocky strata that ran from Burton Cliff to Yeovil and the rain-laden south-westerly gales, or the cold winds, in spring, from the north and east, that could sweep through. Newly settled-in men would be seen out digging in their gardens, far too early in the year. They were not always adequately clad and tackling manual work, that they had never been used to doing, gave them backache and chills.

Men (and their wives, on occasions), could be seen perched precariously on ladders, rubbing down woodwork and painting the outside of the homes. In some circumstances, they soon succumbed to pneumonia or fell victim to accidents. Reg Buckler commented that they were asking for premature death and that one of the couple would be left stranded, miles from their family and friends, which happened in several cases.

Wasn't it stated in Ecclesiates that there was a time for seedtime and harvest? In the countryside, the local people knew exactly when the conditions were right to start digging, planting, harvesting and what would grow and where. Neither was the sea always tranquil. Danger often lurked just feet from the shore and the salt air played havoc with the woodwork and paint.

The cry of the seagulls, the chime of the church clock, the ringing of the bells, the ticking of an electric fencer, dung-laden tractors being driven around the village and the cattle, that brought the streets and lanes to a standstill, twice daily, as well as dropping manure as they went, annoyed many of those who had moved in.

★★★★★★★★★★

News reached the village that Captain Pitt-Rivers's health was failing and in their Christmas card of 1962, to former tenants, Mrs Pitt-Rivers added a footnote concerning 'the Captain's renewed illness'.

★★★★★★★★★★

A recently retired inhabitant to the village reprimanded a workman, who was clad in overalls and covered in oil, thinking that he was trespassing in a private road, only to be informed that he, too, lived along there. A locally born and bred man was walking his dog, as he did daily, along the river bank, when he was confronted and upbraided for doing so. The intruder into the everyday pattern of village life, was soon told to mind his own business and that dogs had been walked there for decades. Another local young man, who was born and brought up in Burton, told a reporter that he lived 'on the reservation', meaning the council housing estate. Such was the initial divide. It would be a long time before the two factions began to understand and tolerate each other.

Letters of complaint began to arrive in the Parish Clerk's mail. There was a lot of building activity in Burton. The Three Horseshoes Inn was redesigned and the land for a car park, purchased at the Sale, was developed. A few months later, the new wall was giving concern. A meeting was held with Tony Palmer, the owner of the local brewery, who assured the Parish Council that it 'would weather'. The alterations to a cottage in Mill Street, for the new post office, was causing annoyance, as rubble, waiting for removal, was being left in the street.

Fallen trees were blocking the river and there was serious danger of flooding. By the end of 1959, a plan to develop Bind Barrow, for residential purposes, was turned down by the Parish Council and then withdrawn. It had all started as Howarth meant it to go on but matters would soon get out-of-hand. Planning applications came tumbling in to the Parish Council. Grants were available to renovate and restore old properties which were too good to miss, as there had rarely been 'something given away', although the conditions imposed presented many a problem and often involved the developer spending out more than had originally been intended. In the past, there had only been a moderate number of council and private development projects. The farm buildings had remained much as before, with the exception of a Dutch barn here and there, as grants had become available and farming methods improved. Planning applications had gone through the simple procedures, generally unopposed.

There were a number of the right sort of privately owned houses for the gentry, mostly service officers, who had chosen to retire to Burton. Some of these grand houses were those rented from the Estate, others privately owned. They had come and gone in Burton, for decades, respected for their position but not often accused of imposing on village traditions and way of life. However, it has been recalled that one new resident, a retired army officer, caused a major upset, when with some of his followers, had voted that moving the headstones in the churchyard would be a good idea and that, consequently, a contractor mowing the grass would be more economic. The churchyard was untidy for some, yet a peaceful place where the wildlife thrived where an annual scalping, usually with a scythe, was sufficient. Simple electric mowers were coming into use and the headstones and curbs certainly made mowing very difficult.

Letters were sent out to descendants who had family graves in the churchyard but not all could be traced. The older tombs had to remain and some families, like the Bucklers and Kerleys refused to allow the stones to be taken away and stood, in a military fashion, around the perimeter of the churchyard. (In time, visitors mistakenly thought that the stones were, in fact, at the head of the appropriate grave). There had been some who moved into the village who were too outspoken and interfering and moving the headstones was a good example of indelicate interference.

There were moans about the dirty state of the village. What was considered dirt by some was only everyday debris to others. Smells that were part of the countryside and seashore caused some upturned noses. It would seem that complaints had come from those who had retired to the village, often from smart suburbs. A large herd of dairy cows along Annings Lane and two hundred head of cattle through the village, twice a day, obviously created problems. The growing amount of traffic, particularly during the Easter, Whitsun and summer holidays, made bringing the cattle in for milking, dangerous, for the motorist, cyclist, pedestrian and the animals, alike and the manure in the streets caused a controversy. A new resident, in Beach Road, complained to the authorities, that the riding school ponies, were dropping manure along the roads. He was, however, quick to run out with his bucket and shovel, to scoop up the piles of dung, for his rose garden!

Edgar Hawkins, Vice Chairman of the Parish Council, caravan camp proprietor and farmer, not wanting to seem uncooperative, decided to attempt to buy a small corner of the Recreation Ground, in order to erect a bridge from his fields, to the farm buildings. This seemed a sensible solution and after a site meeting, the Parish Council sold the plot to him.

A bridge was built, from Corn Croft field across to Shadrach Dairy Farm cutting the number of cattle wandering through the village by half and greatly reducing the number of farm vehicles driving through the streets. Hawkins was fortunate to have an army officer camping at Larkfield and they got talking. It was a time of service cuts and certain types of bridges were obsolete. The officer, no doubt for a consideration, arranged for Hawkins to purchase a defunct bridge, erect it across the River Bride, at a very reasonable price and the army, would undertake the construction as an exercise. The Burtoners turned out to witness yet another unusual spectacle in their village. The soldiers put up tents and set-up their camp in the very field where the Sale had been held. Had a public right-of-way over the bridge been considered at the time, later problems with pedestrians, at risk in the main street, might have been avoided.

The owners of Bay View, unsuccessfully, applied for permission to build a skittle alley at their guest house. The Pitt-Rivers Estate wanted to develop an area of Southover, where land had been retained and a site for housing in the High Street and Bob Frost's application to build a bungalow, went to appeal, after the Parish Council decided to oppose these applications. Eventually, Frost's appeal was won, to build on an old allotment site in Southover, which opened up the way for other development. New caravan sites, were disallowed, even though the influx of campers wanting to come to Burton was increasing by the season. Badly needed revenue was being sent on to other resorts.

More council houses were springing up off Annings Lane, yet, the telephone manager refused to put another kiosk there where few, if any, people had telephones. The River Board authority was not interested in a flood alleviation scheme, although the village was being flooded on a regular basis. Water poured down from Gages Lane into the Grove Road, too. Dogs were fouling the allotments and there was a complaint about Joe Linee's workshop, Lot 12, near the Pound. The road was narrow and dangerous. He had set-up his builder's business store and workshop where similar Estate premises had long existed. By 1961, the Parish Council's attention was drawn to the dangerous parking at The Anchor Hotel. The new "Mine Hosts" were pulling in the customers.

Young people were not forgotten, after the Parish Council was pressurised and it was agreed to allow the village school and Burton Youth Club to use the Recreation Ground.

NEEDING A HAND ON THE TILLER

At Parish Council meetings, general concerns continued to be discussed. The Pitt-Rivers Estate had handed over responsibility of the village greens to the parish and there was talk of putting public conveniences, in the main street, next to the bus shelter, which had been built, during weekends, by Dick Galpin and Bert Adams, assisted by David MacDermott, in 1953, to commemorate the Queen's Coronation. Litter bins were required. Councillors Louis Brown and Ted Hitt volunteered to sweep out the bus shelter each week and empty the litter bin. On his retirement, as the village postman, for thirty-eight years, in February of 1962, Jimmer Norris was presented with a cheque for £23. 11s. 6d, donated, from a house to house collection.

December 29th 1962 and into 1963 heralded the worst winter for some two hundred years. Burton was caught in a dreadful blizzard and conditions were atrocious. Everything remained frozen for weeks.

That year, Rosamond Court, in the High street, (old Market Road), was under construction and two very ancient burials were discovered. The bodies had been placed facing in an east-west direction, inclining towards the barrow on North Hill. One was of

101.Mill Street after the blizzard of 1978.(L) the "New" post office

a boy, aged 14-21 years of age, with a bowl, of similar type to Maiden Castle war cemetery ware, beside him. (This was broken when the site was being cleared for building). The other, believed to be male, was in a grave 6 feet long and 2-3 feet deep. The body was fully extended with the hands crossed over the abdomen. The burial period was thought to be Roman, about AD 1 and concurrently, a coin of circa AD 431 had been found in Barr

Lane. These findings, just under the surface, emphasised the antiquity of the village.

The purchase of the Southover allotments, (valued at £900), had finally been sorted out with the Estate and a £1,000 loan over thirty years was needed. If in the years to come the allotments became obsolete then the land was to be retained as an open space. By then, the Reading Room required slating. The Rural District Council wanted to close the caravan camp at Cliff Farm, much to the councillors' annoyance and the owner's detriment. If the camp was closed then there could be additional 'clear' land along the top of the cliff, adjoining The Hive Beach. Sauce for the goose was sauce for the gander when the Rural District Council applied to colour-wash the council properties in Barr Lane. It seemed an outrageous scheme and was thrown out by the Parish Council.

During 1965, Councillor Lenthall, who by then had been persuaded to represent the 'old hands' on the Parish Council, was unable to obtain reimbursement from the authorities, for clearing a blocked channel, at Freshwater, preventing serious flooding. Shortly after, he emigrated to Australia. It could have been one of the last straws.

Another letter of complaint was received, from a private resident, in the new development in Beach Road, about washing being hung on lines. For the hard-working people of Burton Bradstock, who had lived harmoniously cheek by jowl for generations, this was ridiculous. Washing had to be hung out and always had been, although rarely on a Sunday. No action was taken. The complainant had overlooked the other age-old drying method, whereby bed and table-linen could be found drying on the privet hedges, in the gardens.

However, the workload of the Parish Council was getting much heavier. Miss Edith Bickford, retired Head Mistress of Bridport Grammar School, who had lived in the village for many years, joined the council. Her knowledge, experience and leadership were invaluable, as building applications came in. She put forward the suggestion that a planning sub-committee should be formed to deal with the deluge.

A PLAN FOR THE VILLAGE

T he death of Captain Pitt-Rivers in 1966 was received with great sadness by the former tenants and throughout the county. The threat of nuclear war, went more-or-less unheeded. All that seemed far removed from Burton's concerns.

★★★★★★★★★★

In the September of 1966, the County Planning Authority had realised that a plan, similar to a town plan, was required for Burton Bradstock. In the meantime, no new development applications would be granted. The plan stated that great care should be taken over the architecture and the choice of materials used. Public lavatories should definately be positioned near the centre of the village. (Daily, the village was busy with holiday makers). Emphasis was on road improvement, especially by The Anchor Hotel, where the road narrowed.

More shops were to be approved but not centralised. One shop adjacent to the council housing, in Annings Lane, would be ideal. In the spring of 1958, a young couple's idea to start a shop, incorporating the post office, (the Post Mistress having given notice), in the Shadrach area, at the bottom of Shipton Lane, had been vetoed.

The Burton Village Plan suggested that there should be provision, within the residential areas, for small rural businesses. Manor Farm, having changed ownership, by then, could be developed but the Parish Council was anxious to see the details. Captain Forth, at the old Coastguard Station, received no objections to his proposal to install a shop and office at the camp. It was 'out of the way' and did not affect people in the village. Gordon Cheney, on the other hand, drew a blank over developing land at Barr Lane. His plan to extend the garage was better received. It would seem that it would be a good idea to get elected on to the Parish Council and keep an eye on what was happening, which Cheney, like other businessmen, were encouraged to do.

At Freshwater Camp, the new owner, Stanley Northover, originally from a Chickerell branch of the family, agreed to erect notices to the effect that the bathing there was dangerous. A request for further caravan sites was turned down. The camp was by now, providing a supermarket, a hairdresser, a bar, recreational facilities and a dance and games hall, with a smart snack-bar. As yet, there was no swimming pool. As soon as shops and other amenities were provided at the Coastguard and Freshwater Camps, business in the village began to slow-up. Mrs Thelma Aylott, who was a clerk at the village post office, noted that the number of shoppers, coming into Burton soon decreased.

Sidney Shipp, pressed by his young daughter, who was working at Freshwater, became the camp's first disc jockey. With a radiogram and up-to-date-records he put on entertainments for the youngsters.

Pauline Foot, a qualified hairdresser, recalls that she was approached by the Northovers to set-up, engage extra staff and manage the hairdressing salon, at Freshwater Camp. She was provided with a caravan on the site and lived there throughout the season, for seven years, with her husband and children. For them it was a permanent holiday but for her, it was endless hours, as the salon stayed open from 8am to 10pm!

Cheney's garage was always busy. Residents (especially the farmers and businessmen) and the hundreds of visitors, needed petrol, diesel, tyres and repairs and there was money available to buy new vehicles, usually on a loan. In due course, Freshwater Camp had its own petrol pumps installed, with a slight knock-on effect.

Even with a licensed bar at Freshwater Camp, there was good trade in the three village pubs which were bursting with visitors and locals alike, who enjoyed the convivial atmosphere. The Three Horseshoes went from strength to strength as a lively venue. The Greenfingers Club, at The Dove Inn, entertained a large number of people. Both pub's efforts to raise money for charities, particularly in aid of the Royal National Lifeboat Institution, brought life to Mill Street and Southover. The Anchor hostelry was meeting the needs of the late twentieth century traveller and holiday makers. It had become a welcoming country pub, with trimmings that gave the visitor the notion of seaside and country old world charm, yet with modern comforts. All three hostelries had strong darts' teams and the old fashioned games of Shove Halfpenny, Pontoon and Crib lingered on until all were gone who were enthusiastic to play.

****

At Ingram House, Archer Richards, known as "Dickie", a chatty, jovial little gent, had come to retire. He was immediately elected onto the Parish Council, supported by the new residents. He had some constructive ideas, although not always kindly received. This was 1968 and he suggested that the village should be designated a conservation site. There was no seconder to his proposal.

With more people moving around the village, in the summer months, the footpaths were coming under scrutiny. Jack Burt's application to develop some of his land at Barr Lane was considered *'most undesirable'*. Tony Bishop, too, was looking at development on his farm as he was intending to free himself from the mounting burdens and beaurocracy of farm life and start another enterprise.

Shadrach Farmstead was visualised as a country hotel. Behind, it had ample space for car-parking and other facilities that would be required. Councillor Richards wanted the plan to be rejected outright but he received no support, although the conditions that the planners wanted were too demanding and the saving of a couple of cruck trusses put the Bishops' future in jeopardy. Ten years on, RB Howarth's adamant statement, at the Sale, about controlled development was being adhered to, albeit, on a thin and insecure string. Some decisions seemed very unfair. The new residents were some of the first to oppose further building, especially if it was at their own back-door or blocking the view they thought that they had purchased.

Nothing was consistent and it was questioned as to why one application was successful when others, of equal merit, were turned down. It was a time of utter confusion. Bishop's application to build an agricultural dwelling at the far end of his farm, in Annings Lane, was left undecided and Rosamonds (Dorset), who were the pioneers of good quality, new housing in the district, were refused permission to erect two additional old people's houses in Annings Lane.

Frank Bailey did not fare well when he wanted a twenty-eight day tenting licence, at Cogden. New caravan sites elsewhere were disallowed. Converting a store and derilict cottage, at the Shadrach farmstead, was approved, whilst a licence for a riding school at Freshwater was refused by the parish councillors, as there had been a riding establishment and trekking centre, in Shipton Lane, since 1956, where up to twenty horses, and ponies were utilised through the season, employing half-a dozen seasonal staff.

The Hawkins family's milk-round had taken a back-seat in favour of progressive farming and overseeing the caravan camp, whilst Colin Derryman set himself up, in his father's footsteps, as a milk and dairy produce retailer. He had an extensive milk-round in Burton, through the Bride Valley and Abbotsbury, with the depôt in Rowdens Lane, behind his parents' new home.

The Villa Close caravan camp, situated in the cliff fields, operated by the Hawkins family, had moved to Larkfield and was being extended. This was all part of the plan, to clear the cliffs of caravan camps from Freshwater to The Hive Beach and make it an area of natural, unexploited beauty, free from development. RB Howarth and the immediate backers of the plan (the main one presumed to be the mystery purchaser), set-up a private trust to purchase and administer it but this presented problems and talks with the National Trust officials, seemed sensible.

By 1968, the ownership of the village greens was in question, as there was nothing in Burton Bradstock that came within the Commons Registration Act of 1963. The Parish Council Clerk was instructed to write to the Pitt-Rivers Estate's solicitors. Other business included that the Rector, the Reverend Cyril Ridler, had presented a bill for £5, for the hire of the church mower and the Parish Council had agreed to go fifty-fifty with the Royal British Legion group to repair and redecorate the Reading Room, with a maximum out-lay of £25. Further caravan storage was granted at Larkfield. These caravans had to stay on site, stacked closely together, during the winter months, or be towed to a storage base, when the village would have been clogged-up during the moving of so many caravans. It was agreed they might as well be left on the site. At a Parish Council meeting, in November 1969, approval was unanimous, led by RB Howarth, for a touring caravan site adjacent to Larkfield. Edgar Hawkins declared an interest.

Now the proportion of councillors was four locals to four newcomers. Proposals were often dismissed rather quickly or deferred for investigation. It was all rather chaotic. RB Howarth was still in the Chair. That situation could not go on for ever. A decade after the Sale, Burton Bradstock was rapidly becoming the fastest expanding village in the district, resulting in the Parish Council agendas becoming longer and controversial.

Local families wanted to get out of old, cramped, poky cottages with uneven, flagstone

102. Fishermen, circa 1925, outside Lot 35 Greenwich Cottage, looking as it did until after the Sale. (C) with dog, Joseph Buckler and his brother (R)William. 102a The Cottage standing in flood water 1979.

floors and have space, light, hot and cold water indoors, with modern bathrooms and sanitation, (besides straight walls) and even basic central heating. The townsman was wanting a dream place, in the country, to which he could escape. His wife swooned over the quaintness of the old buildings. With the mains sewer now connected to most properties and gas brought through from the Dorchester Road, modern amenities could be enjoyed. The days of the earth vaults, bucket and Elsan lavatories and a shared cold tap outside, or across the road, were a thing of the past.

The various peculiarities that came with older properties did not seem to bother the new owners at first. It was a sort of adventure to motor down to Burton and 'play house' for the weekend or a fortnight. In some cases, the novelty wore off, or the excessive costs, problems associated with renovation and the general inconvenience of these older properties, led to a sale again.

Coming to the unspoilt beach, the meadows along the river, (still being farmed in the age-old manner), the old-world-charm pubs and friendly shopkeepers and post office staff, giving personal service, very little disturbance, as yet, from traffic and still a reasonable steady pace of life to be had in Burton Bradstock, there was immense interest in buying any of the older properties, that came on the market again or securing newly built bungalows.

Lower Townsend council housing complex was up and running, well before the Sale, land having been acquired from Captain Pitt-Rivers, whilst the South Annings Estate had been started early in the 1960s. There had been condemnation about the colour of the materials that had been used. The glaring white Portland-stone appearance was not in keeping with the mellowness of the village and the complex stuck out like a sore thumb. It all boiled down to costs and availability. No one was manufacturing cheap enough replica stone such as was once hewn from the surrounding quarries.

It was around this period that the Pitt-Rivers Estate made another generous gesture by handing over Green Cliff to be preserved as an open space.

★★★★★★★★★★

A let-up in the wrangle over planning applications was when Donald Ridler, the Rector's son, decided to build himself a boat, on the Rectory lawn, in which he planned to cross the Atlantic. This educated, bright young man, found himself, somewhat, the laughing stock of the "Old Salts" of Burton and West Bay. With £250, great ingenuity, salvaged timber, sheeting and red paint, he completed his plan and named his vessel, "Erik the Red". He was not expected to get out of West Bay harbour, let alone sail some four thousand miles and hadn't he already brought bad luck on his venture, by dubbing 'her' [the boat], with a male name?

By Christmas 1969, the boat was ready for launching. Ridler was aware that the sea off the Chesil Beach could be a death-trap and after meeting a storm in the English Channel and sustaining some damage, he limped back into the harbour. Ridler made repairs and set off for the second time and accomplished his mission. There was a period when his parents did not hear from him and feared the worst. After his return voyage the Burton fishermen and old sailors were the first to marvel at his feat. He was a man from Burton but not a Burton man. They knew full well what he had accomplished. (He had little technological equipment to assist him).

On the beach there were still part-time fishermen at work. Christopher and Philip Hutchings and John Copp acted as crew and Andrew Bullock, Bobby Cammell and Desmond Gape had superseded the old hands. It was said that the best of the younger men to row a boat, in those latter years, was Richard Wylde. No one could match his strength on the oars.

★★★★★★★★★★

RB Howarth, who had steered the village through so much over the past sixty years was getting frail. Through illness, he had missed a few Rural District and Parish Council meetings. This was an exception and he had soon bounced back to lead the councillors and public again. On the 16th of January, 1970 he invited all his past pupils and their partners to a party, in the WI Hall, to celebrate his 90th birthday. It was a double celebration as he had been awarded, a well deserved, recognition for his great service to the community, by being made a Member of the British Empire.

Howarth's death in 1972, when his daughter, Mary and Greta Heal found him in his armchair, was a passing of an impassioned leader with a very extraordinary talent and character.

103. The Rookery from Grove Road, Circa 1960.

104. Swains Row, West Bay, as it is today. Lots 141,142 and 143

106. Ray, Margaret Chapman, née Hawkins and son Andrew, in Australia.

105. Youth club leader Dawn Pattinson, with husband Peter. Inset 105a Pearl Parsons, another leader.

107. Greta Heal, née Hawkins, as everyone knows her.

108. 1976, Jack and Olive Burt on Manor Farm lawn, with their seven daughters, (L) to (R) Bridget, Philipa, Emma, (Front L to R) Heather, Valerie, Julie, (her wedding day), Shirley and four grandchildren.

109. 1965 (R) Master Thatcher, Guy Gale at work on the Three Horseshoes Inn. (L) assistant Jack Lewis, Reg Clarke, Rural Industries thatching officer, (standing on the scaffolding). Inset 109a "The Shoes" in 2005.

110. In the refurbished bar of "The Shoes": (L to R) Bill Jarman, Stanley Williams, Marjorie Jarman, Basil Dent and the hosts Alan Gillett and his wife Joan.

111. Tony Bishop rides a winner shortly after the Burton Sale in 1958.

112. The old flax spinning mill in 2007 awaits a new life.

TWENTY YEARS ON

As the 'flood-gates' were opened, every patch, that was potential building land, was put forward for development. There were now twice the number of dwellings in the village than there had been a hundred and fifty years previously. New building firms were springing up. Not all of the sites were those that had once been part of the Pitt-Rivers Estate, particularly Norburton, which came under different ownership.

Some of those who had purchased at the Sale, were selling off orchards and plots. There were requests to build that were inexplicably turned down. The matter did not rest with the Parish Council now that the central planning authority was having far more say. People were not too bothered about planning applications that did not affect their 'patch' and some were sanctioned that today would be questionable.

Still, nothing seemed consistent. Some thought it was who you knew. There were individuals who wanted a site, on which a family member could build a home but stood no chance. The swathe of new houses and bungalows clung together, without a patch of open green grass between them. There were designated areas and building lines.

Norman Lingard, a self-made market gardener and would-be developer, was refused planning permission to build on one of his fields near Arch Bridge. He already had greenhouses there, in conjunction with the business, vehicles were in and out of the premises and building was going on all around.

Lingard was a clever strategist, even for the planning authorities to deal with and having studied his rights and what might be, in the future, he decided to sit it out and not go to appeal. If he lost, he said, "That would be it. If you wait long enough and pestered enough 'they' would give in." Unfortunately, he did not live to see the application passed, (after he had submitted numerous plans) but he was proved right, posthumously.

Almost twenty years on from the Sale, with the building line extended eastwards, an aerial photograph of Burton Bradstock, showed the extent to which Burton had been developed. Manor Farmyard lay devoid of all its old farming connections. The grand old buildings were put to other uses, or left to the ghosts of the past. Plans for a gentleman's residence, in the former walled kitchen garden, were submitted and passed.

Burton became divided, when a application for a small factory workshop, occupying a disused farm building, was submitted. There were people from both sides who did not want industry in the 'chocolate-box' cover, picturesque village. Had they forgotten, (if they ever knew), that it had once been a working village, thriving on industry with a factory chimney as high as the church tower? There would be noise, smells and extra traffic the objectors pleaded. These objections were considered but a unit to recycle foundry wax, was granted. Yet, once up and running, little was said or heard about the matter again.

In the High Street, Cheney's Garage had the look of a suburban car show-room and Stanley's former home had been modernised, whilst the barn behind, bore no resemblance to his happy-go-lucky store area and workshop. Two smart new properties, double glazed from necessity, along the high street, stood on the site of ruined cottages, beside the mill stream and The Three Horseshoes Inn had been up-dated. The newly sited post office, in Mill Street continued to provide an excellent service and a meeting place. The shop section carried a variety of goods including wool for those who were still knitting.

The landscape had taken on a different aspect, not only with all the new dwellings springing up but the fact that one of the predominant species of trees had succumbed to Dutch Elm disease. Handsome specimens, standing forty and fifty feet high had died off. There was plenty of ready firewood to be had but some familiar landmarks completely disappeared. (To compensate, some tree planting was undertaken, in the village in the 1980s).

★★★★★★★★★★

The mid-to-late 1970s was a time of extremes of weather conditions. The area was always prone to thunder storms and intense flashes of lightning. No one minded the thunder or the rain that usually followed but lightning was best kept out at sea rather than inland, where the thatched properties were very vulnerable. South-westerly gales swept across from the Atlantic Ocean, every year, particularly in November and February.

February 1974 saw one of the worst floods West Bay and the lower reaches of the Brit River had ever experienced. High tides, strong winds and rain brought the sea raging in between the cliffs and finding its way, back up the marshlands, to the Brewery. 1976 was one of the hottest summers on record. The fields on top of the cliff were parched. Livestock were being fed hay in mid-summer! A year later, at the end of August, the Melplash Agricultural Show, held on the Salt Marshes at West Bay was the wettest day anyone could recall. Senior committee members were up to their knees in mud!

In January of 1978, Colfox School pupils from Burton walked to school in wet and windy conditions as a protest at the withdrawal of school transport. Bad weather prevailed and the whole of Dorset was "whited-out" with a blizzard in February 1978 when West Dorset was in a strait-jacket of snow and likened to Siberia. Ice formed in the harbour. A few days later, a rapid thaw brought the threat of flooding. Severe storms followed and West Bay was declared a 'disaster area'. The sea had attacked the promenade and the army, based at Tidworth, was brought in to assist. With dumper trucks, they ferried in 1,500 tons of Portland stone to shore-up and protect the harbour.

Before the year was out, at the end of December 1978, snow fell in a similar manner to that of around a century before, in 1881 and 1891. There was panic-buying due to a lorry drivers' strike and burst pipes added to the problems. That winter of 1978/1979, the roads were impassable again and the hedges were covered with snowdrifts. Everything came to a standstill. To be so severely snowed-in near the sea was uncommon, as the coast usually escaped such weather. Roger Day, mindful that there were a dozen ponies in the fields at Buckler's Bid, crawled his way, a mile up Shipton Lane, to carry hay to them.

The following May 29th heralded a cloudburst over the Bride Valley. Water cascaded down the River Bride and the first places to flood were those that lay the lowest in Burton. It was mid-afternoon. The water was eighteen inches deep in the kitchen at Magnolia Farmhouse, in a very short time and almost to the downstairs' ceilings at Greenwich Cottage. Everything, on the ground floor of these properties, was ruined. Soon, other cottages and shops, in its path, were under water, as was Mulllins's shop [Bridge Cottage Stores] and Stanley's. Mill Street was impassable and the old spinning mill, Shadrach Dairy Farm and Manor Farm were several feet under water. As in the flood of 1886 and 1955, water poured off the hills, down Gages and Shipton Lanes and found its way into houses that lay at the back of Burton.

Freshwater Camp was evacuated (it was the May Bank Holiday week) and the army was called in again to help with the flooding in Bridport and West Bay, as well. Three Sea Scouts received awards for their bravery in rescuing campers at West Bay.

In a Burton cottage, which lay in the path of the surface water coming off the hills, Miss Diana Edwards, found her sitting room awash. Her furnishings were saturated. This was not a new occurrence. Surplus water had caused similar flooding over the centuries but added to this natural phenomena now, was that so much building had taken place, at the northern end of the village. The abundance of new buildings covered many acres and so much of the surrounding bare earth had been covered over with concrete, tarmac and paving stones that the rain water had far less area in which to soak away and it rushed to find an outlet. Old ditches that had bordered Shipton Lane and Annings Lane had been filled in and the Gages Lane ditch had been left unattended.

★★★★★★★★★★

By 1975, The Anchor had its own car-park at the rear. How useful those old gardens were proving. The Barnetts had stayed fifteen years and Vernon Brooks and his wife had taken over and one of their daughters married a young man from the village. At Shadrach Farm, other properties stood in the plot where Frank Bishop had instructed his riding pupils and schooled horses. Beyond the old farm, in Annings Lane, the fields that once formed part of Townsend Farm and butcher Gale's holding, new dwellings, like mushrooms, overnight, in a warm September, had sprung up in clusters.

Everywhere, stark white buildings glared out. Who was it that thought that country properties had always been whitewashed? Charles Road, with its royal sounding name (or was it Charles Moore, the fish merchant or Charles Bullock who had a garden there?) had been built with garages away from the houses. The owners still parked their cars in the street, as many of the garages were used for overflow storage.

Norburton, fashioned around the old North Hill Farmhouse, had lost most of its surrounding private grounds and many of the conifers, planted by Sturdy in 1902, were felled. (The hurricane force winds in October 1987 brought others down.) The unusually designed, Edwardian house was surrounded by a sea of bricks, breezeblocks and concrete.

★★★★★★★★★★

A welcome addition for the youth but incongruous, was a Boy Scout hut overlooking the entrance gates to Norburton. The recent owners of Norburton, to which they added "Hall", had been the Knightsmiths, who had sold their land and property elsewhere and moved to the village in the 1950s. It was inherited by their two daughters, Felicity and Sylvia Knightsmith and son, Nick, all passionate supporters of scouting. The Cub and Scout troops had met in the games-room and used one of the cottages, (once the home of Albert Shipp and his family when he was head gardener at Norburton).

The Knightsmiths soon established themselves, by getting involved in all the local organisations and the three new arrivals, with their exuberance and strong characters and old fashioned principles, came just at the right time to rally the 'two sides'. They were aware of preserving the old village traditions and mode of living and their efforts for the Royal British Legion were outstanding. They were accepted by all the residents because of their undaunted, impartial spirit.

Miss Ruby Gale had started a Brownie Pack and the children enjoyed her kind and thoughtful tutoring. Happily they danced around a Maypole, like the village children of yester-year. (There had once been a Girl Guide Company in Burton, led by Miss Codrington and Miss Fielding). For the teenagers there was a youth club in the village again, in the late 1970s/early 1980s, which was started in the Reading Room and then, courtesy of Jack Burt, moved to Manor Farm. Leaders were Jim Bates, (a man with a story to tell of his war service), Peter and Pearl Parsons and Dawn Pattinson, who strove to interest the young people and many have to thank them for their patience and enthusiasm.

A badminton group used the hall and had a Junior section of keen players, which John Burton remembered well. The village football team went on to win numerous trophies. Basil Dent, Bill Heal, Dennis Bullock, Edwin Aylott, Hilary Youngs and old-hand Bill Jarman and others from time to time, put their knowledge and enthusiasm into coaching and supporting the senior and youth players, with much success. The officials took teams to Cherbourg and Belgium to play and the youths of the 1970s and 1980s were just as nimble as their forefathers had been.

Again, Burton spawned some good players. Marc Aylott had trials with Manchester United but only days into this venture, he was taken ill and lost the chance. He returned to Bridport to be appointed as Head Boy of the Colfox School. So much of the success of the village teams was due to the support received from Jack Burt of Manor Farm, who was more of a cricketer, his daughter, Heather reveals. He lent his field and buildings for the club's use and allowed fund raising events to be held on the premises. Never before had the farm been host to something so remotely connected with agriculture!

★★★★★★★★★★

At the far end of Annings Lane, past Arch Bridge, Peacehaven Farm was new, sprouting as it had, from the main acreage of land that Tony Bishop had purchased. In another of his former fields, one of the most tranquil spots in the village, another holiday camp, had sprung up, designed for a really restful countryside experience. Back towards the village, along a newly surfaced, widened, Annings Lane, more grand properties filled the entire length. Along Shipton Lane, a 'snake' of new residences trailed as far as Kennon Farm.

★★★★★★★★★★

The Bridport News of 21st November, 1986 reported that a mock memorial service had been held at the beach for the café which had been burnt down by no other than the National Trust, allegedly doing it without consulting anyone. According to a National Trust spokesman, it had become an eyesore and the managers, Frank and Patricia Blackmore, who rented it were giving up. This was not the true story from the Blackmore's point of view. The rent was going up and they considered that it would not be a viable project for them, particularly taking into account the amount of work involved in running the café and managing the car park.

The following week, the local paper, reflected the concern of the fishermen who feared that they might be the next to go. Norman Saunders-White, with his wife, Pat, led the protest and rallied those who were dismayed and angered at the demise of the old café. A memorial service was held on the site and a 'stone' erected. (The Saunders-Whites had come to Burton originally as guests of the Harveys at Girt House and had 'stayed').

The Parish Council negotiated with the National Trust, resulting in a proposal that the Trust would build a new, architecturally acceptable café for £60,000, on condition that the Parish Council ran the car park and shared the receipts. A peppercorn rent of £10 a year, for twenty years was requested, to run the café. The first caterers paid over £6,000 a year, on a three year contract and the Parish Council's coffers overflowed! From this the village was able to benefit in many ways. The West Dorset District Council was persuaded to build good toilet facilities and take over the cleaning and sewage disposal.

DISTURBING THE PAST

Every cottage that was left, in Burton, had been smartened up, bathrooms and up-to-date kitchens had been installed, extentions and conservatories added. Room in tiny cottages had to be found for the latest, labour saving gadgets. What the women of the past, with their large families, would have given for a washing machine, let alone a dishwasher, or even the water laid on in the house, in the first place! A handful of the houses and cottages were still owned by those who bought them at the Sale in 1958 but the majority had changed hands and a number had become second, or holiday homes.

New owners had unearthed and opened-up hearths, discovered blocked-up windows and doorways, or put in new ones. Immediately, many new residents, installed the fashionable log-burning stoves which had narrow flues. This constituted a fire hazard, as the chimneys lay low to the thatched roofs and the manner in which, these enthusiastic would-be 'country folk', piled the logs onto the fire, particularly green wood which formed a 'tar', was too much for the artificial chimneys that easily overheated and combusted.

'Open plan' was the fashion and two rooms were often knocked into one, with dire consequences when the load-bearing wall collapsed. Taking down ceilings and beams resulted in roofs caving-in. Plaster was picked off the walls but there was a very good reason why it had been put on in the first place. Outside, it was there to keep out the wet and inside to hold the stones and/or wattle and daub together and to reduce the dust. Apart from "back houses", even the most humble cottages did not have bare stone walls on the inside. Ancient doors and windows would "plim" and jam, only to have wood shaved off that when it dried out, gaping holes were left with the consequent draughts.

Gulleys and drains, that had been put there for a reason, got covered over and water poured into the buildings. Many who had paid large sums, to have their properties re-thatched, were disappointed that the golden yellow coating turned brown and dull and continually weathered. It took a great deal of disappointment and learning to understand the best manner in which to modernised these old places.

Many materials, such as beams and fixtures, were artificial as the plastic era had arrived and the ladies were seeing the latest addition that each other had acquired when attending the Tupperware parties, that were held in people's homes.

****

Ron Guyatt had bought number 47 Burton Bradstock. This was where the Gear family once lived. Joseph Gear, a labourer had been born there in 1826. He ran away to sea at fourteen, walking to Poole. He signed on and worked his passage to Newfoundland, spending the next five years, roughing it as a whaler. He saved sufficient money to return to Burton and marry a village girl, Jane Coombs, setting-up home, at number 60, in Mill Street.

In the bitter winter of 1881, Gear joined the Bridport harbour based coaster "The Why

Not", whose sailing was delayed through icing-up in St Peter Port, Guernsey. Eventually she sailed on Friday the 13th and the old sailors, superstitious about sailing on a Friday and the thirteenth at that, said that she was doomed from the start. With three other Burton men on board, (Simeon Hutchings and his nephew, William and Joseph Gerrard and his son, Joseph), Gear was never to return to his native village. The vessel was lost with all hands, off the Scottish coast. Gear's wife had a premonition that there would be a tragedy. She had seen the ship 'sinking' in the frost on the window pane.

★★★★★★★★★★

Gear's birthplace, on the corner of Darby Lane, opposite the church, had come into the ownership of a Burton born and bred businessman. Here Ron Guyatt had discovered a small shoe, hidden in a niche of the chimney. This was a very ancient custom to ward off evil spirits. Other items came to light, in renovated cottages, such as an old sword blade, wrecked ships' timbers used in the construction, lost keys, some old coins, scraps of letters and old newspapers and bits of shard but there was no pot of gold to be found. The tenants had never been wealthy enough to save anything, except the rent money. One prosperous inhabitant did hide some of his money. A hoard of gold had been found in the 1940s, by a ploughman working on North Hill. Hidden in the bank was a cache of sovereigns, put there, it was supposed, by Farmer Brown, long before, in what he thought was his safe banking system. The find was declared as Treasure Trove.

★★★★★★★★★★

The new arrivals to Burton, who could claim ancestral links, got off to a good start but whilst all the activity and disturbance of the properties was going on in the village, the old Burtoners slept on in the churchyard and the cemetery. Burton Bradstock was no longer the place where they and their ancestors had plied their skills, on the land, at the mills or rowing a fishing boat. The farms were being broken-up with the loss of the staunch countryman and his wealth of knowledge on country matters. The last of the elderly Burton men ambled their way to the old look-out on the cliff or strolled along to enjoy a pint of beer or cider in the pub. The understanding of the sea and local conditions was fast disappearing, too.

One of the last to go was Steve Northover, still active in his eighties, who had been involved in all that had happened in the village. As a young boy he would lower himself over the edge of the cliff, at its highest point, to the ledges below to rifle eggs from seagull nests. (A natural way in which to keep down the seagull population). These eggs were a local delicacy, a welcome addition to the working-man's table and worth a good few extra pence when sold. The best sponge cakes could be made with seagulls' eggs!

Steve, with his incredible head for heights, once walked around the periphery of the church tower for a dare. He had worked at the spinning factory, the corn-grinding mill and as a gardener at The Rookery. His knowledge of the river was unsurpassed and he had the job, like the watermen of old, in all winds and weathers, of closing and opening the [river] hatches to control the flow of water. Steve had rung the bells, played football for the village team, competed in the athletic sports on Burton Veäst Day, tended an allotment and been a member of a fishing crew, throughout his life. There was nothing about Burton that Steve did not know. …. but with his death went not only a man's life but an encyclopaedia of traditions with which he and the ancestors, over hundreds of years, had been familiar.

★★★★★★★★★★

None of 'the old hands' had a good word to say about the changes, in Burton Bradstock that had been brought about in the last couple of decades. Members of the Greenfingers Club tried hard to keep the old traditions alive, managing to succeed for a few years but to some visitors, unfamiliar with village customs, they were looked on as being a bit odd.

All who remained from the families involved in the Pitt-Rivers Estate's Sale of the village, tended to keep to their own. Some still participated on the Parish Council and other committees but the people who had moved into the village had almost taken over. The village was expanding so much and sprawling out in all directions that people could not be expected to know everyone else. In the summer season, the area was swamped with visitors, welcomed by those who depended on them for a livelihood but resented by others. With the man-in-the-street now having more holidays and spare time, part of the pleasure in coming to the countryside was to drive around, viewing from the car windows rather than walking! Motorists and particularly those with touring caravans, found the narrow Dorset lanes caught out their lack of reversing skills.

The only way to become part of the new establishment was to join in with a willing heart. Those who did this, whoever they were, could settle more easily into the type of village that it had now become.

WHAT HAPPENED TO WEST BAY?

Following the Sale in 1958, West Bay continued in much the same manner as it had always done. There was fishing for a living as well as pleasure, visitors flocked in by the thousands and the Municipal Camp, classed as the best in the whole of the country, expanded and then changed hands several times. Sid Gape's shop was modernised, the forerunner of a supermarket and run successfully for a couple of decades by Jack Northover (brother of Stanley Northover of Freshwater Camp) and his wife, Hazel. The post office, across the river, served the 'village' well for a considerable number of years. Cafés came and went but the Riverside Restaurant, under long-standing proprietor, Arthur Watson, was consistent, receiving acclaim from national food critics. It remains an up-market eating house, overlooking the River Brit. Ben and Annette Bryant looked after the visitors with excellent fare at the Bay House Restaurant and had the foresight to set-up a much needed launderette.

Flats were erected in the old shipyard and eventually the warehouses were put to other uses or replaced with residential premises. The Borough Council decided that the life of the majority of the day-bungalows was over and in the 1960s, not before the owners had put up a fight to save them, the majority were pulled down, changing the character of the place.

After the closure of the goods' line the station master's house and the yard lay derelict. Now revived, the old station yard has been put to some use and after a try at being an out-of-town, information bureau and council office, it is another car park with a railway dining place which affords the visitor, a nostalgic experience. The horses that dragged sand and shingle off the beach still worked into the mid 1960s and were replaced by machines until 1984 when the removal of materials from the beach was banned. Goods' yard is kept busy, even so.

Shops selling fishing tackle and equipment for boats, deep-sea diving and the sea in general, sprung up and Clifford Samways, a well known fish merchant and former Town Mayor, who set-up a fish store and retail outlet, handy to the beach, is busier today than ever. A row of units positioned at the entrance to West Bay sold clothing, meat, fish and fruit and vegetables and still do. Jolly kiosks adorned the harbour and retailed everything from buckets and spades to fish and chips, hot dogs and the more modern burger. Ice creams were 'dripped' at every opportunity. Pin tables and games of chance could be played on hot days as well as in poor weather and the annual visit of the fairground amusements, with its cheery merry-go-round music blasting out, across the Bay, sealed the quaint harbour as a trippers' favourite paradise.

The building of the Bridport Leisure Centre, in 1982, on the southern outskirts of Bridport, achieved by a few dedicated people, replaced the Swimming Club activities at West Bay. Health and Safety regulations precluded swimming in the river where facilities there had served their purpose and the new pool was so much safer, in all respects. The end had come for the West Bay Regatta.

Where the meadow grass, opposite Haddon House, once thrived, is a much used and needed public car park. A wall and walkway surrounding the "basin" gives pedestrians better safety, allowing them to amble around the harbour. Under The Mound, alongside the Promenade, there are now well patronised food stalls. The four hotels do good business, some providing seating outside, giving a continental atmosphere. (Is it really warmer than fifty years ago?).

Swains Row has new occupiers and Pier Terrace, built in 1874 on Lord Rivers's land, still dominates the scene. The splendid Golf Clubhouse has been moved further up the coast and the course is still one of the best in the country, bringing enthusiasts to West Bay.

Whilst some things may have changed, people come and gone, since the Sale and West Bay expanded and become busier, its atmosphere is much the same. The tang of the sea-air refreshes and there is still an active working scene. The new harbour is accommodating larger pleasure vessels and visitors return time and time again. The sea has never ceased to batter the coastline and play havoc with the piers and both the East and West Cliffs have fallen away in the past fifty years. Many locals still venture there and stroll around "The Bay", just like their ancestors did, whilst the open-topped and the Jurassic Coast buses bulge with passengers and for those who know, fresh mackerel can still be had as the boats come in.

****

Reminders of the Pitt-Rivers Estate Sale in 1958 have not gone away for the Women's Institute members. Still in possession of the old Boat House, they are sitting-out the latest plans for the site on which their meeting-room stands, after making improvements by putting in a new ceiling. In 1972 the Town Clerk wrote to the spokeswoman, Mrs A Ryecroft, stating that the Council was contracting to purchase the field on which the hut stood and he wanted information about the agreement that had been made with the Pitt-Rivers Estate.

The Bridport Borough Council purchased the whole site from Pitt-Rivers in June 1972 for £4,000. Previously a boat builder had looked at it but on realising that the Women's Institute could not be evicted he had pulled-out. The matter dragged on and on with Midstar Properties submitting a plan for, in the first instance, four houses and garages and twelve holiday flats, which was later replaced with a second application with an access crossing the land on which the hut was standing. The local council was adamant that these developers re-house the Women's Institute.

West Dorset District Council did not approve the plan saying that it was 'piecemeal', the materials were unsatisfactory and that floor levels had to be taken into account as the land lay within the flood plain. A better structure than a pre-fabricated building, was required for the WI, which was going to be costly for the developers, who asked the Institute to contribute £500. The Women's Institute committee had assured the developers that their request was modest and that one hand-basin would be all that was required in the cloakroom. Still, the correspondence flew back and forth. By 1978 the council refused to provide toilet facilities but would discuss relocating.

It still rests with the authorities as the Women's Institute members are adamant that a general hall is needed for West Bay and that if one is built they are willing to quit the present premises, which they have used for over fifty years and move to the new facilities but until that day comes they intend to stay-put. Even very recent refurbishment (2007) of the Salt House has not altered their decision.

★★★★★★★★★★

In 2005, the newly built harbour was opened. This was a multi-million pound scheme that was carried out as an extended local amenity, hoping to bring in more marine business and as a coastal defence, planned to prevent, once and for all, the age-old problem of the harbour entrance being silted-up, by widening it and making alterations to the approach. The elderly men who worked and lived around the harbour, were not so optimistic. They chortled that it would never work and following intense storms soon after, the entrance of the harbour was once again blocked with shingle and a mechanical dredger had to be brought in to extract hundreds of tons of materials.

In the summer season of 2006, there was a faded notice at the top of the new slip-way stating that, *'There is a shingle bar in the harbour entrance'*. There is still a problem, as in the spring of 2007, a considerable amount of mud was dredged up.

★★★★★★★★★★

West Bay is still a quaint little harbour, seen at its best very early in the morning or on cold, windy wet winter days. Beside the river, a number of the brightly painted wooden bungalows have been given a stay of execution, a reminder of the halcyon days of summer holidays at "The Bay", when Bridport families, who owned the bungalows, would pack-up at the beginning of August and move down to West Bay for a fortnight by the sea, which included Regatta Week. One recently changed hands at £170,000. The availability of the Salt House as a meeting centre, that seats fifty people, has provided an amenity and is preserving yet more of Bridport Harbour's history. The remaining warehouses stand proud and are put to other uses.

The air is as bracing as, publicly advertised, two hundred years ago and there are plans to improve and update, the village, (not to everyone's liking). New, modern residences dominate the skyline. The view from the harbour of West Cliff, with its dense covering of new properties, is almost obliterated, by these high-rise apartments which visitors will envy. A 'castle' has been built where the old golf clubhouse once stood and some of the meadows on West Bay Road (a dyke collects the surplus water from these former marshlands), are filled with smart, attractive houses instead of grazing cattle.

West Bay is visited by more and more tourists every year. The Jurassic Coast, from Swanage to Exmouth, now forms a World Heritage Site assuring that the little harbour, which sits in the middle, is destined to see an even greater number of visitors. It remains a much sought-after residential and holiday resort.

West Bay is moderately geared for the increasing annual summer invasion but could easily become saturated. Whatever transpires, Bridport Harbour and its character, that has been forged, by the merchants, tradesmen and tenants of the landlords of old, will still provide some work and be a visitors' haven for many more years to come.

BURTON BRADSTOCK ENTERS THE NEW MILLENNIUM

Justin Mallinson, a man with ideas and understanding, himself a 'newcomer' after the Second World War, headed the Parish Council. In all, he served for twenty-five years. The late eighties and nineties witnessed an era of consolidation when the old and new, in Burton, fused and much attention was given to improving and updating.

Mr Mallinson, a former army officer, who had come to farm at Bredy, had been in the parish at the time of the Sale. He was familiar with how 'it had been' and could see what was needed for the future and was instrumental in a number of projects in Burton as well as planning the celebrations for the New Millennium. With others on the Parish Council and County representatives, including Rear Admiral Gwynedd Pritchard, CB, a naval officer, also retired to Burton and Mrs Pritchard, they steered the village into the new century.

The farming network was fast collapsing all around due to another depressive time for agriculture and in Burton, unexpected circumstances. Fate was to deal a bad hand where all the remaining larger farms were concerned.

Manor and Shadrach Farms were already broken up and at Shadrach Dairy Farm, the Hawkins brothers died, within three weeks of each other in 2000. The farmhouse stood empty and the remaining land was let out. Cogden Farm, on the outskirts of Burton was still in operation but it was soon to change hands. At Pitfold Farm, Shipton Gorge, Robert and Suzanne Bugler continued to farm, with care and consideration for its uniqueness and all it stood for. A few years into the new century there would be a sad and unexpected upheaval there, too.

Retired persons seemed to outnumber the younger generation and some of the original village people were living out their days, in the council estates, off Annings Lane, or in Barr Lane (which was once the exclusive road in the village but had become a threat to pedestrians as speed limits were mostly ignored). A number of the council houses had become privately owned, bought by tenants who had lived in them for a good number of years. The varied, attractive façades, of those in Barr Lane, are a more welcoming sight, at the entrance to the village.

New properties on the Barrowfield Estate and other areas to the north of Burton, as well as on the Bovis Estate, at the far end of Annings Lane, had been bought by some young couples and this was a promising sign, as their children were using the school. Some of the men from these families worked away from home enabling them to earn a far larger salary than could be obtained locally. Annings Lane, with its largely retired residential area, lost its peaceful early mornings and evening shut-down at tea time, when commuters travelled along to and from the village outskirts.

The beach was now almost totally a playground. Rod fishermen found the Chesil Bank inviting and in good weather, visitors flocked there as never before. When the sea

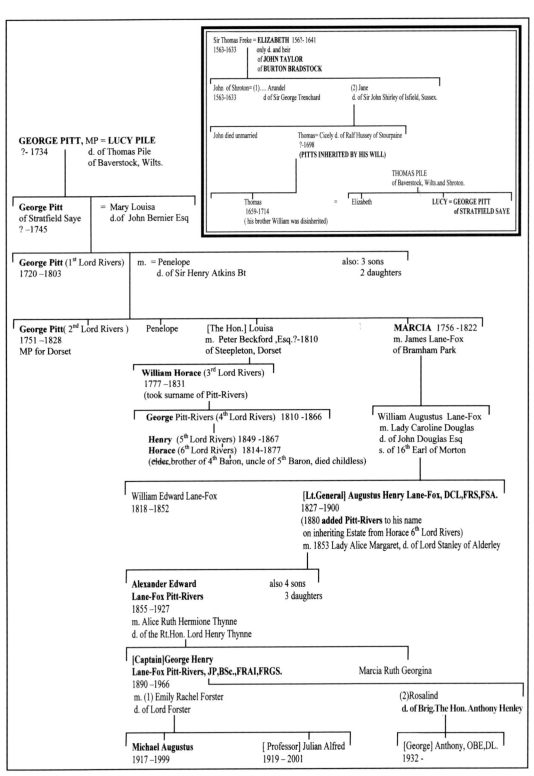

GEORGE PITT, MP **= LUCY PILE**
?- 1734   d. of Thomas Pile
     of Baverstock, Wilts.

Sir Thomas Freke = **ELIZABETH** 156?- 1641
1563-1633   only d. and heir
     of **JOHN TAYLOR**
     of **BURTON BRADSTOCK**

John of Shroton= (1).... Arundel   (2) Jane
1563-1633   d of Sir George Trenchard   d. of Sir John Shirley of Isfield, Sussex.

John died unmarried   Thomas= Cicely d. of Ralf Hussey of Stourpaine
     ?-1698
     (PITTS INHERITED BY HIS WILL)

         THOMAS PILE
         of Baverstock, Wilts.and Shroton.

Thomas   =   Elizabeth   **LUCY = GEORGE PITT**
1659-1714   **of STRATFIELD SAYE**
(his brother William was disinherited)

George Pitt   = Mary Louisa
of Stratfield Saye   d.of John Bernier Esq
? –1745

George Pitt (1st Lord Rivers)   m. = Penelope   also: 3 sons
1720 –1803   d. of Sir Henry Atkins Bt   2 daughters

George Pitt(2nd Lord Rivers)   Penelope   [The Hon.] Louisa   **MARCIA** 1756 -1822
1751 –1828   m. Peter Beckford ,Esq.?-1810   m. James Lane-Fox
MP for Dorset   of Steepleton, Dorset   of Bramham Park

William Horace (3rd Lord Rivers)
1777 –1831
(took surname of Pitt-Rivers)

George Pitt-Rivers (4th Lord Rivers) 1810 -1866   William Augustus Lane-Fox
                                         m. Lady Caroline Douglas
Henry (5th Lord Rivers) 1849 -1867   d. of John Douglas Esq
Horace (6th Lord Rivers) 1814-1877   s. of 16th Earl of Morton
(elder.brother of 4th Baron, uncle of 5th Baron, died childless)

William Edward Lane-Fox   **[Lt.General] Augustus Henry Lane-Fox, DCL,FRS,FSA.**
1818 –1852   1827 –1900
                             (1880 **added Pitt-Rivers** to his name
                             on inheriting Estate from Horace 6th Lord Rivers)
                             m. 1853 Lady Alice Margaret, d. of Lord Stanley of Alderley

Alexander Edward   also 4 sons
Lane-Fox Pitt-Rivers   3 daughters
1855 –1927
m. Alice Ruth Hermione Thynne
d. of the Rt.Hon. Lord Henry Thynne

[Captain]George Henry
Lane-Fox Pitt-Rivers, JP,BSc.,FRAI,FRGS.   Marcia Ruth Georgina
1890 –1966
m. (1) Emily Rachel Forster   (2)Rosalind
d. of Lord Forster   **d. of Brig.The Hon. Anthony Henley**

Michael Augustus   [Professor] Julian Alfred   [George] Anthony, OBE,DL.
1917 –1999   1919 – 2001   1932 -

Freke/Pitt/Pitt-Rivers – Line of Inheritance

was rough the hardier sight-seers crowded on to the beach, watching the waves battering the cliff face. Did any of them think of the sailors of old who were wrecked along that coast when the sea was raging, or those who had jumped overboard and if lucky, were hauled up from the churning sea, on ropes, by brave, strong village men to the safety of the cliff top?

The seine fishing off the beach, was a good escape from the rat-race of the late twentieth century, for those who had hung-on to the old tradition. Dennis Bullock and his son, Andrew, were the last of the long line of Burton Bradstock fishermen who had worked a seine net at Burton Beach. Andrew was dogged by ill health but retained his nets until 2005. He had kept his record book of catches and sales, which he proudly produced for anyone interested, to peruse. Catching fish by the means of echo-sounding equipment had arrived and with the real old fishermen gone, the ancient methods and motivation were gone, too. Decaying boats lay rotting on the beach where their tired, ageing or departed owners had left them. The rusting old winch was a reminder to the few who knew, of the struggle to get the boats up past the high tide mark and the sand and shingle gradually covered what remained of a way of life. Pleasure was now the motive and the car-park attendant was kept busy, the fields used for parking often overflowed and the beach café did good business.

It was to be the new millennium before Burton Bradstock could be seen plainly against the faded background of its quite different past. It was decided that a "Time Capsule", containing items relevant to the day, should be buried at the Parish Pump, with directions left that it was not to be opened for another fifty years and was, it is believed, moved to a safer place. Festivities were organised in the village and a wrought-iron beacon, crafted at Bredy farm, was lit, symbolising the continuity, over hundreds of years, when beacons were lit all along the coast, carrying the news of invasion, victory and celebration. A guided walk around the village, resulted in ninety-four people turning up to learn, *"How it was and how we were"*.

As the twenty-first century dawned and the bells rang out at midday on New Year's Day, 2000, the majority of those directly involved in the Sale, had died. Their descendants had, long before, decided whether to sell or stay. Making these decisions was heart-breaking and not done lightly.

★★★★★★★★★★

The mystery purchaser had been revealed. He had had the foresight to buy-in a most beautiful expanse of countryside and shoreline but had since decided to sell off most that he had purchased those two days, in 1958. It had been Captain Pitt-Rivers's eldest son, Michael, who had purchased Manor and Cogden Farms, as well as the Bridport and West Dorset Golf Course and other parcels of land at the Sale and soon after, the expanse of the Chesil Beach and Pitfold Farm. The tenants that had met with him and agreed to his proposal to purchase the farms and land that they tenanted under his father, had kept very quiet over the intervening years. At the time, the newspapers had underplayed the significance.

Michael Pitt-Rivers had visited Burton Bradstock, prior to the Sale, in 1958 and met with farmers, at Cogden Farm. A lady, Sonia Blair, née Brownell, the widow of George Orwell, who became his wife, that same year, sat outside in the car. She declined an invitation to go into the house for a cup of tea, although it was a very hot day. For Michael Pitt-Rivers, with the village awash with speculators and the curious, this was an out-of-the-way place and as secluded, as could be found, for a confidential meeting. *The Dorset Evening Echo* of July 1958 had got it wrong and had printed (what transpired to be a rumour), that it was Captain Pitt-Rivers who was visiting a selected number of the tenants and struck a deal with them, when it had been his son, Michael.

By 2007, there was no one alive who was present at that gathering. In some ways, it made the way easier for the farmers concerned, not to have to obtain a bank overdraft, or dig deep into their reserves, or sell off stock. Bunny Lenthall would have been faced with a huge bill, if he had bought all that he tenanted and AF Bailey was in a similar situation. In 1958, the Bridport and West Dorset Golf Club was not in a sound enough financial position to attempt to outbid Mr Pitt-Rivers. Even after the pre-arranged meeting and discussions, he did not agree to allow the farmers' sons to take on the tenancies, when the time came, according to the present members of the Lenthall family.

RB Howarth had ideas for saving the coastal stretch and was dependent on the generosity and interest of Michael Pitt-Rivers. Tony Bishop was not invited to take part in the meeting, as the land which he tenanted did not verge along the coast, although Edgar Hawkins held Villa Cliff fields and an arrangement, had been discussed with him, to move the camp to Larkfield.

★★★★★★★★★★

Captain George Pitt-Rivers had handed over the Rushmore section of the Estate to his eldest son, in 1950, (the house was rented to Sandroyd School and later sold to the trustees in 1966) but by 1958, it looked as if Michael was to be denied Burton Bradstock.

Michael Pitt-Rivers was born in 1917. His mother, Rachel, daughter of the First Lord Forster, was a successful actress for fifty years, under the stage name of Mary Hinton. Educated at Eton, and having already gone up to Exeter College, Oxford, he decided to join the army, as the Second World War was declared. He served in the armoured Division of the Welsh Guards, in France and Belgium, remaining in the army after the war, in Palestine and retired in 1953 with the rank of Major. There was a blot on his life, following a scandal in the 1950s, when he and others were imprisoned. Pitt-Rivers was sentenced to eighteen months and the conviction had shocked and angered his father.

This prompted Captain Pitt-Rivers, mindful of the low return the Burton block of the Estate brought in, to sell. He realised that if he sold it off, the capital raised would do a great deal better and as a 'tenant for life', as he had described himself, he was entitled to the interest, the Burton Bradstock Estate having been vested in him as a marriage settlement.

In 1958 Michael Pitt-Rivers, added a considerable section from the Burton Bradstock 'block' to his inheritance, "Ensuring continuity", he said. He saw that the land and farms that he bought-in through an agent, at the Sale, were important assets and for which he probably held some kind of affection. Furthering the great love he held for the county, he wrote the Shell Guide to Dorset, published in 1966. Michael Pitt-Rivers became a dedicated conservationist and custodian of the land, visiting his Burton Bradstock tenants, on numerous occasions, showing kindness and consideration.

Although the Larmer Tree gardens, at Rushmore, continued to open from time to time following General Pitt-Rivers's death in 1900, by the Second World War, the buildings and the gardens had fallen into disrepair. Materials were in short supply and other priorities had to come first. It was Michael Pitt-Rivers who arrested the decline and set about to restore these historic pleasure grounds. In 1961 he organised a pageant there. Taking part were a former Rector of Burton Bradstock, the Reverend Harold Wheeler and Mrs Wheeler.

Michael Pitt-Rivers was a man for trees and just prior to his death he planted his three millionth tree, amongst which was a specimen, like the original Wych Elm that stood there, when his great-grandfather, General Pitt-Rivers, first inaugurated the Larmer Tree pleasure grounds. Today the facilities include, history and botanical courses, the garden and its hire for weddings, a tea room, visitor reception, accessibility for disabled visitors, ample car and coach parking, as well as a welcome to children and dogs, yet it remains unspoilt and much as it was when General Pitt-Rivers laid out the gardens.

In addition to Michael Pitt-Rivers's dedication to his land, he built up a very successful Arabian horse stud and competed at shows throughout the country. When he developed cancer of the throat and suffered a tracheotomy in 1986, he had to relinquish the stud, at the height of its success. He had already sold off the remainder of the part of the Burton Bradstock Estate, that he had so unexpectedly purchased, almost thirty years before, retaining just one field behind Beach Road.

On his father's death Michael Pitt-Rivers inherited the capital secured from the Burton Bradstock Sale and around the same time, had put Manor Farm back on the market in 1966, when Bunny Lenthall could not reach an agreement with him to allow his son, Harry, the right to take on the tenancy. Disillusioned, Lenthall went off to search for a farm in Australia. When he returned to Burton he found that Manor Farm had been put up for sale.

Lenthall was far from happy about his situation and sold the Freshwater Camp, packed-up and the whole family, with the exception of Beverley, the eldest daughter, emigrated to Albany, Perth, Australia, in 1966, naming his new farm, "Bradstock Downs". With the severing of the Lenthall connection to Burton and the break-up of Manor Farm, went another chunk of its history. The locals had been greatly saddened by Bunny Lenthall's swift decision and departure. The heart went out of old Burton.

Michael Pitt-Rivers died in 1999, bearing his illness with great fortitude and was cared for by his companion of forty years, the artist, William Gronow Davis. His plain, unobtrusive headstone stands beside ornate ones of other members of his family, in the churchyard at Tollard Royal, in complete contrast to the Victorian splendour of his great-grandfather's sarcophagus, inside the church. The Estate continues, based at King John's House, Rushmore, in the village of Tollard Royal. It comprises over seven thousand acres, (of which just a total of eight acres are retained in Burton and West Bay) and is administered by a trust.

Michael Augustus Lane-Fox Pitt-Rivers will be remembered for preserving so much woodland and countryside and in particular, saving the Burton Bradstock coastline.

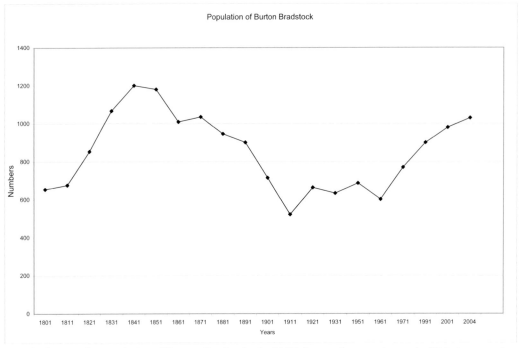

Graph showing the population of Burton Bradstock. In 2007 the number remains static. This is expected to increase when building takes place at the old spinning mill.

316

THE BEST KEPT VILLAGE

Today, tidy, clean streets, smartly manicured greens and lawns, the roses around the doors, as everyone imagined they should be, with no passing cattle to grab a bloom, or foul the streets, greets the visitor to Burton Bradstock. Local builders, painters, decorators, plumbers, (Jim Collins queried whether the sewer would stand the vast increase in households), heating engineers, woodstove merchants, carpenters, glaziers, landscape gardeners, tree-surgeons, woodworm specialists, tilers and thatchers are kept busy on a continuous round, never letting any property fall into, even, a minor state of disrepair and always improving or extending them. In Burton Bradstock, the work has never stopped!

Each time a property changes hands the new occupants want a different kitchen and/ or bathroom, a conservatory or extension and various modifications. There is ample work for local artisans with enough money circulating now to do this, generated by the retired people, the second home owners and holiday makers. The new work, renovations and maintenance have provided the local craftsmen with a steady, good living. The old properties have been saved but the huge expenditure puts them into a palatial category! Visiting family members are only too keen to descend on those living in such a delightful area and tiny cottages and modest sized bungalows, become crowded in the season. Second homes, as some owners prefer to call them, become holiday cottages for friends and relations! Fold-up beds and children's bunks feature in the household inventories.

The village had become a show place and over the last twenty years has won the county's "Best Kept Village" award, on numerous occasions. Defining a village today is far removed from the same of fifty years ago, yet, a heart still exists, centred around the old Parish Pump and there is tranquillity to be found in the back-lanes, out of season.

There are modern facilities such as the well-maintained public lavatories, adjacent to the playing field where a children's play area, with all manner of apparatus, that is required to amuse the children of the new century, can be found. It has been updated to comply with Health and Safety regulations and additional apparatus added, at, it was said, around £36,000. (A similar sum to that which Michael Pitt-Rivers paid, at the time, for a large portion of the village).

To get to the playing field, children have to wind their way through the traffic, that thunders, dangerously, past them. During the summer holidays it proved a huge success, with children being brought by car, from near and far. The garish colours (which like the car park wall of "The Shoes" in the 1960s, 'will weather') and the fairground atmosphere is proving a huge attraction, to the point where not only a safe walkway but a car park is needed!

Many residents and the second home owners, have two or more vehicles. Visitors to the holiday cottages usually come (loaded to the gunwales) in two cars. Can the last of the spaces left in Burton, be used to establish a public car park, such as there is in

Abbotsbury?

Four caravan camps dominate the area; Freshwater, grown to a incredible modern holiday complex, is a village in itself, Larkfield, lies hidden by a screen of beautiful trees, where the latest accommodation is in wooden chalets. Annings Lane Park sits peacefully off the beaten track and there are still campers at the old Coastguard Station, as there were in the 1900s. In addition, temporary camps come to Manor Farm, where members of the Caravan Club and like organisations can enjoy a break in this idyllic part of the world.

Division exists about spoiling the area but the local economy depends on the visitors. Caravans and tents that are eyesores to some are bread and butter to the rest. There is still a working population, even if much diminished over the years. If there is selfishness, then it is in begrudging those who come to lovely Dorset for a holiday, the fresh air and beauty of the place, which the residents can enjoy all the year around.

There is a Village Society, whose members meet to listen to talks from travellers and historians. The old days and ways are romantisised, marvelled at but not envied. The few who class themselves as true Burton people and there are less than a score of them left who were adults at the time of the Sale in 1958, keep a low profile. There are the three Legge sisters who are from true village stock, Mary [Mrs Ward] and the Misses Alice and Gillian Legge. Although, not directly caught up in the Sale, (relatives were involved), they have witnessed the changes first-hand. It has not always been easy for any of the original residents of Burton Bradstock to watch the old traditions and mode of life disappear and be unable to halt the hands of Time.

That is not to say that there was never a migration into the village until after the Sale. Through the centuries people have gone in and out of Burton, on the whole, for work purposes and through marrying into a village family. (The two often going together). The new immigrants who came in soon fitted in to village life and its centuries-old pattern. They were immediately thrust alongside others and became part of a team *'to earn the rent'*.

When education was introduced, the children attended the village school. It was only when people swarmed in, with no work in mind, swallowing up the properties and land, that the locals felt their very roots were being pulled up. However, newcomers to Burton, have over the years, brought their experience and imaginative ideas with them and the village has benefited in many ways.

★★★★★★★★★★

A consistent problem, over the last four decades has been that some new arrivals have put 'their feet in it' by speaking with authority about what they think village life used to be like and often they have not got it quite right.

Their enthusiasm for something, that is definitely a new experience to them, will be a well-tried matter, long-ago thought of, or carried out, or seen, by the locals. Kathy Burton recalled being invited by an excited new resident, to see a bat, in the church.

Bats were an occupational hazard for Kathy and her late husband Dennis, who had both served as church wardens. She had once had a bat land right on her hand, in the church! It was nothing new to her to see one.

The intentions are well meant but the matter is a sensitive one to the few who really know about all that has gone on in the village. It is this, over zealous attitude, which has annoyed the old brigade and the feeling of being taken over that always grieved those left from the days of the Estate. Other villages are fast going the same way but Burton was hit in one fell swoop and the initial changes happened so rapidly.

★★★★★★★★★★

Burton Bradstock is a hive of different and varied, activity nowadays. The social ambiance is good. Two new residents, give a lot of time to the village flower and produce show, and the allotments are tilled with pride and to almost full capacity. A music festival has been held annually for nearly thirty years, the brain-child of Mary Ryan [Mrs Gillham] with the support of her musical family and friends.

The Burton Bradstock Players enthral audiences from throughout the Bride Valley, every year. The Players, of all ages, have produced a pantomime or musical for over three decades but as the years have gone on, the thespians of Mrs Gladys Gale's days and her theatrical legatees have dropped out and their places taken by others new to the area. The memory of Stanley Williams, Freddie Mullins, Albert Shipp, Arthur Bartlett, and Alfie Hutchings's, high standard of singing and comedy and the theatrical talents of Barbara Bishop, Sheila Bullock and Georgie Northover, (herself long ago a 'newcomer' who was sure to bring the house down), all three women having married into Burton families, as well as numerous others, have faded with the photographs.

The Women's Institute is buoyant and has a good workable membership who are always busy with activities which fill many hours for the retired residents. Mrs Cynthia Stevens, a nonagenarian, who has participated in so many of the village activities, all her life, says that when she goes to the Women's Institute meetings she seems to be the only real old Burton person there. She hankers for the days when the village was small, made up of those who had a long established genetic tie with the village.

The hall, with its Stratfield Saye connection to the Pitt family, has been handed over, on a long lease, to a Village Hall committee. Car parking around it, when there is a popular event, can be difficult. Fortunately, there are retired people in the village who are prepared to take on the task of committee work. It is always a struggle to find willing people to do this and those who do, have usually held administrative posts in their working lives but being of retirement age it is only a matter of five to ten years that they will be able to serve. There is a constant turn-over, policies change so often and rumour has it that a few squabbles break out, as there is a surfeit of chiefs!

The others who were caught up in the Pitt-Rivers's Sale and their descendants, are united in their views. They say little but ponder still, even half a century on. Time is fast passing them by and it can only be a few years, now, before those who were directly involved in the 1958 Sale are all gone.

Houses and cottages now carry names that link them with the past. There are Seine and Lerrett, Bengy's, Kitty's, Minnie's, Rose, Stable, Duck and Garden Cottages, The "Old" Bakery, Butcher's, Burton Mill, Little Orchard and Walls tell of what has gone and "Buckler's Bid", is a poignant reminder of the Pitt-Rivers Estate Sale and its tenants. Autumn and September Cottages are, perhaps, a hint at a certain period in life? Questions rest over the name "The Piggeries" as the premises were built and used as a cart shed and store attached to the mill. Any pig housed there was surely short-lived.

Because the population is predominately elderly, there is a steady change-over of properties. The continual upheaval is unsettling. Before the Pitt-Rivers Sale, there was a much greater continuity. In the old days, cottages were held for three lives and families could live in one place, including farms, for several generations.

113. Michael Lane-Fox Pitt-Rivers (pictured towards the end of his life).

114. Burton Bradstock from the air, circa 1985.

115. Burton Bradstock Cars 2007. Inset 115a The proprietor, Saj Vij.

116. Peter Parsons, local builder and decorator. 'There is always plenty of work in the village'.

117. Twenty-first century traffic through the High Street.

118. The Church Fête in 2006.

119. Burton Bradstock village 2007. (Compare with plate 6)

120. Nature will have her way. A recent photograph of a rough sea at Burton Beach.

RUMBLES

An unfortunate occurrence was when a third generation young Burton woman, on clearing-out her parents' cottage, was accosted by a new resident about putting out rubbish bags on a Sunday! Returning to her home and family she was leaving the rubbish ready for collection the following morning. Disillusioned, she sold the cottage and has never returned to Burton. Fortunately, this was not the sort of incident that occurred very often but however, was not an isolated case.

One recent settler has noticed that there are no street lights. There was a definite policy to try to keep a village atmosphere as the multitude of outside lights on the properties, provide more than enough illumination. Street lighting has, however, been axed as the environmentalists were in the majority. The church is flood-lit. A beautiful image and focal point but what of global warming? Solar panelling on the roof could be the answer?

An enterprising man arrived with a mobile fish and chip shop. Even this divided the village. There were some of the original villagers, not to mention others newly moved in, who enjoyed this service. Then, came the 'big bad wolves' who gobbled up the idea of such a common activity in smart Burton Bradstock. The fish and chip van had to go! What would those who hounded it out of the village have thought of the fish hawkers of a few decades before who cried their wares loudly around Burton?

"Visho, Visho!"

★★★★★★★★★★

Behind the roar of the traffic, some tranquillity can be found around the old Parish Pump but this is interrupted by the whoosh of vehicles, or the twice daily motorcade of school transport. Where once there were complaints about the meandering cows strolling through the streets, now it is the school traffic, that annoys some but children are the life-blood of a place. Transport is needed to maintain the village school, as in January 2006, less than half the pupils, of a total of one hundred and six, on the roll, at Burton Bradstock School, live in the village, relates the Head Teacher.

When the Dorset County Library opens its doors, in the old Methodist Chapel, a steady stream, of retired residents and mothers and children congregate. Some drive to the centre of Burton and park around the Parish Pump, clogging up that space. Like the post office and shops, the library is a meeting place, all of which need to be retained.

The ever neutral River Bride flows on 'down to the sea'. Moorhens, kingfishers and other river loving birds, animals and some fish, sport in its comparatively clean water. Only the return of the otter is needed. The paths over the meadows, are well trodden, mostly by strollers, rather than those intent on going about their daily business. Sadly the route has been altered, taking the walker out onto Bredy Road and then back in to the fields. The stone slabs, that formed the stiles, are rarely given a thought. Few people stop to think that those old stones, were hewn, by hand, from the nearby quarry and men had sweated and risked their lives to extract these beautiful blocks from the earth. The old Burtoners were familiar with the names of the fields but they like, the old days and ways have been forgotten. "Timmer" Bridge has lost its rustic look, in the interests of safety and is now a mass of concrete. Although there used to be planks missing and the rails wobbled, no one ever fell into the river!

The villas, (early summer homes), on the cliff, still stand as landmarks and to the memory of a bygone age. The beach, although devoid of working fishing boats, the fields atop the cliffs, the Mere, at Cogden, remain almost as they were fifty, one hundred, even five hundred years ago, with the expanse of sea stretching before the eye. That stretch of coastline could all so easily have become 'another Bournemouth' but what of the hinterland?

★★★★★★★★★★

A survey in 2005 calculated that there were 580 dwellings, (three times the number in 1851), in Burton Bradstock, of which 13. 3% were second or holiday homes, the proportion little altered from the 1890s.

Residents say that the improved bus service is welcome but a doctor's surgery, health centre and pharmacy, butcher's shop and a renewed newspaper delivery are much needed. Milk on the doorstep again for everyone might be out of the question as many prefer to visit the shops. There is indoor short-mat bowling but would an outdoor bowling green be well received? A centre where anyone would feel comfortable to drop-in for a chat and cup of tea or coffee would bolster communications and unity.

A main-street general store and a long established hairdressers have served the villagers well. The recent setting-up, by the progressive business Vij family, of a supermarket, at the garage, caused some raised eyebrows. The well-lit premises signals a different purpose than the beacon for the smugglers who met on that very spot needed. As one person has commented, "The village has a corner shop now!". A weekly market could soon follow. (Abbotsbury was once a town, with its right to hold a market on Fridays).

A kind minded resident, David Barnikel, (who spent part of his childhood in Burton in the 1930s/1940s returning to run a business enterprise in 1979), provides a voluntary service bringing prescription medicines back out to the village. It is said that in twenty years time, that the number of people in the country, over eighty-five, will have doubled and that there will be concern for those living in rural areas, with inadequate transport and the lack of other important necessities. There will be overwhelming pressure on home-helps and personal care. In Dorset, in the next couple of decades, more than half the population is expected to be middle-aged or elderly.

The price of property in Burton Bradstock is some of the most expensive in West Dorset and ranks high nationally. Only a limited number of the younger generation stand a chance of affording a home. Residents, in Burton Bradstock say that they are prepared to put up with the dangerous traffic-ridden main street, that rocks the very ground on which the properties stand, the swathes of houses and bungalows, the need to journey to Bridport so often, as well as the constant invasion by visitors and all the cars, frequenting the roads and lanes or blocking the streets, for the usually mild climate, clean air and beauty of the area.

As in the Estate days, much goes on in Burton. There are annual fêtes, dinners, competitions, outings and get-togethers and numerous fund-raising events as well as dozens of other activities throughout the Bride Valley, which provide plenty with which to interest and to occupy spare time. No one need be lonely. There is always somewhere to go and something to do.

In a report, Professor Neil Ward, Director of the Centre for Rural Economy, said that, " Retirement can release time, energy and resources, which can be very positive for communities. " Dennis Hawkins, shortly before his death in 2000, commented that Burton Bradstock was no longer a working village but one of 'retirement and recreation'. CJ Bailey, of Long Bredy, wrote, 'Sadly it lacks that sense of interdependence which was once the hallmark of village life. '

A seventeen year old boy grumbled there is nothing for them to do but with a bit of effort and thought there is plenty for the youths to do. Like the youngsters of 1958, it needs to be self-motivated. They do face the problem that in a retirement area, any noise they generate is frowned upon but noise and exuberance goes with youth! A place where they can meet to talk, use up-to-date technological facilities, with a coffee bar and a laid-back atmosphere, would please them.

It is the planning applications that will always be the Achilles' heel of the village and that still seem to cause upsets. Now that saturation point has been reached there can be very little further building in Burton except that the two derelict farmyards will be given up. Maybe the 'end' is in sight! Those who sit on the Parish Council, (2007), are people newly settled in the village, apart from Councillor Darren Batten who can claim Burton Bradstock ancestry.

Recently, two women, were overheard, in separate conversations, to say that they were troubled that there might be further building in front of their newly erected houses! That was the great advantage of the close-knit landlord and tenant system. No one was staking a claim on some property or land, (or the view and the 'silence').

★★★★★★★★★★

All too often, it has been claimed that the tenants who were able to purchase at the 1958 Sale were greedy and sold on at a huge profit. This is far from the truth. It was a struggle for most of them and eventually when farms and cottages were sold, there was a back-log of outlay to catch up with and several to share any profit ecrued. Some tenants had been lent money by friends and relations who had to be reimbursed. Although some are owner-occupiers, the fact that there are a number of families living at Lower Townsend and South Annings, who are descended from those who were caught up in the Sale, indicates that fortunes were not made. Profits were made on the sale of building sites but not everyone had land for development. If some of the Pitt Rivers's tenants did come out of it all a bit better off, who could deny them that?

The church, now a part of a team ministry, has been the anchor through the centuries and can still boast a reasonable congregation. It stands mellow and proud. The continuity of worship is strong in Burton Bradstock and there is an enthusiastic team who are motivated to keep the church bells ringing out across the valley. Fifty years after the Sale, little has changed the exterior of the church but very recently there is talk of altering parts of the church interior. This potential 'disturbance' is troubling a number of people although over the hundreds of years there have been numerous alterations to fit the current needs.

The churchyard with its oddly placed headstones, weathered and gathering lichens, allows the grass to be mown easily and with the vast increase in the population, many cremations have been interred. Mr Anthony Pitt-Rivers, youngest son of Captain Pitt-Rivers, still holds the living of the church and is entitled to be involved each time there is a change of clergy.

Will part of the churchyard soon be allowed to become one of Dorset's "living" spaces where wildlife and wild flowers can thrive, reverting to how it was years ago, before the electric mower.

HOW IT IS

Had Captain Pitt-Rivers decided to hold-on to the West Dorset part of his estate, he would surely have had to develop tourist facilities in the village and at the beach and continue to sell off building sites. The rents would have had to be raised for the existing tenants and in the end they would have been the losers. Some properties might have been done-up and long leases sold, as some other estates are doing but that method has its problems. The return on the Burton Bradstock block of the Pitt-Rivers Estate was in the region of £7,500 a year, in 1958. Out of that had to come a number of expenses. Captain Pitt-Rivers's generous assistance to many of the tenants, to leave a large amount of the purchase price of the property and land, on mortgage, gave them a chance that would never have come their way.

When Michael Pitt-Rivers sold-on again what he had retained in the family, most of his tenants were able to purchase from him as they were all in a stronger financial position than in1958. His determination to buy-in so much of the Estate, was a blessing for those caught up in his plan, as well as those who today can benefit and enjoy the coastal swathe, now owned by the National Trust.

★★★★★★★★★★

A modern plan and its perpetrators appear to be addressing what some see as problems but how much will be implemented? Is it all necessary? Someone has come up with the idea that the post office and shops could be moved to the other side of the village and make a new recreation field somewhere off Annings Lane?(If there is a space left). The authorities who set up "A plan for Burton Bradstock", in the 1980s had that in mind. A by-pass was once mooted handy to Shipton Gorge and to skirt around Freshwater! That could never be now that the coastline is part of a World Heritage Site. It looks as if the traffic will continue to rattle through the village.

The listed properties and those of special interest will be kept in check. Will the time come when cars will not be allowed so close to The Hive Beach for environmental reasons? The receding coastline along the Chesil Beach is beyond man's control. Nature will have her will with it, as she has done for thousands of years and who can pin-point what is "in-keeping" architecturally anymore.

Unlike the sixteenth and seventeenth century cottages and houses, which were built by craftsmen with 'time' and centuries of experience, a 'new time' may come when the twentieth century buildings will be out of date. Will they be demolished and some official decree that there must be more breathing space? Is the million-pound flood alleviation scheme good enough to hold? "Serious floods occur twice in a lifetime," the old folks said! More porous surfaces could act as a better soak-away for water and reverting to shutters in the houses would help to prevent heat escaping in cold weather and keep places cool in the hotter summers, just like the shutters on many of the original Burton properties.

Will a future "Plan for Burton", a century hence, put dwellings underground? Can they be built of wood or lined with straw, complete with compulsory solar energy? Materials banned in the 1960s might be recommended, the amount of glazing will be less, similar to the cottages of old and if the sea rises, as predicted, it could wipe out Manor Farm, Mill Street and other old buildings. A substantial sea-wall might be required.

Could everyone have three taps; hot, cold and sea-water? Rain and grey water will have to be used again. Those who fetched and carried the water in 1958 were economical and recycled it. Where will the wind farm be sited? There are several ideal places. Could the river water be harnessed again and will the fields that once produced tons of flax and hemp be sown with bio-crops for fuel? If global warming continues to rise, "they" say that the south of England will enjoy a Mediterranean climate and that resorts will spring up all along the coast. Most people still want to spend leisure time beside the sea. Another Bournemouth! The auctioneer, Arthur Richards, could be right after all.

There are many people, fearing for the environment, who advocate returning to the earth vault. It is not as outrageous as it might, at first, seem. With modern materials and proper management, apart from having to venture outside, (and couldn't that be overcome?), the old system was hygienic and "green"; no chemicals, no wastage of water and a product for recycling.

****

Those who went about their daily toil before 1958 could never have conceived that the village would become saturated with new homes and that it could be difficult to cross the High Street in safety or even to walk along at the bottom of, once quiet and lonely, Shipton Lane without being grazed by a passing vehicle. They could not have imagined the beach without its abundance of boats, nets and the crews, the leathered Old Salts and the men with faces grained with a life on the land, as well as the braiding women - all gone.

The ancestors must have turned in their graves, even the chieftain on the top of Bind Barrow has surely stirred from time to time. Many of the fields where they all worked and played are filled with concrete and bricks, where once acceptable distant noises came from the lowing cattle, bleating sheep, squealing pigs, crowing cockerels and barking farm dogs. From the village, came the sound of the slosh of the water wheels, the spinning-machines thrumming, the grinding-stones pounding, lumbering cart horses, the call "home" for the cattle and the fishermen summoned to rush to the beach, the blacksmith's hammer clanging on the anvil, the rattle of the milk buckets and churns and the fish touts shouting their wares around what was a lively and working village.

Friday and Saturday nights were times for recreation and fun. Music had reverberated across the Bride Valley, from the time of the centuries old August Village Wake when everyone who was able-bodied, joined in. Nowadays, beyond the continuous rumble of traffic in the High Street, acceptable noise appears to come from the clatter of hedge-trimmers and the buzzing of lawn mowers but all is not totally lost. The church bells, the children playing in the schoolyard, the shrill call of the seagulls, are sounds that have been heard in Burton for decades and the steadfastness of the weather vane's predictions, atop the solid church tower, is one thing that is not governed by man.

The majority of the residents of Burton Bradstock are happy with it as it is today. The accents are different and the cars, perhaps rather shinier. Many are "organic vegetable" fanatics, realising that the ancestors had got that right and this attitude bodes well for Burton. The village, in general, is still peaceful in these days of terrorist threats, pollution and environmental scares, Burton Bradstock seems far removed from such issues, yet. Although, a container ship spilling some of its cargo, in February 2007, brought the reality nearer to home.

Those new to the village, arrive in a place which has been capsulated into the modern concept of a village. It is what is sought and expected nowadays. In comparison with life in the cities it is a safe haven. It thrives in a different way.

The one organisation that appears to span any divide that still exists is The Royal British Legion, for its members are from every walk of life, town and village, old Burtoners and the new residents, who had fought, side by side, to defend their country and descendants take a pride in the sacrifices their parents and grandparents made. There is a huge strength in the Bride Valley Group. The Women's section lacked younger members but the men's section, although consisting of mainly aged old servicemen, flourishes.

The Parish Council Chairman, (2007), has a difficult and what could turn-out to be a controversial task ahead, steering the village into what will surely be its next phase. Traffic and congestion, a car park, site for a new hall, two redundant farmyards, The Rookery bridge, the old chapel, affordable housing, (not always welcome on some patches), saving the library and the post office and renegotiating a contract with the National Trust to run The Hive, lie ahead. Heavy responsibilities rest on the shoulders of those who make the decisions. Hopefully they will take time to deliberate and draw on the experience of the past fifty years. Planning applications still cause arguments and it is said there have even been blows exchanged between residents! Like the pre-1958 days, tolerance and understanding are essential. Those who live in Burton Bradstock, either as a result of heritage, moving-in, or as visitors, are now the guardians of this unique village but in looking forward they must not disown the past.

The few who are left, who were witnesses to the Pitt-Rivers Sale, in 1958, may be looking back through rosy spectacles - recalling what were the good old days, the stability and continuity and marvelling at the way in which their ancestors toiled and survived in difficult circumstances, situations that would not be comtemplated, or tolerated today and who for all the long working hours and many hardships, managed to live harmoniously side by side, without envy and found time to enjoy themselves. Their wants were simple. Everyone had a place and knew it. It worked well.

Burton Bradstock, now almost fifty years on from the Sale and a decade into the new century, has a community which is generally content with its present character and charm. There is no question, that over the years, many of the 'newcomers' have contributed to village life in a very positive manner. There have been numerous kind gestures and helpful acts. The school thrives, like never before. The children skip along, chattering and laughing over Timber Bridge along the footpath to the Recreation Ground, for their games and sports, through "Corn Crack", to them, just an ordinary field, yet to those who know, a memorable place where the Sale was held. It was there that so many of the changes began.

Ironically, the Pitt-Rivers Estate Sale catalogue had stated in 1958:

'Burton Bradstock has an atmosphere of its own, springing not only from the beauty of scenery and its seafaring associations and seaside attractions but also because of its extremely mild climate, which is kind to old people and which combined with the exceptional fertility of soil, has made the village noted for the beauty and early growth of its gardens. Burton Bradstock, consequently appeals both to the retiring resident and the more discriminating holiday maker who prefers the exclusive atmosphere of the private beaches and unspoilt coastline. '

That could have been written today!

Now, the custodianship of Burton Bradstock has been handed on. Its rooted inhabitants clung to the old traditions and attempted to be loyal to the past as long as they could but those are summers gone.

Oh! Summer is a pleasant time,
With all its sounds and sights,
Its dewy mornings, balmy eves,
And tranquil calm delights.
I sigh when first I see the leaves
Fall yellow on the plain,
And all the winter long I sing,
"Sweet summer, come again. "

Mary Howitt, 1799-1888

INDEX OF SURNAMES

The principal Lot numbers in the Sale follow the tenant's name in bold print.

Maiden names, where applicable, in italics.

Turner, Sheila see Collins
Vij, family 326, Sajiv 134
Wadham, Gladys see Buckler
Walbrin, Nellie *Burwood* 58, Ray 58, 59
Waller, family 164
Way, Jack 176, 242-244
Wainwright (writer) 266
Wakely, Adrian 208, CJ of Somerton 242, 244, 261, George 145, Marion 137,
   Madeleine ["Toots"] *Williams* 137, 141, 145
Waldron, William 267
Ward, Frank 58, 138, Joe 58, Mary *Legge* 125, 318, Mrs Joe 59, Professor Neil 327,
   Tom 141, 218
Watson, Arthur 104, 307
Warrender, Lady 247
Webb, Phyllis *Foot* 119, **Lot 20**, Reg 109, 119
Welch, Fred 180
West, HP of Woking 251
Wellington, Duke of 7, 252
Wheadon, Hannah 60
Wheatley, Mr and Mrs 221, **Lot 87**
Wheeler, The Rev. Harold and Mrs 315
White, Alice *Bugler* 106, Freda see Moore, Frederick 106, **Lot 10**, Gilbert 275
Whittle, Henry 79
Widger, Barbara 137
Wilkins, Elvina [Viney] *Wrixton* 157-159, **Lot 47**, George 157, 159, Valerie see Aylott
Williams, AE [Bert] 31, 36, 76, 86, 141-143, 145, 175, 176, 255, **Lot 123**, Annie *Hitt* 141, 143, 145, Billy 205, Col. Sir
   David 251, Dick 260,
   Dorothy see Pattinson, Doris see Klopper, Eva 141, 143,
   Frederick 198, Henrietta [Hetty] *Hitchcock* 58, 247, 260, 261, **Lot 128**, James 198,
   Jim 142,
   May 141-143, 251, **Lot 38 (shared occupancy)**, Madeleine "Toots" see Wakely
   Stanley 78, 125, 141-145, 281, 299, 319, **Lot 38 (shared occupancy)**, William 260
Willson, The Rev. Stanley 95
Wilson, Mr C (ecologist) 28
Wratislaw, Major Marc 96, 97 **Lot 3**, Nancy Burrow 81, 96, 97, 160
Wrixon, Elizabeth [Bessie] see Buckler
Wrixton, Alfred 157, Charles 157, Elizabeth 157, Elvina [Viney] see Wilkins, Fred 157, Roy 157
Wyatt, Barbara 155, Joe 155, Jonathan 156, Miss Myrtle 191, SW of Hampton-on-Thames 191
Wylde, Albion 152, Augustus [Gus] 246-248, 254, **Lot 115**, Desmond 248, Jean see Day, Richard 136, 138, 294
Yetman, family 107
Youngs, Hilary 302

OTHER PRINCIPAL LOT NUMBERS
Lots 2 and **13** gifted. **Lot 83** Burton Hive Beach mainly sold vacant. **Lot 90** let to Burton Bradstock Produce
Association. **Lot 97** sand and shingle rights by licence to Woolaway constructions. **Lot 126** Recreation Ground let
to Burton Bradstock Parish Council. Bridport and West Dorset Golf Club part occupants of **Lots 132, 133 and 143.**
Lot 144, Haddon House paddock, West Bay, sold with vacant possession (subject to concession to West Bay WI).
Lots 37, 119, 120, 140 allotments let to various tenants.

List of Burton Bradstock tenants' surnames in the Estate Rent Book, 1784-1791

researched by the author

Ackerman, Angel, Anning, Bagg ,Balson, Barber, Bartlett, Batten, Best, Bishop, Bowler, Boyland, Brown, Bussell, Buckler, Camel, Croom, Chaffey, Chilcot, Chapel, Cox, Darby, Diamond, Dorcen, Farr, Fowler, Gale, Gardiner, Garland, Gover, Gundry, Hansford, Hardy, Hart, Hine, Hooper, Hyde, Knight, Laurence, Mabey, Meech, Miller, Moggeridge, Northover, Parrot, Pitfield, Roberts, Russell, Soper, Smith, Spurdle, Symes, Travers, Tucker and Thurman.

IMPERIAL MEASUREMENTS AND CURRENCY

One perch	$=16\frac{1}{2}$ feet or ($\frac{1}{40}$ th of a rood)
One rood	$=\frac{1}{4}$ acre
One acre	$= 0.4$ of one hectare
One bushel	$= 8$ gallons (dry measure)

12 pence (12d)	$= 1$ shilling (1/-)
240 pence	$= 1$ pound (£1)
20/-	$= £1$
21/-	$= 1$ guinea (£1- 1/-)

ABOUT THE AUTHOR

Elizabeth Buckler Gale was born in the 1930s,in Burton Bradstock, into a farming and fishing background. She takes a pride in her heritage and her ancestors are listed in the Burton Bradstock Lay Subsidy [Tax] Returns of 1327. Her life has been spent working with people through numerous societies and she was recently awarded a Paul Harris Fellowship, for services to the community, by the Brit Valley Rotary Club, one of several organisations of which she is a Founder Member.

Elizabeth Buckler Gale is well known in the agricultural world and is a local historian, giving talks and leading guided walks, as well as writing books and articles.

Sources

Freke, Pitt and Pitt-Rivers copies of Family Tree,
and Pitt-Rivers Estate sale particulars 1951 and Sale Catalogue 1958

courtesy Anthony Pitt-Rivers, Esq., OBE, DL

Pitt-Rivers Papers deposited at the Dorset History Centre

Sale particulars Darby House 1952, *courtesy Mr and Mrs John Bull*

Census Returns 1841-1901, *researched by Amy Knight*

Burton Bradstock Parish Registers, *Dorset History Centre*

Family Trees, privately held: Stone, *Mr Robert J Stone*, Hansford, *Mr Michael Hansford*, Burwood, *Mr Alec W Burwood*, Hutchings, *Mr and Mrs Philip Hutchings*

Bridport News Archive, *Bridport News Office and Dorset County Reference Library, Bridport*

Dorset Evening Echo Archive, *Weymouth*

Western Gazette Archive, *Yeovil, Somerset*

Obituary of Michael Pitt-Rivers, *The Daily Telegraph 1999*

Burton Bradstock Parish Magazines and Bride Valley News, *(author's various copies)*

Hansford Papers, *researched by Michael Hansford*

My Seafaring Family, *Notes from talk by Ken Gollop 2006*

www.measuringingworth.com *for money conversion*

Bibliography

The Story of the Ancient Manor of Hinton St Mary and Annuls of the Pitts, Pitt-Rivers and Frekes, *George Lane-Fox Pitt-Rivers (undated)*

General Pitt-Rivers, *MW Thompson 1977*

Pitt Rivers, *Mark Bowden 1991*

The Pitt-Rivers Museum, *edited by LH Dudley Buxton 1929*

Cranborne Chase, *William Chafin 1818, reprinted 1991*

The Larmer Tree Gardens, *Guide Book, 2006*

Concerning Agnes, *Desmond Hawkins 1982*

Domesday Book, a draft translation, prepared by *Margaret Newman. 1983*

Our Heritage, The Church of St Mary the Virgin, *ET Long, FSA, undated*

Hutchins History and Antiquities of Dorset *Volume 2, 1973 (first published in 1774, reprinted 1863)*

West Dorset-Royal Commission on Historical Monuments, *Inventory Volume I, 1952*

The Bride Valley, *CJ Bailey 1982*

Farmers, Fishermen and Flax Spinners, *Elizabeth Buckler Gale, 3rd edit. 2001*

The Meadows Where We Play, *Janet Sanderson Crouch 1989*

Bridport and West Dorset Golf Club, *George Houghton 1991*

West Bay, *AW Matthews 1901*

Who's Who, *1960 and 1980*

The Bridport Charter of 1253, *Katherine Barker, 2003*

Bridport History Society Journal, *Editor Robert Eveleigh 2003*

The Burton Bradstock Book, *John Eastwood, undated*

Erik the Red, *Donald Ridler 1972*

Eden Phillpotts (1862-1960) The Spinners *1918*, selected Letters, *James Y Dayananda 1984*

My Kind of Town, *Margery Hookings 2005*

From Tolpuddle to TUC, *GE Russell 1948*

The Knocker Up and Seiners, *Cyril Toms 1994*

The Place Names of Dorset, *Anton Fägersten 1978*

The Common Prayer Book

The major archive of monochrome topographical views by James Valentine & Co. is held by the University of St Andrews Library. www.st-andrews.ac.uk/special collections

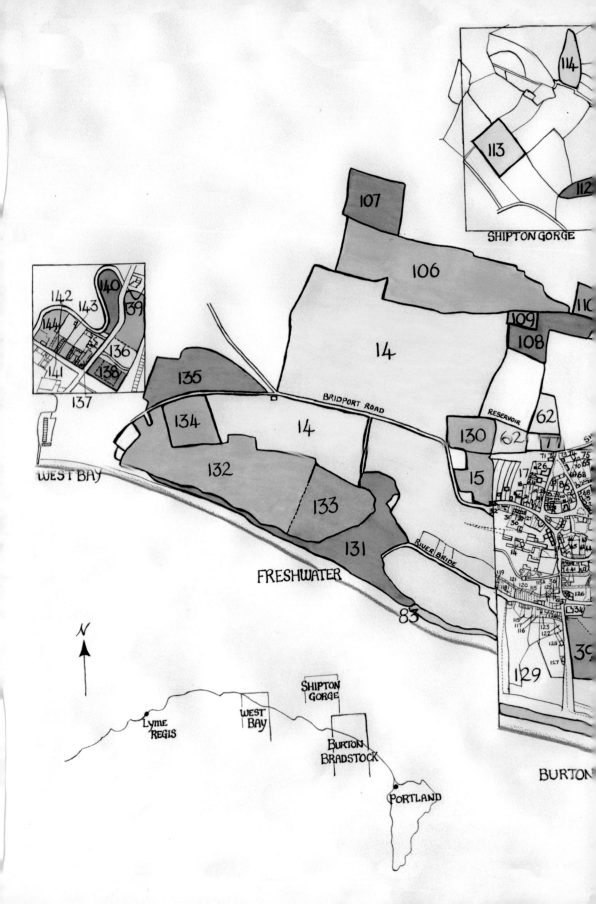

SHIPTON GORGE

114

113

112

107

106

14

109

110

108

142 140
143   39
144 136
141 138
137

135

134

14

BRIDPORT ROAD

RESERVOIR

62

130   62

WEST BAY

132

14

15

133

131

RIVER BRIDE

FRESHWATER

83

129

39

N

LYME
REGIS

WEST
BAY

SHIPTON
GORGE

BURTON
BRADSTOCK

PORTLAND

BURTON

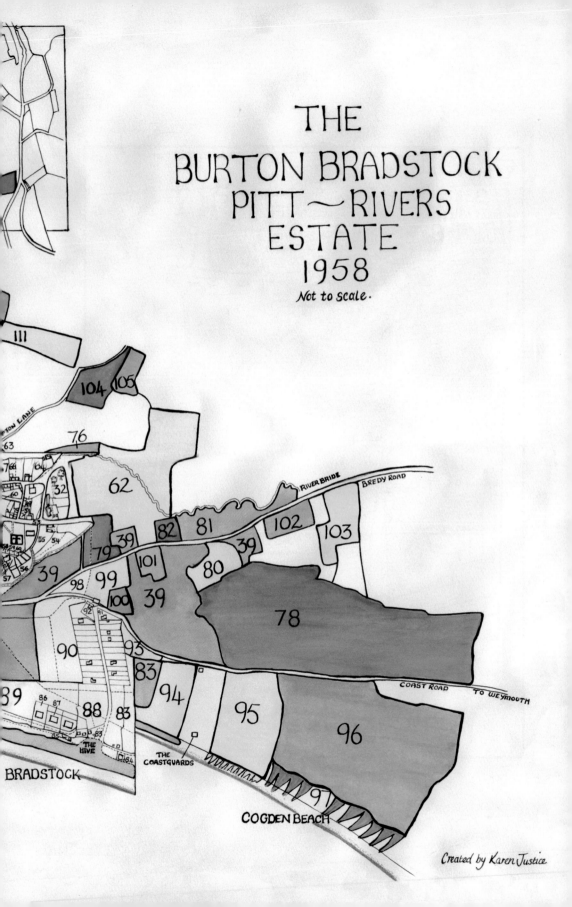

THE
BURTON BRADSTOCK
PITT~RIVERS
ESTATE
1958

Not to scale.

111

104 105

TON LANE

76

63

76

32

62

60

RIVER BRIDE

BREDY ROAD

82 81

102 103

54

39 39

79

101

80 39

99

39 39

98

100

78

90

95

83

94 95

96

39 86 87 88 83

85

THE HIVE

THE COASTGUARDS

COAST ROAD

TO WEYMOUTH

BRADSTOCK

COGDEN BEACH

91

Created by Karen Justice

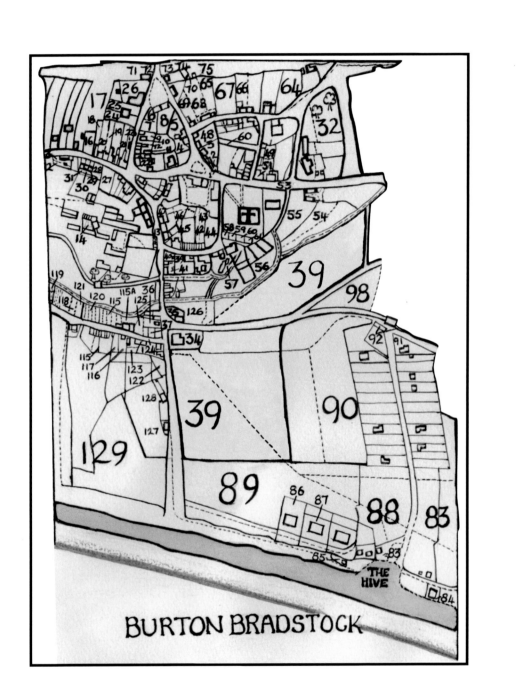

BURTON BRADSTOCK